REMEMBERING THE STICK

REMEMBERING THE STICK

Candlestick Park—1960–2013

STEVEN R. TRAVERS

Guilford, Connecticut

An imprint of Globe Pequot

Distributed by NATIONAL BOOK NETWORK

British Library Cataloguing in Publication Information available

Library of Congress Cataloging-in-Publication Data

Names: Travers, Steven.
Title: Remembering the Stick : Candlestick Park, 1960-2013 / by Steven R.
  Travers.
Description: Guilford, Connecticut : Lyons Press, 2017. | Includes
  bibliographical references.
Identifiers: LCCN 2016054410 (print) | LCCN 2016055914 (ebook) | ISBN
  9781630760717 (paperback) | ISBN 9781630760724 (e-book)
Subjects: LCSH: Candlestick Park (San Francisco, Calif.)—History. |
  Sports—California—San Francisco—History. | BISAC: SPORTS & RECREATION /
  History. | SPORTS & RECREATION / Baseball / History. | SPORTS & RECREATION
  / Football.
Classification: LCC GV417.C36 T73 2017 (print) | LCC GV417.C36 (ebook) | DDC
  796.406/80979461—dc23
LC record available at https://lccn.loc.gov/2016054410

Printed in the United States of America

This book is dedicated to the memory of
John and Jean Strahlendorf

CONTENTS

ACKNOWLEDGMENTS

I especially wish to thank my good friend Bruce Seltzer, who literally came up with the idea for this book. He sent me an email, mentioning how the closing of Candlestick Park might be worth a book recalling its history. I forwarded the email to my friend Rick Rinehart at Rowman and Littlefield, who immediately agreed, and that was that. The easiest sale of my career.

Thanks also to good old Rick, who has worked with me on six books now, with more surely to come. Thanks to my literary agent in New York City, Ian Kleinert of Objective Entertainment, and to my agent in Beverly Hills, Lloyd Robinson of Suite A Management. Thanks also to Stefanie Beasley at *Gentry* magazine for allowing my article from their magazine to be reprinted in this book. Thanks to my wonderful late friend John Stahlendorf, longtime 49ers season ticketholder, who provided me many memories of his years attending their games, as well as a pristine 1962 World Series program.

Rivals

THE SAN FRANCISCO GIANTS AND LOS ANGELES DODGERS MOVED TO California in 1958. Roy Campanella's special night in 1959 was seen as the "debutante ball" of the Dodgers. Five months later Los Angeles won the World Series. For decades, the University of Southern California Trojans and University of California, LA Bruins were America's dominant collegiate sports powerhouses. Crowds of over 100,000 came out to watch football games at the Coliseum; USC, UCLA, and the Rams. The 1932 L.A. Olympics had been the most successful to date. Hollywood was the world's cultural touchstone, and politically the Golden State was now the most important in the nation.

Until the teams moved to California and Dodger Stadium was built in 1962, the Dodgers and Giants were roughly equal rivals. The Giants had won five World Championships (1905, 1921, 1922, 1933, 1954); the Dodgers two (1955, 1959), but they seemed to have achieved an edge in the final New York years and the early California seasons.

That edge had demonstrated itself in the winning of the 1955 World Series followed by the National League championship in 1956. Manager Walt Alston presided over the "Dodger way," a victorious formula of sorts that had been the product of such baseball minds as Lee MacPhail, Branch Rickey, Buzzie Bavasi, Fresco Thompson, and Al Campanis.

The Giants, on the other hand, had fired Leo Durocher and gone through a succession of managers. Dodger Stadium was a shot across the bow at the Giants, but it was also a signal moment in a long-held rivalry that existed before Californians ever thought about Major League baseball.

San Francisco despised Los Angeles. San Franciscans despised Los Angelenos. Los Angeles and Los Angelenos did not particularly care. San Franciscans hated them even more for caring so little. San Francisco was a schizophrenic town with equal parts inferiority complex and superiority complex. They thought of themselves as the Paris of the West, New York of the Pacific; L.A. was a land of rubes. There was no city there, no base, no monument to greatness . . . until now.

San Francisco started out as the important California city, but the building of the Owens River Valley aqueduct and two world wars had changed that. The University of California and Stanford University built impressive stadiums in the early 1920s. Stanford lobbied for the Rose Bowl game to be moved north. Southern California responded by building two stadiums, the Rose Bowl in Pasadena and the Coliseum near downtown L.A. Both dwarfed the northern stadiums. Instead of being compared to Cal and Stanford, they were compared to the "House That Ruth Built" (Yankee Stadium) and the Roman Coliseum.

California's "Wonder Teams" and Stanford under coach Pop Warner were the two great college football dynasties of the early 1920s, but they quickly became overshadowed by Knute Rockne and Notre Dame. When Southern California started their great rivalry with the Fighting Irish, it established the Trojans as the other major grid power, further pushing Cal and Stanford into the shadows. A sense of jealousy pervaded the northern schools, infusing the region in ways that became sociopolitical. Then UCLA came into their own. The Bruins, not the Golden Bears or Indians, were USC's main conference rival, winning the 1954 national championship in football and later establishing themselves as the greatest basketball dynasty of all time.

In the 1950s and early 1960s, reeling from a recruiting scandal in which Stanford "turned them in," California scaled back sports. A program that had produced four national champions in football, two in baseball, one in basketball, plus numerous Olympians became a joke and has never truly recovered.

Political power shifted from the north to the south. Earl Warren was from the Bay Area and attended the University of California. He became governor and was tapped by Thomas Dewey as his vice presidential running mate in the losing 1948 election. Richard Nixon was from the Los Angeles area. He represented a growing, more powerful electorate than Warren, and rose to greater heights. Ronald Reagan would also tap into the same Orange County conservatism that propelled Barry Goldwater to the 1964 Republican nomination, and eventually would become the dominant political ethos in America.

All of these factors, the Rose Bowl and Coliseum being better recognized than Cal's and Stanford's stadiums, the Trojans and Bruins dominating the Golden Bears and Indians, political power shifting to the Southland, leaving Northern California marginalized toward the Left, combined to frustrate denizens of the San Francisco Bay Area. On top of that, they saw that the center of business in the Pacific Rim was no longer San Francisco, but Los Angeles. Then there was Hollywood. The imprimatur of glamour, of beautiful women, hot nightlife, golden beaches, and Tinseltown fame overshadowed foggy San Francisco, which seemed to fall short in every way a city can be measured against another one. San Franciscans looked at their beautiful scenery, their identifiable skyscraper city center, their supposedly more literate cultured population, and tried to look down their noses at the churchgoing Midwestern transplants who made up the L.A. Basin. They seemed to be desperately attempting to convince themselves of their elitism. The harder they tried, the more they failed.

When Dodger Stadium was built, it was the final insult. Now Los Angeles had created pure excellence. It was self-evident truth. It needed no commentary. Los Angeles was superior to San Francisco.

The most successful franchise shift prior to the Giants and Dodgers was the Braves. County Stadium in Milwaukee was a wide-open facility with a large parking lot and easy road access. The car culture was in full swing. It was the Baby Boomer generation, a period of postwar prosperity of unprecedented proportions. The Great Depression, the Dust Bowl, the New Deal, the failed America of John Steinbeck's novels was completely overshadowed by the success of free market capitalism. In Oklahoma, Bud Wilkinson's Sooners were the dominant college football power; their games sold out, eclipsing old stereotypes of Okie poverty. In Milwaukee, attendance topped two million. Families of four came out to the park. They bought expensive new cars, paid for gas and parking. They paid for souvenirs and ballpark food. After the game they frequented local restaurants and businesses. Baseball in Milwaukee was integrated into the economy of an entire community.

During these years, Brooklyn's great rivals, the Giants, suffered attendance downturns. Their stadium, the Polo Grounds, was located in a bad neighborhood. Coogan's Bluff in Harlem was now crime-ridden. Their Bronx neighbors, the Yankees, faced similar problems, but the pinstripers were a dominant team that won the battle for the Manhattan, New Jersey, and Connecticut fan base needed for success. Yankee Stadium also had the advantage of easy freeway access, meaning suburban fans could pop in and out without risking the mean streets as they did in Brooklyn.

When Dodgers owner Walter O'Malley decided to move to Los Angeles, he knew he needed a rival in California, and that would naturally be Horace Stoneham's Giants. O'Malley set about securing L.A. and steering Stoneham to San Francisco. While the well-worn story holds that O'Malley "snookered" Stoneham into making the move, it was in fact Stoneham who announced his club's departure before O'Malley, who was holding his cards close to his vest to secure a good political deal with L.A. Stoneham originally wanted to move to Minneapolis, home of the Giants triple-A farm club. The Twin Cities was viewed as a major region of growth. The Minnesota Twins and Vikings would soon successfully set up shop there.

Despite O'Malley holding off on his announcement until the last minute, New York baseball fans knew it was a fait accompli. When O'Malley announced they were L.A.-bound, it was easy for Stoneham to declare the Giants would play in San Francisco. The Giants' owner was completely fed up with the ancient Polo Grounds, now a war zone. San Francisco, California, a New York–style town steeped in the traditions of Joe DiMaggio and the PCL Seals, was the most legendary of all minor league towns. The rivalry would flourish on the West Coast.

The Boston Red Sox owned the San Francisco Seals. Red Sox owner Tom Yawkey sold his territorial rights to Stoneham in exchange for Minneapolis, at a price of $25,000. On May 29, 1957, the Dodgers announced the move. In August, the Giants followed suit.

"I feel sorry for the kids, but I haven't seen much of their fathers lately," Stoneham said. Stoneham's relationship with his players was the opposite of O'Malley's, who was a cold, sterile businessman. Stoneham was a "real baseball fan as an owner," his close aide, Chub Feeney, said. "Winning meant a lot to him and the team meant a lot to him. He was a rooter." Stoneham was known for his generosity with Giants players, who he viewed as part of a larger family. O'Malley, with slick hair, three-piece suits, and a large paunch, looked the part of a big city bank president. Stoneham, with his rosy cheeks, thinning hair, and thick, dark glasses, was a round-faced man who resembled the comic Drew Carey. His persona was more like a regional branch manager.

Stoneham loved to drink, an occupation that coincided with watching his team. There was a sense that California was one big tropical paradise, with little regard for the enormous physical disparities within its 900-mile north-south borders, not to mention the enormous difference between its coast and its mountain ranges; its Redwood forests and its deserts. Even within the Bay Area itself, temperatures varied greatly. Walnut Creek for example, a bedroom community located over the hill past Oakland, in the east bay, could be steaming hot at 90 degrees on the same day that San Francisco was foggy and wind-swept at 55 degrees.

Stoneham made one thing clear, emphasized above all other criteria: he wanted parking at his new stadium. Parking, parking, parking. Neither L.A. nor San Francisco had much in the way of public transportation. San Francisco's bus service was better than L.A.'s, and a commuter train connected people between the City (its denizens used caps) and the peninsula towns of Burlingame, San Mateo, Palo Alto, and Mountain View, but for the most part its citizenry traversed the freeways and numerous bridges (the Golden Gate, Bay, and eventually the Richmond-San Rafael, San Mateo, Dumbarton, Carquinez, and Benicia) by car.

There was available downtown land near Powell and Market Streets, which would have been an excellent spot. Located not far from where the current AT&T Park is now, it would have offered reasonable weather. Certainly there would have been wind and fog, but it would have been acceptable. Financial district foot traffic, cable cars, ferry service, municipal bus lines, the Southern Pacific train, and eventually the Bay Area Rapid Transit (BART) would have provided easy access. Stores, bars, and restaurants would have benefited from the nightlife and "this is the place to be" vibe that AT&T Park now provides. It was not chosen because local businesses did not want increased traffic congestion. Stoneham lacked the vision to fight for the downtown stadium; all he saw was a big parking lot. In addition, eminent domain laws would have cost the City $33 million to pay off citizens forced to leave properties.

—◆—

The Stoneham family had long owned the New York Giants, the glory franchise of the National League. Well before Jackie Robinson integrated the Dodgers in Brooklyn, the New York Giants were baseball royalty: Christy Mathewson, John McGraw, Bill Terry, Carl Hubbell, Mel Ott . . . the list went on.

Stoneham inherited the club from his dad, and was not unlike the idle rich of the Fitzgerald era. He liked to drink and socialize. Owning a baseball team was the best party favor in America.

—◆—

In the 1950s, the Dodgers-Giants rivalry reached fever pitch. The New York Giants captured the 1954 World Championship, with the Brooklyn Dodgers following suit in 1955. It was deemed a golden era, with all three New York teams featuring center fielders for the ages (Willie Mays of the Giants, Duke Snider of the Dodgers, Mickey Mantle of the Yankees). The New York football Giants were a power, featuring a golden boy all-purpose running back named Frank Gifford.

But under the surface, trouble was brewing. The Polo Grounds was located on the edge of Harlem, and by the mid-1950s was decrepit and crime-ridden. Ebbetts Field was an ancient, smelly little yard with no parking, no freeway access, and its white Brooklyn fan base was fanning out to suburban Queens and Long Island.

Dodgers owner Walter O'Malley could be compared to the Potter character in Frank Capra's *It's a Wonderful Life*: all business. He realized that he was losing a turf battle for a new stadium to a New York

developer and public official named Robert Moses,
who was determined to combine a stadium in Queens
with freeway access and parking. O'Malley's base was
Brooklyn. He was approached by political factions
in far off Los Angeles, who told him if he moved the
Dodgers out west they would grant him a sweetheart
land deal to build a sports palace. Jet travel was
now routine, and expansion to the West Coast was
inevitable. He agreed to move the Dodgers, but he
needed a rival.

O'Malley manipulated Stoneham, who was
losing money and already considering a move to
Minneapolis, where the Giants had a farm club, but
O'Malley painted a picture of a glorious continuation
of the rivalry with the Dodgers in L.A. and the Giants
in San Francisco. Stoneham agreed. He was an amiable chap.

Harney's Dirt

San Francisco Mayor George Christopher saw how O'Malley had manipulated Stoneham. He set out to do the same thing. Christopher had a sweetheart deal with a construction magnate named Charlie Harney. Harney owned tons and tons and tons of dirt. Regular old dirt. He needed a place to put it that would pay him for it. Within the jurisdiction of the City there were only so many places that could accommodate Harney's dirt.

They decided on nondescript Candlestick Point, sitting on a section next to San Francisco Bay. Candlestick Point was located next to the Bayshore Freeway, which connected the City with the airport, almost as much of a boondoggle that was not actually in the City. Stoneham was told of the Bayshore location. He had visions of a baseball version of Fisherman's Wharf, a marina-style stadium perhaps, accompanied by waterfront vistas. In fact, the section of bay that Candlestick Point is located at is one of the farthest from the east bay on the other side. Furthermore, the east bay area across from Candlestick is much flatter than the scenic Oakland and Berkeley Hills to the north, the lights of Oakland and the Bay Bridge providing spectacular visuals. Trying to locate the east bay from Candlestick Point is little more visually spectacular than trying to spot England on the horizon across the channel from France.

A bluff overlooked the site, which was curved away from the downtown Embarcadero area in such a way that there was absolutely no evidence of the beautiful downtown San Francisco skyline to the north, or even the mountainous peninsula to the south. It just sat there. The neighborhoods adjacent to Candlestick Point—Bayside, Hunter's Point, and Potrero Hill—were headed in the same direction as the Harlem slums where the Polo Grounds had been. Stoneham was painted a portrait of racial harmony, of new thinking in California, but in truth the black community of San Francisco lived in sullen isolation, well away from the City's frolicking financial district or the tony neighborhoods of St. Francis Woods, Mt. Davidson, Twin Peaks, and the Sunset.

There was no fan-friendly business for miles and miles and miles near Candlestick, just slaughterhouses, packing plants, and a few liquor stores. An eyesore for the ages, a huge crane dominating a nearby naval shipbuilding facility, blocking whatever views of the bay that there might have been. Fans exiting the 101 freeway found themselves on narrow streets that quickly became boondoggles before and after games with any kind of large attendance. Local kids threatened to vandalize cars unless money was extorted from scared drivers. But all of this was nothing compared to the elements.

Christopher and Harney knew that Stoneham was a man who wanted to get to his drinking early. They arranged for a tour of Candlestick Point in the morning. Mark Twain once said, "The coldest winter I ever spent was a summer in San Francisco." The best time of year there is the fall, the Indian summer months of September, October, and early November. Instead of directing Stoneham to Candlestick on one of those Mark Twain days—cold, drizzly, windy—they drove Horace out on a sunny, clear morning. All Stoneham seemed to see was room for parking. Of course, that room was still part of the bay. This was where Harney's dirt would be dumped, creating landfill and a toxicological disaster. On top of that, nobody understood much about earthquakes back then, other than the Big One had virtually destroyed the entire city only 50-some years before that. Sure, go ahead, build a stadium on the shifting sands of loose dirt dumped into the water!

Stoneham enthusiastically endorsed the whole plan, hook, line, and sinker. Christopher and Harney just looked at each other. This was a savvy New York businessman? The West Coast rubes had pulled the sheet, er, the dirt right over his head. Stoneham was spirited away and by 3:00 p.m. was in his cups. Around that time, a violent windstorm descended on Candlestick Point. It was like something out of Lawrence of Arabia, or biblical fogs that might have killed every first-born child on the point if it had been fit for human habitation in the first place. Dust from the nearby bluffs swirled in a sea of drifting garbage wrappings. Fetid smells filled the air, but Stoneham neither saw, felt, nor smelled it. It was cocktail hour.

In the meantime, Walter O'Malley moved his Dodgers into the Los Angeles Memorial Coliseum until Dodger Stadium could be built. The farther the stands and the screen extended toward center field, the farther away it was from home plate. Deep center field was a considerable distance, and in order to make up for the ridiculous short left field dimensions, right-center field was so deep that Babe Ruth or Barry Bonds would have had little chance of going deep there. Duke Snider, a left-handed slugger in the bandbox Ebbets Field, was completely destroyed by the Coliseum. When Giants star Willie Mays first saw the place, he approached Snider during batting practice.

"Duke, they just killed you, man," he exclaimed in his high-pitched whine.

— ⁓

On April 15, 1958, 23,449 San Franciscans attended Seals Stadium and watched their new heroes defeat their old rivals, Don Drysdale and the Dodgers, 8–0. The Giants drew 90 percent capacity of the stadium located at the corner of Seventh and Bryant Streets in their first year. The club quickly built themselves up on the strength of new, young San Francisco stars like Orlando Cepeda, Willie McCovey, and Juan Marichal. But they never reached the World Series, as L.A. had in 1959. The Giants lost seven of their last eight games to blow the pennant after being in first place all year in 1959.

San Francisco did pass a $5 million bond issue to build a modern stadium. Charlie Harney sold his land to San Francisco for $2.7 million on the proviso that he be put in charge of the construction project. He pledged to complete the park "in eight months." The graft and corruption in San Francisco was rampant, with Mayor Christopher and Harney smiling all the way to the bank. It became a model for bad planning, bad government, and bad bureaucracy.

Dirt from Harney's nearby hill was used as landfill, but it sheared off the windbreakers. Chub Feeney came out to observe progress and saw cardboard boxes blowing around. "Does the wind always blow like this?" he asked with desperation in his voice, visions of the bleak future in his eyes.

"Only between the hours of one and five," answered a crewmember. The workers just laughed. They had theirs, the union had theirs; the suckers from the Big Apple were committed to their incompetence with no recourse. Certainly they lacked the will to insist on excellence.

The smell of clams, polluted water "thicker than Los Angeles smog and fouler than Canarsie garbage" permeated the environment, wrote Southern California writer Arnold Hano, who was familiar with the air quality.

Harney thought the stadium would be named after him. The winning contest name, however, was the uninspiring, unoriginal Candlestick Park. Nobody ever really figured out why it was called Candlestick Point in the first place. It meant nothing and stood for less. Rumor has it the place was built on a five-thousand-year-old Indian burial ground. After Harney heard it was not to be named after him, work slacked off and the completion date was pushed back. Eventually a grand jury probed the payment of Harney's parking contracts, a notoriously crime-addled business run largely by organized crime in San Francisco to this day. The Teamsters' strike delayed installation of key stadium components. Then Harney refused to allow the Giants to observe their future home. The city fire marshal inspected the place and called it a "fire trap." Eventually, Candlestick was reinforced with concrete, the first stadium ever constructed in that manner. But there was one act of genius. Built near the bay waters, partially on landfill, in a major earthquake zone, its original location was moved a fairly short distance to avoid it existing above an active fault. This would prove to be one of its saving graces in 1989.

━ ━

At first, the Giants played at Seals Stadium, a minor league park. They contended in 1959 before blowing the pennant to Los Angeles in the last series of the year. But both clubs needed a new stadium. Walter O'Malley scouted his own locations in Los Angeles before settling on Chavez Ravine. It was a perfect spot located on top of a hill overlooking downtown, with views stretching across the basin, criss-crossed by freeways, plenty of room for parking, augmented by gorgeous hills with trees that could be landscaped into the overall ambience. Stoneham relied on his new hosts to tell him where the stadium would be.

But the fault for Candlestick Park was not all Stoneham's. He did look at a downtown location, not far from where the current AT&T Park sits. In those days, the area south of Market Street was undeveloped. There was land in and around China Basin. Moviemakers liked to make use of it. Alfred Hitchcock found San Francisco to be a great location, and several key scenes from Clint Eastwood's *Dirty Harry* franchise were shot more or less where AT&T Park is today.

But it was the downtown merchants who objected. They felt it would take up too much room, would create too much traffic, make it too hard for shoppers to park, and disrupt public transportation. Rebuffed, Stoneham agreed to take up Mayor Christopher's and Charlie Harney's offer to look at Candlestick Point. Politics and environmentalism aside, other parts of the City that would have been more attractive include the Sunset District, perhaps somewhere near San Francisco State; on the bluffs south of 19th Avenue, affording views of San Francisco and the ocean; or the Presidio (a fully functioning Army base for years after that) that had a lot of open space and could have afforded a waterfront ballpark with spectacular views of the Golden Gate Bridge, the City skyscrapers, Alcatraz, Marin County, and the east bay hills. But none of those locations was feasible for any number of reasons, then or now.

There was a major international airport built south of San Francisco proper, and Highway 101 rolled directly past Candlestick Point. A large population lived on the adjoining peninsula, stretching from Daly City to San Jose, with a growing business climate. The nearby San Mateo Bridge afforded access from the east bay, which included Oakland and Berkeley. Public transportation was dicey, but in those days, the car was king.

The Braves had moved from Boston to Milwaukee and built a stadium with a large parking lot and easy road access. They drew huge crowds, almost all of whom arrived by car. Walter O'Malley convinced Horace Stoneham that any stadium needed these features in order to prosper. Bay Area Rapid Transit was little more than a gleam in some civic-minded citizen's eye in the late 1950s. Bus service was archaic. Big American muscle cars guzzling cheap gas; these were the spoils of war victory.

Landfill

San Francisco's initial bid for greatness, which in the days of Sputnik, the "space race," and the arms race was to get there first. L.A. already had the Coliseum and the Rose Bowl, and in 1959 built the Sports Arena, but Candlestick was the first big-league baseball park.

In reviewing how anxious Mayor George Christopher was to see it built so quickly, we begin to understand why first is not always best. He pulled the wool over the eyes of Giants owner Horace Stoneham, like a ticket scalper who hurriedly sells an unsuspecting fan two tickets to last week's game, only to be in the shadows by the time the ticket-taker rebuffs the swindled fellow.

The big thing in California in those days was *landfill*. There had been a huge earthquake in San Francisco in 1906, another one in Long Beach in the 1930s, and many smaller ones up and down the state, but geologists, engineers, and architects apparently did not yet connect the idea that structures built on landfills were endangered more so by the shifting earth. There was greed to attend to first.

What the ever-increasing population of affluent California wanted were homes, neighborhoods, and businesses built near the ocean, bays, marinas, and waterways. So it was that in Los Angeles, a new development was going up on the sand dunes of Marina Del Rey, ritzy swingers' condominiums built on landfill extending into a spit of water connecting Santa Monica with the south bay. Howard Hughes land.

In Alameda, the Bay Farms project filled tons of dirt into the bay, with little regard for the environment, so the *nouveau riche* could live on sparkling waterways. In San Francisco, the Marina District connecting north beach with Cow Hollow afforded gorgeous waterfront vistas overlooking Golden Gate Bridge.

Then there was Charlie Harney, the contractor. He looked around and saw what he deemed to be the future, in the form of waterfront property south of San Francisco proper, overlooking the bay. It was called Candlestick Point. Basically it was a garbage dump. Next to it was a shipyard. Next to that were the black neighborhoods, populated by African Americans who moved there to work the shipyards during World War II. By the late 1950s it was already decaying, desultory, and crime-infested.

But Charlie Harney had come across a lot of dirt, which he managed to get at a bargain price, because it was, after all, just dirt, but landfill was the big thing back then and, by gum, he would put that dirt *somewhere*. So Candlestick Point looked attractive to him, at least as attractive as a garbage dump can look, but his dirt would cover up all that garbage, environmental concerns or not.

But before he could dump all that dirt into the swamps of Candlestick Point, he needed a lucrative deal to make it worth his while. He was in cahoots with old Christopher, and they were looking around for somebody willing to build on that garbage dump.

Ineptitude and Inferiority

CANDLESTICK PARK WAS BUILT AT A REPORTED COST OF $14,855,990. It has been estimated that some $6 million of that amount was spent on graft and corruption. Still, Candlestick was the first sports stadium built since the Great Depression. It featured a postmodern architectural style popularized by Ayn Rand's novel and movie *The Fountainhead*. Its futuristic design marked the "space race" America was engaged in at the time with the Soviet Union, and indeed Dodgers announcer Vin Scully's first reaction to it was to say Candlestick resembled a "spaceship." In the beginning at least, Candlestick was a model of sorts for Dodger Stadium, completed two years after it. It opened on April 12, 1960, before a capacity crowd of 42,269 fans.

"San Francisco can say this is the finest ballpark in America," stated Vice President Richard Nixon, a native Los Angeleno who at the time was making his way through the Republican primaries, leading to his eventual monumental election with Massachusetts senator John F. Kennedy in November. A year earlier, Nixon called the brand-new Los Angeles Sports Arena (home of the USC Trojans, UCLA Bruins, the 1960 Democratic National Convention, and eventually the Lakers) the "finest arena of its kind."

While Candlestick and the Sports Arena have been impugned over the years, Nixon's words sometimes compared to unfortunate statements he made during Watergate ("I'm not a crook"), the fact is that at least until spectacular places like Dodger Stadium, the Forum, the Spectrum, and new baseball parks in St. Louis, Atlanta, and Houston were built, Candlestick and the Sports Arena were indeed state-of-the-art facilities.

The *San Francisco Examiner* called it "a symphony of gray and concrete." The opener was a resounding triumph. Distinguished guests included Nixon, California governor Edmund "Pat" Brown, Commissioner Ford Frick, and ex-manager John McGraw's widow. The Giants beat the St. Louis Cardinals. Superstar center fielder Willie Mays drove in all their runs.

But these views resonated for about a game or two before fans were literally blown away. On the very first batting practice swing Mays took, he connected and the wind sheared his bat in half.

"Move the fences in," he shouted.

"The wind blew right in your face," said outfielder Felipe Alou.

"I've never been so cold in my life," said first baseman Orlando Cepeda, who hailed from the warm climes of Puerto Rico. But Mays quickly realized he needed to accept the conditions; complaining about Candlestick would not help the Giants.

"Aw, you can't cry about where you play," he stated.

But "Candlestick stories" quickly took precedent. On July 15, the game was suspended 24 minutes due to fog. "It was like a scene from the early days on Earth," said Dodgers coach Bobby Bragan.

The 1960 Giants were managed by Bill Rigney, an old New York hand who hailed from Northern California. He was asked about "handling" Mays.

"Gee, Willie Mays is the last thing I have to worry about because I've got 24 other guys I have to be more concerned with," said Rigney. The quote was meant as a compliment to Mays; his star center fielder needed no "handling," but Mays was struggling to gain acceptance from San Francisco fans who worshipped Galileo High School's Joe DiMaggio, then immediately favored Cepeda and another young first baseman, Willie McCovey, over Mays. Mays took exception to Rigney's comment, but always felt Rigney's firing at midseason cost the club a shot at the pennant, won eventually by Pittsburgh.

"I don't think any team would have done any good that entire first season at Candlestick, the year the park was opened," Mays said.

Both the Dodgers and Giants were close in 1961, but Cincinnati captured the championship. Mays somehow had not excited the populace. He always seemed to pop up in the clutch with the bases loaded. He was a New York creation, Leo Durocher's prodigy, not a homegrown product like the more popular Cepeda.

Candlestick was a liability from the very first season and never improved. Dodger fans who traveled north made fun of it. "The Candlestick weather leaves you depressed," said shortstop Eddie Bressoud. Opponents were just happy to leave. Pittsburgh pitcher Vernon Law said he would not report to San Francisco if he were ever traded there.

"Never mind the hot coffee, get me a priest!" Cardinals announcer Joe Garagiola joked while enduring a game in its cold, breezy broadcast booth.

"No one liked playing there," Giants pitching coach Larry Jansen recalled. "Every team that came in hated it, but I told the pitchers this was our home and we'd have the edge if we just prepared ourselves mentally and physically. Wear longjohns, wear a choker around your neck and warm up an extra five minutes."

Young star Willie McCovey hit an infield pop-up that carried for a homer. Diminutive relief pitcher Stu Miller's glove stuck to the fence and he was "blown off" the mound during the 1961 All-Star Game, causing a balk. On that July day, 100 fans were treated for heat prostration. Then swirling winds caused a huge temperature drop and the infamous gustblown Miller incident. Miller was a little guy who specialized in off-speed stuff.

"He throws a Wells Fargo pitch—it comes up to the plate in stages," Giant executive Garry Schumacher said of him. It was actually one of the more exciting All-Star Games, a 5–4 National League victory that featured many superstars, young and old, but that was not what people remembered.

"The next day in the newspaper, its headline's not 'Miller Wins All-Star Game,' but, 'Miller Blown Off Mound,'" Stu Miller recalled. "There was no wind that day until about the fifth inning."

The wind caused seven errors by both teams, an All-Star Game record. Roger Maris, the superstar right fielder of the New York Yankees, was in shock, saying Candlestick should have been built "under the bay."

"Chewing tobacco and sand isn't a tasty combination," remarked Baltimore relief pitcher Hoyt Wilhelm. To spit in the wind at Candlestick Park was hazardous.

"Whatever this is, it isn't a Major League ballpark," wrote Arthur Daley of the *New York Times*.

On one occasion, a pop fly off the bat of Pittsburgh's Don Hoak was actually lost. It was called foul and the game was held up for 15 minutes. A coiled heating system may have been the most famous example of San Francisco incompetence. Built under the seats in order to warm the behinds of frigid fans, it never did work. Famed attorney Melvin Belli froze his toes and sued, winning full damages: the price of his season ticket, which he paid to San Francisco for the planting of trees, but "not at Candlestick," he said. "They would freeze out there."

Stoneham had a legal waiver printed in the program disavowing future responsibility for malfunctions. Women complained about their nylons torn by the seats. Heart attacks occurred when people walked the steep hills to get to the park in the brutal bayside conditions. "Cardiac Hill" got its name when 16 people died traversing it. In 1962 the elevators failed. A sum of $55,000 was paid to a Palo Alto firm to study the wind, but no answers were forthcoming.

"It's an act of God"!?

It was a waste of dough, just like the money paid to Harney. It had open-ended bleachers, and the monstrous shipbuilding crane loomed beyond like the alien space ship in *Independence Day*. Anything hit in the air was an adventure. Dust swirled amid hot dog wrappers. The players despised everything about the place. It had no redeeming qualities whatsoever, except that people who wanted to leave were allowed to. At night, the fog rolled in like Old Testament Egypt on Passover.

Fans from warm surrounding communities showed up for midsummer games in shorts and T-shirts, then froze to the bone. There was no relief under the stands, which became wind tunnels, even worse than the open spaces. After games, fans were met head-on by the howling elements. Whitecaps roiled the bay. The parking lot immediately had cracks in the cement, since it had been built on landfill. Broken glass was not picked up by the city-employed stadium operations, all of whom were bored and lifeless and made fans feel unwelcome.

The concessions were blasé, hot dogs were cold, the buns were soggy. Beer was warm. Concessionaires were rude. The bathrooms stunk of vomit and urine. It was dirty the day it opened and never got better. The city-built, city-owned, and city-controlled Candlestick was a symbol of government inefficiency. San Francisco, once considered a "can-do" city that, after the 1906 Great Earthquake, had rebuilt itself in time for the Pan-Pacific Exhibition of 1915, lost enormous prestige.

When fans left Candlestick, there was nothing to do for miles and miles and miles anywhere near the place—no restaurants, no bars. Whatever was there was dangerous and uninviting, anyway. South San Francisco, the nearest civilization to the south, had no nightlife of any kind. It was an "Industrial City," which they advertised itself as on a nearby bluff much the way high schools put up a giant "D" or "R" on hills overlooking campuses. Someplace that nobody even knew how to actually get to, called Brisbane, existed somewhere west of the stadium. It was of no use beyond a postal annex.

The downtown fun spots of Union Square, the Marina, and Fisherman's Wharf required a car ride on the freeway, or through the ghetto, then exiting and negotiating major parking hassles. There was little ancillary benefit to the City. Most fans just wanted to get home. If they lived on the peninsula, they never came close to the city center coming or going from Candlestick.

Then there was its effect on Mays. The winds just pushed his powerful shots back onto the field of play. He was forced to alter his swing and become an off-field line drive hitter. Candlestick Park eliminated any chance he had at breaking Babe Ruth's career home run record of 714. The place was a disaster with a capital "D."

—◦—

The building of Candlestick Park compared to that of Dodger Stadium really serves as proof positive that private industry is superior to public works. Mayor Christopher arranged for the city and county of San Francisco to control Candlestick's building and operations, farming out its concessions, parking, and other services to its government friends, some of whom were mobbed up and corrupt. Harney had a place to put his dirt and a sweetheart government contract to build the place.

It opened for business in 1960, and despite all the graft, made a good first impression. There was not much to compare it to, really. County Stadium in Milwaukee was new, but many of the sports stadiums throughout the land went back to the World War I era or the Roaring '20s. Yankee Stadium, the L.A. Coliseum, the Rose Bowl, Cal's Memorial Stadium, and Stanford Stadium had all opened in the early 1920s. Basketball "arenas" were cow barns and B.O. boxes. The L.A. Sports Arena, opened in 1959, was thought at the time to be the best in the nation.

So, nobody had a visual of Dodger Stadium, or the "fabulous" Forum, or the Oakland–Alameda County Coliseum, to compare Candlestick Park to. California governor Edmund "Pat" Brown hosted Vice President Richard Nixon on Opening Day. Nixon announced that the place was the "finest" stadium in the world. Dodgers announcer Vin Scully said the oval architecture reminded him of a spaceship, which was very popular in the science fiction culture of the era.

But that was the end of its good reviews. Famed tort lawyer Melvin Belli sued the club because the heaters built under its seats failed to heat. In 1960, the Giants contended in a crowded National League pennant race, but fell off toward the end when Pittsburgh captured the crown.

—◦—

In 1961, Candlestick's legacy was enshrined forever. Long before "global warming" the midsummer classic of '61 featured extreme climate change all in one afternoon. At the game's beginning temperatures were reported around 100 degrees, a figure likely reached less than 10 times in the park's history. By the late innings, however, the wind was howling and the temps falling precipitously. The Giants' own Stu Miller, a diminutive figure, was brought on and went into his wind-up. A draft of wind caught him and he was called for a balk. The writers said he was "blown off" the mound, which was not quite true, but that narrative carried on for years.

Longtime Giants reporter Nick Peters of the *Sacramento Bee* reported in his book *Tales from the San Francisco Giants Dugout* that Horace Stoneham invited Yankee greats Mickey Mantle and Whitey Ford to the Olympic Club for golf and lunch the day before the game. Mantle recalled that Horace told Ford, "If you get Willie out, I'll sign for everything." If Mays got a hit off Ford, however, the $400 tab was on the two ballplayers.

"So, when Whitey struck out Mays, I came runnin' in from center field, jumpin' in the air like we'd just won the World Series," recalled Mantle. "Nobody could figure it out—except Horace Stoneham."

The first football game played at Candlestick resulted in the Chargers defeating the Oakland Raiders 41–17 in an AFL contest played December 4, 1960. Future congressman and vice presidential candidate Jack Kemp, whose son would later play for the 49ers, threw the first touchdown pass. Charlie Harney was part owner of the original Raiders, who played their first five games at Kezar Stadium. The Raiders moved to Frank Youell Field, a high school facility, after the 1961 season. The Oakland–Alameda County Coliseum, which would have a profound impact on Giants attendance, was built in 1965.

My mother always told me as a child that if I devoted as much time, interest and energy to my schoolwork as I did to collecting and studying baseball cards and magazines, playing baseball, watching the Giants and reading about them in the morning papers, I would have straight A's.

—SAN FRANCISCO RADIO SPORTS REPORTER STEVE BITKER

Superiority Complex

By 1962 there was frustration with the club. "San Franciscans [who expect a pennant] are advised to stay away from coarse foods . . . avoid stimulants that irritate the stomach walls . . . if seized by a choking feeling, lay quietly and well-covered until your physician arrives," wrote Mel Durslag of the *Los Angeles Herald Examiner*. The well-aimed barbs between Los Angelenos toward San Franciscans came early and often.

Candlestick was a model on how not to build a stadium, first learned by the Dodgers. Candlestick Park was the laughing stock symbol of San Francisco ineptitude in the face of Los Angeles excellence. L.A.'s efforts at building Dodger Stadium went smoothly. A New Yorker, Captain Emil Praeger was the chief architect. Vanell Construction built it to perfection; every seat unobstructed, spacious parking for 16,000 cars, all landscaped with exotic tropical shrubs and palm trees.

Despite all of this public evidence of San Francisco's . . . inferiority, San Francisco and San Franciscans insisted on the myth that they were instead superior! The leading lights of this subject were two local gossip columnists, Herb Caen and Charles McCabe, and a politico named Art Hoppe. Caen and McCabe wrote provincial articles extolling the virtue of all things in the City Caen called, in those pre–Saddam Hussein days, "Baghdad by the bay." McCabe had some style. They wrote for the *San Francisco Chronicle*. Its sports section was printed on green paper and called the "Sporting Green." They employed a couple of good baseball writers, but the whole emphasis was on the Giants with a "homer" point of view.

The afternoon paper, the *Examiner*, was better. The contrast with Los Angeles excellence manifested itself, this time in the form of the *Los Angeles Times*. The heart of the *Times* was a brilliant wordsmith named

Jim Murray. Murray, like so many on the West Coast, was an East Coast transplant who came to the paper from *Time* magazine, where he covered Hollywood during an era of true decadence; the last of the studio system, Mob influence, and Frank Sinatra's Rat Pack. Murray once went on a date/interview with Marilyn Monroe, which was broken up when the sex symbol excused herself to leave with another guy. Joe DiMaggio had been lurking in a nearby booth at the Brown Derby.

Murray came to the *Los Angeles Times* in 1961. He wrote with a social pathos, imbuing his sports reportage with observations that the University of Alabama, for instance, was not deserving of the term national champion so long as they neither played integrated opponents, traveled to the North, nor had black players on their roster themselves. It also did not make sense to call the Crimson Tide number one when they lost their bowl game after the final Associated Press poll. Murray was, quite simply, the best sportswriter who ever lived.

The difference between Murray and the San Franciscans' Hoppe, Caen, and McCabe was vast. The elitist view of themselves was embodied by a 1960s column McCabe wrote in which he claimed to have been spared a parking ticket in Paris when the gendarme learned of his San Francisco pedigree.

"You mention that you are from San Francisco and you are immediately a gent, as distinct from the yahoos who bully blacks and throw tear gas at kids . . . and live in ticky-tack houses and go to ticky-tack supermarkets," McCabe wrote.

A San Franciscan, "in the eyes of most Europeans," is really "a civilized European," and the City was an "Arcadian enclave" separated from the backward burgs of America's "fly over country."

"San Francisco, like John Kennedy, has been formally canonized in Europe," McCabe wrote. "It comes as no news to anyone that Europeans hate our guts," he continued. McCabe in his column wailed against our nation's tendency toward wealth and power thrust upon the whole world.

The "traveling American . . . tends to be a quite awful advertisement for his country," he wrote. "He does not care about people in Paris." Apparently, Jack and Jacqueline Kennedy were the sole antidotes to American rudeness.

—◦—

San Franciscans grudgingly acknowledged the greatness of Dodger Stadium. Some things were just too spectacular to deny. They would find
fault with the Dodgers and their fans, who tended to leave in the seventh
inning to beat the traffic, but the stadium itself was a monument.

It certainly did not look good for "Frisco," the name they hated to
be referred to as, in April 1962. The two teams had been in California
for four seasons. The only team to make it to, and win, a World Series
was Los Angeles. Candlestick was a joke. NoCal was getting fed up
with SoCal hegemony. The year 1962 was a particularly good Southern
California sports season. USC went unbeaten, shut out Notre Dame
25–0, and defeated Wisconsin in the Rose Bowl 42–37 to capture the
national championship. The Lakers extended Boston to seven games in
the NBA Finals.

The Trojans and Bruins regularly dominated Cal and Stanford in all
sports. The dynamic of the schools was beginning to take on a political
edge, with Cal and Stanford playing the role of jealous losers.

While L.A. had the Lakers, the Warriors did not move to San Francisco from Philadelphia until the 1962–1963 season. The expansion
Angels looked to be a mini-success. The A's were still in Kansas City, six
years away from their move to Oakland. The Rams consistently had the
upper hand over the 49ers. The Raiders were nobodies. Now this fabulous
new Dodger Stadium threatened to catapult the already-favored Dodgers to a big championship season. Willie Mays and the Giants were the
City's last, best hope to prevent more indignity.

—◦—

Charles McCabe was a columnist, perhaps he might
have been thought of as a "gossip columnist," which
in the era of Walter Winchell in the glory days of
newspapers is significantly different from the work
performed by Leah Garchik in the modern *San
Francisco Chronicle*. Today, San Francisco is thought
of as a liberal city, but until the 1960s it was not. It
was certainly not a Republican lock, but it could be
had by either party. In 1958, when the San Fran-

cisco Giants came west from New York, and in 1960, when Candlestick Park opened, it was presided over by a GOP mayor, George Christopher.

But the City's political shift to the left is largely measured by three columnists at the *Chronicle*: Herb Caen, Art Hoppe, and Charles McCabe. It was McCabe who seemed to capture a vibe, set in the San Francisco of the 1960s, that lasted until Joe Montana and the 1981 San Francisco 49ers put the notion to rest; that San Francisco was an inferior city with a superiority complex in which its denizens did not want "ultimate victory" because, like English gentlemen, it was bad form to be too gifted at "games." Second place, the bridesmaid to a flashy bride, was set in the San Francisco mind as acceptable, almost preferable.

New York City, the New Rome of the American Empire, was a conquering champion of sports, finance, and culture. Los Angeles had the glitz and glamour of Hollywood, then quickly announced its sports presence with authority by winning the 1959 World Series.

But there was something "jarring," according to McCabe, about winning the World Series. It placed too many expectations, it was too showy a display of excellence. It was not fair or egalitarian enough. In those pre-Vietnam days it might even have been a subtle hint that the United States really needed to lose a war every so often to bring it down a peg or two, and that L.A.'s world title was like Howard Hughes winning a contract to develop rocket boosters for NASA.

Bad form for the City.

Alex Pompez and the Latino Pipeline

SEVERAL STRONG SPORTS ORGANIZATIONS WERE BUILT ON THE STRENGTH of enlightened integration policies. The University of Southern California had a black All-American football player as early as 1925, and later coach John McKay turned the Trojans into a juggernaut using superstar black athletes.

UCLA went from being a commuter school to a national sports powerhouse because they took advantage of all the available black talent, not just in Southern California high schools but in the South, where all-white colleges were off-limits to them. John Wooden's basketball dynasty is attributable in large measure to his recruitment of black stars while Atlantic Coast Conference competition, for instance, did not.

The Brooklyn Dodgers, long a laughing stock, became a fabled franchise when they brought Jackie Robinson, Roy Campanella, Don Newcombe, and others into the organization.

The Giants decided to follow a similar strategy. While the New York Giants signed black stars such as Willie Mays and Monte Irvin, they also recognized a new source of talent in Latin America, placing great focus on the region. The early San Francisco Giants were a team with a disproportionate amount of Latino star power.

Latinos had never been banned from Major League baseball. Cuba was a source of talent, producing the likes of pitcher Dolf Luque, a 27-game winner with Cincinnati in 1923. This posed quite the conundrum: black American citizens were denied rights accorded to foreigners.

Long before Robinson's breakthrough, Giants manager John McGraw had employed a black player "disguised" as a Cuban, but the ruse was discovered. Jokes were made of blacks, particularly light-skinned ones, that they were "Cubans" or "Puerto Ricans," but no real breakthroughs occurred. Cubans, Mexicans, Puerto Ricans, and Dominicans could play organized ball as long as they were more Spanish than Negro.

Negro League barnstormers made baseball popular in the Dominican Republican when the dictator Rafael Trujillo recruited them in the 1930s, ostensibly to divert public attention from his oppressive methods. Branch Rickey, the man responsible for Robinson, also opened doors for dark-skinned Latinos in the early 1950s. Robinson had been kicked out the door by his nemesis, Walter O'Malley, but took over the operations at Pittsburgh. The Dodgers had the first shot at Roberto Clemente, a dark-skinned super outfield prospect from Puerto Rico. No longer benefiting from Rickey's leadership, they faltered on the issue of signing Clemente, leaving the door open for Rickey and the Pirates.

The Giants had already taken steps toward fulfilling the promise of Latin America, a place of great political turmoil after World War II. Latin dictators strangely affiliated themselves with Adolf Hitler, who would have considered these brown-skin types to be worthy of the ovens once they had served his purposes. Nevertheless, many Nazis found safe haven in Argentina, Brazil, and other countries. Anti-American sentiment became popular in the 1950s, mainly as a reaction to US business interests monopolizing these "banana republics."

Cuba went Communist, thus ending the steady flow of baseball talent that included the likes of Camilo Pasqual and Tony Oliva of Minnesota. The rest of the region picked up the slack. Excellent year-round weather made it a game played in the winter as well as the summer. Soccer had always been popular, but basketball and football did not take. Baseball did. Fans were gaga over the game. Winter leagues were created in which numerous American stars and prospects honed their off-season skills—sometimes in harrowing political and criminal circumstances—beginning in the 1950s. Coups, revolutions, banditry, and kidnappings were commonplace happenings along with baseball.

The Giants did not land Clemente, but they saw more where that came from in Puerto Rico, an American protectorate and therefore friendlier to US interests, not to mention easier to obtain visas. Their man in charge was Allesandro "Alex" Pompez. Pompez was more than a baseball scout; he was a cultural liaison. The transition for Latino players was a shock to the system in the 1950s and 1960s. Most minor league and spring training towns were in the South, with profound effect on these youngsters.

First, Pompez put a sales pitch on the families, assuring them that he would oversee the development of their children, handling contracts and explaining wages and work rights, not to mention instructing them on haircuts, shoe shines, clothing styles, and myriad aspects of American life. Pompez steered many a Latino player away from other clubs and toward the Giants.

A dandy man, well dressed and stylish, Pompez was a "father figure" to the Latino players. A native of Key West, Florida, he spoke fluent Spanish but was an American who could cross racial, cultural, and national lines. Pompez was a pioneering black baseball executive with the New York Cubans of the old Negro League. He also was involved in the bootlegging rackets of the Prohibition era. His financially successful operation was partnered with Arthur "Dutch" Schultz, known as "the Beer Baron of New York." Pompez supervised Schultz's profitable numbers rackets.

Later, Schultz was murdered in a feud with the notorious Charles "Lucky" Luciano. When New York special prosecutor Thomas Dewey went after him, tying him to the Mob, Pompez escaped to Mexico, but returned when he agreed to testify against organized crime syndicates in return for immunity.

"He became the only guy who ever snitched on the Mob and lived to tell about it," said Negro League pitching star Leon Day.

Pompez regained control of his team, which played at the Polo Grounds. He developed a cordial business relationship with Giants owner Horace Stoneham. When Robinson signed with Brooklyn Pompez was hired as the club's point man in an effort to keep the Giants even with the Dodgers when it came to signing black stars.

But Pompez's Latino background made him indispensable in the Caribbean. He was involved in the scouting and signing of Mays and of course other Negro Leaguers, but the Caribbean was quickly developing as a hotbed of baseball talent. The Pirates and Senators were the main early competition for Latino players, but Pompez kept the New York Giants ahead of the rest.

Many saw California as the future, a progressive place where racial intolerance was not acceptable. The Giants discovered that while it was different, in some ways their Harlem digs had been more accessible to minority players than "liberal" San Francisco. The early San Francisco teams were derided by "poison pen" letters who complained about "Rig's Jigs" (manager Bill Rigney), "Sheehan's Shines" (manager Tom Sheehan), and "Dark's Darkies" (manager Alvin Dark). In their first season in the Bay Area, the Giants' roster included minority players Leon Wagner, Willie Kirkland, Bill White, Ruben Gomez, Sam Jones, Ray Monzant, Andre Rogers, and Valmy Thomas. By 1962, one-quarter of the team was black or Latin.

The Preacher

ALVIN DARK'S STORY IS ONE OF RECONCILIATION, REDEMPTION, AND NEW understanding, followed by sociopolitical restructuring. This describes how the American South struggled to find, as Abe Lincoln called them, "the better angels of our nature." In many ways through sports, the South came to grips with new racial realities, then saw the Republican Party husband the region "back into the Union" until they became not a marginalized New Deal voting bloc, but "rose again" to emerge as an economic and political powerhouse.

Al Dark was that walking conundrum of Dixie: the hardcore Baptist Christian burdened by racial prejudice. Through baseball, he was able to get out of the South and become a man of the world. It led him to New York, where he starred for the 1954 World Champion Giants. A great picture exists of Dark and the black superstar Willie Mays, smiling in each other's company during the team's Broadway ticker-tape parade.

The Giants of the early 1960s were one of the first truly integrated teams. Mays, Willie McCovey, Felipe Alou, Juan Marichal, and Orlando Cepeda were black and Latino stars of the first order.

Dark, who lived in Atherton, appeared at religious functions. The Holy Bible went everywhere with him and he read it . . . religiously. The Giants were in contrast to the secular nature of the City. Aside from Dark, they had a large number of Christian players. The Latinos, in particularly, were strong Catholics. Mays and McCovey, while never known for being outgoing Christians, were from the Bible Belt and could not help but be influenced by that upbringing.

Despite that, Dark refused to make the Giants' clubhouse a church. "He had a rule against presenting his Christian testimony to any of the players while in uniform, a rule I was also to abide by," said Felipe Alou.

"He told me he felt there was ample time to talk about my beliefs, but that while I was in the clubhouse and on the field I was to be dedicated to winning baseball games."

Dark was particularly careful about talking religion with the San Francisco press corps, among which there were Jews and Left Coast secularists. In spring training he did draw a parable, calling the cut-off play "just like the Bible. You don't question it, you just accept it."

Off the field he neither smoked nor drank. On the field he was aggressive, a gambler who "instilled an aggressiveness in that ballclub," recalled catcher Tom Haller. "He wanted us to play hard. Alvin loved to win, but hated to lose. And he did curse. He'd get hot under the collar and could get quite angry at times."

After screaming profanities to umpire Shag Crawford, he "confessed" to the *San Francisco Examiner* that "the devil was in me," that it was "not a Christian thing to do." "Never before have I so addressed any man—and with the Lord's help, I hope to have the strength to never do so again." Dark could be a martinet, lumping the good in with bad after a tough loss, which embittered all.

Dark was born on January 22, 1922, in Comanche, Oklahoma, the son of an oil well engineer. The family moved to Lake Charles, Louisiana, where he grew up in a staunchly religious household. Life in the Bayou state of his childhood was heavily Baptist, strong in racist and segregationist overtones. Laws outlawing integration had been on the books since the Civil War era. When Felipe Alou played in Louisiana in 1956, he and a minority teammate were banned from future action by a law forbidding whites and blacks from playing with or against each other.

Dark's religious convictions were the shield against instinctive racism. His years in New York with black and Latino teammates certainly moderated him further. "Since I had been a kid, the ways I have used to express myself have been mostly physical . . . I was not good at expressing my thoughts verbally or on paper," said Dark.

Dark was not alone in the southern white's interpretation of the racial dynamic. "I felt that because I was from the South—and we from the South actually take care of colored people, I think, better than they're taken care of in the North—I felt when I was playing with them it was a responsibility for me," he said in Jackie Robinson's 1964 book *Baseball Has Done It*. "I liked the idea that I was pushed to take care of them and make them feel at home and to help them out any way possible that I could playing baseball the way that you can win pennants."

Alvin played football and baseball, but his love was baseball. At age 10 he played against 19-year-olds. He was all-state in football, captain of the basketball team. LSU beat out Texas A&M for his services. He played football and baseball for the Tigers. In 1942, his sophomore year, Dark was the running back along with Steve Van Buren, later a Hall of Famer with the Eagles.

Dark was in the Marines during World War II and was assigned to officer candidate school at Southwestern Louisiana State, where he earned football All-American honors. He played halfback on an overseas team in 1945 before going to China. Sports kept him out of major combat, as it did for numerous college and pro athletes. Despite being drafted by the NFL and the All-American Football Conference, Dark went for the Boston Braves, breaking into the big leagues in 1946. He played all of 1947 at triple-A, then helped lead the Braves to the 1948 World Series at age 26.

The middle infield of Dark and Eddie Stanky was distinctively southern. Stanky taught the youngster the intricacies of the game. Dark's .322 average earned him Rookie of the Year honors over Philadelphia's Richie Ashburn. In 1949 Dark and the Braves tanked. Manager Billy Southworth lost his son and drank heavily. Dark learned from Southworth things *not* to do. Dark and Stanky were too opinionated. Both were traded to the New York Giants.

Leo Durocher loved Dark's fiery ways. When Dark turned down $500 to make a smoking commercial, Durocher paid him the money and made him captain. He thought of Dark as a player-coach, a manager on the field.

Over the years, Dark played for Gene Mauch, Charley Dressen, and Fred Hutchinson, all respected baseball minds. "You get the chance to learn managing from a Durocher or a Mauch—that's a pretty good education," he said.

Dark helped New York win two pennants and the 1954 World Series before being traded to St. Louis. He later played for the Cubs, Phillies, and Braves. Whenever a new man joined teams Alvin played for, Dark would take him out to dinner, which was "something as a player that only one other man in baseball did to my knowledge," said ex-teammate Lee Walls, who played for the Dodgers in 1962.

In 14 years he had more than 2,000 hits and batted .289. In late 1960 Milwaukee traded him to San Francisco for shortstop Andre Rogers, and he took over as their manager in 1961.

"I never thought I'd say this about anybody," Willie Mays told writer Charles Einstein a few years later, "but I actually think more of 'Cap' [Dark] than I did of Leo. You know what he did when they made him manager? He sent me a letter, telling me how glad he was we were going to be back together again. How can you not want to play for a guy like that?"

Dark's hiring both fell in line with but deviated from owner Horace Stoneham's normal methods. On the one hand, the Stoneham family had hired former Giants players in the past: Bill Terry, Mel Ott, and Bill Rigney. They liked loyalty and tradition. There was a feeling that to be a Giant was something bigger than to be a Phillie or a Red. But Stoneham also liked hail-fellow-well-met types who he could share a cocktail and camaraderie with. Leo Durocher had not played for the Giants, but was certainly not averse to drinking. So was the Irishman Tom Sheehan.

"Normally, Horace insists that his managers drink with him," recalled Bill Veeck. "It goes with the job. When he drinks, everybody drinks. Especially if he is paying their salaries."

Dark, 39, did not drink. He was loyal to Stoneham and would perform his job 100 percent, but he would not drink. Stoneham understood and did not press the subject. Dark's coaching staff, hired in 1961, came straight out of the great 1951 pennant winners: Larry Jansen (40), Whitey Lockman (34), and Wes Westrum (38). The coaches as well as Dark were all active players in 1960.

"He had a lot of faith in our judgment," said Jansen. "Wes was a solid defensive catcher and a great guy. Lockman really knew how to deal with people, and I guess Alvin thought I knew enough about pitching to help him."

"I know what each of us can do," Dark told the media. "When I assign them their work at Spring Training, I can relax. I know the job is getting done because they know what I want done. And they do it."

Dark's temper was difficult for him to control in those days. "We were playing the Phillies and lost three straight games by one run," Dark recalled. "We had our opportunities, but couldn't score. After one of those ballgames I heard some guys at the other end of the clubhouse laughing. What they were laughing about, I don't know. It was probably something I should have found out before I got so mad. But it hit me all at once. How could anybody laugh in a situation like this?"

Dark picked up a stool and threw it with full force against a door. His finger had lodged into the chair and he lost the tip of his little finger. On another occasion Dark turned over the food trays in Houston, ruining one of Willie McCovey's cherished suits. Willie Mac was a clothes horse. Dark provided the first baseman with a check the next day to pay for a new outfit.

Dark had not been away from the playing field long enough to gain the proper perspective for managing. He wanted his players to play as he had, and was upset at the "new breed" of athlete that was just starting to emerge in the 1960s. It was not just a matter of race, although the game was rapidly changing its "complexion," but the modern player was different, less intense, more worldly.

Great managers and coaches have always been identified as those who could change with the times. That was the key to John Wooden's success at UCLA, and Bear Bryant's at Alabama. Dark was old school. *San Francisco Chronicle* columnist Charles McCabe said that Dark's attitude was a "very dangerous thing," that the manager felt that he needed to "win every game himself."

Dark stood in the dugout "like Washington crossing the Delaware," one writer quipped. He did not have time for jokes or tobacco-jawing, saying that he had seen too many managers let the game pass them by. He had no use for individual achievements, even though his team had some of the greatest individual stars in baseball. It was a challenge for him.

Dark immediately noticed at his first spring training that the team was divided between whites, blacks, and Latinos. He had equipment manager Eddie Logan mix the cubicles so that blacks would be next to whites, Latinos next to blacks, and the like. "It went over like a lead balloon," Dark admitted.

Dark also had a sign posted in the clubhouse that read: "Speak English, You're in America." Dark had a meeting of the Latinos and said the others complained that they jabbered in Spanish. There were worries that they were telling jokes or hatching plots behind teammates' backs. But Cepeda called Dark's complaints "an insult to our language," and the Latinos kept talking in their native tongue.

Felipe Alou understood what Dark was trying to do, which was to assimilate these players into the culture, their new country, and with their teammates, but said it was forced. "Can you imagine talking to your own brothers in a foreign language?" he said, and he should know; brothers Matteo and Jesus were all in the Giants' organization. Besides, many of the Latinos spoke poor English, so it was hard for them.

Dark, however, was not rigid. When he imposed an edict that did not work, he realized it and stopped the practice, as he did with the cubicle assignments and the "only English" rules.

"My intentions were good but the results were bad, so I stopped it," he said.

Unlike Walt Alston, Dark was not a "by the book" manager, said pitcher Billy O'Dell. He thought out every move and had reasons for them. He liked using defensive replacements and went to his bullpen early by the standards of the day. He juggled his batting order, tried to apply defensive strategy based on his interpretation of the shifting Candlestick winds, and warmed up relievers just to bluff opponents.

"Alvin overmanaged, but even he admitted that," said Charles Einstein. The writers called him the "mad scientist." He had fake pick-off plays and other gadget maneuvers.

"I don't think I ever managed thinking some move was the 'safe' thing to do," said Dark. He said he wanted to "have some fun. But you only have fun when you win."

Dark was competitive at everything, including gin rummy (which he was taught by Leo Durocher, a master) and golf. He beat his players on the greens and used that to extract a psychological advantage.

Dark could play "little ball" even with the slugging Giants, and had a grading system that awarded points to players whose obvious statistics were not comparable to a Mays, McCovey, or Cepeda. If a player moved a runner along 30 or 40 times in a season, Dark had kept a record of it and the players were able to use that in contract negotiations.

When Dark told the writers that third baseman Jim Davenport's plus/minus record was excellent, but that Orlando Cepeda's was "terribly minus," he asked that it not be printed in the headlines. The papers ran it anyway. *Look* magazine printed Cepeda's so-called minus-forty rating, and the sensitive first baseman sued for *defamation of character*. He lost.

In March 1962, the conflict between Cepeda and Dark took a turn for the worse when, after a brilliant 1961 campaign, Orlando held out of spring training for $60,000.

Dark's biggest concern entering spring training was the age of his pitching staff. Sam Jones and Billy Loes, both effective pitchers in the 1950s, had nothing left. Dark was relying on 32-year-old Don Larsen and 35-year-old Billy Pierce. Larsen was a hard drinker whose lifestyle made him a decade older. Pierce had been an outstanding pitcher with the Chicago White Sox, but in the Cactus League he was terrible. His spring ERA hovered around 16.00. He gave up a plethora of home runs.

Billy O'Dell held out and Jack Sanford was an unknown quantity, maybe excellent, maybe a bust. Stu Miller was the bullpen ace. A host of untested young pitchers included Jim Duffalo, Bob Bolin, and Gaylord Perry. Twenty-three-year-old Mike McCormick offered huge potential but was always seemingly troubled with arm injuries. Juan Marichal was worried sick about his girlfriend, Alma. Dominican dictator Rafael Trujillo had been assassinated, and violent extremists threatened to throw a bomb through the window of her family's home.

Marichal requested a leave so he could go to the Dominican Republic, marry Alma, and bring her to America. Dark never hesitated.

"He was terribly unhappy and needed to get that gal up here," recalled Dark.

Marichal was deeply grateful and wanted to do something for Dark. He asked Willie Mays for advice.

"Win," said Mays.

Dark certainly could count on Mays to provide veteran leadership, hustle, and his usual brilliance. Ed Bailey was a veteran catcher. Tom Haller was a youngster. Thirty-two-year-old Harvey Kuenn could still hit. Jose Pagan would provide good defense. Jim Davenport was solid at third base. Chuck "Iron Hands" Hiller was the second baseman. Dark decided to make him a project in spring training—to improve him defensively.

"That showed me that Dark could be a teacher, and he made Hiller into a second baseman," said *San Francisco Examiner* sportswriter Harry Jupiter.

First base was a festering controversy, albeit an embarrassment of riches: Orlando Cepeda and Willie McCovey. After Cepeda finally signed, Dark needed to find a place for Willie Mac. Left field was the only solution, but his outfield was also full: Kuenn, the Alou brothers, and of course Mays in center.

Team trainer Frank "Doc" Bowman posted a sign on the clubhouse wall in Phoenix: "Work hard this year—and eat corn on the cob all winter." It did not make a lot of sense but its meaning was clear. They had potential, and if they made the most of it a championship was theirs for the taking.

—— ~ ——

The guy who really messed up the Giants was Alvin Dark. I don't know why they fired Bill Rigney.

—GIANTS SLUGGER ORLANDO CEPEDA

Meet the 1962 San Francisco Giants

FELIPE ALOU, 27, AVERAGED .274 IN FOUR PREVIOUS SEASONS. WHEN he was out with a sore elbow, the club lost six of eight. When he returned they won eight straight. In June Alou was hitting .345, one point from the National League lead. "I just am hitting better through the middle than I ever did," he said. "I have no worry about whether I hit .170 or .300. I have great confidence since Al Dark plays me regular. Don't worry. I just swing."

Batting fifth instead of first as in 1961, the six-foot, 195-pounder said, "This year I like where I am batting. I am too big for a lead-off man. I cannot try to get walks. I am a swinger, not a waiter."

Alou embarked on consecutive-game hitting streaks of 11, 10, 9, and 8 games in 1962. He was also very mature, a solid influence on moody fellow Latinos Cepeda and Marichal, as well as a pathfinder for younger brothers Matty and Jesus.

"Felipe was a very classy person, and a good team ballplayer," said Billy Pierce. "He led a great life and carried himself well. He would try to work with the guys. If some of the Latin fellows got a little excited, he would be the man to calm them down. I don't know if Felipe would ever swear about anything."

Felipe carried his Bible with him at all times, which helped him form a bond with Dark. But he spoke up to writers and was no "shrinking violet," according to writer David Plaut. When Dark kicked over the food table, Alou picked the food off the floor and ate it while staring at Dark. The message was clear: food was a gift from God. Born into poverty, Alou never wasted it.

Alou was born in the fishing village of Haina, Dominican Republic, in 1935, the eldest of four sons. His father, Rojas, was a blacksmith and, like Jesus of Nazareth, a carpenter. He made hand-carved bats for his sons, who practiced by hitting lemons.

In high school Felipe was a track star, but played baseball in the summer leagues. At 16 he worked in a concrete mix facility and became a legend when he *wrestled sharks with his bare hands*! His grades were excellent and he attended the University of Santo Domingo to study medicine. He played on the baseball team, coached by a Giants "bird dog" named Horacio Martinez. Alou's father lost his job and Felipe quit school to support his family. He signed a $200 bonus for the Giants and went to Lake Charles, Louisiana of the Evangeline League.

He was barred by his color and sent to Cocoa Beach, where he led the Florida State League at .308. He impressed the Americans by learning English and in 1958 made it to San Francisco. In 1961 he became a starter, but pitchers could get him out on the outside corner.

He arrived at spring training in 1962 and closed up his stance. It paid off immediately. He hit .500 in the Cactus League and stayed hot in regular season play, was moved from leadoff to fifth, and displayed power. Alou went on a 12-game tear. His homer in Cincinnati shattered the letters on an advertisement atop the Crosley Field scoreboard.

He killed the Dodgers in an April series, prompting a Dodger fan to send a telegram to San Francisco: "Roses are red, violets are blue . . . we'll give our team for Felipe Alou."

He continued hitting well in the first half and made the All-Star Game. He had nine straight hits at one point.

For all of Alou's on-field exploits, however, his greatest contribution might have been when he saved Juan Marichal from drowning off the coast of Haina.

Jim Davenport made the National League All-Star team in 1962. He finally came into his own after years of injuries. He already was generally viewed as the best fielding third sacker in the senior circuit. If he could stay healthy he was destined for greatness. The press dubbed him "a man for all lesions."

His injuries were an anomaly, since he had been a college safety at Southern Mississippi without any health problems. Alabama originally recruited him but 'Bama had a rule against married players. Since Davenport was wed, the scholarship was rescinded and he ended up at Southern Miss instead. In his sophomore and junior years he led his team to upsets over the Crimson Tide. The losing quarterback both times was Bart Starr.

Davenport was an original 1958 Giant, but suffered rib and ankle injuries. In 1959 it was an eye infection. On his 26th birthday he tore his knee up in a collision with Reds catcher Ed Bailey. Larry Jackson's pitch cracked his collarbone. Bleeding ulcers landed him in a Milwaukee hospital. He hurt his groin. His injuries made it tough to run and train properly. The lack of conditioning affected his stamina. The writers speculated that the missing ingredient between 1958 and 1961 was Davenport. Despite his injuries, he led the league in fielding percentage three years in a row.

"Here was a guy who was so quiet, and he never sought out publicity, but he is still the best fielding third baseman I ever saw," said Bob Stevens, a legendary baseball writer for the *Chronicle* who eventually had the press box named after him.

Second baseman Chuck Hiller, on the other hand, was a defensive liability who would lead the National League in errors in 1962.

"One time in Cincinnati, we went to see the very first James Bond movie," recalled Tom Haller. "At the end of the picture, it was discovered that the bad guy, Dr. No, had iron hands.

"So poor Charlie got nailed with 'Dr. No' for a while."

That was interchanged with "Iron Hands." The play-on-movie-words repeated itself two years later with San Carlos, California–born first baseman Dick Stuart of the Boston Red Sox. A power hitter with zero defensive skills, Stuart was given the nickname "Dr. Strange*glove*" after the title character of the film *Dr. Strangelove*.

Hiller had actually led two minor leagues in fielding after being signed by the same Cleveland scout who had inked Bob Feller. The Giants picked him up in 1959 and he hit over .300. Hiller was a talker who Cepeda called "Abner," as in Doubleday, because "he talked like he invented the game."

But Hiller began to press, and the more he pressed the more it affected his play at the plate and in the field. After spending 1961 at triple-A, Hiller was told by Dark he was the starter in 1962. Hiller spent the spring fretting over whether he would blow the opportunity, but when the season started and he was the starter, he was his old "Abner" self again. His fielding, despite the errors, was adequate and he was adept at turning double plays. None of the Giants pitchers was a strikeout artist, certainly not like Sandy Koufax and Don Drysdale, so they needed those twin killings.

Hiller's partner was Jose Pagan, who "has been making me look good on double-plays," said Hiller in 1962. "When [he] gained confidence in me, we started to function as a combination. We're at ease with each other now."

Pagan was probably the least publicized player on the team. He was a Latino on a team of high-profile, high-temper Latinos, but he remained quiet and reserved. "With big stars like Mays, Marichal and so many others, it's too bad Jose never really got the recognition he deserved," said Cepeda. "He was there every day, made all the plays and he could hit."

"You didn't have to worry about Pagan at all," said Billy O'Dell. "He was in the right place all the time. Some of the other guys, you might have wanted to move them a little bit, but not Jose."

Pagan had been signed by Pedro Zorilla, credited with the Cepeda signing. He played five years of minor league ball, and stuck in 1961 when he beat out Ed Bressoud for the job. Teammates called him "Humphrey" as in Bogart because of his nonplussed facial expressions, which the actor effectuated onscreen.

When the club had a scare flying to Chicago in 1962, the cabin went silent until Pagan broke the quiet with a blessed joke: "I say we should take a vote. I'm for taking the bus."

The remark eased the tension. Pagan hit eighth but drove in a lot of clutch runs. His fielding percentage in 1962 led the National League.

Harvey Kuenn was a former American League batting champion. He had hit .300 in eight of the previous nine seasons. Kuenn graduated from the University of Wisconsin in 1952 and announced that he was accepting bids for his services, which came in. Detroit won the "bidding war," signing him to a $55,000 package.

After 63 minor league games the shortstop was brought up in September 1952. In 1953 he was named Rookie of the Year. The 21-year-old picked up the tab for a lavish team party at his hotel. He was barely old enough to consume the alcohol that flowed, and in some ways Kuenn was the first of the "new breed": college educated, rich, and savvy.

He hit .300 every year, switched to the outfield, and was a perennial All-Star. On a team that included Al Kaline, he was the captain. His .353 average in 1959 won the batting title.

In 1960 a controversial trade sent Kuenn to Detroit for Rocky Colavito. Kuenn was booed, but he batted .308 and was the player representative. Cleveland fell below .500 after years of success and general manager Frank Lane traded him to San Francisco for Willie Kirkland and Johnny Antonelli. Harvey chewed Red Man on the field and smoked big cigars off it. *Sports Illustrated* did a piece on him. Writer Tex Maule said he kept the team loose, entertained, and united.

"I don't think there was anyone on the club who enjoyed life or playing in the big leagues more than Harvey," said Billy Pierce of Kuenn, who had married a beauty queen in Wisconsin.

"He's aggressive and a team man," Horace Stoneham said of Keunn.

One day Mays arrived to find a gift-wrapped package in his locker. The box of candy was opened to reveal two dozen decoratively wrapped pieces of horse manure.

"I know you done it," giggled Mays at the laughing Kuenn. "I know you done it."

At midseason Kuenn's dad died, but the club rallied around its friend.

"He taught the younger players about hitting, volunteering his own time which was something Mays didn't do," said Bob Stevens. "He also became very close to Stoneham. He loved drinking margaritas with Horace during Spring Training."

Charles Einstein noted that Kuenn was effective "drunk or sober."

⸺⸻

Matty Alou, the younger brother of Felipe Alou (and older brother of Jesus Alou), was born on December 22, 1938, in Haina, Dominican Republic. At 5'9" and 155 pounds he was much smaller than his powerful brother. He grew up with Juan Marichal and was part of the wholesale exportation of Dominican baseball talent to the United States that has become more than a cottage industry.

Matty played four Major League games in 1960 and 81 in 1961. He was a decent outfielder who threw and batted left-handed.

Carl Boles's only year in Major League baseball was 1962. He was called up from El Paso in midsummer. He would play the rest of his career in Japan. He had one distinctive trait, one reason for being memorable: he was a dead ringer for Willie Mays.

"It was really noticeable when we made a trip back to the Polo Grounds," said Boles. "Willie would get these huge ovations there. That night I came out through the center field bleachers before he did and the crowd thought I was Mays."

The Mets' fans gave him a standing ovation, until they noticed that his number was 14, not Mays's 24. Then they booed him. After games, fans wanting Willie's autograph would mob Boles. Sometimes he would sign Mays's name as a joke. He got excellent service at restaurants and roomed with Willie McCovey, which further made people think he was Mays, since the two Willies from Alabama were linked.

⸺⸻

Catcher Ed Bailey, 31, loved to talk about women, which is the favorite subject of most athletes anyway. His spicy descriptions of girls, alcohol, and his golf game earned him the nickname "Words" and "Mr. Clean."

"He loved to give guys the hot foot," said pitcher Mike McCormick. Wes Westrum was his favorite target because he fell asleep on the team bus.

Hailing from Strawberry Plains, Tennessee, Bailey broke into the bigs in 1953 and developed into a three-time All-Star catcher. In 1961 he was traded to San Francisco to make room for Johnny Edwards. The Reds won the title but Bailey was still happy to be in San Francisco. Cow-milking contests were occasionally held in big-league stadiums, and the country boy Bailey usually won.

Just as Bailey had been traded to make room for young Johnny Edwards, he discovered a young catching sensation on his new team: Tom Haller, 24, the former quarterback at the University of Illinois. Born on June 23, 1937, in Lockport, Illinois, he was the prototypical athlete/catcher. Haller was boyishly handsome, the all-American type possessing great leadership skills, a first-rate throwing arm, and a powerful left-handed bat. He was 6'4", 195 pounds, and had been called up to play 30 games in 1961. He was the Giants' future behind the dish. Bailey was there in case he was not ready, but Haller was ready in '62.

"Alvin told us we were both going to play, but it's only natural for them to want to go with the youngest guy they've got and look to the future," recalled Bailey. "And Dark liked having me available to come off the bench."

Bailey was involved in several "pier six brawls" in his career. In 1962 he followed Cepeda after a homer, and Pittsburgh's Bob Friend went after him. Catcher Don Leppert tackled Bailey. He and Friend exchanged shouts while being restrained. Then Bailey hit a 400-foot home run, giving rookie Gaylord Perry an 8–3 win, the first of his career. It started a 10-game winning streak.

Bailey and Haller provided 35 homers and 100 RBIs out of the catching position.

Billy O'Dell liked Bailey so much that the two operated *without signals.* Theirs was almost a telepathic relationship.

O'Dell was from Newberry, South Carolina; like Bailey, south of the Mason-Dixon Line. Baltimore signed him out of Clemson. Given the name "Digger" after the main character in *Life of Riley,* he never pitched in the minors.

He gained needed weight in the military and in 1957 made the bigs for good. He was an All-Star in 1958. Pitching for Baltimore in front of the Orioles' fans, he threw three scoreless innings in a 4–3 American

League win, but hurt his back the next year. O'Dell's back injury plagued him, and eventually he and Billy Loes were traded to San Francisco.

At first he and Dark feuded over how he was used. He was fined and they had shouting matches. Dark wanted to put him in the 1961 expansion draft but Stoneham insisted he be kept.

In 1962 spring training Dark told him he was the fourth starter "until you show me you can't do it." After an awesome spring he started game two of the regular season, beating the Braves with a four-hitter. The key was his relationship with Bailey. He was effective and consistent all season.

"He never really got credit for being a good catcher, but I thought he was a great receiver," said O'Dell.

——◆——

Billy O'Dell's catcher was Ed Bailey. Jack Sanford's guy was Tom Haller. Sanford was 33 years old and won 16 games in a row in 1962, his best year in the big leagues by far. The six-foot, 196-pound right-handed pitcher from Wellesley, Massachusetts, had been the 1957 Rookie of the Year with the Phillies before a 1958 trade to the Giants.

"Jack wasn't the easiest guy to know," said Haller. Sanford was from the "wrong side of the tracks" in a rough Boston neighborhood. Like all Boston Irishmen, it seemed, he had to "battle for everything in his life."

He was not a prospect in high school, which in cold Massachusetts was not much anyway. The Red Sox rejected him in a tryout, but Philadelphia took a shot at Sanford. He spent eight years in the minors and even drove the team bus. He was the hardest thrower in the Philadelphia organization, but could not control his emotions. He almost punched a club official when told he was being sent to minors. When traveling secretary Johnny Wise told him he was being sent down on another occasion, Sanford tried to plead his case, but Wise just told him he had a bad attitude. Then the Army drafted him. He hurt his arm pitching in an Army game and developed a clot in his pitching hand after a fight. The Army wanted to operate and cut into his clavicle, which would have ended his pitching career. He got up and left.

Out of the service he came back, and in 1957 at age 28 Sanford won Rookie of the Year honors with 19 wins and a 3.08 ERA. But he had worn out his welcome in Philly and was traded to the Giants, where he was 40-35 over the next three years.

He was surly on game days and his family avoided him. He maintained silence all through the pregame routine. He was a loner anyway. The clot made it hard for him to complete games and he was called a "composer of unfinished symphonies." The Candlestick weather did not benefit him, and his reputation was that of a "six-inning pitcher," a bone of contention during contract negotiations.

In spring training of 1962 Dark told the hard thrower to worry less about strikeouts. This and Haller's influence helped him reduce his pitch counts, maintain stamina, and pitch longer into games. He went less for the big strike and more for ground ball outs on the corners. He became one of the best pitchers in baseball, compiling his 16-game streak between June and September. He refused to celebrate it, however, calling it a "fluke." Rube Marquard of the Giants had won the all-time record of 19 straight, but Sanford just said it was "ridiculous" and that the record meant nothing to him. It was his nature to be surly.

———

Billy Pierce was already a veteran star pitcher by 1962.

"If he didn't win, it didn't quite cut him as bad as it did people like Sanford," said O'Dell. Perhaps that was because Pierce had never made a practice of losing much; not in Chicago, certainly not with the Giants, and at Candlestick Park in 1962, never. Twice a 20-game winner with the White Sox, he was a seven-time All-Star and helped the Chisox to the 1959 American League crown, only the second time since 1948 a team other than the Yankees won the flag. He lost a perfect game with two outs in the ninth inning against Washington in 1958.

At 35 the White Sox decided his best years were behind him and he found himself San Francisco–bound. Pierce wanted number 19, Dark's number. Dark said fine. In spring training, however, Pierce was awful, and the Giants had second thoughts. When the regular season started, though, Pierce won his first eight decisions.

Pitching coach Larry Jansen was convinced that the cool Candlestick weather was the key to Pierce's success. Chicago was brutally hot in the summer and could wear a pitcher out. Dark used Pierce as Casey Stengel used Whitey Ford, holding him out for home stands.

"And the results were about as good as I could expect because I won 13 in a row at home," said Pierce.

He missed a month of the season with a spike wound, but that made him fresh late in the year.

—◦—

The player who came over in the trade with Pierce was Don Larsen. He is a legend in New York because he pitched the only perfect game in World Series history, but the native of Point Loma, California, near San Diego, was a legendary drinker. His buddies were Billy Martin, Mickey Mantle, and Whitey Ford—all major drinkers. They called him "Goony Bird."

Mike McCormick said drinking was more common in baseball then than today, but "even I marveled at how much he could consume."

After the perfect game, great things were expected of Larsen, but he never found his form in New York. He was traded to Kansas City then went to the minors. In 1961 Larsen was 7–2 at Chicago, giving life to his career. When the Pierce trade was negotiated, San Francisco insisted on Larsen's inclusion. He pitched effectively in 1962. Against Pittsburgh, Larsen came in with the bases loaded and none out, striking out the side on nine pitches. Larsen enjoyed frog-hunting in the Sacramento Delta and cooked the delicacies.

—◦—

Stu Miller never threw more than 85 miles per hour, but his junk was effective as a closer.

"Stu had the best off-speed pitch of anybody in the history of baseball," said Ron Fairly of Los Angeles.

Choo Choo Coleman went from the Phillies to the Mets in 1962. He said when he swung at a Miller pitch "the ball was THERE! I swung where it was. How could I miss it?"

They called Miller "the Killer Moth" because his pitches resembled one. Dark had felt in 1961 that the staff relied on Miller too much, and forced pitchers to go the distance instead of bowing out in favor of the reliever.

Miller loved crossword puzzles. Miller and Mike McCormick, a native of Los Angeles with great promise, were the only former New York Giants on the staff. Bob Bolin was "the hardest thrower on the staff," according to Bailey. Gaylord Perry was a rookie from North Carolina. At 6'4", 205 pounds he was the younger brother of Jim Perry, who was a star pitcher for Cleveland.

Bob Garibaldi was a huge prospect from Stockton who had starred at the nearby University of Santa Clara, where he pitched the Broncos into the College World Series and earned Most Outstanding Player honors. At the time of his signing, he was considered "can't miss."

—◦—

Felipe Alou took an apartment on Columbus Street in North Beach "with the hippies," despite the club's wishes against it.

—◦—

Haller was by far the best catcher I ever threw to. He was smart, very good defensively and had a good arm.
—GIANTS PITCHER BILLY PIERCE ON CATCHER TOM HALLER, WHO SIGNED WITH SAN FRANCISCO FOR A $50,000 BONUS AFTER PLAYING QUARTERBACK FOR THE UNIVERSITY OF ILLINOIS

—◦—

Sixteen in a row. This is ridiculous. Nobody wins 16 in a row. . . . Boy, what a year!
—GIANTS ACE PITCHER JACK SANFORD ON WINNING 16 STRAIGHT GAMES IN 1962

Death Struggle

At the 1962 opener at Dodger Stadium 52,562 attended and was won by the Reds, 6–3. San Francisco won their opener, 6–0, when Mays hit a homer on the first pitch of the season off Warren Spahn of Milwaukee.

On April 11 Los Angeles won its first-ever game at Dodger Stadium, 6–2 over the Reds behind Sandy Koufax. On April 12 Pete Richert struck out six straight to tie the big-league record in an 11–7 win over Cincinnati. On April 16, the Giants won 19–8 over the Dodgers in their first meeting of the season. Mays, Alou, and Davenport homered. The next day Larry Sherry pitched well in an 8–7 Dodger win, their first at Candlestick since March 1961. On April 24, Koufax struck out a Major League record of 18 (broken with 19 in 1969 by Steve Carlton, and 19 again by Tom Seaver in 1970) versus the Chicago Cubs at Wrigley Field, winning 10–2. On April 25 Bailey hit his home run after a knockdown from Bob Friend, spurring the 8–3 win over Pittsburgh. Four days later, San Francisco defeated Chicago, sweeping two games of a doubleheader with shutouts by Pierce and Sanford, 7–0 and 6–0.

On May 4 an emergency forced the Giants to land in Salt Lake City, Utah, delaying their arrival into the Windy City until 6 a.m. Groggy from a lack of rest, they still beat the Cubs in an afternoon game at Wrigley Field for their 10th victory in a row. On May 21 Los Angeles hammered San Francisco, 8–1 at Chavez Ravine behind three RBIs from Tommy Davis and a dominating 10-strikeout performance by Koufax. Back in San Francisco, the Giants swept the fledgling New York Mets, 7–1 and 6–5 at the 'Stick. On May 30 the Dodgers swept the Mets at the "scene of the crime," in New York, by scores of 13–6 and 6–5. Wills homered from both sides of plate. At the end of May, the Giants were 35-15, the best record in baseball.

"Will the Giants, carving out a whirlwind, pell-mell early pace, as usual in the first month of the season, go kerplunk in June, as has been their pattern the last five seasons, or are they going to prove the bona fide Yankees of the National League?" wrote Jack McDonald of *The Sporting News.*

———

They called it the "June swoon." A cartoon in the San Francisco newspaper depicted a smiling bride and said, "June Bride Happy—What about Giants?" On June 1 the Giants beat the Mets, 9–7 at the Polo Grounds behind two Willie McCovey home runs and a solo shot by Mays, but the Dodgers swept Philadelphia, 11–4 and 8–5, igniting an eventual 13-game winning streak. San Francisco's "swoon" started on June 6 when, after leading by two games over Los Angeles they lost six straight, then went 6–6 over a dozen games to fall out of first. Their sixth straight defeat was a crushing loss at the hands of the Cardinals, by a score of 13–3 in St. Louis. Jim Murray of the *Los Angeles Times* wrote a scathing piece about the seemingly annual June demise of the San Franciscans, stating that "a business executive is standing in his office looking down over the city and is chatting to his secretary. Suddenly, a falling figure shoots past the window. 'Uh oh,' says the man, glancing at his chronometer. 'It must be June. There go the Giants.'"

On June 8 the Dodgers beat the expansion Houston Colt .45s, 4–3 on the road, ascending to the top of the National League standings for the first time all year. On June 12 San Francisco began a comeback, sweeping Cincinnati in a doubleheader, 2–1 and 7–5. On that day, F. L. Morris and two brothers, John and Clarence Anglkin, used spoons to dig out of Alcatraz Federal Prison, located in the middle of San Francisco Bay. They were never found, probably drowned in the swirling, cold waters, their bodies likely swept out to sea. Sanford began his 16-game winning streak with a 6–3 win over the Cardinals on June 17. The next day, Koufax and young Bob Gibson of St. Louis dueled for nine classic, scoreless innings in a game won by a Tommy Davis home run, 1–0 in the tenth inning. On June 29 O'Dell went 12 innings and struck out 12 in a 4–3 win over Philadelphia. On June 30, Sandy Koufax threw a no-hitter, striking out 12 in a 5–0 win over the Mets.

July marked midseason, and on the second Los Angeles swept Gene Mauch's Phillies, 5–1 and 4–0. Johnny Podres retired the first 20 batters he faced, setting a record (broken with 10 in 1970 by Tom Seaver) with eight consecutive strikeouts. On the fourth of July both Los Angeles teams, the Dodgers and the surprising Angels, were in first place, but San Francisco, recovered from the "June swoon," continued to hang tough. Two days later Juan Marichal's 12 strikeouts keyed San Francisco to a 12–3 over Los Angeles. On July 8, the two rivals played a classic October-style game. Koufax, with Don Drysdale coming on in relief, shut out San Francisco, 2–0. L.A. held a slim one-half-game lead at the first All-Star break. They would hold that lead until the last day of the regular season. On July 10, Maury Wills singled, stole bases, and scored twice in leading the Nationals to a 3–1 triumph over the Americans. Marichal was the winning pitcher. On July 17 Koufax was forced to sit down when his mysterious finger ailment became too much for him to bear, but the Dodgers were hot without him.

In late July before the second All-Star break, the Dodgers led by one game. Dodger Stadium held 162,000 fans for a monumental three-game series that had the whole sports world buzzing with excitement and anticipation. Certainly, it appeared that Walter O'Malley and Horace Stoneham were geniuses, the move to California a 20th-century success beyond all previous conception. Milton Berle joked that he was going to fly to San Francisco so he could watch the games on TV, avoiding the congestion but also getting in a backhanded swipe at O'Malley's no-home-games-on-TV policy. Frank "Hondo" Howard hit three home runs and drove in 12 runs as L.A. swept their rivals 2–1, 8–6, and 11–1. Howard was the hottest hitter in baseball, having driven in 47 runs since June 28. The Dodgers were a perfect 5–0 at home versus the Giants and had split the first six games in San Francisco, which accounted for their essential edge so far. On July 29 the Dodgers were threatening to pull away, now up by four games at the break.

The Giants were hoping that the "dog days" of August would favor them, that the cool summer weather in San Francisco would refresh them while the desert heat would tire out their rivals. After all, "The coldest winter I ever spent was a summer in San Francisco," Mark Twain had once said.

"San Francisco isn't a city—it's a no-host cocktail party," wrote Murray. "It has a nice, even climate: it's always winter."

The onset of August had the effect of heightening pennant race sensibilities. First, it was impossible not to compare this with the 1951 drama, but the 1959 race was also fresh in the minds of all concerned. The players, the fans, and the media began to view the season in larger-than-life terms. With the Dodgers now playing in their new stadium, there was a distinct sense that 1962 was truly a "big-league" season, a debutante ball of sorts for the West Coast. John Wooden's UCLA Bruins had not yet won an NCAA basketball championship, but in 1962 they had come close and were obviously on the verge of great things. The Lakers and Trojans were all the rage.

Los Angeles seemed to have everything that San Francisco lacked. The former Los Angeles area congressman Richard M. Nixon looked to be an obvious favorite over the old-style San Francisco pol, incumbent governor Edmund "Pat" Brown. Nixon was the former vice president and standard bearer of the Republican Party. Democrat-heavy San Francisco hated the idea of losing to Nixon and voter-rich, still-Republican L.A.

The Giants were their last, best hope, and if they failed a sense of inferiority would infect the "superior" San Franciscans with a sickness that would be hard to heal. The north-south rivalry took on political and cultural overtones that surpassed the New York years. The papers, particularly the provincial San Francisco dailies, began to give the pennant race front-page space alongside a huge stock market crash, the Israeli execution of Adolf Eichman, the Kennedy administration's obsession with Fidel Castro, and the Mercury astronauts.

"You can talk all you want about Brooklyn and New York, Minneapolis and St. Paul, Dallas and Fort Worth, but there are no two cities in America where the people want to beat each other's brains out more than in San Francisco and Los Angeles," said American League president Joe Cronin, a native of the City.

The writers started to get personal, with particular jealousy and vitriol aimed at the Southland by San Francisco's scribes. The *Chronicle*'s Art Rosenbaum called the Dodgers "Smodgers," sniping that L.A. was a "city whose women would attend the opera in leopard shirts and toreador pants if indeed they attended the opera at all."

"Isn't it nice that people who prefer Los Angeles to San Francisco live there?" wrote Herb Caen.

The players could "feel . . . definite tension in the air," said Maury Wills. "It reminds me of a homecoming college football game. Each time we face San Francisco, it's different than any other National League series."

Veterans taught youngsters like Ron Fairly, who was already imbued by a sense of north-south rivalry against California and Stanford from his USC days, to "hate the Giants more than any other team," he said. "I'm sure the Giants weren't too fond of us, either—and that's exactly the way we wanted it."

Junior Gilliam called Willie Mays "one of the best friends I ever had in my life, but there was no way we would talk to each other on the field. Not even hello."

"Against the Giants, you just tried that much harder," recalled Joe Moeller of the Dodgers. "Even if the Giants had been in last place, we would've wanted to beat them worse than the frontrunners."

"I don't care how you play these games—the Dodger-Giants rivalry is always intense," said Al Dark, insisting it had not lost a thing on the West Coast.

"Usually, in the batting cage, guys on the other teams would come over and exchange ideas, say hi," Orlando Cepeda said. "When we played the Dodgers, we wouldn't talk to them."

"It was a special event that required a much greater level of preparation," said Felipe Alou.

"When you stepped off the plane in Los Angeles, you could hear the electricity," Willie McCovey recalled. "Even the skycaps at the airport were all wrapped up in the rivalry. It carried over to the hotel and finally the ballpark."

"It may not have matched the spirit of the New York days, but it was still a great rivalry," said Podres. "You always got fired up playing the Giants."

If the Giants thought they had a weather advantage in August that would manifest itself into their overtaking Los Angeles, they found that it was not to be. On the third of the month Drysdale beat the Cubs,

8–3, to become the earliest 20-game winner since Jim "Hippo" Vaughn in 1918. The "no man's land" nature of the race, in which both teams had a distinct advantage in their home stadiums, continued to keep San Francisco from catching up.

"It seems to be an incontrovertible fact that neither team can play well in the other chaps' ballpark," wrote San Francisco beat writer Joe King. "The Giants are sad sacks in L.A.; nobody may ever see a team drop dead like the Dodgers in Candlestick."

"We would go to San Francisco with our great pitching staff, and there were games where we'd get blown out, 12–3 or whatever," Ron Perranoski said. "Then they'd come down to Dodger Stadium and we'd win low-scoring games by a run. The two ballparks dictated the action."

With Los Angeles maintaining an overall lead, the tit-for-tat nature of the home-and-home rivalry was not helping the Giants. Both teams built their advantages using dirty tricks that intensified feelings on both sides.

The Giants kept tall grass and a slow infield. The Dodgers used a roller to pack their dirt for their speedsters. The Dodgers sloped the third base line so that bunts by Wills, Gilliam, and Willie Davis would stay fair. Their grass was short. Much of it was meant to gain a psychological advantage over San Francisco more than an actual one. Al Dark instructed the Candlestick grounds crew to water down the paths in order to slow Wills.

On August 4 a "Miracle at Coogan's Bluff" celebration was held at Candlestick Park, with Bobby Thomson, Eddie Stanky, and Monte Irvin attending. San Francisco's own Joe DiMaggio was invited to attended all three games, but had to cancel when his ex-wife, Marilyn Monroe, died on August 5. On August 9 L.A. beat Philadelphia, 8–3. On August 10 the Dodgers came to San Francisco (who had lost three straight at Chavez Ravine) with a five-and-a-half-game lead, their biggest of the year. At 5:30 a.m. Matty Schwab, Candlestick's head groundskeeper, dug a pit where Wills normally took his lead, filled it with water, sand, and peat moss, then covered it with topsoil. During infield practice the Los Angeles players noticed and brought it to the attention of head umpire Tom Gorman. Gorman ordered the pit dug up, but Schwab's crew replaced it with more mud than before. Schwab's wheelbarrow of sand, supposed to dry up the pit, contained all the old, hidden ingredients that had previously been dug up. It was worse than before. Wills said the whole episode "demoralized" him. Mays hit a homer with four RBIs and the Dodgers came unglued in an 11–2 loss.

The next day the Dodgers came out doing mock breaststrokes, and further hi-jinx followed. A Dodger stole San Francisco's leaded bat. A Giant stole L.A.'s practice bat. Dark kept a straight face, saying that unless the infield is watered down, the three o'clock winds kick up the dust. Drysdale started with an 11-game winning streak. Tommy Davis, hitting .452 against Giants pitching, hit a three-run homer off Pierce.

In the third Wills kept stepping out against Pierce to unnerve him, but when the umpire ordered him in, Wills exploded about the field, calling the umpire "gutless." Wills shouted it again and the man in blue thumbed Wills. San Francisco scored two runs in the fourth, and the Giants sensed that L.A. was psyched. Their comeback was on. Then the winds did start to blow. There were delays and the tension was thick enough to cut with a knife.

Clinging to a 3–2 lead, Drysdale allowed a Felipe Alou bloop double. Haller struck out and Drysdale then hit Jim Davenport, causing a hairline fracture. Despite Big D's reputation as a headhunter, it was not intentional. He was the go-ahead run. Drysdale apologized on the spot (and called him later; Davenport was out two weeks). Drysdale struck out Pagan but McCovey pinch-hit for Pierce. Alston came out to talk it over with his ace. Willie Mac always wore him out, and was "the only batter who could consistently destroy Drysdale," said Roseboro.

McCovey had homered off him a month earlier, and a year earlier had hit a 475-foot shot off him, the longest to date in Candlestick history. Alston had Perranoski up and ready but stuck with Drysdale. The count went full, then McCovey slammed a home run and the place went crazy. Stu Miller preserved Pierce's 5–4 win, the 200th of his career. Wills was fined $50 and the Giants were back in it.

On Sunday afternoon, Juan Marichal shoved Dodger bats "where the sun don't shine" in a dominating 5–1 win. Los Angeles was now thoroughly discombobulated, finding excuses for their failings. Buzzie Bavasi called the Giants "bush" and vowed protests, but they were off their game and it would affect the race. Alston said the field was dangerous, that Mays could have broken his leg. Vin Scully called Al Dark "the Swamp Fox."

"One more squirt and the Red Cross would have declared a disaster area and begun to evacuate the Dodgers by rowboat . . . an aircraft carrier would've run aground," Murray wrote.

The Giants exhibited "the most disgraceful case of poor sportsmanship since Major League baseball came to the coast," wrote writer Sid Ziff.

Wills paid his fine in pennies, dragging an 80-pound bag to National League president Warren Giles's desk in Cincinnati, turning it over and letting them spill everywhere. He then asked them to count it and give him a receipt. Alston tinkered with his heretofore successful lineup, putting Tommy Davis at third and veteran Wally Moon in left field. Frank Howard started to slump. The Dodgers were not a good defensive team anyway. Moon's presence made them worse. Also in August, the Alston-Durocher feud reached a head. Third-base coach Durocher had been disregarding Alston's signs for a month.

"Forget the signs," Durocher wrote in *Nice Guys Finish Last*. "We had a manager who sat back and played everything conservatively. To hell with it. Alston would give me the take sign, I'd flash the hit sign. Alston would signal bunt, I'd call for the hit-and-run."

Duke Snider, relegated to the bench, led a cabal of "Leo's guys," all of whom were bench-warmers. Daryl Spencer called Alston "wishy-washy" and called Durocher a decision-maker. Some veterans questioned Alston's decisions. The starters were Alston's loyalists. Against the Cubs, Durocher badgered young third baseman Ron Santo relentlessly, saying he was going to be traded to L.A. Tampering charges were made and Bavasi said it would stop.

Alston called a team meeting and laid down the law, saying, "Leo, that means you." If Durocher missed a sign, Alston said he would be fined $200; the player an additional $200. A few days later Fairly missed a sign and Tommy Davis ran into his own bunt.

"Somebody oughta take some money from these kids," shouted Durocher.

Alston confronted him then and there. "You do the coaching, Durocher, and I'll do the chewing out and fining," Alston declared.

It did not stop there. Alston had to whistle three times to get Leo's attention, and signs were still missed. Mel Durslag castigated Alston for embarrassing Durocher in front of the team. Walt screamed at the writer for his concern over Leo's feelings, but what about his?

"What about the times he has shown me up in front of the players?" Alston yelled. "How much of this do I have to take?" Alston and Durocher moved their cubicles away from each other and stopped sitting next to each other on buses and planes.

Internal dissension was not relegated to the Dodgers, however. After a frustrating loss on August 19, Dark and Cepeda engaged in a shouting match. San Francisco slumped but ended a six losses in seven games stretch with a 2–1 win over New York on August 23.

On August 24, the Durocher-Alston feud took a strange turn. Durocher had a reaction to penicillin, and thinking he was having a heart attack, was placed on a clubhouse table. Alston rushed in.

"I think this is it, Walt," said Durocher, as if it was the "George Gipp scene" from *Knute Rockne: All-American*. "Go get them." Durocher was given dosages of vitamin B, however, and restored to full health. He was still absent from the team for two weeks.

Los Angeles won seven of eight and led by three and a half by Labor Day.

—◆—

The Giants were notorious for slumping in June, what the press coined their annual "June swoon." Murray wrote of their 1962 slump, "a business executive is standing in his office looking down over the city and is chatting to his secretary. Suddenly, a falling figure shoots past the window. 'Oh oh,' says the man, glancing at his chronometer. 'It must be June. There go the Giants.'"

—◆—

The Candlestick Park groundskeepers notoriously watered their base paths in an effort to slow down Maury Wills. Of this sports columnist Jim Murray observed, "one more squirt and the Red Cross would have declared a disaster area and begun to evacuate the Dodgers by rowboat . . . an aircraft carrier would've run aground."

—◦—

The rivalry found its way into the newspapers, for sure. Charles McCabe and Herb Caen had nothing nice to say about Los Angeles, at all. Art Rosenbaum of the *Chronicle* wrote that women in Los Angeles attended the opera in "leopard skin pants," if they attended at all. It made for quite an arresting image, actually.

Jim Murray of the *Los Angeles Times* took exception to the clap-trap from "Baghdad by the Bay," which was Caen's moniker for the City (they gave it caps) in those pre–Saddam Hussein days. In 1962 he wrote San Francisco was a "no-host cocktail party," criticizing the Giants for allowing their groundskeeper to turn the base paths at Candlestick Park into a "peat moss" pit so as to slow down L.A. speedster Maury Wills.

He mentioned Caen when he pointed out that *Sports Illustrated* put the knock on "Frisco," the most hated of all names out-of-towners give to the City, in an article called "Akron of the West." Joe David Brown wrote the place was "Not a big league town. . . . Full of drunks. . . . A citadel of intolerance. . . . Vulgar and cheap." Finally, in perhaps the most unkind cut of all, he wrote the place was "not the lovely lady I had imagined but a vulgar old broad." San Francisco "leads the nation in suicides, mental disease, alcoholism." Murray added that San Francisco has an "insurance against victory better than any Lloyd's can give him."

—◦—

Man, that's what we're playing the season to find out.
—Willie Mays, when asked on Opening Day who would
win the 1962 pennant

—◆—

*One of the most memorable nights of my childhood came on April 16,
1962. My dad, Gerald Miller, and my Godfather, Keith Allen, took me
to my first Major League baseball game at Candlestick Park. I know
how strong an effect that game had on me simply because the memories
of that night have remained so vivid. . . . To wit, I can tell you not only
the extraordinary final score—Giants over the Dodgers, 19–8—but
also the final game totals. The Dodgers out-hit the Giants, 15–12, and
yet lost by 11 runs. The paid attendance was 32,819. Winning pitcher
Billy O'Dell pitched a complete-game 15-hitter. Felipe Alou hit the
first home run I ever saw, and Mays and Jimmy Davenport also went
deep. . . .*

*I wondered, years later, when I came to broadcast the Giants,
"What if the first game I ever saw, they lost 8–0 and weren't good?
Would I have been as big a fan?"*
—Giants Hall of Fame broadcaster Jon Miller

—◆—

What time does the tide come in?
—Dodgers first baseman Ron Fairly joking to Al Dark
over groundskeeper Matty Schwab's swamping the Candlestick base paths in order to slow down Dodgers base
stealing threat Maury Wills

—◆—

I still have a cold from that day.
—Dodgers speed demon Maury Wills recalling the
drenched base paths at Candlestick

September 1962

On September 3 at Dodger Stadium the infield dirt was "as dry as Pharaoh's tomb," wrote Charles McCabe. The biggest crowd of the season, 54,418, came out wearing feathers and doing duck calls. Three thousand duck call sounders were sold by the concessions. Two brought in a real duck and a chicken, throwing them on the field. Dodger batboy Rene Lachemann had to remove them. The Giants came out for batting practice and saw a "gift" on their dugout steps: a watering can. Over the loudspeakers Danny Kaye's popular "Hiller-Haller-Miller" song played.

The Giants had a 10-game losing streak at Dodger Stadium dating back to 1961. Dark shuffled his batting order and Mays, hitting fifth, clubbed a three-run homer off Stan Williams. Sanford walked none in a complete game 7–3 win, his 20th of the season.

After the game the Giants were guests at blonde bombshell Jayne Mansfield's house. It included cocktails and a buffet by the swimming pool, but some Giants were disappointed. Half expected Jayne would be wearing a bikini and the party would be a full-scale sex orgy, with the actress satiating all their "needs." Instead, she was not "anything like her image on the screen," said Pierce, which of course promoted that very fantasy. "She was pleasant, but very businesslike and proper. We knew she was a big baseball fan, but I think there was also some kind of promotion or commercial involved. To the ballplayers, this was a big deal. We went because we wanted to see Jayne Mansfield, her house, and that heart-shaped swimming pool." Wives and girlfriends had a hard time believing the truth, which was that nothing amorous happened.

The next night, perhaps still fantasizing about her, the Giants lost 5–4 when Willie Davis scored from first on a single, Roseboro stole home, and Perranoski struck out Mays and Cepeda to end the game.

On September 5, Mays doubled and singled in a 3–0 win but Marichal, dominating Los Angeles, injured his foot on a play at first base, just as he had a year earlier at the Coliseum. X-rays revealed no fracture but he would miss several starts.

Dark accused Marichal of "jaking" it. It was his 18th and last win of the season.

On September 6, the Armed Forces Radio Network conducted a live satellite call-in interview with the presumed World Series managers, the Yankees' Ralph Houk and the Dodgers' Walt Alston. It did not escape Dark's attention, and he took exception to it.

That day McCovey killed Drysdale again with a single and double, staking San Francisco to 4–0 lead. Los Angeles rallied behind Tommy Davis's single and a Howard home run. Drysdale then knocked down both Willies with furious inside buzz. Billy O'Dell returned the favor, buzzing Drysdale when he came to the plate.

A volatile exchange ensued between umpire Ed Barlick and both managers. Tommy Davis's homer tied it and 54,263 Dodgers fans went wild. Perranoski came on in the ninth. Hiller beat out an infield single. Davenport, back from the disabled list, laid down a sacrifice bunt, and Perranoski tried to get the lead run at second. His throw went into center field for an error, and Giants runners were now at second and third. Felipe Alou walked to load the bases. Mays tapped a force-out at home. Cepeda worked Perranoski to a full count, but the southpaw reliever just missed, walking in the go-ahead run. Perranoski sagged perceptibly. Harvey Kuenn doubled and it was "Katy bar the door": 9–5, Giants.

"Certainly, it was the biggest hit of my career," said Kuenn, which was saying something. Larsen came in to protect the lead. Typical Dodgers fans rushed to the parking lot and their appointments with the Pasadena, Harbor, Golden State, Hollywood, and Santa Monica freeways. In front of growing numbers of vacant seats, L.A. loaded the bases for the "Giant killer," Tommy Davis, who already had two hits and two RBIs in the game. Stu "the Killer Moth" Miller came in. Davis's drive to left field looked to be a homer, but Kuenn speared it. Dark dropped to his knees in the dugout. A run scored but there were two outs. Howard, who hated facing Miller and previously struck out four straight times against him, came to the plate. Miller got him to swing clumsily, but then laid one in there. Hondo hit a towering shot, barely foul down the left field line. Then Howard popped to Davenport and it was over. Dark called it "the most important game I've ever managed."

The Giants returned to San Francisco. It was now September, the best time of the year in the Bay Area. They trailed by a mere game and a half with three weeks left. San Francisco and Los Angeles had no more regular season games left with each other. As if giving thanks for "deliverance" after the Dodger Stadium dramatics, Felipe Alou invited his manager to the Peninsula Bible Church in Palo Alto, where 2,000 people heard the outfielder's testimony on "what the Lord meant to me."

Among Alou's blessings at that time were hits in seven straight plate appearances and the fact that his club was as hot as a pistol. They stayed hot, sweeping Chicago and Pittsburgh to increase their winning streak to seven games. However, L.A., who refused to buckle amid the late-season pressure, demolished both of those clubs. Both teams left for their final road trips: 10 for the Dodgers, 11 for the Giants. On September 12 it was hot and muggy in Cincinnati. Starter Gaylord Perry said the change from the moderate San Francisco weather to the Midwest humidity was "a jolt for everyone." Perry changed his shirt twice that night.

Mays was affected, but not just by the weather. The pressures of the pennant race, in which he was carrying his team on his shoulders, combined with his troubles—a contentious divorce, tax problems, debts, an unhappy personal life—came to a head after the long plane flight from the cool West Coast to the sweltering Queen City. To top it off, he ate junk food that day and it did not sit well with him.

Mays shortened his batting practice turns and struck out his first time at the plate. In the third inning he staggered and fainted in the dugout. Mays was carried by stretcher to the clubhouse and then transferred to Christ Hospital. Mays rested and felt okay the next day, asking to rejoin the team. He was released after 24 hours of observation.

The San Francisco papers treated Mays's health in tabloid manner with rumors of venereal disease, a dugout fight, epilepsy, a heart attack, and even the influence of Kentucky gamblers supposedly slipping him a "Mickey Finn" to affect the betting line. He was simply emotionally, mentally, and physically exhausted. Later Mays was given a clean bill of health by a San Francisco doctor.

But their star's collapse was a blow to the club. The Giants lost two to the Reds and their momentum was gone. Dark sat him some more to be sure and they lost two straight at Pittsburgh. In the last 19 games Mays had missed, his team was 0-19! The Giants blew a 2–1 ninth-inning lead to the Pirates when pitcher Earl Francis hit a homer to win his game. The next night the Pirates broke an eighth-inning tie on Bob Bailey's triple.

Mays returned the next night and homered to send the game into extra innings but Smoky Burgess homered for Pittsburgh to hand the Giants their fifth straight loss. The next night the Pirates beat Mike McCormick to sweep the series. Dark was furious, throwing food around the clubhouse. They trailed by four games.

The Dodgers had won seven straight but struggled. Stan Williams beat the Cubs at home but gave up a grand slam at Wrigley Field in a loss. He was pulled from the rotation and, with no explanation, never returned in regular season play. "It really hurt my pride that they felt I wasn't good enough to do the job," said Williams.

Los Angeles lost two of three in Milwaukee. In St. Louis, a meeting was held on Thursday, September 20 at the Chase Park Plaza Hotel. Traveling secretary Lee Scott assembled Alston, Snider, and the coaching staff. Walter O'Malley flew in. It was an off-day.

"Get tough, Walter," advised O'Malley. "You've got to ride herd on 'em. They're going to blow this thing, sure as hell, unless you can light a fire under them. Warn them that if they blow the pennant, they'll lose more than just the World Series money. It will be reflected in their salaries next year."

Alston disagreed, preferring a vote of confidence. O'Malley responded, "These are not high school kids—they're professionals," insisting that Alston get tough and "make me the heavy."

Alston held his ground, but O'Malley told him that if the team lost, "some heads will roll." Snider told O'Malley not to worry. That night, oddly, the Dodgers attended the Giants-Cardinals game at the old Busch Stadium. The Giants had snapped their six-game losing streak when Tom

Haller homered twice, but that night the Giants blew a 4–3 lead in the ninth on a balk and Ken Boyer's game-winning single, 5–4.

The Giants and Dodgers were both staying at the Chase Park Plaza at the same time. Perranoski told Felipe Alou after the game he would "see you guys next year," and "we win and you won't." On September 7 Wills broke the National League record, previously set by Cincinnati's Bob Bescher in 1911, with his 81st stolen base. "My sincere congratulations," wired league president Warren Giles, apparently willing to let Wills's "nickels, dimes, and pennies" fine-paying incident go. "Now go all the way and break the record held by the great Ty Cobb."

Cobb had stolen 96 bases in 1915. Considered one of the very best players ever to play baseball, Cobb was a portrait of human contrast: a virulent racist who was also a believing Baptist and major contributor to black colleges in the South. One year earlier, Al Stump's article about Cobb had been published in *Look* magazine. It told the story of a bitter old drunk, estranged from friends and family, utterly unable to make sense of the new world he lived in.

Most incomprehensible to Cobb was the existence of blacks in the Major Leagues, not just participants, but veritable matinee idols of sports. One of those very men, the symbol of the "new breed," Maury Wills was about to break his most cherished record. Cobb, wrote many a writer, was "turning in his grave."

But the day of the 154th game of the season, Commissioner Ford Frick did the same thing he had done to Roger Maris in 1961, stating that Wills had to break the record in 154 games for the mark to stand. Because of two ties, Cobb had played 156 games in 1915, two more than the regular 154-game schedule. Frick still insisted that the 154-game standard would apply.

"I wouldn't have minded so much had Frick made his ruling earlier," Wills said. "But why did he wait until the last day?" Wills could have broken the mark earlier had he sensed urgency. "Cobb got 156 games to set his record and I thought I would, too."

On September 16 Bob Buhl of the Cubs shut out L.A., 5–0. Koufax returned in mid-September. The team won 17 of 21 after his injury in

July, opening their five-and-a-half-game lead of August 8, but there was little doubt that his absence had helped San Francisco stay in the race.

"If we'd had Koufax the whole season we would have waltzed to the pennant," said Norm Sherry. "His injury was the opportunity that gave us a chance to get back in the race," said Al Dark.

On September 23, O'Dell won his 19th game, 10–3 over the Colt .45s. On that same day, a classic Koufax versus Bob Gibson rematch of their earlier scoreless duel was in the offing, but Gibby fractured a bone during batting practice.

"There was this tremendous sigh of relief from the Dodgers because they hadn't been hitting, and now they wouldn't have to face this future Hall of Famer," said Scully. "Curt Simmons, who was very much nearing the end of his career, was rushed into the breach to pitch for Gibson."

"I could get out of bed in the middle of December and steal two off Simmons," said Wills.

But Koufax had nothing, giving up a first-inning grand slam. Now the score altered Wills's stolen base strategy. He could not afford to run the team out of a rally just for personal gain. In the sixth, with the Dodgers trailing 4–1, Wills walked and stole number 95. He then took off for third to tie the mark in the 154th game. He had it easily. At the last moment, Jim Gilliam laid down a totally useless bunt. He was thrown out, credited with a sacrifice that was a joke. Wills lost the stolen base. He had no further chances and St. Louis won, 11–2.

After the game, George Lederer of the *Long Beach Press-Telegram* asked Wills if Alston had called for a bunt. "Why don't you ask him?" Wills replied, pointing to Gilliam. Lederer went to Gilliam and repeated the question. Gilliam had had enough. He disliked Wills, was tired of playing "second fiddle" to him all year, and had obviously bunted to deprive him of glory.

"If looks could kill, Gilliam's expression would have struck the man dead," wrote David Plaut in *Chasing October*. "Mind your own Godd—n business," said Gilliam.

"You must have seen that Wills had the base stolen," Lederer continued. "What was going through your mind?"

Gilliam had been caught red-handed, backed into a corner, and reacted angrily by threatening to punch the writer in the nose, but Wills wisely avoided stirring further trouble by repeating the company lie that Gilliam was trying for a base hit with a legitimate bunt try, an effort to spark a rally, not trying to screw up his record-breaking effort.

"I haven't asked anybody to sacrifice for me all season, and I'm not about to now," said Wills. The next night Podres and Larry Sherry combined for a 4–3 win, number 100. Wills did not steal a base. Game number 156 was against the tough Larry Jackson, the most difficult guy in the league for Wills to steal on.

In the third Wills singled and stole second for number 96, as the crowd cheered. But St. Louis went out to an 11–2 lead. Wills batted in the seventh. Alston told him to try for the record regardless of the score. Wills poked a two-strike single and the Cardinal crowd cheered him on. Jackson threw over to first half a dozen times. First baseman Bill White applied hard slap tags to Wills's skull.

Wills shortened his lead to indicate "that Jackson had me buffaloed." Jackson delivered home and the Cardinals relaxed. Then Wills took off for second—a delayed steal, which he never did before, but Al Campanis had suggested he try—sliding in safely. Catcher Carl Sawatski, who was in the process of throwing back to Jackson, had to make a hurried throw to second that bounced. Wills slid head first and had the record.

In the ninth Wills was presented with the bag. Later, Frick backed off his 154-game edict, saying the mark would stand without an asterisk in the official records after all.

Hall of Famer Max Carey, a one-time practitioner of the base stealing arts, had watched Wills closely all year, stealing home, rattling pitchers, and changing the dynamics of the game. "It does me good to see a fellow operate like that," he said.

"I didn't see how I could ever improve on that," Wills said of the club record 50 bases he stole in 1960. "I was even more sure of it the next year, when I only stole 35. Even that was good enough to lead the league."

Wills set a goal of 50 in 1962, but got there by July 27. "I didn't think of the record until I had upped my figure to 72 by stealing three against the Mets on August 26," he continued. "Then, for the first time, Ty Cobb's record of 96 looked possible."

Whenever Wills reached first, fans chanted "Go! Go!" giving him renewed strength and confidence despite the raspberries, fatigue bordering on physical exhaustion, pulled hamstrings, and internal bleeding.

On September 29, San Francisco visited Houston's brutally hot Colt Stadium, home of the Colt .45s before the Astrodome was built and the team became the Astros. Flies said to be as large as a man's fist buzzed about. The Giants won on Friday night, 11–5. On Saturday Miller was wild and Sanford was brought in for a rare relief appearance. Roman Mejias stroked a hit past a drawn-in infield to beat the Giants. They trailed by four with seven games left. It seemed to be over. On Sunday they kept hope alive with a victory, but had gone 3–8 in their disastrous last road trip.

1951 Redux

Los Angeles was 100-56. The Giants, at 97-59, trailed by three. On Monday both teams rested. Both were at home to finish the season. Giants booster Bud Levitas threw a backyard barbecue, and it felt like a farewell party, but Dark made a speech about never giving up. His Christian faith—not to mention the experience of 1951, which he shared with three coaches, Willie Mays, announcer Russ Hodges, owner Horace Stoneham, among others—was the rock he used to maintain strength.

"We're gonna catch these damn Dodgers and we'll beat 'em in the play-offs," Dark exclaimed.

"Everybody thought he was nuts," said Carl Boles.

The Dodgers—Snider, O'Malley, Bavasi, Scully, Leo Durocher—also remembered 1951. But Orlando Cepeda claimed that Dark told him if the club failed to finish second (Cincinnati was pushing and would win 98 games) he would not support their contract demands. Dark denied having done that, certainly not if "we had any mathematical chance to win."

Dark apparently did tell Billy Pierce he had "pitched enough this year," and was free to go home early "as soon as we're out of this thing." Pierce made some flight reservations, but events that week forced him to keep changing them, finally canceling them altogether. By the third or fourth call the airline reservation clerk knew him by name.

On Tuesday and Wednesday, San Francisco beat St. Louis twice while L.A. split with Houston. On Thursday, Gene Oliver's homer sparked the Cardinals to a 7–4 win at Candlestick. In the sixth, Mays lost track of how many outs there were, an unbelievable reversal from his regular baseball instincts, which were flawless. Cepeda struck out and Mays casually

69

walked away from third. The catcher tossed to Ken Boyer, tagging out the stunned Mays while the crowd booed. It got worse when he proceeded to strike out with two men on.

That night, Koufax tried to clinch it at Chavez Ravine. He had good stuff at first, retiring 11 straight with four strikeouts. In the fifth he still led Houston 4–2, and the Dodgers could taste it. But Sandy tired and Alston went to the bullpen. Ed Roebuck, Larry Sherry, and Ron Perranoski were shelled in an 8–6 loss. They still were up by three, but blowing Koufax's lead to an expansion team was devastating to their psyches.

"That loss was the turnaround game," Perranoski admitted.

L.A.'s Daryl Spencer had been with St. Louis in 1961. He said the Cardinals loved the Hollywood nightlife. "There was quite a bit of chasing around out there with some gals," he recalled with a smile.

With nothing to play for, incoming Cardinals players hit the Sunset Strip and hung out until four in the morning. They were loose; the only visiting team to post a winning record at Dodger Stadium in 1962.

"They made pitches that they might not have thrown if they'd gotten a good night's rest," said Ron Fairly. "And that's how they got us out."

In Game 1, St. Louis won, 3–2 in 10 innings. The tension in the Los Angeles clubhouse, what with Wills and Gilliam on less than friendly terms, Alston and Durocher mortal enemies, Drysdale complaining, Koufax's courage questioned, and Tommy Davis giving the "evil eye" to anybody who looked at him askance, was thick and heavy.

On top of everything, the specter of 1951 hung over them like a ghost. The Dodgers hit incessant grounders to shortstop. It got so bad that they laughed, in gallows humor style, as if to say hungover St. Louis needed only a pitcher, catcher, shortstop, and first baseman to beat them. The fans were apoplectic, the media aghast. Doom. Creeping terror. It was 1951 redux.

On Friday a rare September rain canceled San Francisco's game. On Saturday afternoon, Houston's Joey Amalfitano, a talkative native of San Pedro, which serves as the Port of Los Angeles, asked Willie Mays if the Giants "could score a run." Mays just stared at him. Amalfitano told Mays that Los Angeles *could not* score anymore, so all the Giants needed was to score and the pennant was theirs. He was not far from wrong.

In the opener, San Francisco scored 11. Cepeda, McCovey, and Haller provided the offense behind Sanford and Miller. L.A., playing that Saturday night, looked on at the televised game in abject desperation. Marichal started the second game of the doubleheader. His foot still hurt him. X-rays showed no fracture and Dark distrusted the "Dominican Dandy," thinking he was weak-minded and could not handle the pressure of the pennant chase.

"He said very little, but the look in his eye told me that he thought I was trying to quit under pressure," recalled Marichal.

Marichal pitched in pain, but it affected him in a 4–2 loss. After the game, the Latin players gathered at his cubicle. Marichal was hurting and his teammates—friends—felt Dark had risked his career pitching him, but the x-rays of 1962 had mysteriously not caught any fracture.

When Dark benched both Cepeda and Alou on the final Sunday, the Latinos were convinced it was a statement, that Spanish-speaking players could not handle the stress of big games.

That Saturday night, the players went home and listened to a telegraph wire recreation by Giants announcers Lon Simmons and Russ Hodges. It was not unlike 1951, when they took a train from Boston to New York listening to Hodges while traveling through Connecticut, giving them "play-by-play" over the train's loudspeakers of Brooklyn's final game with Philadelphia. Hodges later announced the famed "*Giants win the pennant!*" when Bobby Thomson hit the "shot heard 'round the world."

The bachelor Willie McCovey, a man about town, was out with a date and later recalled San Franciscans straining to pick up the Dodgers' broadcast from Los Angeles, which could be picked up at night. The static voice of Vin Scully was heard on the streets, in cabs, coming out of cars, on transistors in the City. Scully, the ultimate professional, trying to maintain calm despite his team's freefall; Giants fans desperately rooting the other way. At the opera house, the downtown theaters, Union Square, on Market Street, Van Ness Avenue, the Embarcadero, the financial district, Fisherman's Wharf, the Marina, Cow Hollow, the Western Addition, Russian Hill, Noe Valley; out by the Great Highway, the Sunset District, Twin Peak's, from St. Francis Wood to Hunter's Point to Potrero Hill; at Original Joe's, Bardelli's, Trader Vic's, DiMaggio's, Marin Joe's; along the peninsula, across the bridge in Oakland, Berkeley, and the east bay; in the hinterlands of Stockton, Sacramento, and Modesto; down toward Fresno where central California sympathies were evenly split between the Giants and the Dodgers; on the 101 where motorists rooting for both teams traversed the state, past Big Sur and Monterey; Scully's voice told the tale.

Ernie Broglio, who hailed from the east bay, out-dueled Drysdale, 2–0 at Dodger Stadium. San Francisco's hopes were alive, and in all the aforementioned places and a thousand others, cars honked, people whooped and hollered. The Giants were not dead yet. In keeping with St. Louis's "loosey-goosey" style of partying and playing baseball that final weekend, the happy-go-lucky Broglio was throwing curves on 2–0 and 3–2 counts.

"That had to be the best game he ever pitched," said Perranoski. Frank Howard's misplay of a flyball gave Broglio all his support. The next day the *Times* read, "Should O'Malley tempt fate by ordering champagne for the Dodger clubhouse today, he'd best order it on consignment."

They led by a game with one day to go. Amalfitano continued to be right: they *could not score*.

It all came down to September 30, 1962. On that day, James Meredith attempted to become the first black to enroll at the University of Mississippi. A riot ensued and much white and black blood was shed. Mississippi governor Ross Barnett provided no assistance to his fellow Democrat, President John Kennedy, who called it the "worst thing" he had ever seen.

Cepeda and Alou did not see their name on the lineup card on Sunday. Dark started Billy O'Dell against Houston's Turk Farrell, who told the writers he did not intend to lose. In the fourth, Ed Bailey hit a long foul ball, then got the same pitch and hit it fair for a homer to give San Francisco a 1–0 lead. The score was 1–1 when Mays came to the plate in the eighth. He had not had a hit in 10 at-bats and the Candlestick crowd booed him. He was considered a poor clutch hitter, "pop-up Mays."

Organist Lloyd Fox tried to simmer things down by playing "Bye Bye Baby." It was a phrase Hodges used to describe home runs, and a song was made out of it.

Then Mays deposited a Farrell fastball deep into the left field seats for a 2–1 lead.

"It became a blur of white, smashed through the noise of roaring throats, sailing high into the blue," wrote Bob Stevens, "and it gave San Francisco the best shot it has ever had at the long-awaited pennant." Mays had homered on the first pitch he saw in 1962, and now on the last pitch he saw . . . of the regular season, at least.

It was number 48 of the year for Mays, the most in the league. Stu Miller retired Houston in the ninth, striking out Billy Goodman for the last out as the crowd of 41,327 roared to its feet. The Giants mobbed Miller and celebrated on the green plains until the special police escorted them off the field.

The fans stayed in the stands. It was Fan Appreciation Day and five cars were to be awarded to winners of the promotion, but just as important, the score from Los Angeles was not a final. The Dodger game had started an hour later than the San Francisco game.

L.A. entered the final day having won twice in eight days, both times behind the clutch hurling of Johnny Podres. On the final Sunday, Podres faced Curt Simmons. It was Podres's 30th birthday.

The game was scoreless for seven innings. Los Angeles, supposedly the best base-running team in baseball, blew several opportunities. Lee Walls was thrown out trying to stretch a single into a double. Willie Davis was caught on a decoy play. The crafty Simmons picked off Tommy Davis. The Dodgers were reduced to a little league team, their sense of fundamentals completely gone. They were desperate, befuddled, and bamboozled. *They could not score!*

The Dodgers' strong radio station was again heard; at Candlestick during the Fan Appreciation day event, and of course at all the places it had been listened to the previous evening. In addition, Russ Hodges maintained updates on KSFO. Cars pulled up to curbs. At Kezar Stadium, where the team was playing Minnesota, 49ers fans listened in. The Giants gathered around the radio in their clubhouse. A Western Union ticker revealed the play a minute after it happened. The Dodgers' broadcast could not be heard in the Giants' clubhouse.

Podres dominated. He called it one of the best games of his career, better even than his 1955 Game 7 triumph over the New York Yankees in the World Series. But with one out in the eighth, Gene Oliver, whose three-run homer had decided an earlier win at Candlestick, deposited a Podres curveball barely over the left field fence.

Fans were being awarded cars when news of Oliver's homer was announced, and a "Giant roar" came up. When an attractive blonde ambled onto the field to claim her prize, the crowd roared even louder.

At that moment, John Brodie of the 49ers was calling signals at Kezar. It was fourth-and-one at the Vikings' 18-yard line and he suddenly was drowned out by a crescendo of cheers, thinking it was for him. He waved for quiet so his signals could be heard. The 49ers won, but fans stayed at Kezar to hear the Giants-Dodgers reports.

"They just stopped and looked around," recalled Lon Simmons, who was announcing for the 'Niners. "They were thinking what great fans, cheering a huddle."

In the bottom of the ninth, Ken McMullen and Maury Wills flied out. It truly did look as if they simply lacked any capability of scoring, so woeful were the Dodgers offensively. The long season, the dispute between Alston and Durocher, Wills's histrionics, the Koufax injury, Don Drysdale's loud complaints about everything; they were sapped of all strength, like the General Ripper character in *Dr. Strangelove* who feared being drained of his "precious bodily fluids."

The players listened to Hodges. Chub Feeney's footsteps could be heard in the background. Finally, Hodges told them that Jim Gilliam had popped to Julian Javier. There would be a playoff. Bedlam ensued everywhere. Dark proclaimed it a comeback for the ages, and he had been there in '51.

The contrast between the Giants and Dodgers clubhouses was extraordinary. It was also a little different from 1951. On the last day 11 years earlier, the Giants beat Boston and, with the Dodgers losing big against Philadelphia, seemed to have the pennant locked up. Then Brooklyn rallied. Jackie Robinson saved the day with a remarkable catch, and Brooklyn jumped for joy. By evening time, when the Dodgers won, it was the Giants who had the heart taken out of them. This time it was all Giants.

Dodgers players swore and threw things. Podres was beside himself, one of his greatest efforts having gone for naught. He drove to the Mayflower Hotel, his L.A. residence, where friends were waiting to throw a surprise birthday party, but he was in no mood to celebrate. Alston was full of recriminations, self and otherwise. Twenty-one innings had come and gone without a Dodger run, and this was no light-hitting squad. They were stars, winners of over 100 games, World Champions three years earlier, the fabled Dodgers franchise. There were no excuses.

In the last 13 games, San Francisco was only 7–6, but Los Angeles had gone 3–10. "It was like two drunks having a fight in a saloon and trying to stagger to the safety of the swinging doors," wrote Arthur Daley in the *New York Times*. "Both kept falling down. The Giants, however, could crawl better than the Dodgers."

The Dodgers had led for 111 days compared to 54 for the Giants, and entered the final two weeks up by four. The two teams were 9–9 against each other in the regular season, most of their victories coming at home. The L.A. media began an anatomy of their collapse. Aside from internal dissension, defense in particular had failed the club down the stretch. They had finished last in the league in double plays. Koufax's injury, Drysdale's late-season failing after winning 25 games, bullpen collapses, power hitters reduced to an endless stream of grounders to shortstop, bad base running by the so-called swift set, and above all terrible fundamentals were cited. Others said they had "gone Hollywood," tempted by beautiful starlets, too much nightlife, the glitz, their press clippings . . . it went on and on.

San Francisco pitching was seen as the primary reason for the club's success, and in this regard they had benefited from three starters—Sanford, Pierce, and O'Dell—who had come over from other teams, in some cases as reclamation projects. "Sometimes a change of atmosphere helps," says Dark. "It certainly didn't hurt our pitchers."

The year 1962 remains one of those special years.
In retrospect, it stands out as the last innocent
season before John Kennedy was killed and Vietnam
started. African Americans would disagree, looking
on it as the last vestige of post–Civil War segregation,

but there is more to 1962 than that. George Lucas staged his classic *American Graffiti* in that year. John Glenn orbited the Earth and the Cold War heated up over missiles in Cuba in 1962.

It was the height of the Los Angeles–San Francisco rivalry, which has taken on many dimensions, sports, and otherwise, in succeeding years, but may never have been more intense. Whatever it was in New York, it was all that and more in California.

The City's inferiority complex was exacerbated not just by Los Angeles sports dominance in the form of the Dodgers, Rams, Trojans, and Bruins beating up on the Giants, 49ers, Indians, and Golden Bears, but it contained a political dynamic. California was a Republican state. A former US senator from Los Angeles, Richard Nixon, had ascended to the vice presidency. L.A. was a Republican, business-friendly city. The Bay Area squirmed, preferring the Democrats and the unions, but unable to gain national power as did Orange County, the emerging juggernaut of votes and influence. Even a San Francisco Democrat, Governor Edmund "Pat" Brown, seemed to favor the Southland with an emerging plan to pump NorCal water to the Southland.

Every once in a while, he had to stop himself from saying that Mays made a tackle, or Kuenn threw a block, and once he actually did have Davenport gaining for the 49ers.

—Giants announcer Russ Hodges on his partner Lon Simmons, who was also the 49ers announcer, trying to stay up with the Giants final regular season game of 1962 while doing play-by-play of a football game at Kezar Stadium, when the Giants beat the Colt .45s 2–1 on a Willie Mays homer at Candlestick, while the Cardinals beat the Dodgers 1–0 in L.A. to force a playoff

Beat L.A.!

WHO IS THE GREATEST OF ALL BASEBALL WRITERS? A SUBJECTIVE question, to be sure. There is no single answer. Ring Lardner, Red Smith, Jimmy Breslin, Jim Murray, some would say. Others bring up a less-known scribe, Pat Jordan, or the inimitable Richard Ben Cramer, said to have gotten to the heart of Ted Williams while uncovering the mask worn by Joe DiMaggio until his death. But purists oft point to a man with the appropriate name of Roger Angell, for he surely wrote of the game with heavenly words.

For some reason it took until 2014 for Angell to make it to Cooperstown, where he has belonged at least since publication of his 1972 classic, *The Summer Game*. There are any number of fans of any number of teams who if asked to recall the most influential words ever written of their team, would mention Angell's writings in that book, his later works, or his many *New Yorker* pieces. So it is true that nobody captured the baseball ambience of Candlestick Park, and the place the Giants hold in the hearts of their fans, better than Angell.

First, Angell was not a traditional baseball scribe, an "ink stained wretch" of his era, as was the likes of Breslin or Jimmy Cannon. He was with *The New Yorker*, which covered baseball the way *The Sporting News* covered the ballet. For some reason in 1959 somebody on the editorial staff decided to send Mr. Angell to spring training, to get the "flavor" of Florida. They probably figured there was some interest in the subject, since so many elderly, oft–Jewish New Yorkers were now "snow birds" living their retirement years in the Sunshine State.

It was such a popular, well-received piece that Angell was asked each successive season to follow it up with some baseball updates, which in the 1960s generally meant a study of the September pennant chases, followed by in-depth, in-person evaluation of each October's World Series over the course of two decades.

Aside from his *New Yorker* "credentials," Angell did not sit in the citadel of baseball wisdom, the press box. He would take his teenage daughter and sit in the box seats, buying popcorn and peanuts with the other rubes. He observed the fans and stadium attendants, the intricacies of the ballparks themselves, as much as the action on the field or the clubhouse kabuki theater that served as Q-and-A between athletes and journalists.

The year 1962 marked Angell's blossoming. The subject matter, which ripened into full bloom that momentous year, was perfect for his wry, witty observations. It started when he ventured out to the Polo Grounds to see the expansion Mets. At the time, they were simply the worst baseball team of all time playing in a win-at-all-costs town that has zero love for anything but champions.

Somehow, sitting in the stands with his daughter, watching the Mets lose big but valiantly to the new Los Angeles and San Francisco clubs, amid ex-Giants, ex-Dodgers, and haughty Yankees fans, he uncovered not only the magic that would become the love affair between the Mets and their fans, but also the love affair, heretofore not fully revealed, now too late to save them from leaving, between the Dodgers and Brooklyn.

Along with Roger Kahn and Jim Murray, Angell understood and articulated the Giants-Dodgers rivalry better than any writers. In October 1962, his descriptions of Dodger Stadium and Candlestick Park, both based on his first impressions of these two ballparks, remain as vivid and perfect as any written in subsequent years.

After everything, there was still more baseball to be played before the National League could send a representative against the rested, waiting, all-conquering New York Yankees. A coin toss determined that the play-offs would open at Candlestick, then switch for the second and, if needed, third game at Dodger Stadium. Dark, Jansen, Lockman, Westrum, Mays . . . Durocher, Snider . . .

The Yankees had to cancel their flight to Los Angeles. Ralph Houk was concerned that they had been scouting the Dodgers and now they might be facing the Giants, but at least he did not have to deal with Mickey Mantle, Whitey Ford, and company spending three or four days in Hollywood with nothing but "Johnny Grant parties" to keep them busy. They headed to San Francisco's Towne House Hotel to wait it out.

(The Yankees struggled against the expansion Angels in their Dodger Stadium years in large part because they attended wild shindigs in the hills thrown by the so-called mayor of Hollywood, Johnny Grant; they were usually hung over and unable to get around on Dean Chance the next day.)

For the old New York rival Giants and Dodgers, it all came down to October, a best-of-three playoff, just like 1951. Eleven years after the "shot heard 'round the world" the teams started again. It was the fourth best-of-three playoff in Dodgers history.

The Dodgers featured one of the best teams in their long history, Brooklyn or Los Angeles. Unlike the image of later Dodgers teams of the 1960s, this club had power and plenty of offensive punch, but mysteriously lost the ability to score down the stretch, when San Francisco managed to tie them on the last day of the regular season.

Candlestick groundskeeper Matty Schwab went to work on the basepaths. He had already warned the drivers of cars on Fan Appreciation Day not to park on the infield dirt because they would "sink to their hubcaps." Schwab kept it up all night on Sunday. When Wills and company arrived Monday they were again beside themselves, totally psyched by it.

Dodgers public relations director Red Patterson tried to lodge a protest with Warren Giles, who made himself scarce. He then appealed to umpire Jocko Conlan, who approached Dark, who assumed an uncooperative, hard-line stance. Conlan found Schwab, ordering him to dry up and solidify the basepaths. Conlan ordered it rolled, as was the custom at Dodger Stadium, and Dark exploded, saying it was because O'Malley ran the league.

"His word is law," said Dark, as if knowledge of his own team's cheating should not have been allowed. The Dodgers were mollified and encouraged by the October weather, which tends to be the best the Bay Area has to offer; warmer than the summer, mid-70s, no wind, perfect for sailing (a popular pastime).

Koufax started but struggled, allowing a two-out double to Felipe Alou. Mays hit a "Candlestick shot" over the right-center field fence. He had learned to adjust his swing for opposite field power so as to avoid hitting straight into the wind blowing from left field, instead "going with the flow" toward right. An inning later, when Jim Davenport homered and Ed Bailey whistled a single past Koufax, Sandy was sent to the showers, his season over.

"I can't be the same after two months off," said Koufax, largely sidelined after a brilliant first half with a mysterious finger ailment. "My finger is okay, but I felt like the third week of Spring Training."

Billy Pierce breezed past L.A., tossing a three-hit shutout with six strikeouts. "It was the most satisfying game I ever pitched," said Pierce, who upped his record to 12–0 at Candlestick Park and 16–6 on the year. Pierce thanked Conlan afterward, possibly a peace offering after the pregame consternation over the infield rolling. "I congratulated him on calling an excellent game and he congratulated me—sort of a mutual admiration society." L.A.'s scoreless streak was now thirty innings and they had not threatened in any way to break it.

In the opening playoff contest, Mays walked, singled, and hit two homers in four at-bats. The Dodgers played dirty, knocking him down a couple of times, but it only steeled his resolve. His second home run came after Sherry brushed him back. The crowd seemed to adopt him at that very moment. It was the line of demarcation in his relationship with the fans.

"I think it was the moment where the San Francisco fans finally took him to heart," said Pierce.

"I think the fans are starting to warm to me," said Mays, grinning.

"No team can be as bad as we've been," said Alston. "We've got to snap out of it sometime. I still don't know who I'm going to pitch in the second."

Alston then announced he was going with Stan Williams, who had been relegated to virtual obscurity since allowing a grand slam in a key game. It was an odd move, hotly debated by the Dodgers players, brass, and media about their team plane, Electra II, during the flight back to Los Angeles.

"What's he saving me for?" complained Drysdale to anybody who would listen. "The first spring exhibition game?"

The Giants flew to the City of Angels, checked into the Ambassador Hotel (in 1968 the site of Robert Kennedy's assassination), and some watched young comedian Johnny Carson debut as host of *The Tonight Show*. Singer Tony Bennett performed "I Left My Heart in San Francisco."

October 2 was hot and smoggy. A town of notorious front-runners had given up on their team. Cars drove straight into the parking lot. Only 25,231 showed up. The Dodgers had set the all-time attendance mark of 2,755,184 in 1962, eclipsing previous records by the Cleveland Indians and Milwaukee Braves.

Snider was in left field, Tommy Davis at third, and Wally Moon at first. At the last second, Alston went with Big D on two days' rest. He had nothing and tried to rely on his famed spitball, drawing warnings from umpire Al Barlick. In the sixth Drysdale ran out of gas completely. With one out, Haller walked, followed by Jose Pagan's double, a successful sacrifice bunt by Sanford moving them along, followed by singles off the bats of Chuck Hiller and Davenport. The score was 4–0, Drysdale was headed for the shower, and the sparse crowd began to thin out. All that was left, it seemed, were Giants rooters wearing orange-and-black hats and gear; transplanted San Franciscans living in L.A. or those who had driven eight hours on the 101 to be there.

McCovey's RBI single seemed to seal it, and the remaining Dodger "fans" grumbled, booed, left. Alston's team was as done as a Thanksgiving turkey. Thirty-six straight scoreless innings without a peep, they had gone down "not with a bang but with a whimper," as the poet T. S. Elliot so famously wrote. There was none of the dramatics of 1951, of heroism in defeat. They were the French Army in 1940.

"Down in the dugout, manager Walt Alston was poring over the stagecoach schedules to Darrtown," wrote Jim Murray.

The Dodgers "displayed the muscle, the frightfulness, and the total immobility of a woolly mammoth frozen in a glacier; the Giants, finding the beast inert, fell upon it with savage cries and chopped steaks and rump roasts at will," wrote the fabulous Roger Angell.

Gilliam's walk to lead off the sixth scarcely caused a ruffle, but Sanford's reputation was that of a six-inning pitcher. Additionally, the hard-throwing right-hander, already tired from the long season, was nursing a head cold and had to run the bases in the previous inning. Sanford looked "like five miles of bad road," according to Bob Stevens. Dark overreacted and called on Miller, instead of saving him for the closer's role.

Miller had nothing. Neither did O'Dell. Dark was now into his starters, panicking. O'Dell "threw some gas" on the fire that Miller admitted having started. Larsen came in and the Dodgers suddenly were scoring at will. The 36-inning shutout streak fell like the Siegfried Line when George Patton's Army knocked it down. After Los Angeles poured seven runs across, the Giants could see the Promised Land evaporating before their eyes.

"By the end of that inning, they were ahead and I could feel the goat horns sprouting," said Miller.

The sixth inning took an hour and 11 minutes to play. The seventh lasted 10 minutes. Fans started coming back. In the eighth, San Francisco scored twice to tie it, and Dodger frustration was again at an all-time high. Davenport and Mays got hits, Bailey contributed a pinch-hit RBI single, but Tommy Davis threw Mays out at third on a bad call. Stan Williams, now in the game, walked to load bases but pitched out of it. He settled down, gaining some redemption, and in the bottom of the ninth Wills walked. Bob Bolin was lifted for Dick LeMay. Gilliam walked, Spencer hit for Snider, and Gaylord Perry came in. Dark gave him instructions to get the lead man. On the ensuing bunt he had Wills at third but panicked and went to first. Dark ripped the dugout phone off the wall and threw it to the end of the bench, stormed to the mound, wordlessly ripped the ball from Perry's hand, and called for McCormick.

Tommy Davis was intentionally walked to load the bases. Ron Fairly, who was 1 for 31, hit a short pop to center. Wills took a chance. A good throw by Mays would have nailed him, but Willie's effort was up the line and Los Angeles won, 8–7.

The Dodgers picked up Wills and carried him off field. It got so out of hand he had to hide in the training room from teammates, in order to avoid injury. "I didn't want to get killed," he said. "Those guys were acting crazy."

"The feast continued here for a time yesterday," wrote Angell. Trailing 5–0, "At this point, the Dodgers scored their first run in 36 innings, and the Giants, aghast at this tiny evidence of life, stood transfixed, their stone axes dropping from their paws, while the monster heaved itself to its feet, scattering chunks of ice, and set about trampling its tormentors."

It was a total resurrection for Los Angeles. Williams was the happiest of them all, having redeemed himself after a month of purgatory. The Giants were filled with remorse at having blown a sure win. Alston called it "the biggest scrambler I've ever seen. I've never been in a wilder, woolier one, personally." There were recriminations about Sanford's effort.

"One fella said to his face that he'd quit on us," O'Dell said.

The game "is best described in metaphor and hyperbole," wrote Angell, the master of the genre, "for there is no economy in it." The Mets (40–120) "could have beaten both teams."

Suddenly it was the Giants who were arguing and shouting. It looked like all the momentum had swung back to the Dodgers; shades of 1951, after Brooklyn's Clem Labine tossed a 10–0 shutout to force a deciding game. Game 2 required 42 players and took four hours, 18 minutes to play, the longest nine-inning game ever. NBC lost $300,000 when *The Huntley-Brinkley Report* and *Phil Silvers Show* were both preempted. Six years later this game resonated in the minds of NBC executives, who chose to cut away just as the Oakland Raiders were staging a last-minute comeback over the New York Jets in the infamous "*Heidi* game."

Actor Rock Hudson watched Game 2 at a bar in Universal City: "We've got it made," he announced. "Those Dodgers will kill them. The Giants won't have a chance tomorrow. They won't come close. You wait and see."

Director Alfred Hitchcock, dining at Chasen's, sounded like Winston Churchill predicting victory over Adolf Hitler. He said he had "the utmost confidence in the ultimate defeat of the Giants. The good guys always win in our fair city."

On Wednesday afternoon the "what have you done for me lately?" city transformed itself back into a Dodgertown of loyalists. Arriving at Dodger Stadium was 45,693 front-runners, including Doris Day, Rosalind Russell, and Frank Sinatra. The crowd contrasted with the "embarrassing acres of empty seats yesterday, when the park was barely half full," observed Angell. "Los Angeles calls itself the Sports Capitol of the

World, but its confidence is easily shaken. Its loyalists are made uneasy by a team that appears likely to lose. Today, with a final chance at the pennant restored, the Dodger rooters were back, and there was hopeful violence in their cries. Fans here seem to require electronic reassurance. One out of every three or four of them carries a transistor radio, in order to be told what he is seeing, and the din from these is so loud in the stands that every spectator can hear the voice of Vic Scully, the Dodger announcer, hovering about his ears throughout the game."

The modern electronic Dodger Stadium scoreboard invited the fans to sing "Baby Face" and ordered the battle cry "CHARGE!" during rallies. The scoreboard struck Angell, an observer of baseball for years in the venerable Polo Grounds and Ebbets Field, as a "giant billboard . . . like a grocer's placard," and that the "new and impressive Dodger Stadium . . . was designed by an admirer of suburban supermarkets. It has the same bright, uneasy colors (turquoise exterior walls, pale green outfield fences, odd yellows and ochers on the grandstand seats); the same superfluous decorative touches, such as the narrow rickraff roofs over the top row of the bleachers; the same pre-occupation with easy access and with total use of interior space; and the same heaps of raw dirt around its vast parking lots. There is a special shelf for high-priced goods—a dugout behind home plate for movie and television stars, ballplayers' wives, and transient millionaires. Outside, a complex system of concentric automobile ramps and colored signs—yellow for field boxes, green for reserved seats, and so forth—is intended to deliver the carborne fan to the proper gate, but on my two visits to O'Malley's Safeway it was evident that the locals had not yet mastered their instructions, for a good many baseball shoppers wound up in the detergent aisle instead of the cracker department, with a resultant loss of good feeling, and had to be ordered to go away and try again."

These descriptions represent some of the most vivid descriptions of a time, a place, an era, and a stadium ever written.

Ron Fairly told Willie "Three Dog" Davis before the penultimate game that "this one is ours." Durocher wore the same T-shirt, shorts, and socks he wore the day of Thomson's 1951 homer. "I wore them yesterday when we won, and they have magic powers," said Durocher, somehow overlooking the possibility that those items might have a "mojo" that would favor the Giants, not his new team.

The writers asked Dark if he brought along anything from 1951. "Yeah," he said. "Willie Mays."

The starters were the ailing Marichal versus the bone-tired winner of the 1955 game seven, Podres on two days of rest. In the third inning San Francisco took a 2–0 lead on three Dodgers errors, including one by Podres. A Snider double and an RBI grounder by Howard cut it to 2–1. Roebuck replaced Podres with the bases full in the sixth.

"Even so, I pitched pretty good," said Podres of his exhausted effort. "I got us into the sixth inning before Eddie Roebuck bailed me out."

Roebuck, making his sixth appearance in seven days, pitched out of the jam with a force at home and double play. In the bottom of the inning Snider singled and the "Giant killer" Tommy Davis hit a 400-foot homer to give the Dodgers a 3–2 lead. Hope sprang eternal in the breasts of large-busted starlets!

Then the scoreboard flashed news that astronaut Walter Schirra, a USC graduate, had orbited the Earth six times. American exceptionalism seemed to give the crowd a burst of adrenaline, exacerbated by the home team's increasing its lead to 4–2 in the seventh. Wills's fourth hit and 104th stolen base, his third of day, led to the fourth run. A famed photograph shows the throw skipping past Davenport, with Wills totally disrupting him. Durocher ran all the way down the line with Wills as if he were Bobby Thomson and it was over. Durocher *slid* as Maury scored, and the Giants seethed. Felipe Alou said right then and there that it steeled the Giants' resolve.

"For a time today, it seemed that all the recent doubts and discomforts suffered by Dodger fans were finally to be rewarded," wrote Angell, who in his *New Yorker* piece described how the club forged ahead "in the happiest fashion imaginable," behind the "old demi-god" Snider and the "young demi-god" Tommy Davis, "who studies each pitch with the eye of a jewelry appraiser," and Wills was "the ranking deity in Los Angeles this year." The Giants "forgot their newly discovered stratagem for getting Wills out," describing how the previous day Wills had stolen second, only to be cut down at third by "the best arm on the club," the sturdy right wing of Mays.

San Francisco went down quietly against Roebuck's sinker in the eighth. Los Angeles had a chance to increase their lead in the bottom half of the inning. Dark walked two batters intentionally, loading the bases. Roebuck came to the plate. He had thrown three innings and was dead tired. Alston allowed him to hit. The Dodgers groaned. Koufax and Podres begged Durocher to talk sense into Alston, to pinch-hit for the reliever and use Sandy or Drysdale in the ninth. Drysdale shouted and screamed for the chance. One of the best-hitting pitchers of all time, with some managerial foresight he could easily have been used as both the pinch hitter and the closer. Instead, Roebuck made the last out and trudged out for the ninth.

"I'd rather have Roebuck pitching for us with a two-run lead than anybody I've got," Alston later said.

"You're damn right I would have liked to pitch," Drysdale later told writer Bud Furillo. "Only they didn't ask me. I didn't think Roebuck should have started the ninth. He did enough."

Roebuck said Walt's theory was that his sinker would be more effective since he was exhausted, but the pitcher said he was "the most uncomfortable I've ever felt in a game." The smog was debilitating, and he just wanted to get it over with.

In the Giants' dugout, the silence was broken up by Dark. "Matty, grab a bat," he said.

Felipe Alou's little brother Matty, a contact hitter, was the worst guy a sinkerballer like Roebuck could face in that situation. Matty drilled Roebuck's second pitch to right field for a single.

"You can't imagine the pressure I was feeling by now," Roebuck admitted. He made $14,000 that year, and the Series share was $10,000. Wills tried to calm him down. Roebuck got Kuenn to hit a perfect one-hop double play grounder to Maury, but *somebody* had moved Larry Burright two steps away from second base. He was a split-second late in the force at the bag, just enough to allow Kuenn to beat his throw to first base. No double play.

The question would swirl around Dodger circles like the famed "Who lost China?" accusation that dominated politics in 1949. "Who moved Burright?" According to Roseboro, Lee Walls yelled for Burright to play Kuenn as an opposite-field hitter.

Roebuck walked McCovey. Felipe Alou came to the plate. Alston visited the mound. Still no Drysdale. Big D seethed. Roebuck told the manager he just wanted to "finish this thing one way or another." It would turn out to be "or another."

"The clatter of typewriters died away in the press box," wrote Angell. Many writers were already in the elevator headed toward the Dodger victory celebration. Now, silence befell the cramped Dodger Stadium press box. None of the L.A. writers wanted to have to rewrite their stories. Half wanted more drama. Half just wanted it to end. Roebuck had enjoyed success with Mays in the past, but Willie inside-outed a jam sinker up the middle.

"This white blur was coming right at me," Roebuck recalled. He had a large glove he called "the claw." He stabbed, barely missed catching it for the second out and possibly setting up a double play. Instead it squirted off the webbing for an infield hit and a run scored. Bye Ed.

Drysdale?

"Stan Williams!" roared Durocher, not caring who heard him. "He'll walk the park."

Drysdale was beside himself as Williams entered.

The Giants were stunned. Alston had *Koufax and Drysdale* in the bullpen, but went with *Stan Williams*.

"He must have been saving them to pitch in the Series," deadpanned O'Dell. Dark said that if he had Drysdale, "I'm thinking pretty seriously about seeing if he can't finish the ballgame," that in a game of this magnitude "there is no tomorrow."

Williams thought he was brought in because he had pitched well the day before—even though that increased the fatigue factor—and that he had won two playoff games against Milwaukee in 1959.

Alston figured the right-handed Williams would get the right-handed Cepeda, then the southpaw Perranoski could be brought in against the left-handed Bailey. Williams jammed Orlando, who hit a short fly to right. Fairly had a decent arm but was a first baseman, not an outfielder. His throw was late. The Giants tied it at 4–4. Cepeda said it was one of the biggest RBIs of his great career. Consternation bordering on hatred was palpable in the Dodgers' dugout and bullpen, with open, verbal questioning of Alston. A pall fell over the Dodger Stadium crowd, broken up only by the wild shouts of scattered Giants rooters and the San Francisco players themselves.

Alston and Durocher "stalked slowly back and forth in their dugout, staring at their shoe tops and exuding an almost invisible purple cloud of yearning; they wanted the National League season extended by a few more innings or a few more games," wrote Roger Angell. "This wish, like so many other attitudes to be seen in this city, must be regarded as excessive . . . the twitchy, exhausted athletes on both squads was reminiscent of action in the winter softball games played by septuagenarians in St. Petersburg, Florida." The Dodgers had permitted their "gasping pursuers" to catch them, and now they were about to pass them.

Alston *did not go to Perranoski* against the left-handed Bailey, who later admitted he had little chance against Perranoski. Williams threw a wild pitch. Mays moved to third, Felipe to second, and Bailey walked to first. Roseboro came to the mound. He did not want the wild Williams loading the bases; he could easily walk in the go-ahead run, just as Durocher predicted. They looked toward the dugout to get Alston's attention; to come out and get Williams, or at least talk it over, but "*we couldn't find him,*" said Roseboro. Alston was in the runway . . .

Smoking . . . a . . . cigarette . . .

Bailey was walked intentionally.

Davenport, a .320 lifetime hitter versus Williams, came to bat. The first two pitches to him were balls, then a strike. Williams, aiming now, walked him. Alou trotted home and San Francisco led, 5–4. The pall in the dugout and the stands barely concealed indignation.

Finally, too late, Perranoski was brought in. Naturally, Burright booted Pagan's grounder and it was 6–4. Bob Nieman flied out.

The press box loudspeaker announced that United Airlines would have a special flight leaving at seven o'clock for San Francisco and the World Series.

Pierce was called on for the last three outs. He was as calm as a commuter waiting for the 5:15 to Greenwich. Wills grounded out, Gilliam hit "can of corn," and "I knew we were in pretty good shape," said Pierce.

The .205-hitting Walls stepped in for Burright and lifted an easy, soft fly to Mays, who did not make his usual "basket catch." Asked about it later, he yelled, "Are you crazy? That was $15,000 a man." In a year in which he owed money to everybody, he was not about to take any chances. There is a photo of the shirtless Mays, displaying the muscles of a steroid user long before such enhancements were thought of, in the postgame clubhouse. Willie displayed a "million dollar" smile.

The game was over and the stunned crowd spilled onto the freeways, the streets, the bars. The Giants "went into the ritual Autumnal dance of victory in front of their dugout, leaping into the air like Watusi," wrote Angell.

"One of the most dramatic and nerve-racking pennant races in years came to an astounding end today," wrote John Drebinger in the *New York Times*, calling the crowd of 45,693 "incredulous" at the sight of their beloved home nine blowing a two-run lead in the ninth inning of a deciding playoff game for the second time in 11 years.

Park maintenance moved cases of champagne three different times in anticipation of the celebratory locale. The NBC crew barely moved their equipment out of the Dodger clubhouse before the angry home team stomped in. The cramped Giants' clubhouse was a madhouse.

The meltdown in the Dodgers' clubhouse was probably the ugliest and most horrid drunken, all-night blamefest in sports annals, eventually moving to a restaurant on Sunset Boulevard (where Durocher spent the night accusing Alston like Javert from *Les Misérables*), Drysdale's restaurant in the San Fernando Valley (the fact no players were arrested for drunk driving coming or going was a miracle), not ending until daylight the next day. Alston locked himself in his office and fended off bitter players trying to literally get at him, in a scene resembling *Night of the Living Dead*.

"This is the greatest moment of my life!" shouted McCovey, who posed for a wide-smiled photo with his rival Cepeda and pitching hero Pierce in the victorious clubhouse. Then they broke into a conga line. Dark smilingly begged off the champagne.

"If we drink all this stuff, we'd be sick for a week," exclaimed Bailey. "And if we had blown that game today, we'd have been sick for a year."

Former vice president Richard Nixon, trolling for votes in his neck-and-neck gubernatorial campaign against incumbent governor Pat Brown, the election only a month away, told Dark, "Your players have heart. You'll beat the Yankees."

The first game of the World Series was less than 24 hours away. The Yankees had been idling away the whole time; a relatively early pennant-clinching, then waiting out the playoffs. The Giants were loosey-goosey, carefree.

"This was it—this was the pressure," said Mays. "We've got no time to worry about the Yankees now. We'll deal with them as they come."

"Winning those play-offs was better than the Series," Felipe Alou later said. "Because of the rivalry, the animosity between the Dodgers and Giants, the way we came from behind. This was the biggest thing that ever happened to me in baseball—even more than the day I played in the same outfield with my two brothers."

The team started to party in the clubhouse, managed to deal with the press, showered, and were still partying as they made their way to the Los Angeles Airport for the flight to San Francisco.

Dark reminded them that they had a game to play the next day. They managed to cool it, but as the plane approached San Francisco International Airport, pilot Orv Schmidt announced, "There's a little disturbance down below."

People showed up *en masse* at SFO. When the parking lot filled up, many just parked on the side of Highway 101 and walked to the airport. Fans, estimated at between 25,000 and 75,000 strong, overran the runway. The plane circled for an hour and there was talk of landing in Oakland, across the bay. Many feared a crash. Felipe Alou in particular hated to fly.

Eventually, the DC-7 was allowed to land at a United maintenance base. A small gathering of mechanics and the Giants' bus driver politely applauded. The bus would drive the team north to Candlestick Park, where their cars were, but the players who lived on the peninsula, to the south, decided to find their own way home. Cepeda, the Alou brothers, Pierce, and Marichal waded their way through the crowd. They eventually were given rides by fans they had never met before. They all made it.

The rest boarded the bus. At the main concourse, wives and family awaited but beyond that was a semi-dangerous throng. The day had been long and alcohol-fueled. People broke through police barricades, French Revolution–style, converging on the bus.

"Those folks meant well, but they really shook us up," recalled Dark. They started to shake and rock the bus. Several recalled being terrified that the bus would be rolled over and they would be crushed. Writer David Plaut said it was a "miracle" the team escaped without serious incident or injury, to players or fans.

A chant began: "*We want Mays! We want Mays!*" But Willie had found a cab to take him to his peninsula home. Somebody suggested to "throw 'em Boles," his look-alike, but Boles wanted none of it. He literally feared for his safety.

Chub Feeney said that he had never seen anything like it in New York. "It certainly wasn't this way when we won in 1951," he exclaimed.

"But that was all in hysterical New York, not sedate San Francisco," wrote Art Rosenbaum sarcastically.

The event certainly suggested something about the City that nobody ever quite realized before that; exactly what is still not clear, but its image did change somewhat from its sophisticated reputation.

The bus made its way out of the parking lot, but Feeney ordered it to stop at a nearby motel. Because of the late hour, rental cars were hard to come by, and due to the strange events normal plans were askew. Feeney figured that the motel was a good place for players to arrange for rentals rather than at Candlestick, which is off the beaten path.

It was after midnight, the team had to play the Yankees in less than 12 hours, and "We're walking along the highway, across this empty field, in total darkness," recalled Feeney. "I thought to myself: here we are. Here come the champions of the National League."

Los Angeles, Southern California, the Southland, La La Land, Tinsel-town, Hollywood . . . the city that wasn't, they called it, but it was. They had everything: better weather, movie glamour, gorgeous girls, famed nightclubs, the endless strand, a bigger population, political and economic clout, better stadiums filled with more fans, and better teams at every level—high school, college, and professional.

But now . . . finally, San Francisco had *beat L.A.!* In so doing, they had validated, confirmed their superior, narcissistic view of themselves as "gents," not "rubes," as "sophisticates," not "yokels." The great dragon of Los Angeles, not just the Dodgers but the very *idea* of L.A., had been slayed. It was a cultural, sociopolitical victory, a victory for clean air and water over smog, of cable cars over traffic jams, of literature and poetry over celluloid trickery. Allen Ginsberg over John Wayne. Rudolf Nureyev over Shirley Temple. Liberalism over conservatism.

This all seemed to carry forward when, one month later, San Francisco's liberal Democrat Edmund "Pat" Brown defeated Los Angeles's conservative Republican Richard M. Nixon for governor. At the time, it seemed to be Nixon's political obituary, which could not come too soon for San Francisco Lefties. The north had its revenge over the south. They had validation.

Hannibal had crossed the Alps. Lying in wait was the Roman Empire of sports, the Yankees, who represented a city—the Big Apple, New York—that posed a whole new challenge. San Franciscans thought they lived in the City. New Yorkers knew they lived in *the* city! Unlike San Francisco, it was a city that did not consider "ultimate victory" to be "jarring," as Charles McCabe put it. New York City and its Yankees, who had won a war of attrition when the Giants and Dodgers split the scene, who had captured nine World Series since 1949 alone, had absolutely no problem with "ultimate victory!"

But in November the north took their first shot at taking back some of the political panache lost perhaps since the Owens Valley Aqueduct had been built: Governor Pat Brown won re-election against Richard Nixon and all of his Southland political power.

—◆—

They looked beaten. Their looks, their body language . . . they looked so depressed that we caught them.
    —GIANTS HALL OF FAMER WILLIE McCOVEY DESCRIBING
        THE DODGERS WHEN FORCED TO PLAY THEM
            IN THE 1962 PLAYOFF

"It was a lovely ballgame—everything went right," he said.
        —BILLY PIERCE, THOUGHT TO BE OVER THE HILL,
    WAS ACQUIRED FROM THE CHICAGO WHITE SOX AND
    WENT 8–0 AT CANDLESTICK IN 1962, AFTER HE THREW
    A SHUTOUT AND THE GIANTS POUNDED SANDY KOUFAX,
            8–0 IN THE FIRST PLAYOFF GAME

I had to take a tranquilizer to get through the ninth inning.
    —GIANTS ANNOUNCER RUSS HODGES OF GAME 3, '62 PLAYOFF

Man, after that play-off in Los Angeles, I'm all out of tense.
            —GIANTS SUPERSTAR WILLIE MAYS

They couldn't control the crowd. By the time we got off the plane and onto the bus, people started rocking the bus. I thought they were going to turn it over.
        —WILLIE McCOVEY'S DESCRIPTION OF THE AIRPORT
            RECEPTION AFTER WINNING THE '62 PLAYOFF

He thought he was hallucinating. He told us he would take us anywhere we wanted to go. And then when we finally got home, all of our neighbors were out in front of our houses to greet us. We didn't get to bed until early in the morning, and we had to get up to play in the World Series.
    —WILLIE McCOVEY DESCRIBING A DRIVER WHO PICKED HIM
        AND HIS TEAMMATES UP, DRIVING THEM TO THEIR HOMES,
            AFTER ARRIVING FROM L.A.

What the hell are they saving me for, the first spring exhibition game?
—Dodger ace Don Drysdale's reaction to manager
Walt Alston's decision not to bring him—
or Sandy Koufax—in to relieve in the
third and final 1962 playoff game

Wanted, one nearly new 1962 National League pennant, slightly soiled with tear stain in center. Last seen blowing toward San Francisco. . . . Warning: if you return pennant to Dodgers direct, be sure to tape it to their hands.
—Los Angeles Times columnist Jim Murray

It was a terrible year. The Dodgers should have been in that Series, not the Giants.
—Ball Four, by Jim Bouton,
quoting Dodgers star Tommy Davis

"A Festive Prison Yard"

An art exhibit of life-size pastel portraits of Dodger heroes were arranged in a semicircle, each elegantly framed and bearing a gold identifying plate. A velvet rope surrounded it, "like the new Rembrandt in the Metropolitan Museum," Roger Angell wrote, guarded by a uniformed Pinkerton.

It was not unlike a portrait given to Brooklyn manager Charley Dressen mid-September 1951 bearing the inscription, "To the manager of the 1951 National League champions." Not to mention the national TV interviews of the Yankees' Ralph Houk and the Dodgers' Walt Alston in September, previewing a presumed Yankees–Dodgers World Series.

"No one was looking at the pictures," wrote Angell of the 1962 art exhibit. Angell was describing what he saw at his Los Angeles hotel, where he quickly came to gather his belongings before making his way to the airport and departing on that special United Airlines flight reserved for the media, transporting them from Los Angeles to San Francisco. The citywide party was still going strong when *The New Yorker* scribe arrived in . . . the City. The faces of fans "all had the shiny-eyed, stunned, exhausted expression of a bride at her wedding reception," wrote Angell.

Bars and restaurants in San Francisco had been filled to capacity during Game 3 of the playoffs. When it ended, Market Street resembled V-J Day, with cars honking, orange-and-black confetti hung out windows, strangers shaking hands, hugging, and in the case of men and women, some doing a little more than that.

A matinee playing of *Oliver* was broken up by transistor-tilting theatergoers shouting with glee. A restaurant owner poured champagne on the sidewalk, clubhouse style. Handel's "Hallelujah Chorus" broke out at Grace Cathedral.

As the night wore on, the sense of religious deliverance turned into something ugly, with the cops called out to deal with drunk driving, fighting, and vandalism that caused tremendous property damage. Cable cars were tilted and rolled over, roads were closed, and numerous arrests were made.

The San Francisco bar scene was in full swing well past midnight. All of Northern California celebrated the Giants' monumental victory. It was more than just a great win for the Giants over the Dodgers. For the strange, schizophrenic, *superior* San Franciscans-with-an-*inferiority*-complex, it meant much more than that.

Angell's national legend was not yet made when October rolled around, but in reading and rereading *The Summer Game* in the 1970s, the rabid Giants fan gets the sense that here was imprimatur, that when Angell ventured to Candlestick Park and wrote of *their City*, then and only then was big-league status conferred upon her. In so doing, we find that Angell's description of Candlestick upon first sight remains as vivid today as ever, and somehow more poignant than all the words written by local San Francisco scribes over ensuing decades.

Angell was shocked when he got a gander at Candlestick Park, especially after spending two days in what he called "Taj O'Malley" (Dodger Stadium), and a pleasant evening in the salons of San Francisco's cafe society. Candlestick was *nooooo* Dodger Stadium, Angell noted, "with its raw concrete ramps and walkways and its high, curving grandstand barrier, it looks from the outside like an outbuilding of"—yes, Angell got it the very first time he saw the place—"Alcatraz. But it was a festive prison yard during the first two Series games here."

On the evening of the day the Giants won the pennant, the circulation manager of the *San Francisco Chronicle*, which uniquely printed its sports section on green and pink paper, asked the editor what the headline was for the next day's editions.

"It's 'WE WIN!'—white on black," the editor replied.

"How big?"

"Same size as 'FIDEL DEAD!'"

The papers cared only about the Giants. Richard Nixon's campaign was noteworthy because he had appeared in the Giants' clubhouse, a move meant to usurp San Francisco votes normally ticketed to the Democratic Party.

There were human interest stories about little kids using their piggy bank savings, running away from home to buy Series tickets. A constant refrain from the provincial writers harkened back to the "gay '90s," when owner Jim Mutrie called them "my giants." Now, in San Francisco, they were "our Giants." The social set was aghast.

"Good God!" one member of the landed gentry exclaimed. "People will think we're like *Milwaukee*, or something!"

Chronicle columnist Charles McCabe, who was not a sportswriter, normally wrote of the comings and goings at Trader Vic's, city hall, the Sausalito avant-garde scene, and other uniquenesses of San Francisco life. He now directed his attention to the Giants, who he saw as a metaphor for his vision of what America should be. McCabe did not like greatness, as embodied by American Exceptionalism, because for America to be exceptional, other countries had to be unexceptional. That was . . . unfair.

Therefore, he determined that despite having won 103 games, with perhaps the greatest superstar of all time in his prime playing center field, the Giants displayed "lovable incompetence." McCabe warned San Franciscans (who cringed at the moniker "Frisco" applied to them by out-of-towners, of whom thousands were flocking in alarming numbers) that victory would bring on a smugness that would be less comfortable than defeat. It was *not* what George Patton told his troops before they embarked on the rescue of Bastogne.

Roger Angell's political and social sensibilities, which had not cottoned to the Los Angeles scene, were much more attuned to the San Francisco he found in October 1962. The City changed *drastically* with the Free Speech Movement, the antiwar movement, the gay liberation movement, the women's liberation movement, and in particular, the "Summer of Love" (1967). The San Francisco that emerged in the years after that event, after Vietnam and Watergate, bears little resemblance to the City that Angell found in 1962. There are still vestiges of it that will always be there, if one chooses to search them out and find it, but in '62 it was a way of life.

San Francisco was indeed sophisticated, cultured, and foggy. It was the City of Dashiell Hammett's *Maltese Falcon*, with Humphrey Bogart leading moviegoers while "Spade turns up Powell Street." This was a far, far cry from Clint Eastwood's *Dirty Harry* a mere decade in the future. It was a city of men in suits, elegant women, coifed hair, and evening manners, of the theater and the opera, of letters and iconoclasm.

"We've had a lot of trouble in the past few years," a woman told Angell, who by virtue of his *New Yorker* pedigree tended to run in effete literary circles. Thinking she was talking about a scandal in her family or some such thing, Angell was surprised to discover she was talking about the Giants' tendency to lose in September since their arrival in 1958. Instead of pointing out the long history of September pratfalls that afflicted the New York Giants, Angell said nothing to the matron, "for I realized that her affair with the Giants was a true love match and that she had adopted her mate's flaws as her own. The Giants and San Francisco are a marriage made in Heaven."

How they were, and whey they were, is not easy to describe. McCabe had a point, truth be told; they were *almost good enough*, just as San Francisco was. Almost good enough was good enough in these parts. Somehow, these people could turn their noses up at the team, the city, the political figure that finished ahead of them. It was snobbery.

"You win the pennant, then you have to go out the very next day and play the Yankees," said Orlando Cepeda. "That didn't give us much time to savor our win against the Dodgers."

"The way the season ended, and the way the playoffs went, it took away a lot of the excitement of the World Series," said O'Dell. "We never really got the thrill of the Series that I believe everybody else gets."

This may well have been what made them so effective. For decades, National League teams that clinched the pennant early would spend an inordinate amount of time staring at the mounting Yankee forces, and soon they were defeated Gauls slain at the feet of the Roman Legion. Better to know death up close and quick, rather than see it marching toward you over the horizon, across the valley, into their very homes and villages.

—◦—

Longtime Bay Area residents likened the reaction of the victory that day to the celebration of 1945, when the Japanese surrendered to end World War II.

—Veteran San Francisco radio man Bruce Macgowan,
who was a kid growing up in Tiburon, 1962

October 1962

The Giants used 12 pitchers in the playoffs, and the Yankees were well-rested. The only advantages the Giants had was that it opened at Candlestick and they were tired, which *was* a strange advantage.

"Man, I'm tired," said Mays. "Man. We're all tired." Yes, they were exhausted, but they had *adrenaline*.

They also had the advantage of surprise.

"It's funny, we spend a week going over the Dodger hitters and here I am pitching against the Giants," said 33-year-old Whitey Ford.

When San Franciscans got a glimpse of the New York Yankees they felt like Belgians watching the victorious Americans arriving, but these larger-than-life icons were not there to liberate them. It was like somebody had hauled the statues from center field at Yankee Stadium and now they were come to life, walking about Candlestick Park. There is a truth about the Yankees; it existed then and it exists now. They *do* still have Babe Ruth and Lou Gehrig in their lineup. Those guys are *not dead*.

As if Ford, Mickey Mantle, Yogi Berra, and Roger Maris needed Ruth and Gehrig; these guys broke those guys' records. In 1962, there were a very small handful of people walking the Earth who were a bigger deal than Mickey Mantle and company. Dwight Eisenhower and John Glenn. Douglas MacArthur, maybe. The only guys bigger than the Yankees, it seemed, were *former Yankees*, and in this a conundrum was posed. "Joltin' Joe" DiMaggio, San Francisco's own, the pride of North Beach, was unquestionably rooting for the Bronx Bombers.

This being 1962, it was before the Super Bowl; before Larry and Magic and Michael; and baseball still reigned supreme, the World Series a near-religious event, its day-games-played-during-school-days giving off a slight Holy Ghost quality, to be seen by kids whose fourth period teacher had a TV and let them watch; whose fifth period teacher did not. Snippets from the radio, 12-year-olds who were fans feeling superior to clueless classmates who were not.

The West Coast games started at noon to avoid late afternoon winds, which for the Giants, whose trip from L.A. to San Francisco and subsequent scramble for cabs, rental cars, and hitch-hiked rides home, meant little sleep. They would need to rely on that adrenaline, which can often propel one to greater heights than standard preparation, at least in the short term.

The crowd arrived early, bearing picnic hampers for much gin-and-tonic tailgating. It was a polite, cheerful, well-dressed gathering, as if they were attending an outdoor opera concert, or "a country horse show," wrote Angell.

The fans watched the great Yankees take batting practice. A sense of creeping Doubt (with a capital D) began to replace the cheerful optimism engendered from the Dodger Stadium heroics. Mickey Mantle slammed four straight balls over the fence, causing one man to turn to his wife and say, "Well, at least we won the pennant." Berra, Maris, and Ellie Howard put on a pregame show. The sight of Whitey Ford confidently heading to the bullpen for warm-ups caused further shudders. At that point in his career, not only was Ford unbeatable in October play, he seemingly could not be *scored on*!

When the game started fans were in a perpetual state of worry, as in "uh oh, here comes Berra," or "don't relax, Mickey's comin' up this inning." New York jumped out to a 2–0 first inning lead and the crowd feared a blowout. When Mays faced Ford in the second inning, they sensed that a great Hall of Fame treat had been offered them, that all the ups and downs of the crazy season were now well worth it. Mays singled and came around to score, breaking up Ford's World Series record of 33 2/3 consecutive scoreless innings. Ford, who dispatched teams like an executioner, could not get Mays out and knew it.

"It doesn't matter what you throw him," Ford said. "Willie can hit it."

When Mays later drove in the tying run the crowd seemed more relieved than happy, as if they had half-expected their heroes to fall flat on the national stage. The Giants had nine hits against Ford through six innings, but could not put him away.

"Ford stands on the mound like a Fifth Avenue bank president," wrote Angell. "Tight-lipped, absolutely still between pitches, all business and concentration, he personifies the big city, emotionless perfection of his team."

Nevertheless, Mays's success against him and the flurry of hits by the home team did have the effect of demonstrating the possibility, at least, that the Giants could compete. O'Dell had better stuff and racked up strikeouts, but his control suffered. In the seventh Clete Boyer homered. New York added two more runs in the eighth and another in the ninth. The Giants also made mental and physical errors, "clustering under pop flies like firemen bracing to catch a baby dropped from a burning building," and making base running blunders.

"Ford retired the Giants on a handful of pitches and left the mound as if on his way to board the 4:30 to Larchmont," wrote Angell of Whitey's six scoreless innings after the Giants scored in the third, posting a 6–2 victory.

"I'll never forget that homer," Clete Boyer said of his leadoff blast in the seventh, which broke up the 2–2 tie and was the game-winner. "I never got a hit against that guy when he was with the Orioles."

"The big play of the game was Ford," said Dark.

⌐⌐

The night before the second game, Jack Sanford nursed a heavy cold while going over the Yankee hitters with O'Dell and Billy Pierce, two former American Leaguers.

"I need all the help you can get," said Sanford. "The Yankees scare the hell out of you." The game featured 23-game winner Ralph Terry versus the 24-game winner Sanford. Nursing his cold and with antihistamines, using a handkerchief constantly, Sanford was brilliant blending a sneaky fastball, a deceptive slider, a sharp curve and pinpoint control to hurl a three-hit shutout, evening the Series at one in a classic October pitcher's duel, 2–0.

McCovey's monster homer off Terry in the eighth made the score 2–0 and, in this game at least, it seemed like 10 runs. Scoring almost appeared to be against the law. In the seventh and eighth, McCovey's homer, three singles, a walk, two sacrifice bunts, and a Yankee error produced just the one run. Terry pitched three-hit shutout ball until Bud Daley relieved him in the seventh.

"Our staff was in terrible shape but Jack fixed it today," said pitching coach Larry Jansen. "The name of the game is pitching. That's why we're still in it."

"When you pitch a Series victory against the Yankees, you can't complain about anything," said Sanford. "I just kept blowing my nose and pitching strikes. I guess I did pretty good for a dumb Irishman."

"Jack's always had good stuff, but today he had perfect control," said Jansen. "He kept the ball low and he wasn't afraid to go with his slider when he fell behind."

"We know we're in the Series," said Dark. "We played good ball in both games. We're every bit the pros the Yankees are supposed to be."

Giants fans filed joyously out of Candlestick Park filled with hope.

〜⌘〜

As described in this author's previous book:
"When the Series shifted to New York City, it took an entirely different tone. There was none of the hopeful joy of San Francisco. The Big Apple more resembled General MacArthur's forces, having been dealt a blow, re-grouping for the final surge, confident of victory and entirely aware precisely how to attain it; the methodology and the cost. They were in the business of winning. It was not a contemplated possibility; rather, Series victories were accomplished past acts.

"The Yankees were like a veteran writer of books, the Giants a first-time novelist. The veteran scribe knows precisely how and when he will finish his book because he has so much experience and has done it many times. He is confident of his ability because there is no mystery in how he achieves his goals.

"The first-time novelist, on the other hand, is armed with a great idea and inspiration, but is beset by writer's block and procrastination, doubts about his ability, alarmed by the looming deadline. Nevertheless, the Giants were filled with talent and it could not be denied.

"The Yankee crowds were a total 180 from Candlestick. Photo shots reveals fans that more resembled bankers; or Sam Giancana lookalikes, gangsters and their molls in sunglasses, suits and mink stoles. There was little cheering or pleading. They almost looked like foreigners dispassionately watching a game they did not comprehend.

"The San Francisco women had been elegant, and in this regard the New York women looked similar in their expensive coats and coifed hair, but there was none of the noise, no excitement despite the fact that the crowd was a standing room only 71,431. The only emotion seemed reserved for Maris, who was booed lustily.

"'C'mon, bum!'

"Radios were tuned to a New York Giants football game. Conversation seemed more concerned with the latest Wall Street events, or advertising trends. This was the New Rome at the height of hubris. The athletes below were merely paid gladiators brought forth for their amusement. In the sixth inning, large clusters of businessman-fans started to leave, 'preserving their ticket stubs to the persevering verticals,' Angell wrote, so they could 'tell their friends they had been to a Series game.' The *New Yorker* columnist suspected that many of the fans were not even New Yorkers, but rather out of town business execs whose tickets were perks.

"Despite the lack of enthusiasm, however, those athletes on the green plains below engaged in an astonishing brand of great baseball; the building October tension that marks it as the very best of all sports. For six scoreless innings, Billy Pierce and Bill Stafford matched each other in dominating form.

"In the sixth, Maris came to the plate, a tragic hero, unloved despite incredible accomplishments. Had he led Cleveland, or Kansas City, or St. Louis into a similar situation, he would have been elevated to the worshipful status of Rocky Colavito or Stan 'the Man' Musial, but in New York all he was, was not the Mick. Ignoring the flack, like a bomber intent on hitting the target regardless, Maris delivered a clutch single to drive in two runs, breaking up the deadlock.

"'We didn't want to give him anything good to hit, but I missed with a fastball and put it down the middle and Maris had his hit,' said Pierce. The Yankees added a third run. Pierce was gone, replaced by Larsen, another oddly unheroic Yankee returning to his scene of triumph.

"Stafford had a shutout until Ed Bailey's two-run homer closed the gap to 3–2 in the ninth. What was left of the crowd looked on, sure that 'the Major,' manager Ralph Houk, would quell the rebel uprising in time for the cocktail hour. Houk visited Stafford.

"'I didn't see any blood on the mound, so I decided to leave Bill in,' the grinning skipper said. 'He was pitching a great game and I didn't want to deprive him of a chance to go all the way.'

"Houk left, the fans and his team supremely confident that any battlefield decisions he made were infallible. When Stafford got the last out with little trouble their confidence was now full arrogance. There seemed no stopping the Bronx Bombers from wrapping up the Series at home, winning in five as they had done in dispatching over-matched Cincinnati the previous year.

"The fourth game was 'sink or swim' for the Giants. To lose and fall behind, three games to one, giving New York the chance to close it out at home, would be an impossible hole to crawl out of. The crowd also transformed itself from the tourists of game three, replaced by real fans, a fair number of whom were rooting for the Giants. These were the same people who had been witnessing the Giants getting slaughtered at the foot of pinstriped hegemony since their last triumph, when manager John McGraw, pitcher Art Nehf and infielder Frankie 'the Fordham Flash' Frisch led the club to victory over Babe Ruth's Yankees in 1922. At that time, the Giants were the kings of baseball, the Yankees mere upstarts who rented the Polo Grounds and had never won a World Series.

"Beginning in 1923, when the Yankees moved into Yankee Stadium, 'the House That Ruth Built,' they had won 19 World Championships, the Giants just two. Angell described the Giants rooters as 'filled with the same pride, foreboding, and strong desire to avert one's eyes that was felt by the late General Pickett.' For the first time, the full resonance of what this World Series really was hit home.

"It was an East-West Fall Classic. For most of the season, the New York fans and media mentally prepared for the Dodgers and the first re-match of 'subway Series' opponents from the 1940s and 1950s. It was the Dodgers, more than the Giants, who dominated the last decade of three-team baseball in the Apple, and it was the Dodgers whose exodus brought on the most tears, the greatest angst, and now the most yearning. It was the Dodgers, above all others, who seemed to inspire the new Mets, whose line-up was chock full of the former Boys of Summer

"The first greatly anticipated Yankees-Dodgers World Series had not happened. In the odd 1959 season, Los Angeles never looked to be a real contender until they won at the end, while the Yankees stumbled for their only loss of the pennant in what would be the span of a decade. Throughout all of 1962, the battle of titans, Broadway vs. Hollywood, had been built up to fevered anticipation.

"Drysdale and Snider would return, along with the hated O'Malley, and the prodigal son, Koufax. The Yankees' trips to Los Angeles to play the Angels, and their princely reception at 'Johnny Grant parties,' had served as build-up for the eventual arrival of the Bronx Bombers at Dodger Stadium for actual World Series games.

"Dodger visits to the Polo Grounds for series with the Mets had served a similar purpose, whetting the appetite of their legion of Brooklyn fans, now spread throughout the tri-state area in the aftermath of 'white flight.'

"The surprise ending to the season, resulting in San Francisco's victory, had shocked many. It had taken much of the country, including most New Yorkers, a few days to get used to it. The first game of the World Series had been played less than 24 hours after game three of the play-offs, and there had been no time for the press to build up the battle of an inexorable object vs. an impenetrable force.

"But game four at the Stadium changed all that. It was a classic with classic moments that live on in Series memory. The fact that a great October duel was occurring played itself before the eyes of New York on October 8. Suddenly, the realization that the Giants vs. the Yankees had every bit as much panache as the Dodgers vs. the Yankees eased into the conscience of the sports world. It was, in fact, the New York Giants, not Brooklyn who first opposed the great Yankees in the 1920s and 1930s, and in the beginning at least they gave as well as they got.

"Suddenly, memories of Giant glory flooded across. 1951: Joe DiMaggio's 'last hurrah,' the rookies Mickey Mantle and Willie Mays debuting on the world stage, the shadow of Leo Durocher looming larger than life over the proceedings. 1954: the Giants beating Cleveland for the World Championship, with Mays making the Catch, as memorable a moment as any before or since.

"After all, Yankees fans suddenly asked themselves, what was so great about Milwaukee, Pittsburgh and Cincinnati anyway? Boring middle American villages. Sure, L.A. had those 'Johnny Grant parties,' but San Francisco was built in the image of New York City. It had been that way since the trans-continental railroad was completed. Its citizenry, its skyline, and now its baseball team were paeans to Manhattan. What was not to like about a place that practiced imitation, the sincerest form of flattery?

"Plus, they had Willie Mays! It was occurring to these New Yorkers that for all the love they exuded for Mantle, and all the traditions of Ruth, Gehrig and DiMaggio, it was possible, just possible, that the very best of them all was the San Francisco center fielder.

"The game four starters had the ring of a true classic: Marichal vs. Ford. How many times in baseball history have two Hall of Fame pitchers faced each other in the World Series? It has happened; it has not happened often.

"Up until game four, the Giants tended to respond to enemy scores, but this time they staked the 'Dominican Dandy' to a 2–0 lead in the second inning. Marichal seemed completely recovered from his September injuries and dominated New York bats with a two-hit hit shutout through four innings. Watching Juan's high kick and unhittable deliverance of spheres, the Yankees realized that they were in for the fight of their lives; in this game and in the Series, which suddenly seemed inevitably headed back to the West Coast, where anything could happen because in 1962 it already had!

"Then in the fifth Marichal tried to bunt and took an inside pitch from Ford on his hand, clutching the bat. The Giants did not score. Dark looked askance at Marichal, who somehow was still suspect in his eyes. He blamed the pitcher for getting hurt, too much it seemed. Sal Maglie, in Dark's view, would have pitched through it, but it was the end of the line for Juan and Bob Bolin, a flame-thrower but no Marichal, took over in the fifth.

"The 23-year old was inexperienced and the Yankees circled him like hungry wolves, the tension getting thicker by the minute. Bolin pitched in and out of a tough jam, but in the sixth he got wild, walking Mantle and Maris, leading to the Yanks tying the game. At that point, hope was hard to keep afloat for the San Franciscans, minus the great Marichal; trying to stem the legion in unfriendly territory. The fans, who had slowly built up momentum, now were into it, realizing for the first time that their team needed them.

"For the Giants, some act of surprise, of great consequence, needed to occur in order to stop the bleeding, reverse the momentum, and keep them in the World Series. They looked to their most likely heroes; Mays, Cepeda, McCovey were all curiously slumping, but the hero would be the most unlikely of all.

"In the top of the seventh, with Ford out of the game, the Giants loaded the bases on a pinch-hit double by Matty Alou sandwiched in between two walks. Chuck Hiller and his three 1962 home runs stepped to the plate against Marshall Bridges. Hiller, who had struck out with men on in the fifth, got something he could sink his teeth into and lifted a fly ball towards the right field fence.

"A famed photograph taken from beyond right field tells the story. The look on Hiller's face, as he drops his bat and heads out of the box, is one of hope and astonishment at what he may have just done. Catcher Elston Howard looks worried. The fans seated in the expensive box seats behind the screen have that same weary I've-seen-it-all expressions that capture the time and place; the Madison Avenue haircuts, the sunglasses, the mink stoles. But these modern Roman senators are also just realizing that the gladiator, slated to die before thine eyes, has instead won the day against their chosen favorite.

"Hiller, with 21 total homers in eight years, hit a grand slam and suddenly the Giants led, 7–3. Larsen was the winning pitcher six years to the day after his 1956 perfecto and now, whether the Yanks had left their hearts in San Francisco or not, they were returning there, looking for another ring.

"With momentum on their side, the key fifth game was San Francisco's golden opportunity to swing things around some more, giving them the all-important 3–2 lead heading back to Candlestick. But it was the ability to quell just such threats that had always marked the Yankees, and it was to be on October 10.

"The 1962 Series produced a series of classic October photos, and in game five it was Willie McCovey stretching the full length of his 6'4" frame while Bobby Richardson slides safely into first base. Richardson later scored. The Giants made the mistake of handing the unsentimental Yankees a chance to get back in the fifth game. Bailey just missed a tying two-run homer by 15 feet.

"Sanford struck out 10, but a wild pitch in the fourth and passed ball in the sixth led to two New York runs in a 5–3 Yankee win. Tresh, establishing himself as a hero in a Series that increasingly saw little out of Mantle, Maris, Howard, Berra or Richardson, hit a three-run homer and Terry earned the win, his first in five post-season tries.

"'I'm not particularly happy about it,' said Dark. 'I would have been happier if we won three in a row here.'"

—*A Tale of Three Cities: The 1962 Baseball Season in New York, Los Angeles and San Francisco*, by Steven Travers

Joe DiMaggio made his first public appearance since the death of his former wife Marilyn Monroe at the 1962 World Series.

That was the biggest year of my baseball life, winning the pennant and playing the Yankees in the World Series.

—GIANTS STAR FELIPE ALOU, WHO MANAGED THE TEAM FROM 2003 TO 2006

The 1962 World Series was a big thrill, getting to meet Mickey Mantle, Roger Maris and Yogi Berra. But Willie Mays is the greatest I ever saw. Besides being the best ballplayer, he would do anything for you. The day he was traded was the worst.
　　—LONGTIME GIANTS CLUBHOUSE MANAGER MIKE MURPHY

A punch and Judy like me, and to do that? Hell, it made me feel good.
　　—GIANTS SECOND BASEMAN CHUCK HILLER ON HIS GAME 4
GRAND SLAM IN YANKEE STADIUM, '62 SERIES

The East–West Fall Classic

Unlike the playoffs, each Series game had been taut and filled with professional tension. Each club showed not merely a desire to win, but the right to victory, which had not marked the final pangs of the NL pennant race and playoffs. Each game had been decided by a key, game-of-inches play, important strikes delivered, a double play just missed, and it appeared obvious that these were indeed the two best teams in baseball. A classic finish was in the offing.

Nobody on the Left Coast said anything about "global warming" when a freak Pacific storm laid siege to San Francisco just as the two teams were getting ready for the sixth game. There were no games between Wednesday, October 10 and Monday, October 15. The massive storm hit Northern California with hurricane force winds, caused five deaths, knocked out power lines, ravaged property all the way to the Oregon border, and dropped nearly two inches of rain on the City. Commissioner Ford Frick postponed the games until the weather abated. Both teams trekked to the hinterlands to practice and wait it out. Dodger executive Fresco Thompson quipped, "Why call the game? When we play it's wetter than this."

Local and national pundits had ample time to extrapolate on the fate of the Giants, and the increasing awareness that the '62 Fall Classic may indeed be one for the ages. It was the media's opportunity to say all the things they were originally unable to say because of the short time frame between the playoffs and the Series. Many posited the notion that Yankee victory would add to their smugness, but ultimate victory would result in a horn-blowing Market Street celebration, drawing rubes from the outlying provinces of Marin County, San Mateo, and Oakland, all to the consternation of the sophisticates.

"Total triumph is unsettling," wrote Charles McCabe, the resident "oracle of Mission Street."

Future defeat was seen as a fatal virus, and "Giant fans, like all neurotics, are unappeasable," wrote Angell. "I can see it now—the Dodgers should have won the pennant."

When the rain finally stopped, bad drainage on the Candlestick playing surface postponed Game 6 an additional 24 hours. Three helicopters were brought in to buzz the field, but the grass remained soggy. Frick called it "miserable conditions," but play resumed October 15. One man who could not wait for the rain to stop was Horace Stoneham, dismayed to see his booze supply depleted in the hospitality room of the Sheraton-Palace Hotel, where hundreds of writers had nothing to do but get drunk.

The Yankees, in typically smug fashion, made return plane reservations for the night of the sixth game. Instead, Billy Pierce tossed a sweet three-hitter. He was perfect until Maris homered in the fifth, but coasted to a 5–2 win over Ford, now human for the first time, it seemed.

The rain had allowed the Giants to rest, and to get their arms lined up. First and foremost, that meant ace right-hander Jack Sanford, the Game 7 starter. He allowed only a single by Tony Kubek in the first four innings. His opponent was up to the task. Ralph Terry retired the first seventeen batters he faced.

In the fifth, the Yanks opened with two singles and a walk. Tony Kubek then hit a 6-4-3 double play grounder, but Moose Skowron scored and it was 1–0, Yankees. Tom Tresh made a marvelous catch of a long drive to left field by Mays. Another classic photo shows Tresh fully extended, the ball "snow coned" on the tip of his glove.

Billy O'Dell relieved Sanford with the bases loaded in the eighth but pitched out of the jam. It all came down to the excruciating bottom of the ninth inning, with San Francisco trailing 1–0, hoping to get to Mays and McCovey, scheduled fourth and fifth up in the inning.

It looked promising when pinch hitter Matty Alou's bunt single led off the inning. It was Matty whose hit off Ed Roebuck started the fateful ninth inning rally in the Game 3 playoff with the Dodgers. Alou's drag bunt hit was only the third of the afternoon against Terry.

Terry was working hard and had much on his mind. He had given up Bill Mazeroski's "walk-off" homer to lose the 1960 World Series to Pittsburgh and certainly did not want to be the "goat" again. The crowd was pleading, hope against hope, a wall of sound and violent, anguished cries. Bearing down, Terry struck out Felipe Alou and Hiller while Matty stood forlornly at first base.

Now, the moment all had been waiting for, the Giants' *raison d'être*, what San Franciscans had expected since the Giants came west: Willie Mays with everything on the line. Baseball does not get better than this!

Terry worked Mays low and away, which may have been an old scouting report. Mays, reacting to the Candlestick winds, had adjusted his power toward right field. Terry thought he put "real good stuff on it, but Willie opened up and just hit it with his hands." He wristed the ball, powering a shot into the right field corner.

Matty Alou had speed and at first it seemed that he could score the tying run from first base, but Mays's double got stuck in the soggy grass. Roger Maris got to it, whirled, and made a good throw. Coach Whitey Lockman held Alou at third base. To this day, the decision is disputed, but replays seem to indicate that Lockman made the right call.

"I'd make the same decision 1,000 times out of 1,000," Lockman insisted. Dark agreed. Both Maris and the cutoff man, Bobby Richardson, had strong, accurate arms.

"Matty would have been out by a mile," said Ralph Houk.

"Roger Maris was playing me to pull, and he cut the ball off before it could get to the fence," recalled Mays. "If that field was dry, the ball rolls to the fence, Matty scores, and I'm on third."

Instead, Mays was on second, Alou was on third, and McCovey was coming to the plate. Leading 1–0 with two outs, Houk came to the mound to confer with Terry and Howard. McCovey had scorched a triple in a prior at-bat and had hit a homer in an earlier Series game. First base was open but Terry felt, "I could get McCovey out. I felt I had a pretty good line on him. . . . Maybe I was overconfident."

The decisions that were made doubtfully would be made today: leave Terry in, don't intentionally walk McCovey, and pitch to him. McCovey stepped in, a left-handed threat against the right-handed Terry. The odds seemed to favor Willie Mac, but then again . . . these *were the Yankees*!

Terry threw a slow curve, down and away, hoping to fool the slugger. McCovey hit what at first looked like the last out, a fly ball to Maris in right. Then the wind got ahold of it for a three-run game-winning home run . . . except that at the last second the wind pushed it foul.

The crowd was shocked . . . up, down. Of the long foul ball, McCovey stated, "had I realized they were going to pitch to me, I'd have hit that ball out." Standing, imploring, the fans watched McCovey pick up his bat and get back into the box. Next was a fastball, Terry challenging him. McCovey leaned into it and hit one on the screws, a searing line drive. Richardson moved just a step to his left, stuck his glove up as much to protect himself as anything, and caught it. The impact knocked him to his knees, where the devout Christian bowed before jumping up to join his teammates in celebration of the Yankees' twentieth World Championship in 39 years.

"I hit that ball as hard as I could," said McCovey. "I wasn't thinking about anything when I connected, but when you hit it good, you assume it's going to be a hit." In retrospect McCovey said, "I had no problem with Terry." McCovey added of the liner to Richardson, "Obviously they knew what they doing."

Photos of the postgame scene show kids with "flood" pants, varsity jackets, and various officials wearing visors, a popular item of the day, surrounding the celebrating Yankees, who carried Terry off the field on their shoulders.

"I said it would go seven, because you don't beat the Yanks in less than seven," said Dark.

"I was afraid I was going to faint when McCovey hit that ball," said Terry. "I probably would have fainted if it had gone through. . . . A man rarely gets the kind of second chance I did. . . . I was real thankful I had a chance to redeem myself in the seventh game of the World Series, because I'd been the loser in the seventh game at Pittsburgh in 1960."

"This was the best pitched Series game I've ever seen," said Joe DiMaggio. "In fact, the pitching was great all Series."

"It may be noted that the Yankees are the least popular of all baseball clubs, because they win, which leaves nothing to 'if' about," wrote boxing writer A. J. Liebling, in San Francisco during the last two games for a prize fight.

There was plenty to "if" about for the Giants. "What ifs?" cropped up about the length and sogginess of the outfield grass; *if* not "a foot either way" McCovey's liner would have won it, although replays showed Richardson could have gone much further than that to spear it.

Dark was asked if Mays would have scored from second had McCovey's liner gone to the outfield. Dark replied that Willie would have been dressed by the time the Yankees got the ball home, an ode to his instincts as a baserunner and speed.

"I'm just as proud of my players as if they had won the Series," said Dark. "They played just great. When you go down to the last out and the Series is decided by maybe one foot on a line drive, you've battled all the way."

It was the most time-consuming Series since the 1911 Fall Classic, lasting 13 days.

"It was a crazy Series, but it was a crazy season," said Dark. "You never forget a year like '62."

Horace Stoneham threw a party in the stadium club, which included 400 people and all the players. In those days, rings only went to the winners. He bought the players solid gold money clips reading "San Francisco Giants—1962 National League Champions," with crossed bats and balls. Each player's name was carved on the bat, personalized. McCormick said he carried his for years, but stopped because "I think its value is probably too great" to risk theft or loss.

In the end, all the star power on both sides failed to live up to their ultimate billing in a Series dominated by great pitching. Terry was the Series MVP and Outstanding Pitcher, but with a few lucky bounces those honors could just as easily have gone to Jack Sanford, whose hard-luck 1–2 record was accompanied by a 1.93 ERA in 23 1/3 innings pitched.

"We were told he was a six or seven inning pitcher," Mantle said of Sanford. "We figured if we kept it close, Sanford would lose his stuff by the eighth."

"We learned a lot of things about the Giants in the Series, but we were wrong about Sanford," said Houk. "He's a heck of a pitcher."

The Yankees hit .199, the third lowest for a winning team ever. The Giants outhit them by 27 points and outscored them, 21–20, but it was a reversal of fortune from 1960. The batting averages were: Tresh (.321), Clete Boyer (.318), Mantle (.120 on 3 for 25), Maris (.174), Howard (.143), Pagan (.368), Mays (.250), Cepeda (.158), and Kuenn (.083).

Much of the post-Series anguish was directed at Orlando Cepeda, who disappeared against the Yankees.

"I know better than anybody else how terrible I was," said Cepeda. "I do nothing right. I try everything but nothing helps. I feel bad because I let the others down. It's terrible when you're not doing your share. I'm very tired. Between here and Puerto Rico, I play 300 games this year. That is too much."

The Giants thought about trading him. "He just couldn't get his bat around," said Stoneham. "Sometimes he was missing pitches by six inches. That's not what he's being paid $47,000 a year for."

In the Series, Felipe Alou hit third, second, first, sixth, third, and first. His .269 average included a hit in every game but the third and the seventh. San Francisco lost both by a run.

"Davenport surprised me more than any other Giants," said Ralph Terry. "We didn't think he was that good and even though he didn't hit too high, he hit the ball real well."

Charles Schulz, a Bay Area resident, Giants fan, and creator of the *Peanuts* cartoon strip, may have captured San Francisco's sense of longing as well as anybody. In three panels, Charlie Brown sits quietly in a near-catatonic trance, then burst into tears, cursing to the Heavens: "Why couldn't McCovey have hit the ball just three feet higher?"

Decade of Change

"If 1961 was not an 'L.A. year,' 1962 may have been its greatest. It was not just a great Los Angeles year in sports, but in the entire state of California. It was also a key year in the great Los Angeles–San Francisco rivalry. The two cities had battled each other in sports, politics and culture at least since the Owens Valley Aqueduct was completed in 1913, and certainly when USC emerged as a collegiate football power with Stanford and California, then overshadowing them when they began the Notre Dame series in 1926.

"When UCLA took their place as USC's key rival beginning in the late 1930s, a sense of jealousy pervaded the northern schools. By the early 1960s, the L.A. schools were beginning to dominate Cal and Stanford.

"Professionally, the San Francisco 49ers had great players, but the Los Angeles Rams had better teams. L.A. had pro basketball. San Francisco did not. The Dodgers came out west with greater reputation, and in four years on the West Coast still held that distinction.

"By 1962, San Francisco was facing a major crisis of identity. They thought of themselves as being the more elegant, sophisticated city, but everything seemed to happen in L.A. San Francisco had Herb Caen and literature, but Los Angeles had Howard Hughes . . . and Jim Murray. San Francisco had beatniks. L.A. had beautiful women and the Sunset Strip. Who could compete with that?

"But of all the comparisons in the 'who is better?' argument between the two cities, perhaps the quality of the newspapers was the greatest disparity. Otis Chandler effectively accomplished his task by 1962. The *Los Angeles Times* may not yet have won a poll asking what the best paper in the world was. The East Coast bias was still too prevalent, but in truth they were a vastly better paper than the Washington Post and able to compete on par with the *New York Times*. The *New York Times* was very dry. They lived by old journalistic standards, refusing to acquiesce to increasing reader demand for greater color and excitement. Chandler did not publish a scandal tabloid or a wild-headline Hearst-style paper, but he did understand the value of vivid photographs, human interest, and colorful prose, which by then was undoubtedly identified as the 'West Coast style.' Jim Murray epitomized it.

"San Francisco was burdened by a real rag of a paper, the *San Francisco Chronicle*. The *Chronicle* had several talented sportswriters, but the paper was riddled with errors, typos and unprofessional quality. They had three star writers, all of whom had talent but did not come without controversy.

"Herb Caen was uniquely loved in the Bay Area, but his views were very questionable. He seemed to feel San Francisco was the only place worth living in. Naturally San Franciscans fell for this, but his hatred of L.A. bordered on the obsessive.

"Charles McCabe and Art Hoppe were both wildly Left-wing. McCabe openly stated France was a greater nation than America. Hoppe was not yet at full stride, but by the end of the 1960s he wrote in his column he had finally come around to openly rooting for the North Vietnamese Communists over the US. This is a view that really needs no commentary in order to know what it is. The other paper, the *San Francisco Examiner*, was superior, but an afternoon daily with less power and influence. It was certainly not in the same league with the *Times*.

"San Franciscans and Los Angelenos had endless barroom arguments. For L.A. fans, arguing the Dodgers over the Giants, USC and UCLA over Cal and Stanford, the beaches over the bay, the babes over the beatniks; none of these permeated the hardcore San Franciscan. But L.A. had a few aces up their sleeve when it came to bragging rights. They had Vin Scully. Even Giants fans were resigned to admitting Scully's greatness as a broadcaster. They had the *Los Angeles Times*. Nobody was so deluded as to argue the superiority of the *Chronicle*. They had Jim Murray, too. San Franciscans might counter with Herb Caen. Herb Caen was a notorious gossip. He did not care if what he wrote ruined somebody's life. Murray never had that mean edge to him. In the entire history of journalism, Caen was the single most provincial writer who ever lived. Murray was the least provincial. Caen could not carry Jim Murray's proverbial 'dirty jock strap.'

"Murray took exception to the clap-trap from 'Baghdad by the Bay,' which was Caen's moniker for the City (they gave it caps) in those pre–Saddam Hussein days. In 1962 he wrote San Francisco was a 'no-host cocktail party,' criticizing the Giants for allowing their groundskeeper to turn the base paths at Candlestick Park into a 'peat moss' pit so as to slow down L.A. speedster Maury Wills.

"He mentioned Caen when he pointed out that *Sports Illustrated* put the knock on 'Frisco,' the most hated of all names out-of-towners give to the City, in an article called 'Akron of the West.' Joe David Brown wrote the place was 'Not a big league town . . . Full of drunks . . . A citadel of intolerance . . . Vulgar and cheap . . .' Finally, in perhaps the most unkindest cut of all, he wrote the place was 'not the lovely lady I had imagined but a vulgar old broad.' San Francisco 'leads the nation in suicides, mental disease, alcoholism.'

"Murray did not write that he necessarily agreed with Brown's assessment, but he did not entirely disagree. But of all Murray's keen observations in his long career, one of his keenest came when he wrote subconsciously San Francisco does not 'want to win.'

"L.A. went for victory, with all its ugly, jarring connotations, as fervently as Howard Hughes trying to land a contract to build rocket boosters. San Francisco embellished the British tenet that, 'No gentleman ever plays a game too well.' When the City got the best player in baseball, Willie Mays, they rejected him at first. His great talent was almost too vulgar a display of excellence.

"Charles McCabe openly wrote of the strange neurosis, stating that San Franciscans rejected ultimate victory as too jarring. Murray wrote that San Francisco has an 'insurance against victory better than any Lloyd's can give him.' In 1962, it certainly appeared that he was right. The Giants won one of the all-time difficult pennant races ever fought, defeating the Dodgers to capture the National League crown. But they and the City seemed happy to settle for that, when in fact the World Series still had to be played. Everybody appeared perfectly okay with merely making a good showing in an epic seven-game loss to the New York Yankees, a team and a city with no problem handling ultimate victory, in the World Series. Given a chance at redemption in 1963, the Dodgers dispatched the mighty Yankees in four straight in the Fall Classic. The Giants settled for 'bridesmaid' status throughout the decade, never since ascending to the mountaintop.

"Murray, the East Coast native, seemed to put his pulse on the north-south vibe as well as anybody. He loved San Francisco; its ambience, its views, its architecture. He did not quite say it, but he could easily have said it was a great place if only for the people who lived there. Murray had his chances to move up the ladder in the writing game, and in so doing live in Boston, New York, DC, Europe; the salons of international power and politics. He consciously chose to stay in L.A. because he loved L.A., dirty air, congested traffic, cultural plasticity and all. He was L.A. and L.A. was Murray. He instinctively defended it and refused to concede its rival city was superior. He also realized that Los Angeles was now one of the salons of international power and politics, whether they set out to be or not. It was inevitable and already a given by 1962.

"Murray keenly observed the L.A.–San Francisco dynamic over the years. The protest, hippy and gay rights movements of the 1960s did nothing to advance San Francisco's place in the pantheon of great cities. L.A., however, passed Chicago and by 1975 probably even New York as the American and, by extension, global metropolis. It produced two Republican Presidents who were re-elected in landslides. It was the home of political movements that shook the world. Eventually their place faded and San Francisco, only after 49ers symbolically delivered multiple Super Bowl titles in the 1980s, became a power base politically themselves. Murray, the Nixon man, a moderate Republican, was not pre-disposed to identify with the Summer of Love, the 'sexual revolution,' and certainly not to the turning of the Berkeley campus into the de facto staging grounds of American Communism. . . .

"But Murray never lost his admiration for greatness no matter where it could be found. He found it in Willie Mays. As the classic 1962 campaign was heating up, he wrote a laudatory column about Mays on May 23. In reading it, as in so many of Murray's columns, one is almost ashamed to be writing about Jim Murray. Nobody can capture him, or even come close. The temptation is to put quotations on 200 or 300 pages of Jim Murray's quotes, columns and observations, rather than critique or re-hash them. So it is with the Mays piece, an astonishing bit of writing in which Murray wrote in a kind of existential manner, describing Mays almost as pathology, like a doctor or police report breaking him down to his essence: 'iron, calcium, antimony and whatever baser metal a human being is composed of.' It is the sort of approach no other writer—not a Rice, a Cannon, a Lardner, a Smith, a Breslin, even Hunter S. Thompson or William Shakespeare—would remotely think of taking. His brilliance is beyond ability, but in sheer originality of thought.

"In reading this and many of Murray's columns, the greatest challenge is determining what to put commas on and repeat, because every word from beginning to end is too good to, as William Goldman said of editing, 'kill my beautiful little angels.' In the end Murray's columns are in other books in their entirety. This is a biography, but the lack of worthiness of anybody to really 'capture' Murray must be admitted.

"When considering that 1962 column about Willie Mays, it is possible that herein was a confluence of talents reaching rare, Herculean heights. The greatest player of his day, maybe ever, at his prime, being written about by the greatest columnist at the height of his game. Murray could make tiddlywinks sound amazing, but this was Michelangelo commissioned to paint the Sistine Chapel. The best meeting the best.

"The Dodgers-Giants 'death struggle' captured his imagination throughout the summer. In a piece on Los Angeles catcher John Roseboro, Murray wrote, 'On road trips, if John Roseboro isn't at a movie, he's at a laundry. He has more wardrobe changes than Loretta Young.'

"The Giants were notorious for slumping in June, what the press coined their annual 'June swoon.' Murray wrote of their 1962 slump, 'a business executive is standing in his office looking down over

the city and is chatting to his secretary. Suddenly, a
falling figure shoots past the window. 'Oh oh,' says
the man, glancing at his chronometer. 'It must be
June. There go the Giants.'

"The Candlestick Park groundskeepers notoriously watered their base paths in an effort to slow
down Maury Wills. Of this Murray observed 'one more
squirt and the Red Cross would have declared a
disaster area and begun to evacuate the Dodgers by
rowboat . . . an aircraft carrier would've run aground.'

"After Los Angeles blew a 4–2 ninth inning lead
in game three of the play-offs at Dodger Stadium; a
combination of wild pitching, errors, bad scouting,
and terrible managing, Murray focused on beleaguered Dodgers manager Walter Alston, who lived in
small town Ohio each off-season.

"'Down in the dugout, manager Walt Alston was
poring over the stagecoach schedules to Darrtown,'
he wrote.

"Los Angeles blew a four-game lead with a week
to go, capped by defeat in the three-game play-off
a la 1951. Murray came up with this: 'Wanted, one
nearly new 1962 National League pennant, slightly
soiled with tear stain in center. Last seen blowing
toward San Francisco . . . Warning: if you return
pennant to Dodgers direct, be sure to tape it to
their hands.'"
—The Poet: The Life and Los Angeles Times of Jim
Murray, by Steven Travers

It was great coming back to Candlestick Park. I
hadn't been there since the World Series of 1962.
The odor of the clubhouse was strangely familiar, and
I remembered where all the guys had their lockers
and the table in the middle of the room loaded with
ten dozen baseballs for us to autograph.

This was my rookie year and I remember Whitey
Ford hurt his arm and I was going to have to pitch
the seventh game, except that it rained for five days
in a row and Ralph Terry was able to come back and
win the final game 1–0 when Willie McCovey hit a

screaming line drive off him and Bobby Richardson caught it for the final out. And I remember the police escorts we had wherever we went, sirens screaming. Great year for a rookie.
—*Ball Four*, by Jim Bouton

"Billy, You Have to Win Today"
—San Francisco newspaper headline the morning of Game 6 of the 1962 World Series, featuring Billy Pierce starting for the Giants

That game gave me the greatest satisfaction of my life. The sixth game was a game where you're on the spot a little but if you lose, the World Series is over. I was happy to pitch it and do well.
—Giants left-hander Billy Pierce, on winning Game 6 of the 1962 World Series, forcing a Game 7

I never pitched better in my life.
—Giants '62 Game 7 starter Jack Sanford, nicknamed "Smiling Jack" because he always scowled

One of the hardest line drives ever to be caught. Just a bullet.
Giants skipper Al Dark describing Willie McCovey's last at-bat to end the '62 Fall Classic

He was in the perfect place.
—San Francisco's Willie McCovey on Yankees second baseman Bobby Richardson, who caught his Series-ending liner

It was so silent in here. And nothing but celebration there.
—SAN FRANCISCO CLUBHOUSE MAN MIKE MURPHY DESCRIB-
ING THE CONTRASTING MOOD AFTER GAME 7 IN 1962

We thought we'd be back in the Series for the next 10 years.
—GIANTS FIRST BASEMAN WILLIE McCOVEY'S OPTIMISTIC
VIEW FOLLOWING 1962 SERIES

*I was in my first year teaching business law at City College of San
Francisco. I grew up with Joe DiMaggio at Galileo High School and
was more of an American League guy, and was not the big Giants
fan everybody else was. I remember being in the faculty lounge when
McCovey's liner was caught by Richardson. You could hear the groans
all over the building, down the hallways, outside in the courtyard.*
—SAN FRANCISCO NATIVE DONALD TRAVERS

*The 1962 Series was only the second in history where the teams alter-
nated wins in every game. The Yanks won the odd-numbered games,
while San Francisco claimed games two, four and six.*
—*THE WORLD SERIES: AN ILLUSTRATED HISTORY OF
THE FALL CLASSIC,* BY JOSH LEVENTHAL

Why couldn't McCovey have hit the ball just three feet higher?
—CHARLIE BROWN, *PEANUTS* COMIC STRIP, BY SANTA ROSA
RESIDENT CHARLES SCHULTZ

Total triumph is unsettling.
—*SAN FRANCISCO CHRONICLE* COLUMNIST CHARLES McCABE

For the Record: 1962

IN 1962, THE GIANTS AND DODGERS PLAYED EACH OTHER 21 TIMES, with San Francisco winning 11 and Los Angeles 10. One million fans (including the playoffs) watched those games in person, while TV ratings reached 70 percent, plus three-quarters of the radio-listening audience. A Bay Area phone service provided a paid service, providing play-by-play to 25,000 callers per day.

The Giants finished 103–62, followed by the Dodgers at 102–63, one game back. Cincinnati was 98–64, three-and-a-half games behind. Pittsburgh (93–68) trailed by eight. The Braves (86–76) were fifteen-and-a-half back, the Cardinals at 84–78 trailed by 17 1/2, followed by Philadelphia (81–80), Houston (64–96), Chicago (59–103), and at 60 and one-half games back, the lowly New York Mets (40–120).

Orlando Cepeda finished with 35 home runs, 114 RBIs, a .306 average, and 191 hits. Chuck Hiller batted .276 and Jose Pagan .259. Jim Davenport won a Gold Glove while batting .297 with 14 homers. Felipe Alou hit .316 with 25 homers and 98 runs batted in. Willie Mays had one of the best seasons of his career, finishing with a .304 batting average, a league-leading 49 home runs, 141 RBIs, and a .615 slugging percentage (third in the NL). Harvey Kuenn batted his customary .300 (.304). Rookie Tom Haller batted .261 with 18 homers, while Ed Bailey contributed 17 home runs. Playing part-time, Willie McCovey hit .293 with 20 homers and 54 RBIs in 229 at-bats.

San Francisco's ability to match the Dodgers arms was ultimately what kept them in the race. Billy O'Dell was 19–14 with a 3.53 ERA. Jack Sanford was nothing less than spectacular, finishing 24–7 with a 3.43 ERA. Juan Marichal's injury prevented him from winning twenty, but he finished with 18 victories and a 3.36 ERA. Billy Pierce, thought to be an

American League re-tread after his bad spring, was unbeaten at home and 16–6 with a 3.49 ERA on the season. Stu "the Killer Moth" Miller finished with 19 saves and avoided the "goat horns" that he would have been forced to wear after his second playoff game performance. Mike McCormick would take years to reach his potential and finished 5–5. Hard-throwing Bob Bolin was 7–3 and hard-partying Don Larsen was 5–4. Gaylord Perry was 3–1 but in Dark's "dog house" considered timid on the mound after failing to throw out the lead runner at third base on a bunt in a key playoff situation.

A look at the National League in 1962 reveals that it was indeed a golden age of Hall of Famers, veterans and youth, perhaps unequalled. Cincinnati's Frank Robinson, who at .342 was better than his MVP-lead-the-Reds-to-the-pennant year of 1961, followed Tommy Davis's .346. The great Stan Musial of St. Louis did not slow down, hitting .330. Ex-Giant Bill White of the Cardinals batted .324. Milwaukee's Hank Aaron batted .323.

Frank Robinson led the league with a .624 slugging percentage. Aaron's 45 homers trailed Mays, followed by Robinson with 39, Chicago's Ernie Banks (in his initial year as a first baseman after breaking in as a shortstop) with 37, and Cepeda with 35. Davis's 153 RBIs led Mays (141), Robinson (136), Aaron (128), and Howard (119).

Jack Sanford's .774 winning percentage was second to Bob Purkey of Cincinnati (.821), followed by Drysdale (.735) and Pierce (.727). Koufax's 2.54 ERA led Bob Shaw of Milwaukee (2.80), Purkey (2.81), Drysdale (2.83), and Bob Gibson of St. Louis (2.85).

Drysdale's 25 wins led Sanford (24), Purkey (23), another Red (Joey Jay with 21), Art Mahaffey of the Phillies and Billy O'Dell (both with 19).

Elroy Face, the veteran reliever of the Pittsburgh Pirates, led the National League with 28 saves, followed by Perranoski with 20 and Miller's 19. Drysdale's 232 strikeouts were followed by Koufax's 216, Gibson's 206, Dick Farrell of Houston (203), and O'Dell at 195.

Milwaukee ace Warren Spahn, still going strong at age 42, managed a league-leading 22 complete games. O'Dell had 20, Drysdale 19, and despite his late-season injury, Marichal had 18.

Maury Wills of the Dodgers was the National League MVP. Teammate Don Drysdale won the Cy Young Award. Ken Hubbs of Chicago won the Rookie of Year Award, but later would meet a tragic fate when he drowned.

＊

In 1963 the three Alous—Felipe, Matty, and Jesus of San Francisco, all of whom grew up with Juan Marichal in Santo Domingo—became the first trio of brothers to play in the same game together.

＊

Unsung Jose Pagan was named to the Giants All-Decade Team (1960s).

＊

I signed one year after Felipe, but he never told me about Willie Mays—and I was a center fielder.

—GIANTS OUTFIELDER MATTY ALOU

＊

What is wrong with my real name—Jesus? It is a common name in Latin America. My parents named me Jesus, and I'm proud of my name. This Jay, I do not like. It is not my name.

—OUTFIELDER JESUS ALOU (FIRST NAME PRONOUNCED *HAY-SOO*), THE YOUNGEST OF THE THREE ALOUS, ON OBJECTIONS TO HIS BIRTH NAME

Duel

IT WAS HELD ON JULY 2, 1963. IN MOST STADIUMS IN MOST BIG-LEAGUE cities, this would have been a midsummer night's dream, played in balmy weather, a shirt-sleeved crowd languishing amid soft, warm trade winds. Not so at Candlestick in the summer, which as Mark Twain once said of San Francisco was the "coldest winter I ever spent." That night was windswept, as usual, but as the evening droned on toward midnight, the fog rolling in, the 15,921 fans in attendance may have dwindled a bit, but for the most part stayed glued to their unheated seats. Those who left departed reluctantly. They were tired, they had to get up early, they had after-game plans to get to. But while it was a small crowd, some 100,000 fans or more claim to have been there, to have stayed all night and seen it to its eventful conclusion, four hours and 10 minutes after it started.

It was likely the greatest pitcher's duel in baseball history.

The game featured Warren Spahn, already a sure Hall of Famer, a marvel at age 42, on his way to one of his greatest seasons, a year in which the Milwaukee Braves ace would win 23 games against only seven defeats with a 2.60 ERA.

His opponent was a 25-year old phenom, Juan Marichal of San Francisco. He was on his way to a remarkable record of 25–8 with a 2.41 ERA. The Braves' southpaw was 11–3 coming into the game, the Giants high-kicking righty 12–3. His club was battling for the pennant, at 44–34. Milwaukee, a dominant team just a few years prior, was struggling with age, trying to stay above .500. It was a year of pitching, augmented in part by an increase in the strike zone that made for a decade of dominance, not changed until after the "year of the pitcher" in 1968.

The two hurlers seemed total opposites, but had more in common than one might suppose. Marichal's high kick was not unlike Spahn's distinctive leg thrust, which came together in perfect symmetry with his glove curled against his letters. Both were straight over the top hurlers (Juan would mix in sidearm pitches), who got maximum power and torque out of their motions. Neither was a pure fastball specialist. Both had a variety of pitches, great breaking stuff, and total control of the strike zone. So masterful was the control of both Spahn and Marichal as to render them almost mythological, like Satchel Paige, seen by many but not on TV. Had either only pitched a short time, away from the cameras, their skill would have been whispered about as something that needed to be seen to be believed. But both enjoyed long, fabulous careers, which in an odd way makes what they did seem a little more ordinary. Neither man was ordinary, on the mound or in life.

Spahn came from the Oklahoma dust bowl, although he attended high school in Buffalo. He angered manager Casey Stengel of the Boston Braves with his lack of aggressiveness. When Stengel sent him down to the bush leagues he told Spahn he lacked guts and would never amount to much. Before Spahn could much prove his worth on the field, he found himself sent off to war. His war was as high-action as it gets: the Battle of the Bulge, a monstrous winter conflict between the American airborne fighting off a last desperate offensive by the Nazi wehrmacht. The man who lacked guts showed he did not, earning a Purple Heart for bravery and valor in helping the Americans win the last big battle of the European Theater.

When Spahn returned, lucky to be healthy, one of the most decorated athletes from the war, he seemed invigorated by his experience and found success in baseball. While Stengel was managing in New York Spahn, who had less than 30 career wins before age 30, embarked on a decade-plus that may not be exceeded by any hurler, before or since. He would win the Cy Young Award in 1957, lead Milwaukee to the World Championship that year, and eventual induction into Cooperstown. By 1963, he had one last thing to prove. Spahn wanted to break Christy Mathewson's and Grover Alexander's career National League record for victories (373).

Marichal was a different story. Growing up a devout Christian in the Dominican Republic, he battled poverty, sickness, and several life-threatening episodes. Like Spahn, he experienced more trials and tribulations in his youth than most kids, and like Spahn he had to prove himself to his managers. He sustained a strange injury in the World Series when he was hit by a pitch while trying to bunt against the Yankees. He was out of the game and the Series. In a seven-game set lost by the barest of margins, perhaps his presence might have been the difference between victory and defeat. This was hanging over his head in 1963.

Then there was Sandy Koufax. Throughout the 1950s, Spahn had unquestionably been the greatest pitcher in all of baseball. But Marichal found himself pitching in an era in which several other hurlers rivaled him, depriving him of Cy Young Awards and the full measure of glory that his unbelievable career might otherwise have engendered.

American League aces of the 1960s and early 1970s included Jim Palmer, Whitey Ford, Denny McLain, Mickey Lolich, Sam McDowell, Camillo Pasqual, Catfish Hunter, Dean Chance, and Nolan Ryan. In the senior circuit, such all-time greats as Spahn, Phil Niekro, Tom Seaver, Jim Bunning, Bob Gibson, Steve Carlton, Ferguson Jenkins, his teammate Gaylord Perry, and in Los Angeles, Don Drysdale and Koufax, plied their trade during Marichal's heyday. In an era in which only one Cy Young Award was handed out in both leagues (until 1967), despite Hall of Fame seasons seemingly piled on top of one another, it was always somebody else. In 1962, Drysdale won 25 games and the Cy Young Award. In 1964 it went to Dean Chance and his 1.64 ERA. In 1967, Marichal sustained an injury while his teammate Mike McCormick walked off with the honor. In 1968 it was Bob Gibson after posting a 1.12 ERA. In 1969, Tom Seaver attained superstardom. By 1970, Marichal was beginning to deteriorate while Gibson captured his second, and in 1971 Ferguson Jenkins was given the honor. After that, Juan was never close to his magical 1960–1971 self, while both Seaver and Palmer captured three. Perry would probably not rank quite as high as Marichal in the pantheon, if their contemporaries were polled, yet his lifetime records, due to longevity and mastery of the spitball, allowed Gaylord to surpass Marichal in several crucial statistical categories, not to mention land him two Cy Youngs. Then there was Koufax, winner of three Cy Youngs (1963, 1965, 1966) and an MVP award (1963).

The '63 season stands out, as Marichal found himself standing in a most frustrating and improbable shadow; that of Koufax, whose own "guts" had also been challenged by his manager, Walter Alston, until this, his breakout season. Aside from Marichal's 25–8 record and 2.41 ERA, he completed 18 games. How much better could any pitcher get? Many baseball historians might argue that the answer to that question came in the form of Koufax's 25–5 year, complete with a 1.88 ERA and 306 strikeouts, arguably the best season not just of his career, but in all history. After facing him in the World Series, New York's Yogi Berra expressed amazement that he managed to lose five times. The Dodgers won the World Series in a four-game sweep, but the '63 campaign was a huge disappointment for Marichal's club.

"After '62, we felt we'd win it every year for eight or 10 years after that," remarked slugging first baseman Willie McCovey. Instead, the Giants were victimized every year by an odd symbiosis called the "June swoon," when they would tank, fatally, every season in that month. They would usually be "bridesmaids, never the bride," as writer Pat Frizzell described them, finishing second to a succession of rivals. In 1963 they finished third, 11 games back of Los Angeles. For San Francisco, it was like reliving the frustration of the Series loss to the Yanks a year earlier.

The Braves' .500 record was not the result of any lack of offensive punch. The game featured teams that had two of the best righty-lefty home run combinations of all time. For Milwaukee, that meant Hank Aaron and Eddie Mathews, both in their prime years. For San Francisco, that meant Willie Mays and Willie McCovey (both at their heights), although on July 2, 1963, Dark inserted Mays in the number two slot in the order, followed by McCovey, Felipe Alou (fourth), and Orlando Cepeda (fifth). This was not a game between two inept hitting clubs.

Marichal and Spahn went through the first three innings each yielding a single hit and no runs. Marichal featured all his assorted pitches, but was beginning to settle into fastball mode. Spahn's vaunted screwball was his out pitch. Both were relaxed and confident.

"When you have confidence, you can relax," said Marichal. "It's an important point of pitching. . . . It's not wrong to think you're the best."

He used his screwball to get the dangerous Mathews, but against singles hitters like Frank Bolling, Roy McMillan, and Don Dillard, stayed with the heat because "if you let a little guy get on base, when the big guy comes up," then trouble awaits. The "big guy" was Hank Aaron. "Throw the ball and close your eyes," he said of his strategy against Hamerin' Hank. When Bolling singled, it might have ended up that way, but Marichal retired Aaron on a foul out and struck out Mathews.

"Once you're ahead of the batter, you take away the options of the other team to run and steal and play aggressive baseball," Spahn said in *The Greatest Game Ever Pitched* by Jim Kaplan.

It was important that Spahn retire Harvey Kuenn, a former batting champion, so he could concentrate on Mays without men on. Mays had enjoyed great success against Spahn, just as he did against Sandy Koufax. His first big-league hit was a homer off Spahn and it broke a long slump in 1951. Pitching fluidly, Spahn struck out Mays.

In the third, Marichal faced Del Crandall, a break of sorts since he was Spahn's preferred catcher. The club's other young backstop, Joe Torre, was a major threat. Crandall reached second on a throwing error by third baseman Kuenn. Men in scoring position served to make Marichal pitch better, however.

"I used to win a minor bet in the clubhouse by betting that a run couldn't score from third with no outs against Juan," recalled teammate and fellow Hall of Famer Gaylord Perry. McMillan flew out to center field.

"They had so many great pitches," Perry recalled of the Marichal-Spahn duel. "They weren't overpowering, but they had great control and a high kick that made them hard to pick up."

Challenging Aaron in the fourth, Marichal benefited from the conditions when his long flyball was caught at the warning track in left. "Did you see him hit that ball?" Marichal asked later. "It was going out of the park, and then that wind caught it. What a break that was!" He struck out Mathews again, but walked Norm Larker before Mack Jones singled. Crandall singled to center and Larker headed for home, but was thrown out by Mays "in one amazing motion," wrote Bob Stevens of the *San Francisco Chronicle*.

"He made a perfect throw," recalled Marichal.

Norm Larkin testing Willie Mays? "The indignity!" wrote Jim Kaplan.

In the fourth, a major threat was removed. Mathews, who had come back too soon from an injury, was replaced by Denis Menke. In the bottom of the inning, Mays grounded out but McCovey singled. Alou hit into a force and Cepeda popped out. The Braves put a man on in the next frame but Bolling lined to Keunn, ending a threat.

By the seventh everyone's attention was on the two men who stood like "minor deities 15 inches higher than anyone else—the height of the mound," wrote Kaplan. "They were conducting a clinic for the ages: Marichal stylish and blazing, Spahn as Shakespeare said, 'firm as rocky mountains.'"

Aaron was especially flummoxed by the Dominican Dandy. "The foot's up in your face, and that's bad," he said of facing him. In the seventh Crandall was thrown out at second on a botched hit-and-run, rendering a double by Spahn—one of the best-hitting pitchers ever—irrelevant.

In the bottom half, the Giants mounted a threat and Dark went to Jim Davenport, normally the starting third baseman, as a pinch hitter. He flied to center. The Giants went down one, two, three in the eighth, as did Milwaukee in the top of the ninth. There was no activity in either bullpen. With one out in the last of the ninth, McCovey faced Spahn. He hit one completely out of the stadium, but in a call bitterly disputed by San Francisco, umpire Chris Pelekoudas called it foul.

"It was so high and far that after it passed the fair pole you could see it curve into foul territory," recalled Marichal. "It was hit so far it landed in the parking lot."

Then McCovey grounded out, Alou singled, but Cepeda grounded out. It was now on to extra innings. Marichal was working on a six-hitter with three walks and three strikeouts. Spahn had surrendered five hits with a strikeout and one walk.

As the game progressed, the fans got colder. The 10th passed with little action. Aaron struck out to open the 11th, a key out for Marichal. He got the next two men, seemingly stronger than ever, but Spahn set San Francisco down in their half—one, two, three. That was how Milwaukee went down in the 12th, and the same with the Giants. The game threatened to go on forever. Marichal had retired 16 straight until Bolling got a hit in the 13th, but Aaron fouled out. A Giants rally in the 13th, in the form of Ernie Bowman's single, was snuffed when Spahn, who featured one of the great pickoffs ever, caught him wandering off the bag. Neither pitcher considered the possibility of leaving for a pinch hitter. There were so few baserunners that their at-bats did not seem to be promising opportunities, anyway. Dark visited the mound a few times, but never to consider removing his ace. By the 14th it seemed to be too much to leave him in.

"I begged Mr. Dark to let me stay a few more innings, and he did," Marichal said. "In the 12th or 13th, he wanted to take me out, and I said, 'Please, please, let me stay.'" Catcher Ed Bailey seemed to be caught up in the excitement, and argued for Marichal to continue, as well. In the 14th, Marichal told Dark, "Alvin, do you see that man pitching on the other side? He's 42 and I'm 25, and you can't take me out until that man is not pitching."

"When Juan said that, it was a great tribute to Spahn—and to Marichal," remarked Perry.

Dark recalled that he and pitching coach Larry Jansen, his teammate along with Willie Mays during the miracle 1951 season, were keeping pitch counts, a relatively new thing, and he thought, "I don't want this kid to get hurt." Whenever he asked him if he felt alright, the pitcher "always said he was."

Both pitchers were cruising. Based on performance and ball movement, neither showed any sign of fatigue or wear, but in the 15th Marichal told Dark he had enough. But when Spahn retired the Giants, Marichal impulsively grabbed his glove and went to the mound. "For a while I thought there were going to be two pitchers on the mound because the guy from the bullpen was coming in," he said. "They had to call him back."

It was 12:20 in the morning when the 16th inning began. "Hardly anyone had left the park," wrote Jim Kaplan, which seems hard to believe and is difficult to verify. After retiring the Braves, Marichal told Willie Mays he really needed to call it quits.

"Don't worry, I'm going to win this game for you," Mays told him.

In the bottom half of the inning, Spahn used screwballs to retire Kuenn. He had reached 200 pitches.

"Hit one now," Marichal called to Mays as he approached the plate.

"I will, Chico," Mays, who called Juan "Chico," said to him.

He was hitting only .257 and was in a slump. The fans had even booed him recently. Spahn had owned him all night. He was exhausted. Spahn was also tired! The wind had died down, a blessing.

Spahn threw a screwball . . . that did not screw. Mays swung and connected. Spahn knew it was over, walking to the dugout before the ball cleared the left field fence, and the best-pitched game ever was over: 1–0, Giants. Marichal finished with 227 pitches and the victory.

"We were riveted," recalled famed sportswriter Ron Fimrite. "It was the best game I ever saw."

"I never saw anyone like him," said Orlando Cepeda. "I've talked to Hank Aaron, Frank Robinson. They all say the same. Marichal never gave you an inch, never gave you a break."

"With Juan, on the field, there are no friends, no family, no compadres, no countrymen," said Felipe Alou of facing Marichal. Alou was traded to the Braves the next year and had to face his old friend many times after that.

It was Spahn's last great season. He would even be Marichal's teammate for a brief time in San Francisco before retiring with 363 wins, 10 shy of the record 373.

—◦—

One year after the Marichal-Spahn duel, in 1964, another memorable extra inning game involving the Giants was played, this time at Shea Stadium in New York. The lowly Mets and the contending Giants were tied late in the 13th inning when Gaylord Perry was called on in relief.

Perry was a tall, lanky right-hander out of North Carolina. He had tremendous ability; an above-average fastball, a wicked slider, all the tools. Despite this, he had yet to materialize in his first two years in the Major Leagues. Al Dark was losing confidence in him, and worse, Perry was losing confidence in himself. The word, unspoken and perhaps even spoken to Perry, was that this was his last chance to show what he was made of before deportation back to the farm, or a demoralizing trade.

There were 57,037 fans packed into the brand-new Shea to see a double-header. In the second game, the score was tied 6–6 when Perry was brought on in the 13th inning. It was Dark's last gasp. He was out of pitchers. Perry immediately floundered, getting into trouble, and with Mets all over the sacks, it looked like the end, for the game and for Perry.

But Perry had been experimenting in the bullpen with a spitball, an illegal pitch but an effective one. Nervous, desperate and out of options, he decided to load one up. It dipped all over the place, producing the desired result. He stayed with more "wet ones," pitching out of the jam, and then for nine more innings—10 scoreless in all—until San Francisco finally scored two in the 23rd inning to end the marathon with an 8–6 victory.

It did not have the classic line of the Marichal-Spahn masterpiece, but to Gaylord Perry it was the game of his life.

"I was determined not to be sent back," said Perry of his "motivation."

—◦—

Jesus Alou had six hits vs. Chicago on July 10, 1964.

—◦—

From 1964 to 1968, Jim Ray Hart averaged 287.8 homers and 89.4 RBIs.

—◦—

He could have been the best of all right-handers in that time.
—GIANTS OUTFIELDER MATTY ALOU ON JUAN MARICHAL

—　⌣　—

They each had intense pride, so it was like the Dominican Republic against Puerto Rico.
　　　　　—Hall of Fame Pirates star Willie Stargell
　　　　　describing Juan Marichal's battles with teammate
　　　　　and fellow Hall of Famer Roberto Clemente

—　⌣　—

First I thought I'd like to go to college, but the team's manager came to my house. He said if I signed a contract, he wanted me to study baseball in America.
　　　　　—Masanori Murakami, the first Japanese pitcher in
　　　　　Major League history, who came to the Giants in 1964

—　⌣　—

We changed managers in the middle of 1960 and look where that left us.
　　　　　—Giants star Willie Mays advising ownership not
　　　　　to fire manager Alvin Dark until the end
　　　　　of the 1964 season

—　⌣　—

I was surprised I got traded by the Giants. I'm not afraid to say they made a mistake.
　　　　　—Felipe Alou, traded to Milwaukee before the 1964
　　　　　season, had many excellent years in baseball

—　⌣　—

His power is beyond our fondest expectation.
　　　　　—Batting coach Hank Sauer

The Roseboro Incident

THERE IS A GREAT DEAL OF BACKSTORY TO THE INFAMOUS 1965 DRUBBING Juan Marichal gave to Dodgers catcher John Roseboro, with a baseball bat, witnessed by a large throng at Candlestick Park. Perhaps it started in 1964, the last year of manager Alvin Dark. Dark felt that he was losing control of the clubhouse. The team disappointed in 1963, watching the hated Dodgers go all the way. In 1964, they began to slip out of a tight pennant race late in the season, and the pressure was getting to Dark, passed down to the team. He had trouble with the Spanish-speaking players using their native tongue in the clubhouse and on the bus. He also had a problem with Marichal, who experienced back pains the year that Dark considered suspect.

"Periodically, he seemed to think I lacked 'guts,'" Marichal recalled. "Dark seemed to undergo a great change during 1964. I do not know all the reason for this."

Dark made a strange request; that Juan pitch the lowly New York Mets, a team he was unbeaten against, "different than you've been pitching them up till now." Then Dark gave an incendiary, racially charged interview to an Eastern publication, basically saying that neither black nor Latino players "subordinated" their needs to their clubs, or had "pride" in the American teams they labored for.

Marichal was extremely fair in his assessment of Dark, insisting he never saw Dark punish a player for racial reasons, but added "those quotes didn't help anything." Nevertheless, after the club languished behind the National League leaders, Dark was fired and replaced by Herman Franks, a totally different personality type.

But when the 1965 season rolled around, Marichal and many of his countrymen were in a state of "ferment," because the Dominican Republic was undergoing a revolution.

"I do not think it is difficult to realize that injury and illness can be brought on by other things besides physical causes," Marichal stated, adding that sometimes he had to pull over to the side of the road to get his wits together. In reflecting upon the events of the 1965 season, few sportswriters ever focused on this aspect of Marichal's life until a 2014 book by John Rosengren (*The Fight of Their Lives: How Juan Marichal and John Roseboro Turned Baseball's Ugliest Brawl into a Story of Forgiveness and Redemption*). All that was ever written about was what he did to Roseboro, without much consideration of the cause beyond verbal jousting and a nicked-ear return throw to the mound by the feisty Dodgers catcher.

The street battles in the Dominican, followed by President Lyndon Johnson sending troops to quell the unrest in our own hemisphere, truly worked on Marichal, to the negative.

"But with troops in the streets, and people being hurt and killed, it gives you a strange feeling to talk political abstractions when you are thousands of miles away, playing baseball for a living," Marichal stated.

Marichal was getting up-to-the-minute reports on the Dominican uprising from Rod Ryan, a Western Union unit chief at Candlestick Park. This was the "comic opera," as Juan called it, that enveloped the beginnings of the eventful 1965 campaign. For one thing, 1965 was the year the "McCovey question" was resolved once and for all. Since 1959, McCovey and Orlando Cepeda had traded off playing first base. Both were tremendous sluggers who needed to be in the lineup every day, but without a designated hitter, one of them was always out of position. Neither was much of a left fielder, but there was no alternative. But in '65, Cepeda sustained an injury and McCovey played first base, blossoming into a star. Cepeda was eventually traded to St. Louis.

"There were some hot words in midseason of '65 in Los Angeles, after Drysdale had put Mays down two times with close pitches," recalled Marichal. "I said: 'If that keeps up, somebody's going to find out we can protect our hitters.'"

When league president Warren Giles heard Marichal say that, he issued a stern warning. Of the Dodgers-Giants rivalry, *Time* magazine wrote, "Now the principals are San Francisco and Los Angeles, two cities

325 miles apart whose partisans hate each other's guts . . . in ordinary times . . . August 22, 1965 was no ordinary time."

While Marichal was distressed over riots in the Dominican Republic, Dodgers catcher John Roseboro, an African American, had similar worries. He was "deeply concerned about race riots in the Watts section of Los Angeles near his home," *Time* continued. "For tinder, there was the tension of the tightest National League race in history, for fire, a provocative trading of beanballs, curses and the threats. In the third inning, with the Dodgers leading 2–1, Marichal came to bat. The second pitch was low inside; Roseboro dropped the ball, then picked it up and deliberately fired it as hard as he could back to the mound—right past Juan's ear."

Marichal claimed that the ball nicked his ear. He turned to Roseboro.

"Why did you do that? Why did you do that?" he screamed. Roseboro then charged Marichal, who was still holding a bat. In front of 42,807 Candlestick denizens, frazzled by the rivalry and tense race relations resulting from the Watts riots, Marichal clubbed Roseboro three times on the head with his bat.

"One man stopped it all," wrote sportswriter Arnold Hano. "Willie Mays took John Roseboro's face in his hands and said in a voice that scarcely hid tears, 'Oh, John, I'm so sorry. You're hurt.'"

Mays and the Dodgers trainer, Bill Buhler, began to lead Roseboro toward the clubhouse, but the sight of blood reignited the catcher's anger. He struggled to get to Marichal, but Mays placed himself between the two men. He cupped Roseboro's face. They were good friends, despite the rivalry; they shared the tempestuous African-American baseball experience of the era.

"You're hurt, John," Mays said softly, as he led him away. In the radio booth, Giants announcer Russ Hodges wondered aloud whether Mays might be unnerved after the bloodshed.

"They can thank Mays there wasn't a real riot out there," said the Dodgers' Lou Johnson, one of the most vociferous in his efforts to get at Marichal.

"Peacemaker he had been," Hano wrote. "Brandisher of the warclub now he was."

Facing Koufax—the man who truly *was* unnerved—Mays bashed a homer over the center field fence, leading to a rare victory over L.A.'s ace.

Marichal was fined $1,750 and suspended for eight days, what amounted to two crucial starts in a pennant race that promised—and eventually did—go to the last day. Roseboro was not punished. The incident served to spur L.A. to greater heights. Conventional wisdom holds that it took the air out San Francisco's tires. The Giants were 19–9 prior to the incident. L.A. would later win 14 straight, propelling them to the pennant and a seven-game triumph over Minnesota in the World Series.

"Neither Juan nor the Giants ever regained their form," wrote *Time* magazine.

Not so fast; San Francisco won 14 straight after the Roseboro incident, and Marichal, who won 22 games on the season, won three of those games. As late as September 16, 1965, San Francisco led Los Angeles by four and a half games. But Marichal also pointed out that the suspension, which covered eight *games*, covered nine *days*, a distinction he pointed out was very important.

"*Time* also was incorrect in saying I hit Roseboro three times with the bat," Marichal pointed out.

"Most of all, *Time* was incorrect saying that Roseboro did not answer when I asked him why he had thrown the ball the way he did. He did answer, if you call what he said an answer. What he said was 'f—k you.' I had the bat on my shoulder. If he didn't do it on purpose, he didn't have to give me that kind of answer. If he didn't say that, then I think nothing would have happened."

Marichal said there had been a lot of verbal jousting between the two benches, and several brushback pitches, but nothing serious. He also said he and Roseboro had "talked pleasantly" before the game just the day before. The real reason Roseboro felt the need to nick Marichal in the ear with a throw was because Koufax simply did not like to pitch inside, unlike his teammate, the notorious Drysdale. He had thrown a "courtesy pitch" over Mays's head earlier, but that scared nobody. Roseboro felt the need to make up for Sandy's lack of aggressiveness.

"Now I knew Koufax wasn't throwing at me," recalled Marichal. "I never dreamed it would come from behind."

Roseboro, he said, dropped Koufax's curveball "on purpose, I believe," in order to align himself right behind Marichal. As for using his bat, Marichal told Harry Jupiter of the *San Francisco Examiner*, "He's got everything on. He's got the mask, the chest protector. I don't think I can fight with a guy like that. I know from the way he was coming toward me he was coming to fight. I only hit him one time—the first time."

Roseboro sustained a severe gash and a lot of blood was evident. Marichal continued to wield his bat, which many have found their greatest fault in him for. "I know if they take the bat away everybody will hit me," he stated, adding that the Dodgers were closer to him at that point than his own teammates.

Immediately, Marichal realized the magnitude of what had occurred. "I was very sorry about what happened," he stated.

Mays entered the Dodgers clubhouse several times during Giants at-bats to check on Roseboro. Marichal's subsequent suspension hurt even more since a twi-night doubleheader in Philadelphia and a rainout meant the club had to go an extra game without his services. He also believes the timing of the suspension was specifically worked out so he would not be pitching in front of 56,000 fans at Dodger Stadium in San Francisco's next swing to L.A. The reaction to Marichal from the Roseboro incident was only partially responsible. There was still grave fear due to the recent Watt riots. Marichal was not even allowed to make the trip to L.A., where protests at the airport or outside the hotel might have occurred.

When Marichal pitched on the road after that, he was booed mercilessly, but he still heard cheers at home. Ultimately, Los Angeles prevailed and went on to glory, which most everybody considered to be a sense of justice; the white hats beating the black hats, the villains.

It took a while, but Marichal and Roseboro managed to bury the hatchet and even become friends. Marichal also redeemed himself in subsequent years, obviously as a pitching sensation, but also as a gentleman. What he did was wrong, but it did not reflect his true character.

—◦—

He had the devil inside him that day.
—Teammate and friend Matty Alou on Juan Marichal,
August 22, 1965

Roseboro was just as guilty as Marichal was.
—GIANTS HALL OF FAME ANNOUNCER LON SIMMONS

Then Willie Mays reached the scene. He pulled Roseboro out of range of Marichal's bat, and helped the umpires to restore order. Only a man for whom the other players had complete respect could have waded into that explosive situation and broken it up.
—GREAT PENNANT RACES OF THE MAJOR LEAGUES, BY FRANK GRAHAM JR.

He's a guy who everybody should have as a friend.
—GIANTS TEAMMATE JIM BARR ON JUAN MARICHAL

I just figured that if I wanted to stay in the big leagues, that was my job.
—FRANK LINZY, THE 1965 NATIONAL LEAGUE ROOKIE PITCHER OF THE YEAR WITH 21 SAVES AND A 1.43 ERA

Take a hike.
—THE ONLY ENGLISH WORDS JAPANESE PITCHER MASANORI MURAKAMI LEARNED IN TWO YEARS IN SAN FRANCISCO

The kid has more range at second base than any Giant I've seen.
—GIANTS ANNOUNCER RUSS HODGES ON INFIELDER HAL LANIER

Year of the Pitcher

By 1968, Juan Marichal and Gaylord Perry were one of the great one-two pitching combinations in all of baseball. Marichal was likely a Hall of Fame lock already, if not at the season's start, certainly by its end. He built on his masterpiece win over Warren Spahn to go 25–8 with a 2.41 ERA in 1963, then followed that up with a 21–8 mark and a 2.48 ERA (1964) and 22–13 with a 2.13 ERA (1965). The '65 campaign of course was marred by the Roseboro incident, but Marichal pitched brilliantly after returning from his suspension. In 1966 he was joined by Perry, now a bona fide star.

Marichal's 25–6 record in 1966, to go with a 2.23 ERA, was almost superhuman, but again the Cy Young Award evaded him, as Sandy Koufax won 27 games with a 1.73 ERA to lead Los Angeles to the pennant. Perry was 21–8 with a sterling 2.99 ERA. In 1967 Marichal sustained an injury, limiting him to 14 wins. Perry had a 2.61 ERA but poor support limited him to 15 victories. With Koufax retired, Mike McCormick's 22 victories earned him an improbable Cy Young Award, but it was St. Louis and Bob Gibson who took the Dodgers' place, breaking San Francisco's hearts.

In 1968, Perry was 29 years old. Once he started loading up the spitter against the Mets in a 23-inning marathon at Shea Stadium in 1964, he never looked back. He finished 12–11 with a 2.75 ERA that season, then joined the 20-victory circle two seasons after that. But the '68 season was one of the most frustrating in Giants history. Orlando Cepeda had been traded to the Cardinals in 1966. He responded by winning the 1967 MVP award, leading the Birds to a World Series victory over Boston. Ray Sadecki, who came over from the Cardinals, where he had been a 20-game winner, was far less effective with the Giants.

Willie McCovey was *The Sporting News* National League Player of the Year in '68, blasting 36 homers with 105 RBIs, but Willie Mays declined for the second straight season. Bobby Bonds broke into the league with a grand slam home run, but the club, like all of baseball, did not produce offensively as in past seasons.

Marichal was possibly better than *ever*. All season long, he and Denny McLain of the Detroit Tigers pursued the magic 30-victory mark. McLain attained the goal, finishing with 31. Marichal fell a bit short at 26–9 with a 2.43 ERA. But the frustration, the "bridesmaid" status they endured when Los Angeles achieved glory, then the Cardinals, continued. Bob Gibson's ERA was a modern record low 1.12 to go with 22 wins, and it was impossible to deny him the Cy Young Award *or* MVP. Marichal easily could have had three . . . *or more* . . . Cy Youngs if not for the likes of Sandy Koufax, Dean Chance, and now Bob Gibson.

Also in 1968, Don Drysdale of Los Angeles pitched 58 2/3 scoreless innings. San Francisco's Dick Dietz was batting when Don Drysdale "hit" him with the bases loaded, supposedly ending Big D's effort to break Walter Johnson's all-time record, but umpire Harry Wendelstedt called him back, saying he failed to get out of the way of the ball. The runner was returned to third base, and Drysdale pitched out of the bases load jam to eventually achieve the mark. "It was the worst call, without a doubt, that I have ever seen," said Dietz.

So it was that by September 17, when St. Louis arrived at Candlestick Park, the Cards had already clinched the pennant. The events of the next two days mark an anomaly of baseball, the result of a decade in which the strike zone had been lengthened, and pitching was so dominant that after that year the mound would be lowered.

It was a year in which the American League featured but one .300 hitter (its champion Carl Yastrzemski at .301); the combined ERAs of both leagues was below 3.00; the All-Star Game was a 1–0 affair; both league MVPs were pitchers (Gibson and McLain, the first 30-game winner since 1934); Catfish Hunter of Oakland tossed a perfect game; while a plethora of other hurlers tossed no-hitters.

In fitting with this theme, on September 17 and 18, 1968, at Candlestick Park, for the first and only time in baseball history, back-to-back no-hit games were thrown, by pitchers on opposing teams. The two games mark a mirror of the whole season.

Perry was a hard-luck 14–14 entering the game. His opponent? Gibson, already a winner of 21 games, but incredibly the recipient of poor offensive support from his team, despite their championship status. He was so dominant in '68 he could have won 30, or more, as McLain did. The game that night was a microcosm of this lack of support, for this was the only kind of game that could beat Bob Gibson that year.

Ron Hunt improbably touched Gibby for a first inning homer, circling the bases fast, not wanting to look up and catch the disbelieving glare of Bob Gibson contemplating the scrawny middle infielder daring to take him deep. Not to bring forth the wrath of Gibson, a notorious headhunter, Hunt was already the leader among hit batsmen, but the contrived nicks he took from too-close curveballs and changeups was no comparison with a 100-mile an hour heater near his ear from this guy.

From there, Gibson and Perry dominated the scene in a one-hour, 40-minute game played before a mere 9,546 fans. Perry, a seven-year veteran two days past his 30th birthday, walked Mike Shannon in the second and Phil Gagliano in the eighth. *The Sporting News* reported that he featured "a slider that was breaking about three inches on the outside," according to catcher Dick Dietz, but made no mention of added movement courtesy of saliva, licorice, or slippery elm. Perry threw 101 pitches.

Perry, a good fielder and all-around athlete, helped himself with two good defensive plays on a bouncer and covering first in time to get the speedy Bobby Tolan after a hard smash to McCovey.

It was some redemption for a hard-luck campaign in which he lost three games by 2–1 scores and three others by 2–0, but his third win in four decisions against the Cards. It was his first no-hitter since his high school days in Williamston, North Carolina. Perhaps St. Louis was a bit hung over, as this was their first game since clinching the flag, but it does not take away from Perry's gem.

"Any pitcher can get lucky and pitch a no-hitter," said Perry, "and let's face it—you've got to be lucky to pitch one."

This is a ridiculous statement. Perry's lack of ego is admirable, but to throw a no-hit game against a Major League Baseball team is an act of pitching skill with few comparisons. Some luck is normally attached, but it remains one of the great feats. Perry struck out nine. Gibson surrendered four hits with 10 strikeouts. In later years Gaylord changed his tune a bit.

"I was very excited about it because the Cardinals were the best, and there was nothing close to a hit that day," he recalled.

"Perry regarded it as the best game he ever pitched," wrote Nick Peters in *Tales from the Giants Dugout*.

It seemed to take a no-hitter, a shutout or near-shutout, for Gaylord to win in 1968. In his next start, Atlanta defeated him, 2–1.

"You can't let it stay in your mind," he said of a lack of run support. "It's easy to get upset, but if you stay upset you're never going to win a ballgame. You've got to stay positive, keep trying to do better."

Owner Horace Stoneham rewarded Gaylord with a $1,000 bonus.

The only prior no-hitter thrown by a San Francisco Giant prior to that evening had been by Juan Marichal in 1963. In 1938, Johnny Vander Meer of Cincinnati threw a no-hitter in consecutive starts, a feat never accomplished before or since, but a similar accomplishment was in store the next day when Ray Washburn of the Cardinals returned the favor, tossing a no-no marked by five walks and eight strikeouts in a 2–0 victory.

"I never saw a guy throw a curve much better," said Mays. "It floated, but you couldn't hit it."

Washburn had come up a red-hot prospect but an injury sustained in 1963 had derailed his success. The slow curve he developed compensated for his lack of an overpowering fastball. He used 42 curves to go with 89 fastballs against San Francisco. He only averaged 1.5 walks a game that year, but worked extra carefully to the dangerous Giants lineup.

The right-hander from Kirkland, Washington, never allowed a baserunner past first base after the first inning. His strikeouts of Mays and Dietz prevented a Giants score. Bob Bolin of the Giants had a shutout through six innings, but Mike Shannon's double drove in Orlando Cepeda. The Cards added a run in the seventh.

That pitch was as dry as a Baptist wedding.
—Giants Hall of Famer Gaylord Perry describing a
pitch he used to strike out Hank Aaron,
who said it was a spitter

⌣

You think it was hard trying to hit that SOB? . . . I complained to the umpire, "Come on, you know that's a spitter." The umpire says, "Quit bitching. There's only one side wet. Hit the other side."
—Ron Hunt, teammate and opponent of Gaylord Perry

⌣

Now Gaylord, well, he became famous for throwing a spitter even though he always said he didn't. He later switched from saliva to Vaseline. He became an expert, the best. Gaylord Perry and I were like brothers. I love him and I'm pretty sure he loves me.
—Juan Marichal: My Journey from the Dominican Republic
to Cooperstown, by Juan Marichal with Lew Freedman

⌣

When I was called up, I hadn't slept the whole night in Phoenix. Herman Franks, the manager, asked me if I wanted to play, and I said no at first because I was dead tired. Then I thought more about it, and I figured I was in the big leagues, so I might as well play. I batted seventh and it was a tremendous thrill to play in front of 40,000 people.
—Giants star outfielder Bobby Bonds on his
call-up to the Major Leagues, 1968

⌣

Bonds made history in his very first game when he hit a grand slam, the first time that happened in a rookie's debut in the twentieth century.
—Willie Mays: The Life, the Legend, by James Hirsch

⌣

Talk about making a grandiose appearance.
THE *GIANTS ENCYCLOPEDIA*, BY TOM SCHOTT AND NICK PETERS, DESCRIBING BOBBY BONDS, BILLED AS "THE NEXT WILLIE MAYS," HITTING A GRAND SLAM HOME RUN IN HIS DEBUT VERSUS THE DODGERS ON JUNE 25, 1968, AT CANDLESTICK PARK

Willie Mays had a locker near mine, and it took me one-half hour to get dressed because I kept watching him.
—BOBBY BONDS

He is a superstar, but not a superman.
—SPORTSWRITER ARNOLD HANO ON WILLIE MAYS

If you were a 21-year old living in San Francisco in 1967, there was a whole other kind of scene happening, and in a lot of ways I'm very much a product of the sixties. The passion for the game was still there, but I must confess that I didn't pay attention in the same way as I had when I was younger.

But I remember watching and reading about this kid Bobby Bonds and learning about his family.
—*SAN FRANCISCO GIANTS: 50 YEARS,* BY BRIAN MURPHY, QUOTING BAY AREA NATIVE DANNY GLOVER, STAR OF *LETHAL WEAPON* AND *ANGELS IN THE OUTFIELD*

The Giants finished second for the fourth consecutive year, establishing a Major League mark they are not apt to brag about.
—*OFFICIAL BASEBALL GUIDE—1969,* HARRY JUPITER'S SUMMATION OF THE 1968 SEASON

The 600/3,000 Club

WILLIE MAYS NEEDED 13 HOME RUNS AT THE START OF THE 1969 SEASON to become only the second player to reach 600 career home runs. He wanted to do it at Candlestick, but the struggle to get to the milestone wore him out. He finally hit it on September 22 in San Diego off rookie Mike Corkins.

"It was my most satisfying home run," he said, "because of all those guys waiting for me when I crossed home. There was nobody left on the bench. That really got to me." Also in 1969, Mays was awarded by *The Sporting News* as the Player of the Decade (1960s). Mays took "pride" in being "one of the few hundred ballplayers out of tens of millions of Americans who dreamed one day of becoming a big leaguer."

In 1970 he acknowledged that Babe Ruth's 714 was out of reach, but he chased another milestone: his 3,000th career hit. He needed 74 to get there. He got hot and closed in on the record with a 10-for-23 stretch, and on July 18, at Candlestick this time, reached number 3,000 with a single off Mike Wegener of the Montreal Expos.

Mays said "the main thing I wanted to do was help Gaylord Perry win a game." Perry came into his own that year, winning 23 games with a 3.20 ERA and 23 complete games. While he had been a great star for four years, he always labored under Juan Marichal's shadow. In 1970, Marichal had a down year, his first ever. Perry may well have won his first Cy Young Award, but Bob Gibson of St. Louis walked away with his second in three seasons. The 1970 Giants were like so many San Francisco teams of the Mays era, an enigma of sorts. They featured offense in mega-doses. All-Star catcher Dick Dietz drove in 107 runs and batted .300. McCovey did not tail off in the slightest: 39 bombs, another 126 RBIs. Second baseman Ron Hunt batted .281. Mays had a fine season, rebounding from off-years in 1967–1969, by swatting 28 homers and batting .291. Bobby Bonds was a conundrum; he set a record striking out 189 times from the lead-off spot, but that did not stop him from getting 200 hits, 26 homers, with 49 stolen bases, and a .302 average. Left fielder Ken Henderson batted a creditable .294. But after Perry, the Giants' pitching staff—starters and bullpen—could not get the job done. There was no beating Cincinnati's Big Red Machine, one of the great National League teams to emerge in years. San Francisco finished 86–76, in third place.

—◦—

> After the 1970 season, legendary Giants announcer Russ Hodges passed away. The torch was passed to his protégé, Lon Simmons. Simmons was a prep pitching star in Southern California recruited by USC coach Rod Dedeaux before signing and playing in the minor leagues for the Boston Braves and Philadelphia Phillies organizations. He needed to come up with a suitable home run description that did not copy Hodges's famed call. Simmons's signature call was, "You can tell it good-bye."
>
> "He used to say to me that a lot of our listeners were casual listeners. Ladies doing ironing, or guys driving a delivery truck. So if he said 'Bye-bye baby,' they would know the Giants had done something good . . .
>
> "I had to come up with something, because Russ had his 'Bye-bye Baby.' I wanted something low key, too, so that's how that slogan developed . . . Russ had a fabulous sense of humor—we got along so great—and I never enjoyed working with anyone more . . ."
>
> Simmons did end up with another enjoyable and friendly partnership when he joined with his old teammate from Burbank High School, Bill Thompson, in the Giants radio booth.

—◦—

The greatest thing about Mays was his anticipation. If the ball was out on the dirt away from the catcher, Mays moved up a base. . . . Mays ran before the ball hit the ground, because he knew it was going to hit the ground.

—Giants announcer Lon Simmons

⌒⌒

Willie Mays was "as monumental—and enigmatic—a legend as American sport has ever seen."

—Sports Illustrated

⌒⌒

Willie Mays never hit a homer off me, and don't think I'm not proud of that one! He was the greatest, flashiest, do-it-all player there may have ever been.

—Three-time Cy Young Award winner Tom Seaver

⌒⌒

The trip resulted in a spread of handsome photographs in Ebony but not much romance. Mays spent most of his time on the golf course and visiting his former teammate Andre Rodgers.

—Willie Mays: The Life, the Legend, by James S. Hirsch, describing Mays's chaperoned date with actress Judy Pace to Nassau, Bahamas, after she selected him on The Dating Game

⌒⌒

That season produced one of the truly memorable images of Mays's career. In an April game at Candlestick, the Reds' Bobby Tolan smashed a ball deep into right center. Both Mays and Bobby Bonds sprinted to the track and leaped at the same time, their gloves reaching over the fence. In a sequence of four wire service photographs, the two men collide in mid-air, with their legs entangled, their glove hands outstretched, with Mays's belt flush against Bonds's midsection. Next, their feet land, though their bodies are entwined as one. They then

collapse to the ground, with Bonds on his left side, Mays flat on his back, the ball visible in his glove.
—*WILLIE MAYS: THE LIFE, THE LEGEND*, BY JAMES S. HIRSCH

I don't feel I'm ahead of Willie, because Willie's my mentor.
—GIANTS STAR BOBBY BONDS

When it came to the plate, it looked like an exploding fastball, like there was smoke coming from it.
—HALL OF FAMER SECOND BASEMAN JOE MORGAN OF THE ASTROS AND REDS (LATER THE GIANTS) ON FACING GAYLORD PERRY'S SPITTER MIXED WITH RESIN

Gaylord, tell me, where do you get it?
—PRESIDENT RICHARD NIXON QUERYING GAYLORD PERRY ON WHERE HE HID THE VASELINE, DURING A 1970 WHITE HOUSE VISIT

He had ways of going about what he had to do to get the job done.
—GIANTS CATCHER TOM HALLER, WHO WAS TRADED TO THE DODGERS PRIOR TO THE 1968 SEASON

Last Hurrah

In 1971 the *Saturday Review* declared "The Age of Willie Mays." He was 40 years old. He engendered such awe from teammates and opponents alike that when the Dodgers' Don Sutton accidentally beaned him, Don looked on "in horror, as if he had just thrown a dart through the Mona Lisa or cracked a statue of St. Francis," wrote Jim Murray of the *Los Angeles Times*.

It was a magical, final year of glory for the superstar and his team. They had known disappointment in their years since coming from New York, but the club succeeded, and they had numerous stars at the top of their respective games. Few teams outside of the Yankees have featured so many Cooperstown-level players wearing the same uniform.

The year 1971 was a replay of the 1960s, in particular the rivalry with the Los Angeles Dodgers. Koufax was five years retired, and Don Drysdale was forced to call it quits after an injury sidelined him early in the 1969 season. But Maury Wills was back after exile to Pittsburgh and Montreal, and a young team some referred to as the "mod squad" after a popular TV series came into their own.

San Francisco had hit the ball hard in 1970, but pitching betrayed them. The key in 1971 would be Marichal; if the "Dominican Dandy" returned to form, all would be well. Indeed, he demonstrated early that he was again in top form, and the club got off to an explosive start, threatening to run away with the Western Division in the manner of the 1970 Reds, who seemed to have eaten all their press clippings along with banquet food in the off-season, looking terrible early and never recovering.

Roger Angell made a return to Candlestick Park, which he had called "a festive prison yard" during the 1962 World Series, but found little to praise in the stadium construction project, meant to enlarge and "modernize" Candlestick in order to accommodate the 49ers. He sat in a "westerly gale," but was impressed with the Giants, who at the time opened with an eight-game lead on Los Angeles, now visiting the park. A home run by "Willie Howard Mays . . . disappeared in the direction of San Leandro," and the 40-year-old center fielder was "playing the game with enormous visible pleasure."

But the inevitable "June swoon" combined with a hot L.A. rally promised a long, hard summer, and that is exactly what they got, every bit as exciting as the 1962, 1965, and 1966 pennant chases. In July at Tiger Stadium, Mays led off for the National League in the All-Star Game in Detroit. That game is shown often on ESPN Classic and the MLB Network, hailed as the greatest confluence of talent at least since the first All-Star Game that featured the likes of Babe Ruth, Lou Gehrig, and Jimmie Foxx.

The American League came to play, bound and determined to end a near-decade losing streak with the likes of Minnesota's Rod Carew; Baltimore's Frank Robinson, Brooks Robinson, Jim Palmer, and Mike Cuellar; Boston's Carl Yastrzemski and Luis Aparicio; Detroit's Al Kaline and Mickey Lolich; New York's Thurman Munson; Oakland's Reggie Jackson and Vida Blue; and Washington's Frank Howard.

The Nationals featured Pittsburgh's Roberto Clemente and Willie Stargell; Atlanta's Hank Aaron, St. Louis's Joe Torre and Lou Brock; Chicago's Ron Santo and Ferguson Jenkins; Cincinnati's Johnny Bench and Pete Rose; New York's Tom Seaver; and San Francisco's Juan Marichal, Willie McCovey, Bobby Bonds, and of course Willie "the Say Hey Kid" Mays.

There are other all-time greats who for various reasons do not appear in the box score of the American's league 6–4 victory, including Catfish Hunter, Bob Gibson, Steve Carlton, and Dick Allen, just to name a few.

The last month of the season threatened to be a reversal of the 1951 and 1962 seasons, this time featuring a furious late rally by the Dodgers. San Francisco, so powerful and fluid, seemed to tire and as John Wooden once said, "Play not to win, but rather not to lose" down the stretch. When it was all said and done, however, San Francisco emerged with the division crown by a single game, 90–72 over the Dodgers at 89–73.

"Sometimes I still wonder how we won," said first-year manager Charlie Fox. "The Dodgers had a better team, but we played very well together."

McCovey, whose knees ached, slumped perceptibly to 18 home runs. A big plus was 6–6 newcomer Dave Kingman, a pitching ace and slugger who had led USC to the national title. Legendary Trojans coach Rod Dedeaux said Kingman was the finest player he ever coached. Kingman was drafted by San Francisco, quickly ascending to Candlestick. Rookie shortstop Chris Speier provided much-needed spark on defense.

"I had been playing ball all winter to be ready for Spring Training, and Charlie Fox took a liking to me," said Speier.

Mays batted .271 but his steady, veteran leadership was never more evident or needed. He was just what the doctor ordered for Bobby Bonds, who at this point in his career seemed almost a lock for the Hall of Fame, slugging 33 home runs with 102 RBIs to go with a .288 average and 26 stolen bases. Not since Mays in the 1950s had a Giant, or perhaps any player, demonstrated such a combination of power, speed, and outfield defense.

But the 1970 Giants hit the ball hard, too. The '71 version won because they played baseball the way winning teams play it. That meant sterling infield defense led by Speier, third baseman Al Gallagher, and second baseman Tito Fuentes.

"It took guts to be a Giant," said Gallagher. "You couldn't buy it. You had to earn it."

"We love each other," said Speier.

"I played with four organizations, and not one compared to the Giants," said Fuentes, who was thought to be something of a "hot dog." "I never understood why they didn't like me. Now, I think I know, now that they do like me."

"He would never shut up," Speier said of Fuentes.

"His hands were so fast on the double-play, it was like the ball never hit the glove," pitcher Jim Barr said of Fuentes.

"They said, 'Hey, you cannot play like that. You're too flashy,'" Fuentes recalled.

"Tito had a lot of talent—he could really play," recalled Fox. "We always had trouble turning the double-play until Tito and Speier got together and hit it off right away."

Of course, more great defense was provided by Mays, McCovey, and Bonds. "He didn't say much, but he set an example by what he did," recalled teammate George Foster of Mays (he went to Cincinnati and hit 52 home runs in 1977). "I just watched and learned." Speier came to play every day. He grew up in Alameda, literally looking at the twinkling lights of Candlestick Park across San Francisco Bay.

"I saw Mays and McCovey in the field, and Juan Marichal on the mound," Speier recalled of his first impression of big-league life. "I said, 'What am I doing here?' It was a great feeling." Speier was a hardcore ballplayer in the mold of old-timers depicted in Lawrence Ritter's *The Glory of Their Times*.

"I took my failures really, really hard in the beginning," he said.

But Marichal's return to form, which included a division-clinching win over San Diego on the last day of the season, was the difference. Kingman's homer propelled the win. Juan won 18 games with a 2.94 ERA, while Perry won 16 with a fine 2.76 ERA. Hard-throwing Jerry Johnson provided some bullpen stability, and it was enough to push the club over the top. "If his control wasn't great, the leg kick would have been useless. It might have helped with his deception, but the overwhelming stuff and control were what set him apart," said pitcher Steve Stone.

Perry won the first playoff game over Pittsburgh, 5–4 at Candlestick Park. Perry "pitched resolutely and intelligently, and survived, while his younger opposite number, Steve Blass, pitched brilliantly and dashingly, and did not," wrote Angell.

But the Giants fell into a funk against a club they had dominated in the regular season. Clemente, Stargell, and the "Lumber Company" won the next three games, then rallied to beat Baltimore in a seven-game World Series classic. Mays himself had given all he had just to get to the postseason. "I'm dead tired," he declared. "I was a guy who tried to do everything," he would later say.

"Had we had a rested Marichal, I think we would have beaten the Pirates," said Fox. Speier batted .357 versus Pittsburgh in the playoffs.

Candlestick Park . . . is in many ways an excellent place to avoid—a dour, wind-whipped gray concrete tureen that is currently being enlarged, of all things, so that it may similarly test the loyalties of pro football fans this autumn.

—THE SUMMER GAME, BY ROGER ANGELL

Losing to World Champion Pittsburgh in the National League Championship Series couldn't dim the Giants' feeling of satisfaction and achievement.

—OFFICIAL BASEBALL GUIDE—1972

If it were up to me, I'd have finished my career with the Giants. It was Charlie Fox's idea because he really wanted Sam McDowell. If he tells you otherwise, he's a liar.

—GIANTS PITCHING ACE GAYLORD PERRY,
TRADED TO CLEVELAND FOR "SUDDEN SAM" MCDOWELL
AFTER THE 1971 SEASON

It seemed like you were always 0–2 against Gaylord Perry.

—1971 NATIONAL LEAGUE MVP JOE TORRE

Favorite Candlestick memories: Bat day with our little league team. Thousands of kids pounding bats in the stands in rhythm and cheering. Also, my mom agreeing to take us to the game on cold nights so she could see Chris Speier (she thought he was handsome). Cold as those summer nights were at the park, we still found a way to eat a frozen chocolate malt.

—PEBBLE BEACH ATTORNEY JIM LOWELL

Here Comes the Niners

THE GIANTS AND THE SAN FRANCISCO 49ERS BEGAN TALKING ABOUT converting Candlestick into a multipurpose stadium for football in 1965, not coincidentally the year the Oakland–Alameda County Coliseum was completed, the Raiders moving in the next year (the A's arrived in 1968). Phase one of the conversion of the facility began in 1969 with moveable right field stands. Projected to cost $9.1 million, it actually cost $14 million.

In 1960, Candlestick featured one of the first all-electronic scoreboards. The nine-story scoreboard was moved from right to left field at a cost of $238,000 for the renovation. It required two men to operate, had a 900-button console and 7,500 lamps.

The natural grass was removed, replaced with synthetic turf, which required a layer of asphalt spread on the stadium floor. Carpet layers installed the Astroturf.

The left field buildings, housing restrooms, and concessions were demolished to make room for new double-deck stands. Trenches were dug for roll-out stands providing seating on the east sideline for football, to be stored for baseball. It was designed by John Bolles, the original architect. Construction continued during the 1970–1971 seasons. The football press box was completed in June 1971. The stadium would not support steel so it was built out of aluminum. The old wooden seats were replaced by red and orange plastic seats. The upper deck in right field went up in June 1971, two months before the first exhibition football game. An additional light tower was added. The old towers were strengthened with a total of 1,100 lights, triple the previous intensity.

The right field stands rolled out for football. They were designed like pullout bleachers at high school gymnasiums. The last roof panel was placed in 1972, finishing the full enclosure of the structure. It was supposed to reduce the wind, but in keeping with the unimpressive nature of the design and planning since its inception, it increased it by causing negative air pressure, thus the swirling hot dog wrappers.

Gate F on the east side completed the modernization. It featured the longest outdoor escalator in the world, with a similar one at Gate A. They were part of the original plan but had been cut in 1960 by budgetary concerns.

The first 49ers game was an exhibition with the Cleveland Browns played on August 8, 1971. Football had been played at Candlestick before, most notably the East-West Shrine Game and, in the early 1960s, assorted Raiders games. The new configuration allowed for ample parking, creating the famed tailgate scene. Seats replaced benches and the park had better restrooms and concessions. It also became one of the best-lit stadiums, with nine towers featuring 350 candles worth of illumination. Seating increased to 62,000 for football, 59,000 for baseball.

A 27-foot-tall statue of St. Francis of Assisi (San Francisco is named after him) was erected at the entrance to the 'Stick. It had been commissioned by Charlie Harney but was not erected until after the modernization, designed by artist Ruth Cravath, who built it out of plexiglass. The increase in parking meant car demonstrations and driver education classes were held there when there were no games.

The new Candlestick seemed to usher in a successful era. In 1971, both the 49ers and Giants won their division championships, but the Giants folded and had a poor decade. The 49ers won again in 1972, but they too went into the doldrums for a decade after that.

My first Monday Night Football game: 'Niners vs. K.C. Chiefs. Sat low in the end zone and could not see much, but the atmosphere was energized. Dave Martin and I walked all over the stadium that night. Probably around 1972.

—PEBBLE BEACH ATTORNEY FAN JIM LOWELL

A Black Day by the Bay

THE DATE WAS DECEMBER 23, 1972, A DATE THAT WILL LIVE IN INFAMY in the San Francisco Bay Area. That year, 1972, was star-crossed in many ways. In the spring the baseball players had struck, interrupting the beginning of the season. The gaudy, hairy Oakland A's still managed to win the American League West, then captured thrilling playoff and World Series victories over Detroit and Cincinnati to deliver the first professional world championship to Northern California.

In September everything that could go wrong went terribly wrong when sports and politics met in an ugly confrontation at the Munich Olympics. The Soviet Union literally stole the Gold Medal from the United States in basketball. Bay Area swimmer Rick DeMont had his Gold Medal taken from him because his asthma medication was on the banned substance list, which had been updated after the original list—one that did not include his medication—had been submitted to his coaches. Then Palestinian terrorists murdered Israeli athletes.

Richard Nixon won by the largest margin in presidential history that fall, but his Watergate imbroglio was already a done deal waiting to be exposed by the *Washington Post*.

Football was successfully played on both sides of the bay by respective division champions Oakland and San Francisco. The dream of a Bay Bridge Super Bowl just 400 miles down the road, at the Los Angeles Memorial Coliseum, gave hope to many. The same prospect hung in the air two years earlier, only to be dashed when the Raiders lost at Baltimore and Dallas upended the 49ers at Kezar Stadium in the conference championship games.

The odds were not in favor of the two teams. Miami was unbeaten, a team for the ages that would have to be overcome in the AFC. In the

NFC a more egalitarian landscape prevailed. Dallas was the defending Super Bowl winner but strangely inconsistent in '72.

On December 23, fans were hoping for early Christmas presents. What at first appeared to be shiny toys for both clubs turned out to be lumps of coal. Such hope there was at first—a great day of football viewing with logs burning in the fireplace, the smell of holiday smoke emanating from neighborhood chimneys, packages under trees, friends and family gathered for holiday good cheer.

With morning coffee came Oakland at Pittsburgh. It was one of those nerve-wracking defensive struggles, with the young Steelers, led by Terry Bradshaw, clinging to a 6–0 fourth-quarter lead over the veteran Raiders. Then Ken Stabler, a legend in the making whose star would shine almost as brightly as Joe Montana's, ran 30 yards for the go-ahead score.

Bradshaw went to the well three times with nothing to show for it, leaving fourth-and-desperation with a few seconds left. His pass bounced off either Frenchy Fuqua, Jack Tatum, or both of them simultaneously, landing in the hands of Franco Harris just inches above the ground. His "Immaculate Reception" resulted in a touchdown and a 13–7 Pittsburgh win that took the air out of the Raiders.

Now, there was no love lost between the Raiders and 49ers, whether it be late Oakland owner Al Davis or fans of both teams. Nevertheless, there is a natural tendency among sports fans to root for other local teams. A Raiders–49ers Super Bowl looked intriguing. In pro sports, it's a little different than college, where Cal and Stanford almost have a vested interest in each other's failure. Especially for kids, local pride and rooting interests are not burdened by old animosities. They just want the local guys to win.

That said, the 49ers Faithful shrugged off the Immaculate Reception and got ready for the formidable threat of Roger Staubach and Dallas. The Cowboys under coach Tom Landry were almost a dynasty. In the 1960s they had lost two straight heartbreaking NFL title games to Vince Lombardi's Packers. Under the Texas good ole boy Don Meredith and ex-California All-American Craig Morton, Dallas developed the reputation of a team that couldn't win the big one. This was a reputation that alternately hung around the necks of the Cowboys, the Raiders, the Vikings, the Rams, and the 49ers in the 1960s and 1970s.

After beating the 49ers in the 1970 NFC championship game, the Cowboys lost to Baltimore but shed their can't-win-the-big-one image the following season when ex-Navy Heisman hero Staubach finally took over as their quarterback for good.

In 1972, their first full season at the thoroughly modern Texas Stadium, Dallas found themselves in a dogfight with a team that had no business beating them, but managed to do it anyway. George Allen's "over the hill gang" captured the NFC East. The intense Cowboys-Redskins rivalry hit full stride. Dallas made the playoffs as the wild card but lost home field advantage. The first round found them at Candlestick Park on a sunny afternoon.

San Francisco was a solid pro football franchise but a notch below the best. Throughout the 1960s, George Allen's Los Angeles Rams dominated them. The Rams of that era were one of the best teams never to win a Super Bowl. They were snakebit in freezing Minnesota or found some other excuse not to win, but the 49ers were just a bump on their winning road. When Allen left Los Angeles and took over in Washington, UCLA's Tommy Prothro became the coach of an aging team in L.A.

From 1970 to 1972, an odd conundrum shadowed the rivalry. After beating L.A. in 1970, the 49ers could not overcome the Rams at home or away. But the Rams fell over themselves against the rest of the league, allowing San Francisco to win three straight division crowns.

Coach Dick Nolan's squad was veteran, experienced, and injury-prone in 1972. Star quarterback John Brodie went down in the fifth game, but was capably backed up by ex–Florida Heisman Trophy winner Steve Spurrier. He kept the team in contention for nine games until Brodie's return, when the former Stanford signal-caller relieved Spurrier, engineered two touchdown drives, and beat Minnesota 20–17, clinching the West.

Nobody was confusing the Niners with the 1966 Green Bay Packers, but nobody else in the NFC resembled Lombardi's champions, either. The power had shifted to the American Football League, now the AFC, and with a few variations on the theme remained for many years, with the exception of San Francisco (and Dallas) dominance in the 1980s and early '90s.

Dallas, their first round opponent, was in a state of confusion all day long. Behind Morton they had defeated San Francisco in the 1970 NFC title game. Staubach directed them to a 14–3 victory on January 2, 1972, en route to a Super Bowl victory over Miami. The '71 Cowboys are regarded as one of history's better teams, but success in Dallas leads to the kind of pagan idolatry that makes it hard to maintain the discipline that is necessary to win year after year.

It seems hard to believe in the retelling, since Staubach is a Hall of Famer, a winner, and a quarterback who gets more than a little support in the "he's better than Montana" argument, but he was inconsistent and *on the bench* while the Niners built a seemingly insurmountable lead.

Brodie engineered drives that resulted in a field goal and two touchdowns on the ground, good for a 21–13 halftime edge. The Candlestick crowd smelled blood. San Francisco looked fast, and Dallas looked confused; arguing among themselves, the taskmaster Landry threatening to "delete" them from his famed computer. It was the kind of home-field celebration that builds momentum until the snowball cannot be stopped. The radio and TV announcers all but declared victory for the 49ers and prognosticated the results of a 49ers-Redskins title bout when Larry Schreiber scored his third TD, giving the home team a 28–13 lead entering the fourth quarter.

Dallas came out in the fourth quarter and turned it around immediately . . . not! Instead, they seemed to have given up. Consternation and recriminations were the order of their day. There was always something controversial brewing below the surface with these guys, a fact exemplified by books, novels, and movies that told tales out of school about them.

The clock kept ticking. Dallas foundered. The crowd celebrated. The 49ers congratulated themselves. The scribes wrote their game stories and worked their way toward the locker room. Victory was secure.

Staubach came off the bench. The man who had led his team to the Super Bowl a year before had been benched. It was back to the old quarterback question that had haunted Dallas as they transitioned from Meredith to Morton to Staubach . . . and now what?

Deep, *deep* down in the guts of only the most hardened, bitter, veteran fans were two sensibilities. One: San Francisco chokes. They had done it in 1957 against Detroit. In the world of pro football, there were ultimate champions and it was not them.

Second: Staubach already was a mythological figure of sorts. Those who had seen Montana weave his magic at Notre Dame could not shake the image of the '77 national title, the '78 USC game, and the '79 Cotton Bowl from their minds as Joe delivered the goods at Candlestick. The same with "Roger the Dodger," who had beaten Notre Dame while at Navy. He had served as an officer and a gentleman. He was so upright, so clean. Could nice guys finish first?

That said, the notion was *ridiculous*. The 49ers, like the movie mogul in that year's best movie, *The Godfather*, had said, they "could not afford to look *ridiculous!*" Staubach delivered no horse's heads, just touchdowns. Not with five minutes left. Not with two minutes left. An earlier Toni Fritsch field goal had "cut" the lead to 28–16. Whoop-de-do. Roger hit Billy Parks on a meaningless 20-yard scoring strike with *1:30 remaining*.

Okay, Bay Area fans remembered the 1968 *Heidi* game, when the Raiders came out of nowhere to beat the Jets after the movie about a little Swiss girl took over East Coast TV screens, but this was *ridiculous*. Wasn't it?

With the score 28–23, Dallas went for the inevitable on-side kick. Every human being from San Jose to Santa Rosa and beyond knew it was coming. All the "good hands people" were there. So, it seemed, was God favoring His Chosen People, and they were not the guys playing for Baghdad by the bay, as *Chronicle* columnist Herb Caen dubbed the place.

Dallas had it, and now Staubach looked like the Colossus of Rhodes. *Can he lead his team to a touchdown?* The Niners faithful watched like bystanders at a traffic accident. It had to be a TD, not a field goal. Suddenly, it was inevitable. The sensibilities of 60,000 people pleaded for San Francisco to hold on but knew they would not. They were right. Roger had a chisel and took a few well-placed stabs at his Hall of Fame plaque when he hit receiver Ron Sellars for the 10-yard touchdown pass that gave Dallas victory, 30–28.

Few, if any, comebacks have been more improbable. Silence was broken only by the whoops of those Texans who made the trip, or who lived in the Bay Area. The Dallas players' shouts mixed with the *yee-haws*.

The Candlestick denizens were too stunned even to boo. Eventually they moved, but they did not awaken for nine years. Brodie was ancient. The team was old. Everyone knew it was their last hurrah before the age of mediocrity that made up the remaining years of the decade, although few could have predicted the team would be quite as bad as they would actually be.

Salt would be added to the wound. Los Angeles became a dominant team again from 1973 to 1979.

Jimmy Johnson was a five-time All-Pro cornerback who played his entire career with the 49ers. He started on offense and defense at UCLA. His brother was another famed Bruin, 1960 Olympic decathlon champion Rafer Johnson. Growing up in Kingsburg, a San Joaquin Valley town, Jimmy was saved from drowning by his "hero" Rafer as a child. He intercepted 47 passes and also played wide receiver early in his career. Johnson twice won the Len Eshmont Award for inspirational play and earned a Hall of Fame plaque in 1994.

Dick Nolan took over a moribund 49er team in 1968. A Maryland alum, Nolan led San Francisco to their greatest success prior to the Bill Walsh era. He was in charge from 1968 to 1975, and helmed three consecutive Western Division champions (1970–1972). His son, Mike Nolan, grew up hanging around the 49ers practice field, and in 2005 was named coach of the team.

Worst moment was Preston Riley's fumble against Dallas in fourth quarter of NFC title game in 1972.
    —San Francisco business executive Peter Cooper

1970 Redux

The similarities between the 1973 and 1970 San Francisco Giants are quite numerous. In both seasons, the club featured offense galore, one outstanding pitcher surrounded by second rate mound performances, all of which left them completely unable to compete with Cincinnati's Big Red Machine. The season ended up being a harbinger of down times. Bobby Bonds, high flying and on the very edge of superstardom, slumped, never recovered, and was eventually traded. The hated Dodgers, not the Giants, were young and talented, emerging as the next great rival of the Reds. It would be Los Angeles and Cincinnati dominating the National League over the next years, which would be among the worst in Candlestick history.

While there were similarities to the 1970 club, this was the new Giants. Bonds had been around since 1968; he was a veteran. He finished with 39 home runs and 96 RBIs, batting .283 with 43 stolen bases. MVP of the All-Star Game, he was the favorite to capture the league Most Valuable Player trophy, but in September folded, thus failing to become the first-ever with 40 homers and 40 stolen bases. Jose Canseco would achieve this milestone in 1988, and Bobby's son Barry would repeat the trick. But the inability to reach 40 homers or 100 RBIs cost Bonds the MVP, which was won by Pete Rose of Cincinnati.

Between 1970 and 1973, there were moments of great importance to the San Francisco Giants. There was the '71 division championship. Chris Speier hit .269 with 15 home runs, making the 1972 All-Star Game. It was one of the few bright spots in a desultory season. There was "Dirty Al" Gallagher, a local San Franciscan from the Mission District.

"If he got a couple of base hits, he didn't want anything washed," Giants clubhouse manager Mike Murphy said.

Then there was the Willie Mays trade, to the New York Mets prior to the 1972 campaign. "The first time I saw Mays coming out of the dugout in a Mets uniform, I had tears in my eyes," said Lon Simmons.

"Willie was probably relieved. Willie also rejuvenated and rejoicing as new Met, out from under the heavy 20-yr. burden as Giants deity and leader," wrote Roger Angell, notes taken upon observation of Mays, who had an initial hot streak with the Mets early in the 1972 season.

Mays played two years in New York, hanging up his spikes after the 1973 season.

"The fans in other cities began giving him tributes, starting in Los Angeles, where Mays received a raucous cheer when he pinch-hit in the final game of the series," wrote James Hirsch in *Willie Mays: The Life, the Legend.* "In San Francisco, he received one final standing ovation when he loped to the dugout after grounding out in his last at-bat. And so it went, from San Diego to St. Louis, from Montreal to Philadelphia."

For the record, Willie Mays's final game at Candlestick Park was an 8–7 Giants victory over the New York Mets on August 11, 1973, before 15,762 fans. It was not his last playing appearance in the Bay Area. The Mets improbably captured the National League East and the National League playoffs, before playing Games 1 and 2, then 6 and 7, versus the Athletics at the Oakland–Alameda County Coliseum in the World Series. Mays had several rough moments in the seven-game loss to the two-time World Champion A's.

━━

Early in the 1973 season, San Francisco rallied from a 7–1 deficit with two outs in the ninth inning, thanks to a grand slam by Chris Arnold and a three-run double by Bonds, winning 8–7 in probably the greatest comeback in Candlestick history.

"In that particular year," Bonds remembered, "I was the best player. I should have hit .300 every year, and maybe I would have if I didn't have to hit for power. But if I had to do it all over again, I'd do the same thing because my team needed power, and I always played for what my team needed."

Willie McCovey's knees ached, but he enjoyed a memorable year with 29 home runs and 105 RBIs. Outfielders Gary Matthews and Garry Maddox were bona fide stars, both .300 hitters with power and excellent gloves. Dave Kingman slammed 24 homers. Tito Fuentes and Chris Speier shored up the middle infield.

Left-handed pitcher Ron Bryant was a journeyman pitcher given plenty of run support, which he rode to 24 wins, but the baseball writers recognized the superlative work of Tom Seaver, who failed to get 20 wins with feeble Mets run support, but whose ERA was below 2.00 almost all season, earning him the Cy Young Award.

If any of the other Giants pitchers had been particularly effective, the 88–74 Giants would have challenged Cincinnati's 99 wins. But Marichal was at the end of his road, injuries ending his dream of 300 lifetime wins. Eventually his number 27 jersey was retired after his career, which included six 20-win seasons. He is in the Hall of Fame.

Sam McDowell was an alcoholic (he has since beaten the addiction) acquired in the trade with Cleveland for Gaylord Perry that remains among a host of all-time San Francisco front-office flops, that also include the loss of Orlando Cepeda to St. Louis and George Foster's trade to Cincinnati.

—◦—

Did you know that famed broadcaster Al "Do you believe in miracles?" Michaels was the Giants broadcaster in the mid-1970s?

—◦—

The Giants had Bobby Bonds, so I had no idea I'd be the next center fielder after Mays. . . . I would hit .319 and I would hear about Willie hitting .340 or something.
—Giants center fielder Garry Maddox (1972–1975),
who did a tour of Vietnam before
signing with San Francisco

—◦—

Gary accomplished things you really couldn't have expected from a first-year player.
—GIANTS STAR BARRY BONDS ON 1973 ROOKIE OF THE YEAR
GARY MATTHEWS, WHO BATTED .300 WITH
10 TRIPLES FOR THE ORANGE-AND-BLACK

I just didn't believe I had the ability to do that when I turned pro. I didn't think I had a good enough fastball. . . . You can't call me a spectacular pitcher.
—GIANTS SOUTHPAW RON BRYANT,
WHO WON 24 GAMES IN 1973

Ron looked like a bear with his chunky build.
—CLUBHOUSE MANAGER MIKE MURPHY ON RON BRYANT

You can't compare Joe and me. I had 660 home runs. He had 363. There is no comparison.
—WILLIE MAYS, WHEN ASKED A QUESTION HE PERCEIVED TO
BE REGARDING A COMPARISON BETWEEN
HIMSELF AND JOE DIMAGGIO IN 2001

It Is Darkest Just before the Dawn

CLICHÉ TIME: IT IS DARKEST JUST BEFORE THE DAWN. RICHARD NIXON: "To appreciate what it is like to be on the highest mountain top, one must tread through the lowliest valley."

For the San Francisco 49ers, the period from 1973 to 1980 represented the longest, darkest night of their history; a period in which the team tread in the "lowliest valley." The 49ers were born into the old All-American Football Conference as part of the post–World War II expansion. They were adopted into the National Football League beginning in the 1950 season. AAFC teams Los Angeles (Cleveland, later St. Louis, now again the L.A. Rams) and the Cleveland Browns (now the Baltimore Ravens, not to be confused with the new Cleveland Browns) were immediately successful. The 49ers were not, but they were competitive.

They had a good season in 1957. In the 1960s the Rams dominated, but San Francisco fielded entertaining teams with star quality players like John Brodie, Jimmy Johnson, and Dave Wilcox.

From 1970 to 1972, San Francisco had playoff teams, but after the disastrous fourth-quarter blowout loss against Dallas in the first round in '72, they got old, discouraged, and bad—fast.

From 1973 to 1979, San Francisco was terrible. Only the birth of the expansion Tampa Bay Buccaneers prevented them from being the worst team in the league, but even Tampa under coach John McKay rose to the NFC title game by 1979. The 49ers stayed mired in mediocrity.

San Francisco was a failed team. Their young players did not develop. Veterans came in by trade, only to show their age. What made the period even more galling was that it represented a golden era in the league and in the state. San Francisco's failure was accentuated by the fact that their rivals attained the heights of glory.

New Yorkers speak wistfully of the 1950s, when three superstar center fielders—Willie Mays of the Giants, Mickey Mantle of the Yankees, and Duke Snider of the Dodgers—roamed outfield pastures. Rivalries were intense in baseball. Frank Gifford's New York Giants enjoyed a strong football run. But New York cannot compare to what happened in the Golden State from the 1960s until the 1990s.

Obviously this period encompasses 49ers greatness. There were the three division titles of the early 1970s and the five Super Bowl titles of the 1980s and '90s. The Giants were strong in the 1960s. The Angels contended in the 1980s. The Rams were excellent, for the most part, in the 1960s and '70s. Stanford went to two Rose Bowls (1970 and 1971). The Chargers of Dan Fouts were a high-powered early '80s offense.

But the proverbial "glory days" are centered in the 1970s. The cross-bay Raiders were dominant in the 1960s, more dominant in the 1970s and 1980s. USC football was probably as strong from 1962 to 1981 as any collegiate power in history. Their best teams were in the 1970s. UCLA basketball under John Wooden (1964–1975) put together a string like none other, highlighted by an 88-game winning streak in the '70s. The Lakers were contenders in the 1960s, champions in the 1970s, a dynasty in the 1980s. The Golden State Warriors won the 1975 NBA title. The Dodgers were terrific in the 1960s, 1970s, and 1980s. Then there were the Oakland Athletics. While the 49ers stumbled and bumbled, the A's put together one of the great sports dynasties in history. All these champions relegated the Niners to the back of the newspapers.

In addition to all these great teams, the 1970s saw a rise in California prep, junior college, and "other" sports. Redwood High of Marin County and Lakewood High of L.A. County had dynasties in baseball. Verbum Dei of Los Angeles rose to unprecedented prep basketball heights. High school football in the Southland took on a new status above and beyond Texas, Ohio, and Pennsylvania. Cerritos Junior College enjoyed a baseball run like none ever seen, and Fullerton College was a junior college football powerhouse. Stanford tennis became a juggernaut. USC and UCLA track dominated (Cal won the 1971 NCAA track title before losing it to academic ineligibility). Had USC or UCLA been countries, they would have been among the top medal winners at the 1976 Montreal Olympics. USC baseball captured five straight College World Series titles. After Title IX, women's sports took a giant leap forward, with California becoming the trendsetter.

The mid-to-late 1970s were tough times in San Francisco, however. Greatness abounded all around them, across the bay and in hated Los Angeles. But the Giants and 49ers represented mediocrity. Candlestick Park, not yet 20 years old, was immediately declared ancient, dirty, a symbol of all things second-rate, low-rent, unimpressive.

The Oakland–Alameda County Coliseum was considered safe, warmer, comfortable, fan-friendly, and accessible. The adjacent Coliseum Arena was modern and filled to capacity. Down south, Trojans, Bruins, and Rams games at the Coliseum were played before enormous throngs at a stadium considered a shrine of immortality. Anaheim Stadium and San Diego Stadium were modern marvels. The Fabulous Forum was home to Hollywood's "in" crowd. Dodger Stadium was the Taj O'Malley.

Then there was San Francisco itself. The city was dirty, corrupt, seemingly taken over by organized crime and peep show booths. Tourists found other, better destinations. Homeless were camped out on the streets, at city hall, and in front of restaurants that patrons chose not to patronize. Once a vibrant city famous for its wild celebrations at the end of World War II—a favorite of sailors and other servicemen—San Francisco by the 1970s was a moribund hangover in the aftermath of the drug-addled Summer of Love, the hippie revolution, the drop out generation, and the protest movement.

The fan base at Candlestick was not generally *from* San Francisco, anyway. Their people came from the suburbs of Marin, San Mateo, and Santa Clara counties. The teams they fielded gave them little incentive to drive through dangerous Bayview streets, leaving their parked cars to the tender mercies of tire thieves and vandals. There was certainly nothing worth doing after the game near Candlestick, and little incentive to venture into the heart of the City itself.

Amid this desultory atmosphere, a football team lived down to expectations. The year 1973 marked the end of John Brodie's and defensive tackle Charlie Krueger's careers. Injuries killed the club in a 5–9 year against the league's toughest schedule. Center Forrest Blue and linebacker

Dave Wilcox were rare bright spots, both voted All-Pro. Tight end Ted Kwalick out of Penn State was a top performer. That year the Rams made a big comeback. New coach Chuck Knox installed a conservative, ground-oriented offense around the experienced veteran John Hadl, obtained from San Diego when San Francisco native Dan Fouts took over. Los Angeles was 12–2. The Rams' success symbolized the difference between the two cities. L.A. was the "city of the future," hailed as innovative in the arts and technology, a place that supposedly had "gotten it right" in terms of harmonious race relations.

In 1974 heir apparent quarterback Steve Spurrier was injured, and his four replacements failed to make the grade. After opening with two hopeful wins, they dropped seven straight in a 6–8 year. One bright spot was Rookie of the Year Wilbur Jackson. Jackson is a historic figure. He was the first full scholarship black player ever recruited by Bear Bryant at the University of Alabama. To "grease the skids" for Jackson's acceptance, Bryant scheduled a game against integrated powerhouse Southern California in 1970. When the Trojans won big at Legion Field, 'Bama fans were clamoring for fast black players . . . like Wilbur Jackson. By the time his Crimson Tide career was over, Jackson had been voted team captain, and the South had risen again.

"Football's religion in the South," said Jackson. "When I got out to California I heard about the Big Game [Cal versus Stanford]. I checked it out. It wasn't like any game in the SEC in terms of excitement. Fans out there were laid-back, but I enjoyed my time in the Bay Area."

Dave Wilcox finally had to retire when a knee injury ended his excellent career. The Rams again won the Western Division, but the balance of power had shifted well in favor of the American Football Conference, winners of 8 of 10 Super Bowls in the decade.

In 1975 the Rams were a dominant defensive team, but Dallas ended their momentum in the NFC title game at the Coliseum. San Francisco was an afterthought at 5–9, although their 24–23 win over L.A. ended an embarrassing 10-game losing streak to the Rams.

New coach Monte Clark seemed to have turned things around in 1976 (8–6). Enormous hopes were pinned on quarterback Jim Plunkett. A local product from James Lick High School in San Jose, Plunkett captured the 1970 Heisman Trophy at Stanford. After leading the Indians to a Rose Bowl upset of Ohio State, he was selected with the first overall pick of the 1971 NFL Draft by New England.

In his first game at Foxboro Stadium, Plunkett engineered a victory over the mighty Oakland Raiders, but went downhill after that, losing his job to Steve Grogan. Still youthful, the move to San Francisco seemed a natural fit for Plunkett, and indeed in 1976, improvement was made. But after a 6–1 start that had everybody excited, the Niners tanked.

Running back Del Williams rushed for 1,203 yards, and UCLA center Randy Cross made the All-Rookie team. The great Jimmy Johnson retired after 16 years. A four-game losing streak ended playoff hopes and left Plunkett subject to much criticism. The Rams again captured the West, but even worse, the cross-bay Raiders finally broke through after years of dominant, yet ultimately disappointing seasons to capture the Super Bowl, which was played in Pasadena sunshine.

In 1977 Eddie DeBartolo Jr. bought the team and brought in Joe Thomas as general manager. There was little indication that this would improve things as the club lost their first five in a 5–9 campaign under new coach Ken Meyer. But there were indications, in faraway places, that something new was in the air.

Halfway across the country, junior quarterback Joe Montana led Notre Dame first to a green-shirt upset of Southern California, then a Cotton Bowl win over Earl Campbell's Texas Longhorns, en route to the national championship.

Closer to home, a short drive down Highway 101, the former coach at Washington High in Fremont, who had been an assistant under Marv Levy at Cal, under John Ralston at Stanford, under Al Davis in Oakland, and under Paul Brown at Cincinnati, finally got his chance as a head man. His name was Bill Walsh. When he returned Stanford to respectability after a few down years, people started to take notice of his "new ideas."

The year 1978 was the nadir of the decade. Plunkett was discarded like stale French bread, but hope was placed on another local legend. Orenthal James Simpson grew up in the Potrero Hill section of San Francisco. He prepped at Galileo High, then set every junior college record imaginable at City College. At USC, his legend was made: a national championship and a Heisman. National icon status came to him in Buffalo, where he was the first overall pick of the 1969 draft. OJ broke Jim Brown's single-season rushing record, becoming the first ever to gain 2,000 yards in 1973. In his prime, OJ had many pundits contemplating whether he indeed had replaced Brown as the greatest football player ever. While he probably fell just short of that, OJ was a hero and major superstar, not just on the field but a Hollywood hero, a commercial spokesman, the most popular sports figure in the pre–Michael Jordan era.

He was brought home to San Francisco in 1978 along with his Potrero Hill, Galileo, CCSF, USC, and Buffalo Bills teammate Al Cowlings. OJ was well past his prime, however. He was cheered, but offered no magic in a 2–14 season. Failed coach Pete McCulley was let go, and the decision was made: a youth movement; a new direction; no more failed, injured veterans. OJ hung up his cleats, heading to Hollywood and an unfortunate destiny.

This meant two things. First, Walsh was hired after leading Stanford to a bowl win and two strong seasons. Then Walsh drafted Montana, still available, *incredibly*, in the third round. He considered his own Stanford signal-caller, Steve Dils, but was impressed by Montana's winning ways at Notre Dame.

Walsh installed a high-powered passing scheme, and quarterback Steve DeBerg was effective with Montana learning the ropes behind him, but their 2–14 record had nobody thinking that greatness lay just around the corner.

In 1980 progress was sure. They started out strong and finished strong in a 6–10 year. Wide receiver Dwight Clark set the club record with 82 catches. Montana took over as the starter and completed 64 percent of his passes. Heading into 1981, the 49ers were hopeful. Nobody could predict anything like what would transpire in that and subsequent seasons, but one thing seemed apparent: after a long, black night, the first dawn of a new day was peeking over the horizon.

After winning three straight division titles, there was still hope that Dick Nolan's team could continue to hold their own, and that the transition from John Brodie to Steve Spurrier would be a winning one. It was looking good in the second half of the first game of the 1973 season, when the 49ers were threatening to end world champion Miami's winning streak. But in searing heat and humidity before 68,276, the Dolphins recovered to win 21–13. Their streak was ended the following week at Cal's Memorial Stadium in a 12–7 loss to Oakland, playing away from the Coliseum because the A's had a game that Sunday.

There were good players on the bad 49ers teams of the 1970s. Wide receiver Gene Washington had been one of Jim Plunkett's targets at Stanford. Tight end Ted Kwalick was a former All-American at Penn State. Defensive end Cedrick Hardman and center Woody Peoples were All-Pros. Defensive tackle Charlie Krueger was a picture of the tough pro football player.

Did you know that Monte Clark, who coached in San Francisco for one year (1976), had been a star player at the University of Southern California?

Celebrity Corner

AMONG CELEBRITIES WHO ROOTED FOR THE SAN FRANCISCO 49ERS AND Giants, the most identifiable San Francisco image is that of Clint Eastwood. His 1966 Sergio Leone "spaghetti Western" *The Good, the Bad, and the Ugly* has become a touchstone cultural phrase that describes most everything in life.

Eastwood may be the most accomplished Hollywood figure of all time, surpassing the actor he is most often compared to, John "the Duke" Wayne. Eastwood has longevity, box-office success, critical praise, Oscars, and diverse achievement. He was the leading box-office name in the 1960s, 1970s, and 1980s. He is one of the most successful directors in Hollywood history, and has done it all: screenwriting, producing, television work.

Eastwood is a Bay Area native who graduated from Oakland Tech High School, which produced A's superstar Rickey Henderson along with a number of other sports stars. Drafted into the Army, Eastwood landed soft duty: lifeguard at the Ft. Ord swimming pool near Monterey. Honorably discharged, Eastwood—tall, ruggedly handsome, chiseled features, muscular with *perfect* hair—blew into Hollywood like so many other hopefuls.

He was discovered and immediately cast as a cowboy type: Rowdy Yates in *Rawhide*. By the mid-1960s he was a well-known, successful TV actor. He starred in a moderately successful film, *Coogan's Bluff*, playing a "duck out of water" cowboy investigating a crime in New York City. It became the template for the Dennis Weaver TV show, *McCloud*.

Then Eastwood had the opportunity to star in a series of Westerns made improbably in Italy. *The Good, the Bad, and the Ugly* was the third and best of those. Directed by Leone, it was one of those movies that might be described as "so bad it was good."

For years, the film was regularly shown on a big screen in San Francisco's Matrix, an upscale Triangle bar located where the old Pier Street Annex once was. On crowded Saturday nights, surrounded by young professionals and mingling singles, film buffs were often mesmerized by the "silent" film, mouthing the words of Eastwood and Eli Wallach.

"Blondie, you can't die, Blondie," people would mimic Wallach when he tries to revive the thirsty Eastwood, who he previously left for dead in the desert, but must keep alive when he discovers that "Blondie" knows where the treasure is buried. Hilariously, groups of guys at Matrix would repeat the words while their irritated dates stared at them impatiently.

By the late 1960s, Eastwood's films were the leading moneymakers in the world. Then in late 1971 came the movie that defined the actor, identifying him with the City. The screenplay was written by a USC film school graduate named John Milius, who attended USC with George Lucas.

Milius created "God's lonely man," who bucks the rules, the trends, and the coddling of bad guys. He set the film in San Francisco, using corrupt city officials, inept police brass, and odd bystanders as props for a tall, handsome, rugged macho man known as "Dirty Harry" Callaghan. It was the role Clint Eastwood was born to play.

One of the most famous of all scenes from *Dirty Harry* was filmed right there on the 49ers' home turf, Kezar Stadium. Andy Robinson was given the role of "Scorpio," a take-off on the real life serial killer who dubbed himself the "Zodiak Killer." Director Don Siegel chose Robinson because he wanted "a murderer who looks like a choirboy."

America fell in love with the movie and the actor. The love affair continues to this day. All the subsequent *Dirty Harry* films were shot in San Francisco or Northern California. *The Enforcer* (1976) features a scene in which the mayor of San Francisco (played by John Crawford) attends a Giants game at Candlestick Park. Advised by his aide to leave early to beat the crowd, he says, "I really thought the Giants might win this one." He is then advised that the home club is being no-hit by what looks like the Houston Astros.

From Candlestick their car makes its way back to City Hall via the bay route, which means crossing the Third Street Bridge. A terrorist, anticipating this, has the bridge raised and armed men then shoot up the car, taking the mayor for ransom. That Third Street Bridge is now called the Lefty O'Doul Bridge, crossed by thousands of fans making their way from the parking lots to the adjacent AT&T Park, modern home of the Giants.

The Enforcer was not the first time San Francisco or Candlestick Park was featured in the movies. Famed director Alfred Hitchcock had long made San Francisco a backdrop for many of his films. The movie industry followed suit by utilizing its vistas, skylines, and bay. *Experiment in Terror* was a thriller starring Glenn Ford, Lee Remick, Stefanie Powers, and Ross Martin (later Robert Conrad's sidekick in the TV program *The Wild, Wild West*). In it, a murderer kidnaps a young woman. The climax occurs at Candlestick during a Giants-Dodgers game.

"They told us they were going to film the game that night," recalled San Francisco pitcher Mike McCormick. "We all had to sign releases and were paid $50 apiece for being in it. They just said to go play and not even think about what they were doing.

"I pitched a complete game win that night, so I was on the post-game show in the clubhouse when they brought Lee Remick down and we were introduced. I signed my cap and gave it to her. Then she left because they were setting up to shoot other scenes.

"All the shots with fans in the stands were done after the game. They were there until three or four in the morning. We had no idea what it was all about until we saw the finished film in."

Directed by Blake Edwards (*Peter Gunn, The Pink Panther, 10*), Vin Scully's play-by-play was integrated into the film. Henry Mancini's score provided a stunning soundtrack.

Eastwood moved to the Monterey area, where he eventually was elected mayor as a moderate Republican. His real life politics never matched the ferocity of most of his characters. Aside from Eastwood, many other celebrities have rooted for the 49ers. This includes local favorites like Chris Isaak, Huey Lewis, Carlos Santana, The Grateful Dead, and all the band members of Journey, all of whom have sung many National Anthems.

—

"Show me the money!"
—ACTOR TOM CRUISE IN CAMERON CROWE'S 1996 HIT *JERRY MAGUIRE*; ACCORDING TO SPORTS AGENT LEIGH STEINBERG, THE MODEL FOR CRUISE'S CHARACTER, THAT TERM WAS VOICED BY A 49ERS STAR, HIS CLIENT TIM MCDONALD

—

Marilyn Monroe: Joe, Joe, you never heard such cheering.
Joe DiMaggio: Yes I have.
—SAN FRANCISCO NATIVE JOE DIMAGGIO, WHO STIRRED THE CROWDS AT YANKEE STADIUM, GIVING AN ICE COLD RESPONSE TO WIFE MARILYN MONROE GUSHING OVER HER REACTION FROM TROOPS ON A USO TOUR OF KOREA

"A festive prison yard": aerial of Candlestick Park in the 1980s. PHOTO COURTESY OF THE LIBRARY OF CONGRESS

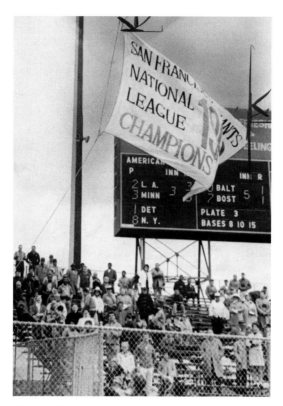

National League banner flying over Candlestick Park, 1963. PHOTO COURTESY OF SAN FRANCISCO HISTORY CENTER, SAN FRANCISCO PUBLIC LIBRARY

A full house for a Jehovah Witnesses gathering in 1961. PHOTO COURTESY OF SAN FRANCISCO HISTORY CENTER, SAN FRANCISCO PUBLIC LIBRARY

A helicopter was used to dry out the basepaths in this photo from 1961. PHOTO
COURTESY OF THE LIBRARY OF CONGRESS

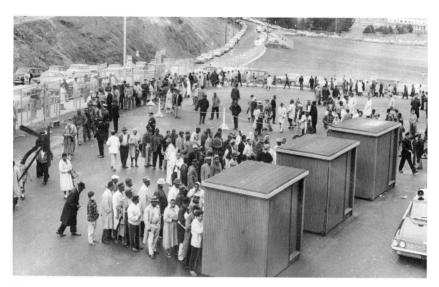

Fans wait in line to buy tickets on opening day, 1963. PHOTO COURTESY OF SAN
FRANCISCO HISTORY CENTER, SAN FRANCISCO PUBLIC LIBRARY

Making history at the 'Stick: Juan Marichal pitching a no-hitter againts the Houston Colts, June 19, 1963. PHOTO COURTESY OF THE LIBRARY OF CONGRESS

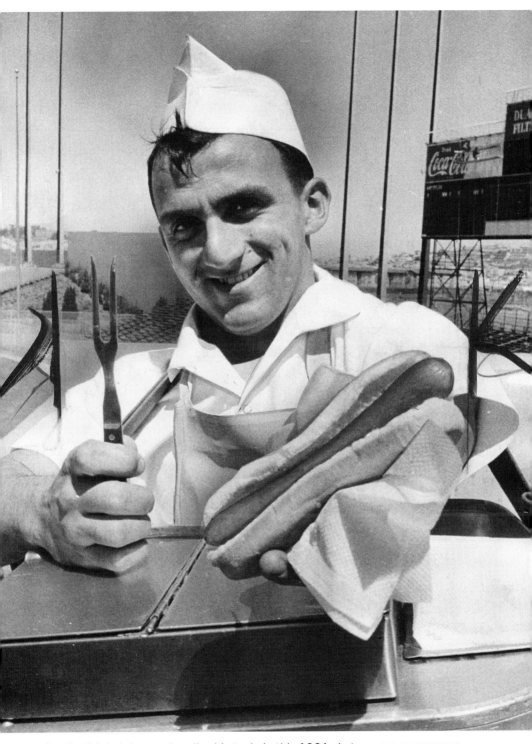

Candlestick hot dog vendor plies his trade in this 1964 photo. PHOTO COURTESY OF
SAN FRANCISCO HISTORY CENTER, SAN FRANCISCO PUBLIC LIBRARY

Iconic yet controversial, Barry Bonds is shown here acknowledging the crowd at Candlestick after hitting an opening-day home run in April 1993. PHOTO COURTESY PHOTOFEST

A less controversial hero of the 'Stick was Joe Montana, four-time Super Bowl champion and three-time Super Bowl MVP who led the 49ers from 1979 to 1992. PHOTO COURTESY PHOTOFEST

Damage from the Loma Prieta earthquake of October 1989. PHOTO COURTESY OF SAN FRANCISCO HISTORY CENTER, SAN FRANCISCO PUBLIC LIBRARY

Workers inspect the stands following the 'quake, which interrupted the 1989 World Series. PHOTO COURTESY OF SAN FRANCISCO HISTORY CENTER, SAN FRANCISCO PUBLIC LIBRARY

Halicki's No-Hitter, Montefusco's Boasts

ON AUGUST 24, 1975, A PERIOD OF GIANTS DOLDRUMS, 24,175 PEOPLE saw a highlight, pitcher Ed Halicki tossing a 6–0 no-hitter versus the New York Mets. He struck out 10. Second baseman Derrell Thomas stole three bases and scored twice. He also made an error on a ball that bounced off Halicki's leg, but the scorekeeper ruled it an error.

"I was aware of it from the fifth inning on, but I didn't think it would become a reality until the eighth inning when I saw I needed only six more outs," Halicki said. "In the last inning, I had to face Felix Millan, Mike Vail, Jesus Alou and Wayne Garrett.

"I knew Millan was a good contact hitter, and that if anybody was going to break up the no-hitter, I felt he was the guy. I ended up striking him out on a hanging slider, which I couldn't believe.

"Then I walked Vail and got two strikes on Alou. He fouled off about seven pitches and popped out to third. I think I threw Garrett a breaking ball inside, and he hit a two-hopper to Willie Montanez at first, and that was it."

The Giants of 1974–1977 were certainly not very good, and attendance, which had never come back to pre–Oakland A's levels (1968), suffered terribly. The A's won their third straight World Series in 1974, captured the division in 1975, and contended in 1976 before the club was completely disbanded due to free agency, which helped open the door to a Giants comeback. San Francisco had to suffer through two pennant-winning seasons by rival Los Angeles, not to mention back-to-back World Series victories by their vaunted division opponents from Cincinnati.

The Giants, however, were not a wholly untalented club. "I would think in that era we were the fastest outfield in baseball," said Gary Matthews of himself, Garry, Maddox, and Bobby Bonds.

The trading of Bonds, coming on the heels of Willie Mays's, Gaylord Perry's, Willie McCovey's, and Juan Marichal's departure, ended an era. "After Mays, McCovey, Marichal and Perry were traded, we knew anyone could be traded," said Bonds.

Bobby Murcer came to San Francisco from the Yankees in the Bonds deal. A talented center fielder once ticketed as Mickey Mantle's successor, he had no love for Candlestick. He provided some spark here and there, but overall was disappointing.

"He was always bitching. 'That would have been a homer in Yankee Stadium,'" Chris Speier said of Murcer.

"He was a Yankee guy," recalled clubhouse man Mike Murphy. "He used to walk around saying, 'I'd pay somebody to blow this place up.'"

But despite this, there were highlights and even stars. The Giants had three very talented starting pitchers. Aside from Halicki, John D'Aquisto struck out 168 to set a Giants rookie record in 1974.

"We were losing, and there were no fans in the stands," he said.

"He had such a great arm, but he could never be consistent," said Lon Simmons.

That September one of the most colorful players in Giants annals arrived. John "the Count" Montefusco predicted a shutout of Los Angeles and backed it up with a 1–0 win. "If it's this easy I'll win 30 games next year," Montefusco boasted to announcer Al Michaels.

The Count was 15–9 with 215 strikeouts to earn 1975 Rookie of the Year honors, then won 16 with a 2.88 ERA in 1976, complete with six shutouts. "If you can strike out people when you're in trouble, the game is easy," he said.

In 1976 Montefusco tossed a no-hitter versus the Atlanta Braves. "If you're going well you can back it up," Montefusco recalled. "I wanted to do something to entertain people." While many took exception to Montefusco's boasting, the Giants averaged only 6,456 fans in 1975 (owner Horace Stoneham's last year), and they needed *something* to create excitement.

"If you want to know how good he was, just ask him and he'll tell you," joked broadcaster Joe Angell.

"I could be rated with Tom Seaver or Don Sutton. . . . Who am I hurting by popping off?" Montefusco exclaimed.

"His mouth got him in a lot of trouble," D'Aquisto said. Most notably was the day Montefusco predicted, as he had before shutting out L.A., that he would duplicate the feat against the World Champion Reds, and for good measure strike out Reds Hall of Famer Johnny Bench four times. Instead Bench and his teammates raked him out of the box early.

"If I had to do it over again, I wouldn't be as outspoken as I was," he said. "I was a young kid, and my mouth worked faster than my mind did. I said some really stupid things that I shouldn't have said. It was just because I was naive and immature. I still haven't grown up, but I do watch what I say now.

"I'd like to take back my prediction about Johnny Bench. But a lot of my predictions did come true."

There was an additional strong pitcher on the Giants staff during this era. Like Dave Kingman, Jim Barr had starred on national champions at USC for coach Rod Dedeaux.

"During the off-season, he would make me his catcher," said Emmy Barr, his eldest daughter. Barr won 90 games for the San Francisco Giants (81 of those coming in the 1970s, making him the winningest Giants pitcher of the decade).

"I was the kind of pitcher who didn't strike out very many guys, but I put the ball in play," said the control artist Barr. That control resulted in his once retiring over two games a Major League record 41 straight batters.

"Wow, you got to be kidding," Barr said after learning that he had set the record. "I had no idea what I'd done. I just knew I'd put two pretty good games back to back."

Barr was 15–12 with a 2.89 ERA on a mediocre club in 1976. "He didn't have that fantastic stuff that blew people away, but he had a real bulldog mentality," teammate Chris Speier said of him.

⌐⌐

Right-hander Jim Barr was a good pitcher on bad teams during most of his Giants career, winning 64 games in a five-year period,

1973–1977, but his greatest achievement was a record-setting performance as a rookie.

Barr retired 41 consecutive batters without a hit—the equivalent of 13 and two-thirds innings—over two games against Pittsburgh and St. Louis. The previous record was 36, so Barr regarded it as his proudest moment in baseball.

—TALES FROM THE GIANTS DUGOUT, BY NICK PETERS

The Bay Area is the center of devil worship, radical groups and homosexuality in the country. It is a Satanic region.

—RELIEF PITCHER GARY LAVELLE (WHO COLLECTED 20 SAVES OR MORE THREE YEARS), A "BORN-AGAIN" CHRISTIAN, LED A SPIRITUAL REVIVAL OF LIKE-MINDED CHRISTIANS ON THE 1970S GIANTS

The next two days I studied The Bible. I wanted to know the truth.

—GIANTS SHORTSTOP JOHNNIE LEMASTER (1975–1985) AFTER SURVIVING A HEAD-ON COLLISION IN HIS NATIVE KENTUCKY

We had games where the same fan would get five or six foul balls.

—GIANTS PITCHER JOHN MONTEFUSCO ON THE CLUB'S DISMAL MID-1970S ATTENDANCE

I know where Patty Hearst is. She's in the upper deck at Candlestick Park. They'll never find her.

—GIANTS COACH JOEY AMALFITANO, JOKING ABOUT ATTENDANCE AT A TIME IN WHICH NEWSPAPER HEIRESS PATTY HEARST HAD BEEN KIDNAPPED BY LEFT-WING RADICALS, THE SYMBIONESE LIBERATION ARMY

—◦—

It looked like Toronto was the answer.
—ALL-STAR SHORTSTOP CHRIS SPEIER DESCRIBING THE
SEEMINGLY INEVITABLE SALE OF THE GIANTS AFTER THE 1975
SEASON TO CANADIAN INTERESTS, BEFORE NEW OWNERS BOB
LURIE AND BUD HERSETH STEPPED IN TO SAVE THE DAY

—◦—

Bob Lurie and I are the reasons the Giants stayed in San Francisco.
—PHOENIX MEAT-PACKING ENTREPRENEUR BUD HERSETH,
WHO FORMED A NEW OWNERSHIP GROUP WITH
BOB LURIE BEFORE THE 1976 SEASON

—◦—

*The most exciting last-minute rally in baseball this season came on
March 2 in San Francisco, when Robert A. Lurie, a local real estate
nabob, put through a telephone call to Arizona and talked to Arthur
(Bud) Herseth, a Phoenix meat-packer, whose name he had heard just
a few minutes before. Lurie asked Herseth if by any chance he would
like to put up four million dollars and become half owner of the San
Francisco Giants. Herseth asked a few questions and then said sure,
why not?*
—FIVE SEASONS: A BASEBALL COMPANION, BY ROGER ANGELL

The Melancholy Story of Jim Plunkett

JIM PLUNKETT IS NOT A 49ERS HERO. HE IS, IN FACT, A 49ERS BUST. THERE are no great stories of Jim Plunkett leading the 49ers to glory, or even much beyond marginal half-season success. But Plunkett cannot be fit into either the bad or ugly categories.

Plunkett's story is a wonderful one, and while his 49ers history is not much to write home about, it is a part of the bigger, wonderful picture.

First, let it be stated that Jim Plunkett was born to be the 49ers' quarterback. He grew up in San Jose. While the 49ers are of course named after San Francisco, it can be argued that they belong more to the peninsula and the south bay than to the City proper. Their 2014 move to Santa Clara seemed to confirm this.

The point is that the 49ers are kings in San Mateo County, Santa Clara, San Jose, Marin County . . . but not so much in San Francisco. Its fan base, its season ticketholders, come more from the suburbs. San Franciscans from San Francisco are as likely to head north to the wine country on beautiful Indian summer gamedays as they were to make their way to Candlestick Park, which was easily accessible from the peninsula.

San Jose is 49ers country, an area known as the south bay, which spans roughly from Stanford University and southward. Plunkett starred at James Lick High School, but he was not the marquee quarterback in the Bay Area. That was Mike Holmgren, out of Lincoln High in San Francisco. Lincoln High, located near Golden Gate Park and Kezar Stadium, where the 49ers played until 1971, also produced coach George Seifert. Holmgren went for USC, but never won the starting job. He was a Trojan for four years, while fellow San Franciscan OJ Simpson won the Heisman and his team the national championship. Holmgren later became a coach under Seifert, then led Green Bay to the 1995 world championship.

When USC went for Holmgren, Plunkett decided to stay in Northern California. Notre Dame showed interest, but there was little enthusiasm. They had all their cards on Joe Theismann.

"I rejected California because the Free Speech Movement was underway in Berkeley, and I didn't want to be bothered by student protests . . . I knew all along it would be Stanford," said Plunkett.

Stanford and the 49ers are almost joined at the hip. Frankie Albert, who led Stanford to football glory, was a star 49ers quarterback and later their coach. John Brodie was a hero at Stanford before leading San Francisco to three straight division titles (1970, 1971, 1972).

Bill Walsh returned Stanford to success before leading the 49ers to ultimate glory, then returned to lead Stanford back to success. The 49ers won their second of five Super Bowls at Stanford Stadium. They train at Santa Clara, just a short drive from Stanford. It is a comfortable, affluent community, and members of the team have long been integral members of it.

Plunkett had to fight for everything he had at Stanford. A Mexican-American from a poor neighborhood, the product of an unglamorous high school program, with parents suffering from physical maladies, Plunkett felt out of place with the rich kids and scholars who populate the Farm.

But he outworked his competition, becoming the starting quarterback as a 1968 sophomore. He returned the Indians (they became the Cardinals in 1973) to national prominence. In 1970 he entered the season considered a Heisman hopeful. Plunkett was asked what was more important to him, the Heisman or the Rose Bowl. The Rose Bowl seemed a longshot, real estate seemingly endowed to the mighty University of Southern California, who had gone there so consistently under coach John McKay that the place was their second home field.

"The question had hardly left the writer's mouth when Jim replied, 'The Rose Bowl, because I can do that with my team,'" recalled Indians coach John Ralston. "That tells you something about Jim Plunkett. Tears came to my eyes."

The year 1970 came to be known as the "year of the quarterback." Aside from Plunkett, the collegiate landscape was dotted with star signal-callers Archie Manning of Mississippi, Rex Kern of Ohio State, Lynn

Dickey of Kansas State, Bill Montgomery of Arkansas, Dan Pastorini of Santa Clara, Ken Anderson of Augustana, and of course Joe Theismann of Notre Dame.

But it was a dream year for Plunkett. First, he defeated the mighty Trojans to get Stanford into the Rose Bowl. Then USC beat Theismann and Notre Dame, which gave Plunkett the Heisman.

In the history of the Rose Bowl up until this time, there may never have been a bigger underdog than Stanford was against Ohio State. Woody Hayes's team was unbeaten and untied. His 1968 Buckeyes had finished number one with sophomores. Now they were seniors, led by Kern and safety Jack Tatum, but Plunkett led Stanford to the stunning upset, ending their surefire national championship aspirations, not to mention infuriating Woody. He despised most everything on the West Coast, especially Stanford (by now home of much antiwar protest).

Despite all the talent at the quarterback position, it was Plunkett who was the number one pick in the 1971 NFL Draft, by the New England Patriots.

"Thus far, I believe, Jim Plunkett is the best college quarterback I have ever seen," said TV analyst Bud Wilkinson.

"Plunkett is the best pro quarterback prospect I've ever seen," said UCLA coach Tommy Prothro.

Plunkett played professionally for one decade prior to leading the 1980 Oakland Raiders to a Super Bowl title. In that decade, he had one legitimate highlight. That occurred in his very first game, the initial contest played in the brand-new Foxboro Stadium.

The Patriots were one of the lowliest teams in pro football, their opponent, arguably the most successful: the Raiders. Plunkett stunned the silver-and-black with a 20–6 victory in 1971. That was it, however. New England was an also-ran in the Plunkett years. He lost his job to Steve Grogan, who got them into the playoffs.

In 1976 Plunkett was traded to San Francisco in a widely heralded deal. He was still young. There was still enough luster, especially in the Bay Area, from his Stanford days to believe that the return home would mark his personal comeback and a return to contention for a franchise that had not been in the hunt over a three-year stretch.

The popular mythology is that Plunkett was a big-time bust in San Francisco, but before that happened, he returned hope to their fans.

Under new coach Monte Clark, Plunkett engineered a fantastic 6–1 start. The media was agog. All of his Stanford promise seemed to be coming to fruition in San Francisco. With the Raiders off to a fantastic start, talk of an all–California Super Bowl—to be played in Pasadena's Rose Bowl, the site of Plunkett's greatest triumph—had football fans giddy with excitement.

Then San Francisco fell flat with four straight losses. Plunkett was barely mediocre after that. The final 8–6 record was respectable, but not playoff-worthy. In 1977 Plunkett was a virtual nonfactor. San Francisco lost its first five games, finished 5–9, and Plunkett was gone.

He was dealt to Oakland, but became a Raider only after seriously thinking of retirement.

"I'd never been a Raider fan," he explained. "Growing up, the 49ers were always my team. I didn't like that Raider silver-and-black color scheme or the team's attitude."

For two years, his presence on the Raiders roster was for all practical purposes nonexistent. Then in 1980 Ken Stabler was dealt to Houston, and Dan Pastorini, one of those "year of the quarterback" names from 1970, where he starred at Santa Clara, was brought in. Pastorini was at first inconsistent, then gone when he broke his leg. Oakland turned to Plunkett out of shear desperation.

In one of the greatest comeback stories ever told, Plunkett took charge and led the Raiders to the World Championship. In 1983 he again took the L.A. Raiders all the way, beating another 1970 college quarterback, Joe Theismann, in the Super Bowl. He engineered winning Raiders clubs in 1984 and 1985, retiring an all-time Raiders great, a color analyst on their radio broadcasts, and an icon of the organization on par with Ken Stabler and Fred Biletnikoff.

Plunkett has remained a faithful Stanford alum, too. His 49ers past is downplayed. Neither the team nor Plunkett make much of it. He filled a dismal period between John Brodie and Joe Montana. Obviously, as his Raiders record proved, he could have, under the right circumstances, led San Francisco to success. In retrospect, a lack of supporting talent or great coaching was at least as much or more to blame for the failures of 1976–1977 as Plunkett.

He never did team with OJ Simpson, who was brought on in 1978. The idea of a Plunkett–OJ "dream ticket" might have seemed a nice idea, but the truth is the 1978 49ers could only be cured by something like, oh, a new coach named Bill Walsh and a new quarterback named Joe Montana—but what were the chances of such a thing?

17.9—Gene Washington's 49ers record for average yards gained per catch in his career (1969–1977). In 1968 Washington hooked up with Stanford sophomore Jim Plunkett to lead Stanford to a 20–0 beating of California in the Big Game.

If only Niners coach Monte Clark, who directed the team to a respectable 8–6 record in 1976, had not been let go in a dispute with the ownership group, partly out of differences regarding the future of Jim Plunkett, he may have been the 49ers coach for a number of years. If so, when the window of opportunity for Bill Walsh to take over had come, they might not have gone for the Genius, with results that surely would never have approached their 1980s success.

Jim Plunkett was acquired from New England for quarterback Tom Owens (1976–1977), number one draft choices, and Houston's 1976 and 1977 number one picks.

After Jim Plunkett, Steve DeBerg from San Jose State University was a competent NFL quarterback despite the record of 49er teams he quarterbacked before Joe Montana took over. In 1979, under the

tutelage of Bill Walsh, he broke Fran Tarkenton's NFL
record for completions with 347.

—

*The success that I always felt I had with the Giants or the 49ers is that
I sort of announce as though I'm sitting in the stands with the people.
I sort of echo their feelings. I'm an interested fan.*

—Longtime 49ers and Giants
play-by-play man Lon Simmons

Renaissance in '78

THE YEAR 1978 REMAINS AN ISLAND OF EXCITEMENT IN A SEA OF mediocrity. From 1974 to 1977, for the most part the Giants were unimpressive noncontenders. The Los Angeles Dodgers and Cincinnati Reds dominated the division, trading championships, fiercely competing with each other in thrilling races.

But the Giants announced their presence with authority early in the '78 campaign. They ventured into Dodger Stadium and ripped up the vaunted L.A. pitching staff. Both defending champion Los Angeles and perennial contender Cincinnati got off to slow starts while San Francisco remained hot well into the summer. Attendance, which had dipped since the late 1960s and gotten so bad at one point the club practically moved to Toronto, was way up. It was not just crowd size. It was especially about *enthusiasm*, which was sky high all summer: 1,740,477 fans entered Candlestick, excellent numbers for the era. But there were several sellouts and near sellouts that produced huge victories for the Giants. A weekend series May 26–28 demonstrated that baseball was *back*. Crowds of 43,646, 45,865, and 56,103 packed Candlestick to see the home team beat L.A. in two of three games. The club broke the 50,000 mark a number of times after that.

The Oakland A's, the dominant champion of the early part of the decade, were now struggling mightily, and at last in '78 it appeared the Giants had won a decade-long battle for the soul of the Bay Area baseball fanatic. Many waited for the other shoe to drop; how long could this club expect to beat the Dodgers and Reds, filled with superstars? The old north-south inferior/superior dynamic was well in play. Dodger Stadium was a gleaming palace, filled to capacity night after night. The Dodgers wiped out the old Dodger Stadium attendance records, drawing an unbelievable 3,347,845 fans to their park. *Sports Illustrated* quoted various big-league players saying that only when they came to the Dodgers, with their private plane, their state of the art spring training facility, with their shining city on a hill and their "Dodger way," did they finally feel they were "in the big leagues." A recent *Forbes* analysis determined the Dodgers to be the most valuable sports franchise on Earth, at the time worth $50 million.

But Giants manager Joe Altobelli consistently got the most out of his club, and for those who were there, 1978 was a magical summer of fireworks and fury at Candlestick. The club featured both old and young. The young was represented by a magnificent talent, outfielder Jack Clark. They called him "Jack the Ripper." At 22, he established franchise records with 46 doubles and a 26-game hitting streak.

"The bat feels like a magic wand—I shake it and it gets hits," said Clark, who slammed 25 homers with 98 RBIs and a .306 average. "I grew up in Southern California, but I always liked the Giants," he added, stating that he rooted for all the "big boppers" in the San Francisco lineup. After his career, he was a Dodgers batting coach, but refused to take his jacket off because "I'm not a Dodger."

"The Ripper hit the ball harder than anybody I've seen," recalled teammate Dan Gladden, adding that infielders "would back off when he took batting practice."

The old was represented by two veterans, both come over in trade. One came from across the bay. Vida Blue had been a Cy Young Award winner and Most Valuable Player on the Oakland A's dynasty. When owner Charlie O. Finley realized he could no longer compete in the free-agent era, he unloaded all his stars. The last to go was Blue, who took his southpaw act across the bay and, in 1978, won big game after big game, his high leg kick propelling smokin' fast balls that the National League batters could barely catch up to. He won 18 games. Fans were on the edge of their seats, cheering and hollering as "the Blue Blazer" would close in on strikeout victims and victories at his new home.

"Pure contentment—I never had so much in years," recalled Blue, adding that the crowds pumped him up like never before.

"The beautiful part of the Vida Blue trade was that even though we gave up seven players, it didn't hurt our big league club at all," said Alto-belli. He had his team in first place at the All-Star break and ultimately won Manager of the Year honors. General manager Spec Richardson won Executive of the Year honors. The Giants long had a reputation for bad trades—Orlando Cepeda for Ray Sadecki, George Foster for Vern Geishert, Gaylord Perry for Sam McDowell—but the Blue acquisition was gold!

The other "old" player acquired in trade the previous season was a familiar face: Willie McCovey. "You know you're loved when you come back as a visiting player, and you get a bigger ovation than the home team," McCovey said of his return to Candlestick during his short sojourn with the San Diego Padres.

"I've never heard anyone say a bad word about him," Cincinnati superstar Pete Rose said of McCovey.

"I'd never been given a 'day' before, and to drive in the winning run on your day, after they've given you all those gifts and you know that 90 percent of the people in the stands are there for you—that's special," McCovey said of Willie McCovey Day given in his honor at Candlestick on September 18, 1977, the year he returned to Giants from the Padres and earned Comeback Player of the Year after hitting 28 home runs.

At age 40 in 1978 he contributed huge hits in key situations, which included a home run to ignite a 6–1 win over the Dodgers before a huge throng during the first game of a key series in May. The cheers he received dwarfed even those given to Willie Mays in his prime.

"They had guys like Mays and Hart, but it always came down to McCovey," recalled Dodgers ace Don Sutton. "He was awesome, easily the most feared hitter in the league." Also during that series, journeyman Mike Ivie blasted a grand slam off Sutton in the May 28 win. Bill Madlock batted .309.

Bob Knepper complimented Blue—two southpaw stars—as he won 17 games with a 2.63 ERA, anchoring a veteran pitching staff that included John "the Count" Montefusco, Ed Halicki, Jim Barr, and Gary Lavelle out of the bullpen.

Montefusco broke in a few years earlier, a brash, outspoken talent who was the Rookie of the Year in 1975, but after he broke his ankle in 1977, "I was never the same again." He still contributed some big performances early in the '78 campaign. Barr was still an effective hurler.

Finally, in late August and September, the club slumped and was surpassed by both eventual National League champion Los Angeles and Cincinnati, but at 89–73 it remains one of the bright spots in Candlestick Park history.

I didn't do much on the field when I played, so I'm trying to afterward.
—Rob "the Rock" Andrews, who played three seasons in San Francisco, batted .264 in 1977, and ran the Giants' fantasy camps after he retired

Would I have been as big a fan without the summer of '78? Would hundreds of thousands of others, too?
—*San Francisco Giants: 50 Years*, by Brian Murphy

In 1978 the Dodgers' Reggie Smith charged into the stands at Candlestick Park to take on a fan who was throwing things at him. Smith did it again in 1981, but a year later he signed with the Giants as a free agent.
—*Giants Past and Present*, by Dan Fost

I took a date to her first baseball game at the 'Stick in the late '70s and baseball fans know your first game you buy a program for your memory of that first game you attend. Well my date refused to buy a program and I ended up getting one anyway. Well that particular game the paid attendance was around 840 and about the seventh inning the public address announced if you turn to page such and such in your program and the moon in the ad for Seiko watches was signed by Greg "Moon Man" Minton you won a his and her watch. Well, sure enough the program my date refused to buy which I ended up purchasing was the signed program. My date mentioned she had not purchased a present for her dad who's birthday it was the next day. Of course I felt sorry for her and gave her the men's Seiko watch for her dad's birthday. Of course I gave her the woman's watch to insure another date or at least a kiss goodnight. What happened was I lost two Seiko watches that night to a lady who never dated me again and my Giants losing in sub-freezing weather. What was a highlight of this experience at a Giants fantasy camp years later I was able to share this story with Mr. Minton.

—Giants season ticketholder Brad Beedle

The Catch

WHEN IT COMES TO THE SAN FRANCISCO 49ERS, EVERYTHING COMES down to this day, this game, this moment: the Catch. It is the Holy Grail of the franchise, the parting of the Red Sea by which a flood of glory days follow. It is most likely the greatest event in Candlestick Park history.

The date was January 10, 1982. It had been an unusually rainy season in the Bay Area. Major floods created havoc on the Russian River and in Marin County just two weeks earlier, but the City was drying out when the Dallas Cowboys rode into town for the NFC championship game.

The Cowboys were still the Cowboys. Roger Staubach was no longer their quarterback, replaced by Danny White, but Tom Landry was their coach, and they had all the swagger of the 1970s teams that went to five Super Bowls and won two of them.

Up until that day, the 49ers were suspects. They had been desultory in the mid-to-late 1970s. Bill Walsh was a successful college coach, but by no means the Genius. They were coming off a 6–10 year and under Joe Montana had gone 13–3, but Joe was not yet the Greatest Quarterback of All Time.

This was Caesar crossing the Rubicon, Grant taking Richmond, the Von Rundstedt plan in 1914. It was San Francisco's bid for immortality.

While the 49ers are remembered for the offensive exploits of Montana, it was defense that powered them. Jerry Rice was years from becoming a Niner. They had little in the way of a running game. But they had a rookie defensive back from USC named Ronnie Lott, who put the fear of God in opposing ball carriers. Veterans Fred Dean and Jack "Hacksaw" Reynolds had come over via trades. Hungry for championships that had eluded them throughout their careers, they spurred the team on.

"Going to the 49ers was like a breath of fresh air for me, a new start," said Dean. "They were underestimated in '81, and we took a lot of teams by surprise. But by the Dallas game, people knew we were for real. That game was important for the franchise. And the Catch? Well, the Catch was the most important play of the season. Getting to the Super Bowl is every player's dream. It was the Catch that put us there."

The Catch was thrown by Joe Montana, whose name resonates in the world of sports and celebrity like that of Babe Ruth, Joe DiMaggio, Muhammad Ali, and Michael Jordan. But *the Catch* was made by Dwight Clark. Clark was a southerner out of Clemson University. The year 1981 was a particularly good year for him, as his new pro team, San Francisco, went all the way the same year his alma mater captured an equally improbable national title.

Clark is an all-time great 49er who went on to a successful front office career, but unlike Montana, he lives off the Catch above all other accomplishments. He is like Bobby Thomson and his "Shot Heard 'Round the World," or the Craig Fertig–Rod Sherman combination who teamed up to throw and catch the winning touchdown for Southern California, ending Notre Dame's title hopes in 1964.

Clark remembered feeling "very confident," and felt his team matured that day in ways that resonated not just in the subsequent Super Bowl win over Cincinnati, but in the entire "team of the decade" 1980s.

The 49ers had struggled early in the season, although those September and October struggles were successes compared to the dismal previous eight years. They lost to Cleveland at home, prompting a rendition of hometown band Journey's "Don't Stop Believing," as fans filed out of Candlestick. But they won a defensive struggle at Green Bay and beat the Steelers.

The turning point win at Pittsburgh, according to Clark, was the game that propelled them to ultimate victory. Pittsburgh was the "team of the 1970s."

Now they were facing "America's team," Dallas.

"I could never describe in words what it was like," Clark recalled. "At the time, it happened so fast, it's hard to put into words. On the other hand, I look back, and everything happens in slow motion. My friends always kid me that the play could have been 'the Drop.'"

Football fans watching on national television got a good look at the contrast in climate between the Midwest and the Pacific Coast. The early AFC title game featured the warm weather San Diego Chargers almost freezing to death in their loss at Cincinnati to a Bengals team that probably would not have beaten Dan Fouts and company on a neutral field. After that "ice bowl," the relatively sun-splashed Candlestick looked like paradise. It at least offered even playing conditions.

San Francisco started things in good form when Montana hit Freddie Solomon for an eight-yard touchdown pass four minutes and 19 seconds into the first quarter. Dallas clawed back in with a field goal. A 49ers fumble set up a two-play drive. Ex-Arizona State quarterback White hit Tony Hill from the 26—10–7, Dallas.

San Francisco sputtered as the two teams settled into trench warfare, but the Niners' historian-coach, Bill Walsh, knew he needed a football version of the Meuse-Argonne Offensive in order to give his team confidence that they could beat Tom Landry's Cowboys. Unable to move the ball on the ground, and with the vaunted "West Coast offense" out of sync, he called for a big play and got it: Montana bootlegging to the right, finding Clark deep for 38 yards. But Dallas met the challenge and held. All 60,000 fans groaned, and "it could be heard for miles down the Bayshore Freeway from the Stick," wrote Michael Tuckman and Jeff Schultz in *The San Francisco 49ers: Team of the Decade.*

"That was a little depressing," said linebacker Keena Turner.

Back to the trenches. On Dallas's next possession, San Francisco won the battle. With field position shifting in their favor, Montana knew he needed to take advantage of it. Starting at the Dallas 47, he put it all together in the style that he would come to be known for. Montana could overcome confusion, replacing it with vision, like none other. The result this time was a four-play touchdown drive, with Joe scrambling out of the pocket to his left, mostly avoiding Everson Walls (whose interception interrupted the last drive). With Dallas committed to the rush, Clark was wide open if only Montana could unload it, which he did, but not without paying the price in the form of some 1,000 pounds of blue-and-white Dallas beef on top of him. When the crowd went wild, Montana under the pile knew he had succeeded, and perhaps those Cowboy pass rushers knew that the man buried beneath them was truly special.

"I kinda like when that happens," Montana said.

"America's team" had no intention of relinquishing the throne easily. After an 80-yard drive, their own Hall of Famer, running back Tony Dorsett, scored from the 5, and they led again, 17–14.

Ronnie Lott made a rare mistake when he was flagged for pass interference to help Dallas keep the drive alive. Later, Lott questioned the call, as did Walsh. Walsh saw that the game would be won not by the infantry but by the air force. After the half, he had tried for a big strike, but Montana was intercepted. So was White. It was not a perfectly played game, but the adrenaline was at fever pitch with the realization that the struggle would go on to the end.

San Francisco struck with a 2-yard Johnny Davis touchdown run to lead 21–17, but nobody felt safe.

"Going back and forth like that with the score, it must have been fun to watch," said Turner.

Maybe for fans of the Bears, or perhaps Bengals supporters already secure in their team's Super Bowl fortunes.

A slight 49ers edge was gained when Dallas was held to a Rafael Septien field goal, cutting it to a razor thin 21–20. When San Francisco fumbled in the fourth quarter and Dallas converted it into a 21-yard touchdown pass from White to tight end Doug Cosbie, the game had all the earmarks of past 49ers horrors: blowing the 1957 NFL Playoff game to Detroit; letting Roger Staubach destroy them in 1972. Their opponents were the masters of the fourth quarter comeback, the two-minute drill, the thrill-a-minute comeback.

But this time, the 49ers had Joe.

"They took the lead, and a big hush came over the crowd, and it was as if the coffin had closed on our season," said tight end Charles "Tree" Young, now a preacher who speaks in a dramatic pulpit manner. With Montana, however, "We rose to the occasion. Nothing could stop us."

What is forgotten, however, is that Montana did not lead San Francisco to victory right after Cosbie's catch. He threw a seeming game-breaking interception. Landry decided that *their* infantry would close it out. For nine excruciating plays, Dallas held the ball, the lead, and time of possession. There was no room for error; a Septien field goal would ice it. The big crowd expected the worst. After all, this was San Francisco, not across-the-bay Oakland where the comeback win was as commonplace as it was in Dallas.

But San Francisco held. Solomon fair caught Danny White's punt at the 49ers' 11 with 4:54 to go. The lights were on in the January gloaming; a crowd begged, a nation waited to see the presence of greatness. Montana had shown more than glimpses of it on national TV before: in 1977 when he led Notre Dame to the national championship, in 1978 in a noble defeat against USC, in 1979 against Houston in a college performance perhaps unrivaled in history.

Walsh kept it short. The "West Coast offense" churned up yards—and time—to mid-field. With two minutes left, they were in Cowboys territory. Dallas, like the Romans almost 2,000 years earlier, was determined to keep the modern version of Hannibal in the Italian countryside. Montana was determined to be the Barbarian who broke through the gates. The duel was personal on the sideline, the defensive mastermind Landry versus the new passing guru of the West, Walsh.

Solomon gained 14 on a reverse, Clark caught a 10-yarder, and then Solomon caught a 12-yarder to the Dallas 13. A timeout was called with 1:15 to play. The field was now narrowed, to the defensive advantage.

Montana threw an incomplete pass, but Lenvil Elliott gained seven on a sweep to the 6. Another timeout was called. Faced with defeat or glory, the two legends-to-be, Montana and Walsh, decided to go for Solomon in the air. Walsh told Montana to hold on to the ball until the last possible instant, looking for the speedy Solomon, but if he was covered, the secondary receiver should be Clark. If the Clark option was exercised, however, "hold it or throw it high" so that "it'll be thrown away" instead of intercepted, with another play to go to if this failed, according to Walsh.

According to offensive tackle Keith Fahnhorst, the huddle was bridling with confidence, which no doubt can be attributed to Montana and also to Walsh. "Sprint right motion" was set up for Clark to line up slot on the right, run an inside hook, with Solomon taking three steps and then heading up the sideline. Walsh wanted something that would be deep in the end zone for either man. Landry gambled that his rushers would get to Joe before he could find Solomon or Clark. With almost any other quarterback, he would have been right.

Ed "Too Tall" Jones, however, "looped" around the linebackers, recalled Fahnhorst, but when Earl Cooper blocked his man, he also knocked Fahnhorst down. Solomon slipped, and Clark was double-covered. Montana sprinted to the right, chased by Dallas defenders like giant policemen hoping to bring down a robber. D. D. Lewis was a few feet from Montana. The sideline approached dangerously, looking like the ground approaching a skydiver whose parachute was not yet open. Montana kept his cool. He had an extra play if he had to go out of bounds or throw it away, but he did not want to waste the play unless he had to. If he went out of bounds or was sacked, the loss of yards would be an obstacle almost impossible to overcome. Instead of giving up, Montana then backpedaled a few feet. Solomon was covered, but Clark broke free.

Montana unloaded one for the 6–4 Clark, tossing it high enough to avoid an interception but seemingly beyond Dwight's reach. Montana later said he was surprised that Clark had to "jump that high," disputing the notion that it was a throwaway, and thus a fluke.

Montana, sitting under all that high-priced Dallas defense, did not see it, but observed replays, marveling at Clark's leaping ability. As great as Montana was, it is called the Catch, not the Pass, because it was Clark's superlative leap and sure hands that brought it down.

"I thought I had jumped too soon," recalled Clark, but he came down with it.

The 'Stick went utterly ballistic. All-Pro center Randy Cross had been knocked on his keister and was a spectator.

"I saw the whole thing," said Cross. "It was really pretty."

The extra point gave San Francisco a 28–27 lead, but the collective conscience of millions pictured Dallas making a patented Cowboy comeback to win on a field goal by the reliable Septien. When the kick was returned to mid-field, it looked somewhere between possible and probable, but White was not Staubach, and San Francisco held.

Rookies Lott, Eric Wright, Carlton Williamson, Lynn Thomas, and second-year man Montana represented an incredible future. Clark was now an instant legend.

"That one play didn't make me financially wealthy or anything," said Clark when his number 88 was retired on "Dwight Clark Day" at Candlestick in 1988. "I didn't all of a sudden get a ton of commercials. But not a single person who knows anything about football doesn't know about the Catch."

—◦—

Dwight Clark was a 6'4", 204-pound receiver drafted 10th in the 1979 draft by the 49ers out of Clemson University. Clark obviously is a 49ers legend because he made the Catch against Dallas in the January 1982 NFC championship game. Clark played for San Francisco until 1987 and was Joe Montana's best friend. Later, he was a high-ranking, well-respected 49ers executive, a protégé of Bill Walsh. But Clark was not a Hall of Famer, as in a Canton Hall of Famer. He was not particularly fast, and while talented, he was a product of Walsh's system. When Jerry Rice and John Taylor came along, Montana had better targets. As good as the team was with Dwight, they were better with Rice and Taylor.

—◦—

Edward J. DeBartolo Jr. was a flawed human being, but nobody can argue that he was one of the most effective owners of a sports franchise in the history of Northern California. He came from Youngstown, Ohio, a town notorious for organized crime. DeBartolo's family made their millions through real estate, mostly shopping centers. The term "mob ties" has attached itself to his name, possibly unfairly because he is Italian. He liked to party, was known to favor strippers, and got in some trouble from time to time, but the players loved him. He paid them well, beginning with his 1977 purchase of the club and on through their "team of the decade," four-Super Bowl, 1980s dominance.

—◆—

Top 10 Northern California Sports Owners

1. Al Davis, Oakland Raiders
2. Charlie O. Finley, Oakland A's
3. Edward DeBartolo Jr., San Francisco 49ers
4. Peter Magowan/Larry Baer, San Francisco Giants
5. Walter Haas, Oakland A's
6. Joe Lacob/Peter Guber, Golden State Warriors
7. Franklin Mieuli, San Francisco/Golden State Warriors
8. Horace Stoneham, San Francisco Giants
9. Lou Spadia, San Francisco 49ers
10. Joe and Gavin Maloof, Sacramento Kings

—◆—

To this day I've never heard a roar as loud—nor experienced goose bumps as intense—as that day at Candlestick.
—49ERS FAN DAVID KAUFER ON THE CATCH

—◆—

I wasn't going to take the sack. I could see Dwight. I knew he had to be in the back of the end zone. I saw his feet hit the ground. I heard the crowd screaming.
—SAN FRANCISCO 49ERS HALL OF FAME QUARTERBACK
JOE MONTANA DESCRIBING THE CATCH

—◆—

It's probably going to be just like it was in '81.
—NOSE TACKLE PETE KREUGER BEFORE BEATING DALLAS IN
THE FIRST 49ERS-COWBOYS MEETING SINCE THE CATCH

Birth of a Dynasty

THE SAN FRANCISCO 49ERS VICTORY OVER THE CINCINNATI BENGALS at the Pontiac Silverdome in Michigan on January 24, 1982, at first appeared to be just another surprise World Championship by a previously bad sports team. Obviously Bill Walsh was the "flavor of the day" among coaches, Joe Montana was an emerging star, and Ronnie Lott had the makings of greatness; but overall there was scant evidence that a dynasty was in the works. They had little running game and did not have the star power of the great teams of the 1970s: the Steelers, Cowboys, Raiders, and Dolphins.

But as it turned out, San Francisco's victory served as harbinger of more than simply the franchise's ascendancy. It was a paradigm shift in Bay Area sensibilities. Up until 1982, virtually all sports greatness in Northern California resided in Oakland. The Giants had made their bid in 1962, falling just short, but in the 1970s they were a joke, playing in dilapidated Candlestick while their rivals, the Dodgers, rose to a position of glamour, winning pennants in front of capacity crowds and admiring Hollywood crowds at beautiful Dodger Stadium.

Oakland billed itself as the "home of champions" for good reason. The A's captured three straight world championships (1972–1974), the Warriors one NBA title (1975), and the Raiders two (1976 and 1980). San Francisco had lost the Warriors to the east bay in the early 1970s. The Rams dominated San Francisco and played a "hometown" Super Bowl at the Rose Bowl in 1980. USC and UCLA just killed California and Stanford. Los Angeles was seen as the most trendsetting American city, surpassing crime-infested New York with no competition from San Francisco. In 1982 they "stole" the Raiders.

The City was at a low point. Political power resided in the Southland, where Los Angelenos Richard Nixon and Ronald Reagan had ascended to the White House. San Francisco's national image was one of corruption and ineptitude, its streets dirty and filled with the homeless. In 1977 Superintendent Harvey Milk and Mayor George Moscone were shot to death by a colleague who avoided conviction using the "Twinkie defense," but later committed suicide. Clint Eastwood's *Dirty Harry* series did little for the City's image. San Francisco's financial district lacked the panache of Wall Street. Its restaurants and nightspots were "so yesterday." Tourists and suburbanites found little appeal. Strip clubs were controlled by organized crime. Broadway was dangerous. Polk Street was a haven for "anything goes."

San Francisco Bay Area sports fans resorted to class envy and boorishness. Cal students dumbly waved credit cards in an effort to "mock" the rich USC kids, who just laughed at them. Giants fans showed up for the Dodgers and little else. They threw garbage at Tommy Lasorda, soiling the air with foul epithets, impressing nobody who counted.

When the San Francisco 49ers won the 1982 Super Bowl, however, it all started to change. Thousands of people descended on the City. Cars jammed the Broadway tunnel, and people celebrated at the Triangle in the manner of patriots on V-J Day. It was this event that created the birth, or Renaissance, of the trendy, yuppie Marina District, Cow Hollow, and Pacific Heights areas. In conjunction with the computer revolution, it led to the gentrification of Broadway, the growth south of Market, and eventually the building of Pacific Bell Park in 2000.

It is not inconceivable to state that the popularity of the Montana-Walsh-Lott 49ers created conditions leading to political revitalization, spurring city growth and leading to the City's hosting of the 1984 Democratic National Convention and two San Francisco women, Dianne Feinstein and Barbara Boxer, being elected to the US Senate. Los Angeles lost clout amid riots, a major earthquake, the OJ murders, dry spells at USC and UCLA, and the loss of both the Rams and Raiders.

It had started a few years earlier when Eddie DeBartolo, scion of a shopping center empire in a town notorious for organized crime—Youngstown, Ohio—improbably spent $16 million to take over the

Niners. The "carpetbagging" DeBartolo had hit all the right buttons, however. Bill Walsh came over from Stanford. Joe Montana was still available when Walsh took him in the third round. Walsh scooped Ronnie Lott up in the draft like a hungry man presented a free cheeseburger and fries at Original Joe's. Seattle took UCLA's Kenny Easley, who they felt was a better prospect.

In 1981 everything clicked: 13–3 to win the West; slaying the Rams; victory over Dallas; and a trip to Michigan, where the NFL had gambled that a Super Bowl party could be pulled off despite frozen conditions. Had the game been played outdoors, Cincinnati may well have prevailed as they had against San Diego at Riverfront Stadium, but the Silverdome was just that . . . a dome.

"It was definitely a new experience for us," said Keena Turner.

Walsh broke the tension by meeting his team at the hotel dressed as a bellhop. His calming influence kept the team focused even when a traffic jam through the snow-covered streets caused San Francisco to arrive at the Silverdome late.

The Bengals were not from a major media market, and San Francisco's sports enthusiasm was questioned, but surprisingly the ratings were high to see the new order after years of Steelers, Cowboys, Raiders, and Dolphins domination. Fans were interested in Walsh and Montana. Walsh scripted the first 20 plays or so, and it worked to perfection. San Francisco sprinted out to a 20–0 halftime lead, threatening to turn the game into a rout.

"We felt satisfied that we'd done what we wanted to do in the first half," recalled Fred Dean.

Hacksaw Reynolds, however, had played on a Rams squad that had gotten off to a good start before losing to Pittsburgh in the Pasadena Super Bowl two years earlier. He knew the game was not over.

Cincinnati got the ball to start the second half. Led by quarterback Ken Anderson, they drove 83 yards to make the score 20–7. For a young team, panic was a natural component, the threat of blowing a big lead hanging over their heads.

Cincinnati seemed to have solved Montana. Ross Browner sacked him. A pass to Freddie Solomon was broken up.

"We definitely lost our momentum at that point," said Turner.

Another three-and-out and field position advantage to Cincinnati made DeBartolo suddenly stop thinking of victory speeches. Anderson went after the 49ers' young secondary, hitting receiver Cris Collinsworth for 49 yards to the 49ers 14. Cincinnati worked their way down to the 3, first-and-goal.

Big Pete Johnson, perhaps the best power runner in the NFL in such a situation, was sent up the middle. He had scored more touchdowns at Ohio State than Archie Griffin. He pulled a coterie of 49ers with him to the 1.

"Everybody was pretty hyped up in the huddle," said Dean. "My feeling was, either we could stop them here and be champs, or we could lose it and think about it for the rest of our lives."

Ex-Packer and now Bengals coach Forrest Gregg no doubt wanted a repeat of Bart Starr's quarterback sneak for a touchdown that overcame Dallas's goal-line stand in the 1967 "ice bowl." After Johnson's carry, Gregg decided that he would play it as a four-down situation, touchdown or nothing. Johnson got the ball behind left guard Dave Lapham, but John Harty, Dwaine Board, and Archie Reese met him. Harty brought him down, no gain.

Former LSU star Charles Alexander "the Great" got the ball on a swing pass and ran wide. Linebacker Dan Bunz, a blonde kid who looked like a typical Southern California beach boy from unheralded Long Beach State, had lost his starting job. This would be his only tackle of the game. He would not be an All-Pro, Canton was not waiting, greatness was not his destiny, but in the annals of 49ers lore, his stop of Alexander in the open field ranks with the Catch or any of Montana's touchdown tosses.

Alexander had blundered by cutting off his pattern before he could reach pay dirt. Now it was fourth-and-goal. Momentum favored San Francisco, but Pete Johnson was a momentum-buster. He hit the line hard, but it was crowded, and he was stopped. Archie Reese rolled onto the pile, waving his warms in exultation.

The 49ers sideline went nuts.

"We were ecstatic," exclaimed Randy Cross.

"From that point on, we realized we could win this thing," said wide receiver Mike Shumann.

The inches differential reminds one of Al Pacino's locker room speech to his team in *Any Given Sunday*, a film coproduced by ex-49er Jamie Williams.

"You've gotta fight for those inches," Pacino's Tony D'Amato says. "Because those inches are the difference between winnin' and losin' . . . between livin' and dyin.'"

So true.

The poor field position left San Francisco vulnerable when they were unable to move the ball, allowing Cincinnati to come back and score to make it 20–14. But the goal-line stand had given them confidence. The kickoff field position was restored, allowing two modest 49er drives that were just enough to allow Ray Wersching to kick two field goals and put the game out of reach for Cincinnati.

Cincinnati scored late to close it to 26–21, but Walsh's team hung on for the first World Championship in city history. The only other "ultimate championship" won by a team within San Francisco city limits was USF's 1955–1956 NCAA basketball titles, led by Bill Russell and K. C. Jones.

Not only had the 49ers shed their loser's image, they had shed San Francisco's loser's image; or more appropriately, restored their image as a great city, tarnished in the previous decade, 19 years after *Chronicle* columnist Charles McCabe said "ultimate victory was too jarring."

Suddenly, the "genius" Bill Walsh and the golden boy from Notre Dame, Joe Montana, represented S.F. excellence in the manner of local boys like Joe DiMaggio and Frank Crosetti . . . names seemingly from a bygone era that was no more, at least until the Niners brought glory back to the city by the bay.

As if carried by the new popularity of San Francisco, local acts such as Huey Lewis and the News and Journey seemed to be propelled to national stardom on the backs of the 49ers. A new golden era had been embarked upon. The people who descended on the City's streets and bars the night of January 24, 1982, felt a new energy that would indeed lift the entire region over the next 15 years.

Charles "Tree" Young was a prototype tight end who came out of Edison High School in Fresno to the University of Southern California, where he played in the famed 1970 game at Alabama that is credited with ending segregation in Southern football. He was an All-American in 1972.

"I only got two or three passes a game, but averaged 20 yards a reception," he said. The '72 Trojans are considered the greatest team in college football history. Charles played for the Philadelphia Eagles and the Los Angeles Rams. He participated in the 1980 Super Bowl for the Rams before coming over to San Francisco. A total team player, he was used mainly as a blocker but was a key element in Bill Walsh's "West Coast offense" and a member of the 1981 World Champions. He finished his career in Seattle, where he is to this day a respected Christian minister.

The 49ers got off to a hopeful start in 1981, but nobody knew if they were for real. Then they traded a 1983 number two draft pick and option to exchange 1983 number one draft choices to the San Diego Chargers for veteran defensive end Fred Dean. All Dean did was earn the UPI Defensive Player of the Year award, the NFL Outstanding Defensive Lineman of the Year award, the NFC Defensive Player of the Year award, and a Pro Bowl spot. Another key acquisition was linebacker Jack "Hacksaw" Reynolds, a longtime Rams nemesis. He and Dean anchored the defense with Lott in the secondary.

Did you know that the 1981 49ers featured three rookies in the secondary? Aside from Ronnie Lott, there was Carlton Williamson and Eric Wright.

Well awwrrright! Take yer clothes and let's have a look at'cha!
—Rolling Stones frontman Mick Jagger when a nubile
young lass managed to make it onto the Candlestick
Park stage and practically throw herself at him,
during a Stones concert in October 1981

Morgan Breaks Dodger Hearts

THE 1978 GIANTS MANAGED TO CATCH LIGHTNING IN A BOTTLE. IF THE performance of the 1974–1977 and 1979–1981 Giants is to be considered representative of their abilities, the single year (1978) in which San Francisco streaked to a lead must be viewed as an anomaly of sorts. Their fold at season's end foreshadowed three more mediocre seasons.

By 1980, the club finished 11 games under .500, attendance down to 11th among 12 National League clubs. That was also the season Willie McCovey called it quits. Unlike Willie Mays, who was traded, and in a return to Candlestick (among other appearances) uttered bitter recriminations over perceived injustices that nobody else could understand, Willie Mac went out a class act.

"The ovation he received was heartwarming," recalled announcer Hank Greenwald of McCovey's farewell at the 'Stick in 1980. "It was all you could do to choke back tears."

The Giants established the Willie Mac Award, presented annually to the player who best exemplifies the spirit and leadership displayed by McCovey throughout his career.

"Like our cable cars, Willie McCovey will endure in the hearts of all those who love San Francisco," said former Mayor Dianne Feinstein.

"I played my whole career injured, my whole career," McCovey said.

"When McCovey told me, in a faraway voice, that he sometimes listens to old radio tapes of his final days as a Giant, it seemed so private. I felt as if I were eavesdropping," wrote Brian Murphy in *San Francisco Giants: 50 Years*.

"In *The Wonder Years* episode 'Odd Man Out,' best friends Kevin Arnold and Paul Pfeiffer get in a fight following a dispute over Willie

McCovey's baseball card," wrote Jesse Russell and Ronald Cohn in *Willie McCovey.*

McCovey remains among an elite core of great Giants stars who are still regularly seen at what is now called AT&T Park. "I believe the most important part of the Giants tradition is the great players that this club has," former star outfielder and manager Felipe Alou said. "This is the team of Willie Mays, Orlando Cepeda, Willie McCovey, Bobby and Barry Bonds, Gaylord Perry, and Juan Marichal."

In 2003 a statue of McCovey was erected outside AT&T Park. "I guess I've come a long way from that young guy in Mobile, Alabama, to having a statue here in San Francisco," McCovey was quoted saying in *San Francisco Giants: Where Have You Gone?* by Matt Johanson and Wylie Wong.

The 1982 Giants are very similar to the 1978 version, in that they had been a bad club in the years prior to that season, were contenders for a year, then slipped back into mediocrity until the arrival of Roger Craig and Will Clark.

"This organization is a loser," Jack Clark said. "We weren't handed a very good formula or a very good team, but we showed up anyhow."

"He was a guy who was somewhat misunderstood," broadcaster Hank Greenwald said of Clark. "People thought of him as petulant at times."

While they were not very good in the years after it, in '82 they contended. The Giants featured several old-timers who still had some gas left in the tank. Former Dodger Reggie Smith, a switch-hitter, slammed 18 home runs at age 37. What was the greater shock? For the fans, looking at the native Los Angeleno and ex-Dodgers star Smith, who literally attacked fans at Candlestick Park a few seasons earlier? Or for Smith, now wearing orange and black in a season in which his old hated rival would tear the heart out of his old team?

Another ex-foe, 38-year-old Hall of Fame second baseman Joe Morgan batted .289 with 14 home runs. Darrell Evans, age 35, contributed 16 longballs.

"Joe Morgan's greatest strength was as an offensive player, but he was a great all-around player as well," former teammate Tom Seaver recalled. "He could beat you in any one of three ways—with speed, with defense or with the bat."

Jack Clark was in his prime, hitting 27 homers with 103 RBIs and a .274 average. Old reliable Duane Kuiper hit .280 and Bob Brenly batted .283. Jeffrey Leonard, at 26 years, had come over from Houston and was in his sixth season. Chili Davis hit 19 home runs.

No pitcher won more than 13 games, but a strong bullpen helped the club stitch together 87 victories. Greg Minton pitched 269 1/3 innings without allowing a homer between 1978 and 1982. He saved 125 games in 13 years (1975–1987), and was an All-Star in 1982, finishing 10–4 with a 1.83 and 30 saves.

"My adrenaline flowed. I craved it," he said. "I'm a sinkerball pitcher, and you're not supposed to give up homers if you keep the ball low."

Minton was known to add a little something. "Just shows what sandpaper and Vaseline on a baseball will do . . . I had more fun than most people."

The club was led by feisty manager Frank Robinson, an all-time legend. He came from the playing fields of cross-bay Oakland, as had Morgan, and forged a Hall of Fame career that included MVP awards in the National League (1961) and American League (1966). After becoming the first African-American manager in Cleveland, he returned home and took over the Giants.

"I think Frank Robinson was such a gifted athlete that he found it hard for players not to play like a Frank Robinson," said Dan Gladden. "But there are very few people who can play at his level."

"He's underrated as a player," said Morgan. "He's underrated as a manager. He never gets credit for everything he's done. I don't know why."

"He didn't want any silliness out there," said Felipe Alou.

In 1982, the Atlanta Braves opened the season with 13 straight victories, but defending World Champion Los Angeles rallied and made a race of it. It looked to be a Braves-Dodgers horse race, but San Francisco stuck around and would not go away. On September 30 versus Houston

Ron Pruitt's "super blooper" keyed a Giants win that set the stage for the L.A. series.

It came down to a final three-game set at Candlestick Park. On Friday night, Jerry Reuss of Los Angeles shut out the Giants, 4–0 before a crowd of 53,281. On Saturday 46,562 fans had their hearts broken via a 15–2 Dodgers wipeout. On Sunday 47,457 fans came out to see if their favorites could play the role of spoilers, as L.A. still had a chance to catch Atlanta.

"But for me coming out of Cleveland and not having a chance of winning anything, that week and that whole year were exiting," recalled middle infielder Duane Kuiper.

By 1982, Candlestick Park was a real snake pit for the Dodgers. The rivalry with Los Angeles had always been intense, but loud, arrogant Dodgers manager Tommy Lasorda brought out the worst in San Francisco fans, who threw things at players and yelled the worst kind of epithets.

"I loved going there for that alone," said Dodgers third baseman Ron Cey.

"I remember walking back to the tunnel after a one-run loss, and something whizzed by me. It was a gin bottle," recalled star first baseman Steve Garvey, a particular target of Giants supporters.

Reigning Cy Young Award winner and Most Valuable Player Fernando Valenzuela went six innings but was removed by the despised Lasorda. Hard-throwing Tom Niedenfuer came on, but equally hard-throwing southpaw Terry Forster was called in with two men on and the left-handed hitting Morgan coming up. Lasorda was playing the percentages, which worked against Morgan getting around on a southpaw. But Morgan did get around on one and launched a home run over the right field fence, which ultimately held up in a 5–3 victory that sent the Dodgers home for the winter, and Giants fans home happy.

The date was October 3, the same as the final days of the 1951 and 1962 campaigns.

"I wanted this one for the Giants and the fans," said Morgan. "It meant so much for the Giants and their fans to beat the Dodgers that day."

"I was standing next to Frank Robinson outside the dugout and didn't think it was going to go out. . . . Half the fun was watching Lasorda squirm," Kuiper said. "When you see him rub his forehead and take that palm and drag it over his face . . . it's worth it."

⸺⁓⸺

The author of this book was a minor league pitcher in the St. Louis Cardinals and Oakland Athletics organizations. In 1982 he pitched in a Major League spring training exhibition game for the Oakland A's against the San Francisco Giants at Phoenix Municipal Stadium. He tossed three innings of scoreless work, the game announced back to the Bay Area by no less than Bill King and Lon Simmons. Joe Morgan, Rob Deer, Rickey Henderson, Joe Rudi, Mickey Tettleton, and Shooty Babitt all played in that game.

⸺⁓⸺

In 1983 the Giants began to issue Croix de Candlestick badges to fans who stayed until the last out of extra-inning night games. They read "Vini, Vidi, Vixi": "I came, I saw, I survived."

⸺⁓⸺

Darrell Evans hit three home runs in one game versus Houston at Candlestick Park in 1983. He hit 30 on the season.

⸺⁓⸺

Atlee Hammaker was 9–4 in the first half of 1983, and started the All-Star Game, but gave up a grand slam to Fred Lynn.

⸺⁓⸺

Mark Davis grew up a Giants fan, hating the Dodgers. His first Giants victory was an 8–0 shutout over L.A. at the 'Stick in 1983. Later he beat them 1–0 at Candlestick, then beat them again at Dodger

Stadium in a nationally televised Game of the Week. The Dodgers won the West that year. "To play for the Giants and beat the Dodgers three times, twice on shutouts," he said. "To me, that's a big deal."

—◦—

The second All-Star Game played at Candlestick Park was held on July 10, 1984. The first one, held in 1961, went a long way toward establishing Candlestick's reputation for inclement weather when a 100-degree day turned chilly and windy in a few hours, and reportedly Giants reliever Stu Miller was "blown off" the mound, causing a balk. In 1984 only Bob Brenly (.291, 20 homers, 80 RBIs) represented the Giants, but the weather was no factor in a 3–1 National League triumph played before 57,756 fans. Huey Lewis and the News sang the National Anthem. Gary Carter of Montreal was named Most Valuable Player.

—◦—

We used to get on each other in the clubhouse. We yapped it up and kidded around. It was a lot of fun. . . . When the game started he gave you every ounce he had. He never dogged it.
    —GIANTS PITCHER MIKE KRUKOW ON JOEL YOUNGBLOOD,
                 WHOSE BEST YEAR AS A GIANT WAS 1983
                      WHEN HE HIT 17 HOME RUNS

—◦—

Hitting in the leadoff spot was a dream come true.
    —JOHNNIE LeMASTER, NAMED AS THE SHORTSTOP ON THE
               GIANTS' ALL-DECADE TEAM (1980s)

—◦—

He was more valuable than anyone ever knew.
    —ALL-STAR RELIEVER GREG MINTON ON JOHNNIE LeMASTER

—◦—

People don't realize what his wife feels like in the stands.
—Pitcher Bob Knepper on Candlestick fans
booing Johnnie LeMaster

I wanted to be it cold and windy and foggy and gnarly.
—Mike Krukow on the "advantage" of
pitching at the 'Stick

I've got so many memories of the 'Stick that are baseball related, but here's one on a more personal note.

Candlestick was the perfect place to court a girl, especially one that loves baseball. It was so cold during night games that it was "snuggle to survive" and I always brought a blanket. It was the summer of 1984 when my first four or five dates with my wife Ann were Giants games. Our first game was in early August when the Giants faced the Mets and a 19-year-old kid named Doc Gooden, and by October we were married. Although attendance was low and you could move down into box seats with no problem, we used to move up under the overhang near the mezzanine level to avoid the biting wind and fog.
—Sir Francis Drake High School
graduate Greg Clementi

Super Bowl XIX: 49ers 39, Dolphins 16

IN 1983 THE 49ERS ADVANCED TO THE PLAYOFFS AGAINST A TREMENDOUS Washington club, led by Joe Theismann. In a battle of Notre Dame greats, San Francisco rallied with three fourth-quarter touchdowns, but two questionable calls did them in late. A Redskins field goal sent Washington, not San Francisco, to the Super Bowl.

"That bitter loss could have motivated or crushed us," said Montana. "If we had wanted it to bring us down and affect our play in 1984, we could have let it. It would have been easy. But we didn't do that because we had guys like Ronnie Lott, who wouldn't allow us to think like that. Ronnie was extra motivated because he had been called for the second penalty before Mark Moseley's winning kick, so he was one of the guys who pushed the team to get back to the play-offs the next season."

Though it can be argued that it was or was not their best season, 1984 remains a special year in 49ers history. Their 15–1 regular season record was the best. Several subsequent teams were 14–2, but the 15–1 mark remains a record few teams have ever matched. Only the 1972 Miami Dolphins, 14–0 in the regular season and 17–0 after the Super Bowl, are better.

The 1984 49ers did not have the running game of later teams, when Roger Craig came into his own. They did not have Jerry Rice yet, and their victory over Miami in the Super Bowl was impressive, yet not as thorough as the 1990 whipping of Denver, or even the 1994 destruction of San Diego.

However, they defeated Dan Marino and a Dolphins team that looked almost unstoppable. If San Francisco were to prevail, it seemed, Montana and company would have to score at will in a shootout. Montana indeed did lead his team to an offensive explosion, but the defense bottled up Marino.

Perhaps what separates this year from others was the fact that ultimate victory came before a partisan Stanford Stadium crowd. This made it a unique game in all of NFL history.

One loss to Pittsburgh prevented an unbeaten season. San Francisco rolled to their last nine wins in a row. The New York Giants and the Chicago Bears were no match in home playoff wins, 21–10 and 23–0 respectively. A victory over Miami at Stanford would make them pro football's first 18-game winner.

It was a team of leaders: Lott, Montana, Randy Cross, but "everybody on that team knew his job without anybody saying anything to them," said Montana.

Bill Walsh used psychology on the 49ers, especially Montana, who despite his status was still a young man in 1984. Walsh rarely complimented Montana, leaving the understood message that his performance was what he was capable of, and so it was just his job. When Montana would suffer a slight injury or take the bench at the end of a big win, Walsh would tell his back up something like "Great game." Montana at first was upset that he never got those small words of encouragement until he understood that he was expected to be great.

"Bill expected that high level of me all the time, so for him to say something like that to me, I had to do something that was way-out-of-the-ordinary great," said Montana.

Roger Craig was an immediate-impact rookie from Nebraska in 1984. Wendell Tyler was a talented running back from UCLA, although he had a lifelong problem with fumbles. Dwight Clark, Russ Francis, and Freddie Solomon were excellent targets for Montana in the "West Coast offense." This was still the heyday of Walsh's mastermind offensive schemes, still considered novel concepts. Later, when John Taylor and Rice came on and added extraordinary speed, their passing game spread the field, but the 1984 team still played ball control on the ground and in the air.

Some 49ers and members of the media claim in retrospect that nobody gave San Francisco any respect prior to the Miami game, as if Marino's team had it won already. This is not entirely true. The game was expected to be close, but nobody wrote off Joe Montana and the 49ers.

Marino's targets were Mark Duper and Mark Clayton, two fabulous pass-catchers. He had thrown for over 5,000 yards and 48 touchdowns.

An offensive line of Bubba Paris, John Ayers, Keith Fahnhorst, Randy Cross, and Fred Quillan protected Montana. The game started, and Montana had a 25-play script, a staple of the Walsh strategy, although there were divergences based on situations.

"There were very few games where we went past eight or nine—maybe 10—plays of the script," explained Montana.

"Stay on an even keel; don't let any one thing be any bigger than any other," Walsh told his team ahead of time. The familiar surroundings of Stanford Stadium also relaxed the coach and his team.

San Francisco was held on their first possession and punted. The defense of Lott, Hacksaw Reynolds, Keena Turner, and Fred Dean squared off against Miami's no-huddle offense. They scored on their first two possessions, an Uwe von Schamann field goal from 37 yards out, and then on a short touchdown pass. In between, Montana led San Francisco downfield for a TD. After the Dolphins went ahead 10–7, the Niners felt they might have to score every time they had the ball, so they amped it up. And that was what they did. Montana hit Craig from eight yards out. Montana scored on a six-yard run. Craig carried it in from the 2. Now it was 28–10.

"You want to give us short yardage; we'll take short yardage," Montana explained.

When Miami began to drop their linebackers, Craig and Tyler pounded for gains. Montana also had the chance to make some yards scrambling.

Miami's Reggie Roby, the best punter in the NFL, had an off day, helping the Niners in the field position war. Leading 28–10 was nerveracking "because Danny was so dangerous—and I mean *really* dangerous," said Montana.

But Lott, Eric Wright, and Jeff Fuller stepped up big time. Still, two Miami field goals narrowed the halftime score to 28–16, and it wasn't over. But San Francisco scored on a Ray Wersching field goal and a Roger Craig slant to make it 38–16, and that's how it ended up. Miami coach Don Shula said his team suffered a "total breakdown."

"As soon as it's over, it's like, 'Oh, God, now what do we do?'" said Montana, which explains the conundrum of sports greatness, or political victory, or life in general: always another hill to climb. The 49ers would have a letdown and not repeat the trick for three more years.

"I know one thing I'll always remember fondly about Super Bowl XIX is that we didn't go away to play it," recalled Montana. "It's always nice to go some other place to play a Super Bowl because it is something special, but I don't think I would have preferred going away. It felt good to stay home, despite the many distractions. It gave us an opportunity to play in front of the home crowd and for the people of the Bay Area to see us win one Super Bowl in person."

A famous photo shows Walsh, carried on the backs of his team, the rim of the familiar Stanford Stadium in the gloaming background, the sun having set in the west. It does not get any better than that.

—◦—

1980s 49er backup quarterback Jeff Kemp is the son of former Buffalo Bills quarterback, New York congressman, and 1996 Republican vice presidential candidate Jack Kemp. Kemp threw the first touchdown pass in the history of Candlestick Park, against the Oakland Raiders in 1961.

—◦—

3: the number of times in a row tackle Keith Fahnhorst was named All-Pro (1983, 1984, 1985).

—◦—

Has anybody ever seen actor Tom Selleck and 49ers tight end Russ Francis (1982–1987) in the same room? Francis greatly resembled the popular *Magnum P.I.* actor, an athlete in his own right at USC. Francis is a native of Hawaii, where *Magnum P.I.* was so famously shot.

—◦—

1,502: yards gained by Roger Craig in 1988, establishing a club record.

Craig and Clark and Mitchell and Dravecky and . . . "Humm Baby!"

Roger Craig was one of those guys who was "good enough" to lose 20 games. The North Carolina native broke in with the 1955 World Series champion Brooklyn Dodgers and was a key member of the first Los Angeles World Championship team in 1959. He was allowed to become subject to the expansion draft, however, and was selected by the original 1962 New York Mets. His 10–24 and 5–22 records with the 1962–1963 Mets look awful on paper, but in truth a man has to be an effective pitcher simply to stay in the rotation long enough, and to have enough decisions to lose 20 games.

While the late 1980s is looked back upon as a golden era dominated by Craig, it was as much the doing of general manager Al Rosen. It started when Bob Lurie called him for some advice on selecting a new GM and direction for the beleaguered club. Rosen, one of the most respected men in baseball, had been a star third baseman for the Cleveland Indians.

"And don't forget about me, Bob?" Rosen said to Lurie, assuring him he was interested in the position of Giants GM. Rosen was hired, and so was Craig. Prior to Craig, few pitchers were ever managers, but his success changed that perception. Today it is less rare for pitchers to manage. "He was an honest man who knew pitching," said Rosen. "And when you're going to make changes, you start with pitching."

"What Al Rosen was doing was eliminating all excuses for failure," said Mike Krukow. "He and Roger were like the winning couple from *Dancing with the Stars*—they were in sync."

The Giants team Craig took over in 1985 was a total disaster, but Craig turned them around very quickly. In 1986 catcher Bob Brenly hit

16 home runs, second baseman Robby Thompson batted .271, while Jeffrey Leonard, Dan Gladden, and Chili Davis contributed. He turned Mike Krukow into a 20-game winner.

But the entire team dynamic, which had changed when slugger Jack Clark was sent to St. Louis, materialized with the arrival of 22-year old Mississippi State All-American first baseman and 1984 Olympian Will Clark. Clark was one of the most ballyhooed prospects ever to arrive at Candlestick. "He became the story of the spring," recalled pitcher Mike Krukow, explaining that the team did not need to talk about losing 100 games in 1985. "It took a lot of pressure off us."

In the 1986 opener Clark came to the plate against the legendary Nolan Ryan in the first inning, announcing his presence with authority by slamming a home run to spur an 8–3 victory.

"As I was going to second," said Clark, "I just said to myself, 'Good it's 1–0.' Then I realized I had hit it off Nolan Ryan, and it was my first big-league at-bat. You have to smile about something like that." Catcher Bob Brenly then gave him his nickname: "Will the Thrill."

"It was just one of those things that seemed to roll off the tongue," recalled Brenly.

"He comes off cocky to some, but there's no questioning his ability," said Chili Davis. "He's a natural."

"Most young hitters are mistake hitters, not great hitter," said Ryan himself. "Will is a great hitter, a pure hitter."

"In those first couple of years, he was the heart and soul of the Giants," said longtime San Francisco media personality and ex–Giants announcer Ted Robinson.

Clark was a serious baseball man from the beginning, so some of the veterans decided to lighten things up. "It really got serious in 1986 because we had a ton of rookies on the team, guys like Will Clark, Robby Thompson and Bob Melvin," recalled Krukow.

"We're going to Wrigley one day, and as we pass the statue, I get up on the bus and make this speech about Giants tradition. I was fired up, telling the rookies that this was a ticket to a 10-year contract and gaining acceptance."

Krukow told the players of a special "tradition," which was to paint over a famed statue of an American hero named General Philip Sheridan on Lakeshore Drive in Chicago. "It was amazing," Krukow continued. "We had a big group of guys all over the statue, and they really did a job. They came back on the bus with paint all over themselves, and I told them they missed a spot; so they went and did it again.

"The upshot was that we had a Bay Area TV crew filming a documentary on the club. They asked if they could come along, and I told them OK on the condition they would just make copies for us and not air it.

"When we get back to San Francisco Al Rosen calls me into his office and reads me the riot act. He was hot, telling me he turned on the TV and all he saw was drunkenness and vandalism. It was difficult to keep from laughing."

(The Cubs got their revenge years later when one of their batboys became a Chicago vice cop and entered the Giants' visiting clubhouse to make mock "arrests.")

But Krukow backed it up on the hill. On July 3, 1986, Krukow defeated defending champion St. Louis 1–0 before 47,167 at the 'Stick. When Krukow won his 20th victory, an 11–2 win over Los Angeles on the final day of the '86 season, he recalled something teammate Candy Maldonado told him. "We were talking one day this summer," Krukow said, "and Candy told me, 'You're going to win 20 and I'm going to clinch it with a grand slam in L.A.' He really said it."

Maldonado *did* hit a grand slam that day, driving in six runs in total. "I had a dream it was going to happen," he recalled.

"That was a remarkable season because we turned it around and became a winner after losing 100 games in 1985," said Krukow. "Winning 20 has become more important to me through the years. I'm introduced as '20-game game winner Mike Krukow.' They don't do that when you win 19."

A series of young players came on the scene, the likes of which were Clark, Robby Thompson, and Matt Williams. Those young players became the inspiration for one of the more successful Giants marketing campaigns, spurring billboards throughout the Bay Area advising:

"YOU GOTTA LIKE THESE KIDS."

Also in 1986, Steve Carlton, who vowed not to speak to the media, briefly joined the Giants. "We will discuss nothing about the press," Carlton told a press conference. "I haven't talked in 10 years, and that's the way I like it."

"If he talks, I talk," said Jeffrey "Penitentiary Face" Leonard of Carlton. Leonard and Clark were too completely different cultural types who took some time to understand each other. "I knew I could get to Will. . . . I wanted to test him, but I never doubted his ability," Leonard recalled.

A natural left-handed line drive hitter with good power, in 1987 Clark drove in 91 runs and hit .308 with 35 home runs, but it was Craig who changed the entire culture and dynamic of the San Francisco Giants. The Giants had great players before Will Clark, but were deemed "losers," a term no less a star player than Jack Clark applied to them. Their ballpark was a "prison yard" . . . or a mausoleum. Coincidence or not, perhaps it was the unbridled success of the 49ers, displaying excellence in that very "prison yard," that gave the Giants no reason to make excuses. That and Craig's sunny optimism.

Craig's nickname came from his constant utterance "Humm baby." "We didn't have a lot of big name players," he said of the 1986–1987 Giants. "But we had youngsters like Will Clark, Matt Williams, and Robby Thompson and the next year, we were in the play-offs."

"Roger Craig came in and changed the personnel, and more than anything else, changed the attitude of the ballclub," said Bob Brenly.

"I don't want to hear any more complaints about this ballpark," Craig told his team.

In 1987, he was 57 years old. The Houston Astros were the defending division champions, while the Mets were the defending World Champions after a spectacular, rollicking, 108-win campaign. Both clubs would fail to meet the standards of 1986. The Dodgers, consistent contenders throughout the 1940s, 1950s, 1960s, 1970s, and 1980s, suddenly went into an odd tailspin in which the club either attained ultimate glory or fell flat on its face. The division was up for grabs, and after an 83-win season in 1986, Craig's club had an air of confidence about them. An amazing 52,020 fans packed Candlestick Park for the opener and got their money's worth in a typical Roger Craig baseball game: Giants 4, Padres 3 in 12 innings. Mike Krukow pitched eight gutsy innings before giving way to the bullpen. Chili Davis's single off future Giant Dave Dravecky plated Leonard and the Giants were off to the races.

The club finished April with 16–7, but on July 4 were a game under .500 (39–40). Under general manager Al Rosen, the Giants were no longer the bumbling fools who traded stars for washouts. The next day (July 5), Rosen traded Chris Brown, Keith Comstock, Mark Davis, and Mark Grant to the San Diego Padres for Dave Dravecky, Craig Lefferts, and Kevin Mitchell. Davis in particular would have great success, but in retrospect this was one of the best trades in Giants history, not just leading to victory in 1987 but a World Series appearance two years later.

First there was the acquisition of Mitchell. Mitchell had been a key figure on the Mets' World Series winners, which included a base hit that kept their rally alive against Boston. He was considered a "bad guy," however, a rough kid from a tough San Diego neighborhood. Despite his potential, the Mets unloaded him to San Diego, and now the Padres were telling him good-bye. A player like that was trouble.

Craig felt he could handle a player like that, harness his great talent and awesome power. Rosen made the move. Dravecky would become one of the most beloved figures in Giants history. The 31-year old lefty was in his sixth season. He was 3–7 with San Diego at the time of the trade, but was 7–5 down the stretch with San Francisco, winning key games to help the club win 90 games and the West by six over Cincinnati.

"That's the stuff you dream about in the backyard playing wiffleball," said Mike Krukow of clinching the division.

Rick Reuschel won 19 games that year. It was a period of baseball renewal in the Bay Area. The A's had resurrected their franchise a few years earlier when Charlie O. Finley finally sold the club to the Haas family of the San Francisco jeans dynasty, Levi Strauss. The A's featured the "Bash Brothers" and would become a near-dynasty. In 1987, 1,917,168 fans jammed Candlestick Park, a tremendous improvement over the 1970s and significantly greater attendance than their 1960s heyday, before the stadium was enclosed. It was good to see fans fill what for so many years were so many empty seats.

When San Francisco lost the playoff opener to St. Louis their backs were against the wall. Dravecky's masterful two-hit, 5–0 shutout in game two completely turned the tables, sending the series back to Candlestick Park on the strength of Giants momentum. That remains one of the greatest games ever pitched by a member of the San Francisco Giants.

"No question, this was by far the best game I ever pitched," recalled Dravecky.

The largest crowd in Candlestick history (57,913) met the club on October 9. After three innings, the home team led over St. Louis lefty Joe Magrane, 4–0. Leonard aggravated the Cards when he homered and circled the bases with his signature "one flap down" trot. But Giants starter Atlee Hammaker fell apart and St. Louis rallied to win, 6–5.

The next day, the Giants' backs were again against the wall, and they again rallied. Trailing 2–0, Mike Krukow settled down and Leonard hit his fourth home run in as many games. Krukow went the distance, scattering nine hits, but three double plays kept him out of trouble.

"If you were going into a battle in which your life or death depended on it, you'd better have Mike Krukow on your side," Al Rosen once said. Bob Brenly's eighth inning homer clinched the 4–2 victory over one of their great nemeses, Cardinal right-hander Danny Cox.

The next day 59,363 frenzied patrons jammed Candlestick. This time the hero was journeyman relief pitcher Joe Price. St. Louis got out ahead of Rick Reuschel early, but Kevin Mitchell drove Robby Thompson home with a single to tie the game. When St. Louis went ahead, it was Mitchell again, this time with a home run to tie it at two. A rare Will Clark error contributed to another Cardinal lead in the fourth, 3–2, but a four-run Giants bottom of the fourth made it 6–3. From there it was "hold 'em Joe Price" time, and he did, preserving victory and sending the series back to the Gateway City with San Francisco leading, three games to two.

At that point, the confidence in the Giants reached sky high levels. KNBR sports talk host Ralph "the Razor" Barbieri jinxed it for everybody when he "guaranteed" a San Francisco victory. As if to confirm Barbieri to be a speaker of untruths, the Giants were shut out twice at Busch

Stadium. The first wasted another Dravecky masterpiece as John Tudor out-dueled him, 1–0. In Game 7, Danny Cox was unhittable in a 6–0 put-away. A lasting memory of the series, however, remains Jeffrey Leonard's four home runs and .417 batting average, earning him the MVP award.

"When it's all said, Hac Man was one of the sweetest human beings I've ever met," Krukow said of Leonard, who masked his soft side with a tough exterior. "He was tough, but a tough lamb down deep."

"I put my heart and my life on the line right there," recalled Leonard, who was originally left off the Game 1 playoff lineup card but put back on when he showed his passion to the manager. "And Roger Craig respected it, embraced it and gave me the opportunity to play."

"It was uncanny," Matt Williams said of Craig's ability to make the right moves. "He would put the hit-and-run on first and second and nobody out, and it would work. He knew it would work."

"I don't want to take credit for anything," said Craig.

<hr />

The year 1988 was another one of those frustrating years that marked the entire Giants' Candlestick history. San Francisco would contend and come close, but as Charles McCabe had written more than two decades earlier, "ultimate victory is unsettling." By 1988, the old "second best is good enough" mentality did not hold water. The 49ers were a dominant pro football franchise that had zero problem going all the way, but the Giants were still bridesmaids to the glamorous Dodgers, who defeated cross-bay Oakland, four games to one, in the World Series. Giants fans had to sit and watch while fans of their hated rivals from the Southland, led by Tommy Lasorda, cheered with joy while Kirk Gibson hit a miracle homer off Dennis Eckersley.

The Dodgers of the 1980s were often in a strange miasma. Since the 1982 campaign, after which they lost the core of their famed infield (Steve Garvey, Davey Lopes, Bill Russell, Ron Cey), they either won divisions (1983, 1985) or were under .500 (1984, 1986, 1987). In 1988 Tom Lasorda pulled off a miracle. Led by ace pitcher Orel Hershiser simply pitching out of his mind, in the process breaking Don Drysdale's consecutive scoreless innings record with 59, they managed to capture the West, defeat a heavily favored Mets club in the National League Championship Series, then won Game 1 of the World Series when league MVP Gibson powered the homer, prompting announcer Jack Buck to say, "I don't believe what I just saw!" The powerful Athletics were seemingly a team for the ages, but fell to Los Angeles like Eastern Europe under Joseph Stalin.

This was no fun for Giants fans. While the 49ers, who captured their third Super Bowl a few months later, elevated sports expectation in the City, it was still Los Angeles who attained "ultimate victory" in baseball. The Giants were always second best.

Prior to the 1989 season, former Mets Cy Young Award winner Tom Seaver wrote in *Tom Seaver's 1989 Scouting Notebook* that Will Clark's "attitude is not as galling and arrogant as many observers surmised it would be. In fact, he even could be called a 'gamer.'"

It was faint praise at best, but that was the best Clark could hope for at the time. He then went on a season-long tear as if to show not that he cared what his critics said, but that his performance would rise above it.

While the season would be dominated by the offensive fireworks of Clark and left fielder Kevin Mitchell, it was the miraculous series of events revolving Dave Dravecky that mark the era and set in stone several dates as perhaps the most memorable in Candlestick Park history.

In 1988 Dravecky noticed a lump in his arm, but did not think it serious at first. Finally a doctor diagnosed him with cancer. He then met with pitching coach Norm Sherry and manager Roger Craig. "That meeting set the stage for what became a love affair with San Francisco," Dravecky recalled. Determined to make a comeback, he rehabilitated, and after a stint in the minor leagues, now felt recovered enough to try again. On August 10, 1989, 34,810 arrived at the 'Stick to see him pitch. Incredibly, he pitched seven shutout innings to earn a dramatic victory over Cincinnati. A devout Christian, Dravecky's performance had *miracle* written all over it.

"The highlight today was to be able to stand on the mound and give thanks to almighty God for the miracle that enabled me to perform," said Dravecky.

"When I first saw his arm, I didn't think he'd ever pick up a baseball again," said Craig. "I've seen a lot of things in baseball, but I can't remember a game with more drama than this one."

The entire story was yet to be written. On August 15 at Olympic Stadium in Montreal, Dravecky literally broke his arm throwing a pitch to Tim Raines of Montreal. He collapsed and had to be carried off on a stretcher. Eventually his arm had to be amputated, but Dravecky survived and remains a popular ex-Giant and incredibly inspiring figure.

"I've had so many challenges as an amputee that I try to be everything I can," said Dravecky.

"Obviously, he's as good a Christian and human being as there has ever been on the face of the Earth, but you gave him the ball, he wasn't afraid to knock an opponent on the ground," Brenly said of him.

"He was the most inspirational man I ever played with," recalled Chris Speier.

"I saw, with my own eyes, a miracle," said Craig. "It was almost spiritual how it happened."

"It was incredible. It was an amazing memory forever etched in my heart, simply because of the circumstances of the situation," Dravecky recalled. He helped raise $200,000 for a six-year-old San Mateo boy with leukemia, needing a bone marrow transplant, among numerous other acts of grace and inspiration.

"Baseball was just a stepping stone to something more important, and it culminated with that day," he said of the event. "My life is about my relationship with God, my relationship with my wife, kids, friends, and associates."

<hr />

In 1989, Roger Craig's charges came out with renewed purpose, but if they needed added inspiration, the dramatic events surrounding Dave Dravecky made them sure they were a team of destiny.

For the first time in franchise history, 2,059,701 fans passed Candlestick's turnstiles, breaking the magic two million mark. At that point in his career, the 25-year-old Clark looked like a good bet to make the Baseball Hall of Fame. He played in 159 games, hitting 23 home runs with

111 RBIs and a .333 average. Second baseman Robby Thompson teamed up with shortstop Jose Uribe to provide sterling defense up the middle. Outfielder Brett Butler was a sparkplug and defensive standout.

Then there was Kevin Mitchell. Indeed, Roger Craig, the good old boy from North Carolina, did more than "handle" the "rough" kid from the San Diego projects. He turned him into a bona fide superstar. Perhaps Mitchell's signature moment occurred on April 26 in St. Louis off the bat of Ozzie Smith. Smith hit a twisting, slicing liner down the left field line, not unlike the ball Yogi Berra hit that was caught by Sandy Amoros in the 1955 World Series. This one was foul, and Mitchell over-ran it toward the stands. The ball looked like it was going to drop behind him, but at the last second Mitchell instinctively stuck his *bare hand* out and caught the ball. Announcer Hank Greenwald sounded stunned, and ex–big leaguer Duane Kuiper, in the booth with him said, "In my entire life I've never seen that happen."

But Mitchell's bat was what propelled San Francisco. He had one of the best offensive seasons in Giants history, hitting 47 home runs, driving in 125, and batting .291 to earn the league MVP honors.

"The hard work I did before the season really paid off," he recalled. "I hit 12 home runs in spring training. And instead of getting weaker late in the season, I was getting stronger."

Former Braves and Dodgers slugger Dusty Baker had been brought in as a batting coach. He helped fine tune his swing. "I would hit two home runs in a game, and Dusty would say, 'I see something wrong in your swing', and he'd take me into the cage late at night to work on it."

"It was amazing the power he could generate," recalled Hank Green-wald. "It was almost as if at times the game was too easy for him."

"The Giants have been such an awesome team for me." Mitchell said of the turning point not just in his career, but in his life. "They've always been my team, and they're still my team."

"Best trade I ever made, but I had no idea Mitchell would be so good for us," Al Rosen said of acquiring Mitch.

On the mound, Rick "Big Daddy" Reuschel was 17–8 with a 2.94 ERA. He started the 1989 All-Star Game at Anaheim. While Juan Mar-ichal may have established a tradition of Giants pitching dominance at the midsummer classic, subsequent S.F. hurlers like Atlee Hammaker and Reuschel gave up monster shots. In 1989 Bo Jackson of Kansas City hit a memorable blast against "Big Daddy," but aside from the All-Star Game he pitched well and won a Gold Glove, too. Scott Garrelts added 14 victories with a fabulous 2.28 ERA. The bullpen stitched together 47 saves, 20 by Craig Lefferts, one of those brought over with Mitchell in the San Diego trade. Steve Bedrosian added 17 saves.

Nearing the season's end, Los Angeles exacted some satisfaction when they denied the Giants the opportunity to clinch, sweeping three straight at Dodger Stadium before the Giants won at San Diego to capture the West with a 92–10 mark, three games better than the Padres.

Future Hall of Famer Greg Maddux squared off against the Giants in the playoff opener between the Chicago Cubs and Giants at Wrigley Field. Clark's performance ranks among the greatest single-game efforts not just in San Francisco history, but in all of baseball annals. He hit a double and two home runs, good for six RBIs, in an 11–3 romp. Mitchell added a three-run homer for good measure.

This game also marked a new trend. Prior to one of Clark's home runs, a confab was held on the mound. Clark claimed to read Maddux's lips and knew what he was preparing to throw him. He promptly deposited it over the fence. When Maddux later learned of this, he took to holding his glove over his mouth so hitters—or spies—could not see what he might be saying. In subsequent years, this practice has made more sense. Obviously the chance that somebody watching the game in the clubhouse—or elsewhere—could communicate with the dugout was prevalent then and now, but recent technology like cell phone cameras and apps increase the possibility of such a thing being stolen.

The two clubs came to San Francisco tied at a game apiece. More than 62,000 people were on hand to witness Robby Thompson's two-run home run, propelling a 5–4 Giants win. A bullpen-by-committee held Chicago scoreless the last six innings to preserve the key victory.

Maddux may have been more careful in preventing Clark from reading his lips like the Lone Ranger, but there was no stopping his bat. Clark reached the Cubs' ace with two doubles and a single, plus Matt Williams, finally reaching his promise, provided a two-run homer and a two-run double to give San Francisco a 6–4 win and 3–1 series lead before 62,048 fans. It was again a combined bullpen effort—Kelly Downs and Bedrosian—that held Chicago in the last 4 1/3 innings. Clark was now six-for-six off Greg Maddux on the series. He must still see "the Thrill's" visage in his nightmares.

Finally on October 9, before a throng again surpassing 62,000, "27 years of waiting," as announcer Hank Greenwald described it, came to an end in one of the most exciting games in the 'Stick's long history. In 1962, when the Giants beat the Dodgers in Game 3 of the extra playoffs, it was at Dodger Stadium. This was a pennant-clinching win at home, a first.

Reuschel started and held the Cubs to a run in six innings. Will Clark, on a tear for the ages, tripled off Andre Dawson's glove and tied the game on Mitchell's sacrifice fly. In the eighth, tied at one, San Francisco loaded the bases . . . for Clark. Facing hard-throwing southpaw Mitch "Wild Thing" Williams, Clark fell behind 0–2, then fouled off two pitches. Then Clark lined a two-run single into center field, and that was enough to send the Giants to the World Series. Kevin Mitchell also batted .353 with two homers and seven RBIs in the playoffs.

In the postgame interview, doused in champagne, Clark was asked about the "pressure" by a TV interviewer.

"*Pressure?!*" he said in his squeaky voice. "I didn't feel pressure. This is why we play this game." It was typical Clark bravado. "He had a high squeaky voice, always making noise in the clubhouse," recalled owner Bob Lurie.

"He had a knack for knowing when everybody was looking at him to do something," said Brenly. "Those were the situations where he seemed to thrive."

"I hesitate to ever say it, but Will reminds me of Stan Musial," said Craig.

"He reminds me of myself," remarked Pete Rose.

Their opponent in the Fall Classic: cross-bay rival Oakland, at the apex of their Bash Brothers glory. While that Series would be remembered for things other than Giants victory or even baseball, in many ways it represented a real turning point in the Bay Area.

Since the 1950s, Southern California sports teams and Republican politicians held sway over liberal San Francisco, on the fields of play and at the ballot box. But in 1989 both Bay Area teams, the San Francisco Giants and Oakland Athletics, faced each other on the world stage. In football, the Rams were completely dominated by the four-time Super Bowl champion 49ers. This was a year of breakthrough; a few years later two San Francisco Democrats would turn the state "blue," and California would remain that way ever since. The Raiders would return to the Bay Area, abandoning L.A., and the Rams would move to St. Louis.

The '89 Fall Classic offers no Giants highlights, beyond a home run by Bill Bathe in his first Series at-bat, and Mitchell's blast off Mike Moore in Game 4. It was the Oakland dynasty, all the way; two wins at the Coliseum and two at Candlestick, for a 4–0 Athletics sweep. A well-worn posting on Oakland Athletics social media shows Dennis Eckersley and his teammates jumping for joy after sweeping Game 4 at the 'Stick, mockingly calling it the greatest event in the history of the old stadium.

"1987 and 1989 were highlights, pitching in the play-offs and doing well and winning for the first time as a team was sensational," said Krukow. "When you win, there's nothing else like it. When you lose, it's miserable."

—◆—

"I was living in Los Angeles in October of 1989 when my friend Howard Gibian called to tell me he had two tickets to game three of the World Series between the A's and Giants and Candlestick Park. I drove up on Monday and stayed at Howard's apartment in Walnut Creek. We decided to take BART to the game, scheduled for around 5:15 on Tuesday, October 17. We picked up the BART train around three or so, and at 3:30 give or take were riding under the San Francisco-Oakland Bay Bridge, at the bottom of the bay. About 15 or 20 minutes later we exited at the Daly City station, then boarded special buses for Candlestick Park. There was a lot of banter, many arrogant A's fans in their green-and-gold garb declaring the supremacy of their team, up two games

to none, predicting there would be a sweep and no
return to the east bay.

"But Candlestick, as Roger Angell said in 1962,
was 'a festive prison yard' with heavy accent on
tailgating, beer-drinking, and colorful bunting inside
the stadium. More than 62,000 fans packed the old
park, and most Giants fans just seemed happy to be
there, absent much in the way of expectations.

"The pre-game festivities were underway a little
after five p.m. Howard and I had several cold beers
and were thoroughly enjoying the ambience when the
stadium began to sway like crazy. We were sitting in
the second deck, but neither of us felt any danger. At
first we thought it was 'the wave,' the crowd stomp-
ing its feet, some kind of man-made act meant to
generate excitement. We quickly realized it was an
earthquake. Howard and I, native Californians, had
experienced many of those. This seemed no less
powerful than others we had lived through.

"The crowd, feeling the same way, cheered, as if
this was a sign from God stirring the Giants perhaps. Then I heard somebody say, 'The Bay Bridge
is down.' This was a report hitting the news, mostly
via radio as many TVs were off due to an electrical
outage, but radios were turned on and this was the
original report.

"We were not hearing, 'A section of the bridge
is down,' but rather 'the Bay Bridge is down.' This
was a monumental, shocking, incredibly disturbing
image; one of the great structures on Earth gone in
an instant, hundreds of cars, maybe 1,000 human
beings, hurtling to their deaths in the waters below,
or crushed by steel, or suffocating in the tunnel on
Yerba Buena Island. It was something out of a movie,
an epic disaster, *War of the Worlds* or something.

"People were aghast, talking about this event. I
recalled a book or novel I once read in which a Japanese spy living in San Francisco before World War II
watched every day while the Bay Bridge was being
built. Finally, when it was complete, a marvel of
engineering no other nation in the world was at that
time capable of duplicating, this spy wired back to

Tokyo that 'war with a nation capable of doing such things can never be won.' Yet, here Mother Nature had, at least we all felt at the time, destroyed something as remarkable as the trans-continental railroad, the L.A. Aqueduct, even the moon landing.

"So the players gathered on the field, their wives dressed to the nines, we were told the game was canceled, there was no electricity, and we filed out. Now what? How to get home? Howard and I thought about finding a bar and waiting it out, but figured alcohol was not our ally; we needed to keep our wits about us.

"We did not have a car, having taken BART. BART was completely out of the question. Had we driven, and been running late, we could have been on the bridge when the section collapsed, crushing an auto. We did find out on the radio, thank God, that this was the only thing that happened; the bridge was damaged but not destroyed. Hundreds of lives had not been lost, although many did die in the 'pancaking' of a freeway in Oakland, which was also on our route back to Walnut Creek if traveling by automobile.

"Had we had a car, I suppose we could have returned via the San Mateo Bridge, or we could have spent the night at my parents' house in Marin County, requiring a drive through a city no doubt snarled in traffic, over the Golden Gate Bridge that apparently was still operating.

"But this was not an option. A bus took us back to the BART station, which at least got us away from Candlestick. From there we found a nearby house, where two very nice young ladies kindly allowed us to come in, get a bite to eat, call our parents to tell them we were okay, and figure out what the heck was happening. My parents informed me our house was just fine; a relief. Electricity was on in their place and we saw news reports suggesting that there was ferry service back to the east bay, with a bus shuttle to Walnut Creek. Municipal buses were running for free. We figured where we could pick one up nearby and off we went.

"Sure as heck, a muni bus came and took us, without pay, to the Embarcadero in the downtown financial district. It was quite a display of civic mindedness, not charging money at a time of need. We walked across the street to the ferry terminal, where a line of people stretched around the block. I guess I am not proud to say this, but there was some kind of break in the line that allowed us to slip in way ahead of others, and we were on a ferry in an hour or so instead of two or three hours.

"That was eerie. We floated more or less under the bridge, staring up, with only the moonlight to see the damage. The city was silhouetted in darkness, no electricity, or little of it, on either side of the vast bay. It was a warm beautiful fall night, the best time of the year, the reason people move to the City in the first place. The people were very quiet. It reminded me of the survivors found walking the halls in *The Poseidon Adventure*. Few people had cell phones, so communication was not what it is today. Would their house be damaged, still standing? Their kids, their relatives, their friends, their schools, their places of business? Radio and news reports were exaggerated and while alleviating the initial shock of a destroyed Bay Bridge, still left many with images of the downed freeway, oil and gas leaks, or other affects. At that point we were figuring thousands had perished, many were trapped in buildings. Or worse.

"Eventually the boat landed and we identified a bus back to Walnut Creek. The streets were empty in Oakland as I recall, but we had to take an alternate route because the pancaked overpass at the Oakland maize was our normal route back. I cannot recall; we may have stayed on surface streets all the way, or most of the way back. Finally we arrived at the Walnut Creek BART station, where Howard's car was, and from there back to his apartment, undamaged. Walnut Creek looked pretty good and I think had electricity.

"It was probably midnight or later when we got home, some seven hours since the earthquake hit.

Maybe we had a beer or two and talked it over, went to sleep, and the next day I drove back to L.A. on Interstate 5, which parallels the San Andreas Fault.

"I've felt pretty darn strange about bridges ever since."

—San Francisco–born baseball fan Steven Travers

Catcher Bob Brenly was playing out of position, third base, on September 14, 1986, versus the Atlanta Braves at Candlestick Park. In the fourth inning he tied a Major League record, committing four errors in a single frame. Atlanta led, 4–0.

In the fifth, he hit a homer, and his two-run single tied the game at six in the seventh inning. Finally he hit a two-run homer off Paul Assenmacher in the bottom of the ninth to give his club a dramatic 7–6 win.

"This isn't your typical storybook finish—it's a novel," said Mike Krukow.

"This is the greatest 'Humm Baby' game of the year," declared Roger Craig,

"I went from the outhouse to the penthouse," said Brenly. "I was the Comeback Player of the Year in the afternoon. When Roger told me to catch, I thanked him. I didn't want to see another ground ball. I can laugh about it now, but I wasn't too pleased about the four errors at the time.

"It was frustrating, and I was supposed to start the game as the catcher. But Chris Brown showed up with a sprained eyelash, or something like that, so I'm at third base hoping they would hit the ball to somebody else. That game was like an out-of-body experience."

Chili Davis played for San Francisco from 1981 to 1987, and was a fan favorite. However, he was allowed to leave and sign as a free agent with the Angels after the 1987 division-winning season. This was viewed as comparable to the loss of Gaylord Perry, George Foster, Garry Maddox, and Gary Matthews in terms of bad deals.

John Lennon of The Beatles, who once created controversy by suggesting the musical group was more popular than Jesus Christ, was proven wrong 21 years after the group played to a half-empty Candlestick Park. On September 18, 1987, the Pontifical Mass attracted 70,000 Christian worshippers to the 'Stick.

The "Monsters of Rock" featured Van Halen and Metallica at Candlestick Park on July 16, 1988.

Will Clark broke the 100 RBI mark in 1988, and in 1989 drove in 111 with a .333 average. "Will the Thrill" left for Texas after hitting .283 in 1993.

Robbie Thompson was the 1986 Rookie of the Year and an All-Star in 1988 and '93. In 1991 he hit for the cycle versus San Diego at Candlestick. The former University of Florida Gator hit 19 home runs that year.

Giants GM Al Rosen believed his biggest mistake was allowing Brett Butler to go to Los Angeles after his three-year Giants career (1988–1990). He stole 31 bases for the 1989 pennant winners.

On July 29, 1990, Scott Garrelts fired a one-hit shutout to defeat that year's World Champions, the Cincinnati Reds, 4–0 at Candlestick Park.

⌐⌐

This season has been like 20 years for me.
—GIANTS SHORTSTOP JOSE URIBE, ACQUIRED IN THE JACK
CLARK TRADE PRIOR TO THE 1985 SEASON, ON HIS WIFE'S
DYING OF A HEART ATTACK, LEAVING HIM WITH THREE
CHILDREN TO RAISE; HE HIT .291 IN 1987 AND CONTRIBUTED A
GAME-WINNING SINGLE OVER THE CARDS IN A
PLAYOFF GAME AT CANDLESTICK, BUT WAS
NEVER THE SAME AFTER THE TRAGEDY

⌐⌐

*It means a lot. I never won anything in my life. Will was great. He
helped me out a lot. We were like batteries to each other. . . . Will and
I fed off each other.*
—KEVIN MITCHELL, WHO SOMEHOW SEEMED TO FORGET HE
WAS PART OF THE METS WORLD CHAMPIONSHIP TEAM THREE
YEARS EARLIER, RECALLING HIS CHEMISTRY AND WINNING WAYS
WITH WILL CLARK IN 1989

⌐⌐

*There is no such thing as Texas Leaguers in Candlestick. They all
become pop-ups for the catcher.*
—EX-GIANTS INFIELDER, CURRENT
BROADCASTER DUANE KUIPER

⌐⌐

*I don't have memories that I can specifically associate with the 'Stick,
but after Dravecky underwent his initial treatment for his cancerous
arm, he came back to pitch for a minor league team, San Jose, I believe
it was.*

*A couple of my buddies and I drove to San Jose to see his first game.
He pitched well, without problem, but I can't recall the final score or
his stats. However I most certainly remember the incredible support he
got from the small crowd in the stands. Around the same time I had*

been invited to a surprise birthday party to be held at a private golf club near Redwood City. The rather wealthy host wanted to surprise his wife with a huge turnout. Among the invitees were John Brodie, and some other active or retired professional athletes, including Willie Mays. I don't know how he knew these guys, but they showed up.

The birthday girl was to be driven to the site well after the guests had arrived. When she finally showed up in the parking lot, all of us guests were told to push back against the walls. The guy in front of me stepped on my foot. It was Willie Mays. He turned, and stuck out his hand, which was much bigger than mine, and apologized. He was just about my height, six feet, broader in the shoulder, with just the hint of a belly.

I told him I'd seen him play at old Seals Stadium when the Giants first came West. In very gentlemanly fashion he said, "You don't look old enough." He chuckled when I told him, "I was on my father's knee," so I admitted I was actually in college.

—Balboa High graduate Ray Batz

❧

This incredible feeling came over me. Everything seemed to go in slow motion. It was almost as if I was watching myself do this.

—San Francisco Giants: Where Have You Gone?, by Matt Johanson and Wylie Wong; quoting Bob Brenly on the day he made four errors in an inning, then redeemed himself to win the game

❧

I'd never make it as a player, so I thought maybe there was another way. . . . I try to make the dead spots of a game interesting. A bad game doesn't have to be a bad broadcast.

—Giants announcer Hank Greenwald (1979–1986, 1989–1996), a Syracuse University graduate who started with Lindsey Nelson, and later partnered with Ron Fairly

We make the best of it. Try to make money and come home safe.
—GIANTS 1986 ALL-STAR CHRIS BROWN, WHO DROVE A
TRUCK FOR HALLIBURTON DURING THE IRAQ WAR

*He was the greatest rookie in the history of the Giants franchise, not
for what he did in the field, but how much fun he was in the dugout
and in the clubhouse.*
—DUANE KUIPER ON MARK GRANT,
GIANTS PITCHER OF THE 1980S

*From that moment until the end of time, I promised myself, I would
always consider Candlestick my favorite sports venue anywhere.*
—*CANDLESTICK PARK,* BY TED ATLAS, ON THE STADIUM
HOLDING TOGETHER AFTER THE 7.1 LOMA PRIETA
EARTHQUAKE ON OCTOBER 17, 1989

"It Ain't Over 'Til It's Over"

UNDER COACH BILL WALSH, THE SAN FRANCISCO 49ERS WON THE SUPER Bowl in the 1981 and 1984 seasons. After both of those years, they experienced letdowns. In 1982 the NFL players struck, limiting the regular season to nine games. The Niners never got untracked and failed to contend.

The 1984 team is considered by some to be the best ever. Unlike 1981, they were a perfect combination of youthful veterans, superstars and team players, running and passing, quick-strike offense and stifling defense, and brilliant coaching. They were a dynasty, all but unbeatable. The great Dan Marino and his high-powered Miami Dolphins fell like the North Korean defenders at Inchon, with the MacArthur-like Montana leading San Francisco to resounding victory.

It seemed after that game nobody could stop San Francisco except San Francisco and their own hubris. In reality, the Niners did not completely fall apart in 1985 or 1986. The '85 Chicago Bears and '86 New York Giants were juggernauts who could beat anybody, which they did in those seasons.

By 1987, however, the 49ers appeared to be just another good team in a conference that had finally found its power base after years of falling to the AFC. Pundits questioned whether Walsh was looking for another challenge. Hotshot quarterback Steve Young was brought in by trade from Tampa Bay, causing immediate controversy. Having "failed" to lead his team to Super Bowl victories over the previous two seasons, Montana now faced the fickle San Francisco "What have you done for me lately?" crowd.

Another strike hit in 1987, and again it seemed to throw the team off stride. The fractured season produced a Washington–Denver Super Bowl. John Elway, anointed as the next great quarterback—a "replacement" for

Montana—was totally outplayed by Washington's Doug Williams, the first black quarterback to lead his team to a world title.

San Francisco's regular season performance in 1988 had nobody talking about their place in history. The Niners opened 5–2 but slumped to 6–5, two games out of first place in the NFC West. Then they beat defending champion Washington to launch a four-game winning streak. Their 10–6 mark was good enough to capture the division crown, but they were not a big favorite to go all the way. That said, they had Montana and Jerry Rice. No one was betting against them either.

San Francisco had the good fortune of getting healthy in time for the playoffs. Eric Wright had a combination of ailments and age plaguing him, but he was ready to contribute at the end. Tim McKyer was able to come into his own that year. John Taylor missed some games early but was back. Montana had a bad back, but Steve Young filled in nicely. Joe was ready to go for the playoffs.

The team was "very loyal to Joe," said Wright, an All-Pro cornerback. "We had played with him over the years and in two winning Super Bowls, so we were supporting him 100 percent.

"We knew that when he was in there we could be down by a touch-down with two minutes left and he would bring us back."

The Rams had faltered late in the season to give San Francisco the edge they needed in winning the division crown, and with it better home-field advantage rather than the wild card. Neither Minnesota (34–9 loss at Candlestick) nor Chicago (28–3 losers) was a match for them.

The Bears game was a very important one in that it was played in freezing conditions at Soldier Field. Pacific Coast teams are notorious for their inability to meet the cold-weather challenge (e.g., Chargers, Rams), but the great ones do (e.g., 49ers, Raiders). With two weeks to rest and prepare, the Super Bowl now represented the prospect of a reward in the form of Miami temperatures.

However, the Miami experience was not all bikini-clad models and South Beach revelry. Race riots in Miami's Overtown section cast a pall over the proceedings, although the hotel of their opponents (Cincinnati again) was closer to the riots than was the 49ers'.

According to Wright, the team managed to enjoy the nightlife, but they maintained their work ethic through veteran leadership, not heavy curfews. Bill Walsh was never big on that kind of thing, preferring to treat his charges like adults.

The Bengals featured a terrific southpaw quarterback, league MVP Boomer Esiason, and running back Ickey Woods. Cincinnati coach Sam Wyche had once been mentored by Bill Walsh when he was an assistant under the legendary Bengal taskmaster Paul Brown. What no one realized before the game was that it was Walsh's last as a pro coach, not to mention star center Randy Cross's final contest.

Cincinnati was not going to let Walsh's scripted offensive scheme roll out to a 20–0 lead this time out of the gate. Bad omens reared their ugly head for the Niners when offensive tackle Steve Wallace broke his leg early. Then nose tackle Tim Krumrie broke *his* leg. The field conditions were not good as a result of a poor "vacuum system" put in place before the game. A lesser team would have been put off their game by the conditions and injuries. This team had Montana and Lott.

They "had to put it into your mind that was just a normal thing that happened in the course of the football game," recalled Wright. "We didn't want to be wary about the field because it would slow us down."

The "trademark" opening drive for a TD did not happen, setting the team off its confident pace. Instead of allowing it to be "disconcerting," according to Wright, it was "just up to the defense to stop the Bengals offense. Our defense prided itself on keeping the other team in check until the offense got going—that was a formula for winning."

Cincinnati got the ball, bound and determined to score and give their ebullient star, Woods, a chance to do the famed "Ickey Shuffle." He picked up yardage but was held short of the end zone.

Michael Carter, Charles Haley, Keena Turner, and of course both Wright and Lott came to play. Despite the ballyhoo of both teams' offenses, it was quickly determined that Super Bowl XXIII would be a hard-hitting, grind-it-out defensive battle. Because of the "West Coast offense," featuring a short passing scheme and creative patterns, the 49ers were thought of as a "finesse" team, which of course is ridiculous considering the true nature of pro football. "But the defense wasn't like that," said Turner.

Lott was a maniac on the field. Corner Don Griffin and safety Jeff Fuller emulated him as best they could. Mike Walter and Turner would alternate, depending on whether it was a passing or running down. Jim Fahnhorst stayed in most plays.

The strategy was to play the fast Bengals receivers—Cris Collinsworth, Tim McGee, and Eddie Brown—aggressively instead of trying to contain them. It was risky but it worked. Collinsworth broke for a long gain early against Wright, forcing Eric to respect his speed.

Montana broke the early logjam by driving his team from inside their own five to a Mike Cofer field goal and a 3–0 lead. In the first half, Walsh stayed with ball control: short passes and handoffs to Roger Craig (1,000-plus yards rushing that season) and Tom Rathman. San Francisco had a chance to create some breathing room, but Cofer missed an easy field goal. Then, after a long John Taylor return of a punt, they drove deep into Cincinnati territory only to lose a fumble. Jim Breech managed a field goal to tie it for Cincy at the half, 3–3. The announcers all expressed amazement that their prognostications of a wide-open offensive "bonanza," as Niners broadcaster Joe Starkey liked to call it, had not been realized.

Cincinnati established themselves as a major challenge, taking over in the third quarter. They maintained a nine-minute possession resulting in another Breech field goal to forge ahead 6–3. While the Bengals were disappointed not to have scored a touchdown, they had put Montana and company on their heels, forced to watch from the sideline, while wearing out the defense. The 49ers were listless and punted, but Bill Romanowski's interception of an Esiason pass reversed momentum at a critical juncture. Cofer's subsequent field goal tied it 6–6. It was obvious that this was shaping up to be a Super Bowl for the ages. Very few Super Bowls up to this point had lived up to the hype.

The hype was increased and the Niners momentum totally stifled when Cincinnati's Stanford Jennings ran the kick back all the way to make it 13–6. Luck then played a role. Montana veered away from the close-to-the-vest style he had heretofore employed, hitting Jerry Rice and Roger Craig with long passes to push close to the Bengals' goal. Then a

Montana pass intended for Rice or Taylor was dropped by cornerback Lewis Billups. Given reprieve, Montana hit Rice for a touchdown to tie it 13–13.

Cofer missed a field goal, and Breech made his to give the Bengals a 16–13 lead, but most of the world had one thing on their minds as San Francisco took over with some three and a half minutes remaining. Joe Montana, starting at his own 8-yard line, was in his element.

Montana, a legend, an athlete of mythological proportions, a San Francisco icon perhaps over and above all others—Walsh, Lott, Joe DiMaggio, Willie Mays, Barry Bonds—will be remembered for directing his team to four Super Bowl championships, countless big victories, and many "two-minute drives." In 1982 against Dallas the Catch was thrown by him but pulled down by Dwight Clark. In the 1985 Super Bowl the Niners dominated from start to finish. Montana was less "clutch" in 1989 than he was polishing his Canton statue.

His performance down the stretch against Cincinnati in Super Bowl XXIII, however, epitomized his cool nature. One particular incident stands out above all others. He hit five passes in a row, several to Rice, and had his team driving. The mindset of the club had gone from that of a tying field goal to a winning touchdown. With time called on the field, Montana stood amid his "band of brothers," each looking at him as if he were Henry V at Agincourt.

Then Montana noticed the comic actor John Candy, at that time one of the biggest stars in Hollywood, standing on the sideline.

"Hey, check it out," he remarked. "Isn't that John Candy?"

With the weight of the world on his shoulders, Montana appeared to be as calm as a stargazer on Hollywood Boulevard. It was the roly-poly Candy, observing Montana, who realized he was in the presence of *true* greatness.

Having taken their "Candy break," San Francisco resumed the drive with cool efficiency. A long pass to Rice, almost a touchdown, put the ball inside the Cincinnati 20. Montana had done it to Sam Wyche's team in a similar manner in 1987. Everybody *knew* he would come through again. Montana hit Craig down to their 10. Now they had the field-goal option, but wanted a TD first and foremost. Time-out was called with less than a minute remaining.

Cincy figured it was Rice, who had gotten all the throws in the drive. John Taylor went into the middle, breaking for a split second, which was all Montana needed to hit him in the end zone, breaking Bengal hearts.

Rice was named MVP, having caught over 200 yards' worth of passes. Montana threw for over 350 on the game, with two scores. Many 49ers say it was their sweetest victory of all, for good reason. They had struggled, yet succeeded. Walsh's retirement made him a rare thing in sports. Few leave on their own terms at the height of their success. Walsh has his detractors. He was a man of big ego and rubbed some the wrong way. His moniker, the Genius, is felt to be over the top by some. It was not. He is to football what Steven Spielberg is to filmmaking, Ernest Hemingway to writing, Abraham Lincoln to statesmanship.

In the 1981 draft, San Francisco got Chicago's second round draft pick via trade. With it, they selected 6'1", 180-pound cornerback Eric Wright from Missouri. Dwight Hicks, Keena Turner, Carlton Williamson, and even Jeff Fuller may have been more heralded players in the 1980s than Wright, who was platooned depending on defensive play situations. In San Francisco, Wright's success can be attributed to his role in that system, which he thrived in from 1981 to 1990 (making All-Pro in 1985).

49ers Greatest Overtime Games

1980: 49ers 38, Saints 35
1988: 49ers 16, Broncos 13
1990: 49ers 20, Bengals 17
1996: 49ers 19, Redskins 16

Most Super Bowl Championships

6—Pittsburgh Steelers
5—San Francisco 49ers
5—Dallas Cowboys
4—Green Bay Packers
4—New York Giants
4—New England Patriots
3—Oakland/Los Angeles Raiders
3—Washington Redskins

"It was also a defining year in the L.A.-San Francisco rivalry. For years, Los Angeles teams destroyed Bay Area teams. There were exceptions, mainly in the form of an Oakland A's dynasty and great Oakland Raiders squads, but until Joe Montana and the 49ers lit up pro football, the scales were heavily weighted in favor of the south. In the 1980s, however, the Dodgers slumped a bit, the Rams slumped a lot, and USC fell precipitously, at least by their lofty standards. California and Stanford were not exactly bringing back memories of Brick Muller and Frankie Albert, but they would over the next few years compete on a relatively even playing field with Southern California and UCLA. Certainly the old Bruin basketball dominance was a thing of the past.

"In 1989, the Detroit Pistons ended the Lakers' run. Kareem Abdul-Jabbar retired and Murray wrote that he finally shut his many critics up. 'God made him more than seven feet tall,' he wrote. 'He took care of the rest.' He was finally 'winning with class.'

"Then came the baseball season. The defending World Champion Dodgers struggled and the Angels never contended. Our National Pastime was a Bay Area affair, its teams exciting, featuring thrilling players like Will Clark, Kevin Mitchell, Matt Williams, Jose Canseco, Mark McGwire, Rickey Henderson, Dave Stewart and Dennis Eckersley. The A's in particular looked at that time like a collection of future Hall of Famers. In the case of Henderson, Eckersley and manager Tony LaRussa, they were.

"The sight of winning A's teams were not new, but for Dodgers fans, who for years laughed at the incompetent Giants playing in front of rude, foul-mouthed fans in the fetid Candlestick Park, the sight of the orange-and-black beating the Chicago Cubs in the NLCS to advance to the Fall Classic, the biggest of stages, well, that was an affront. Coming in confluence with utter 49ers dominance, it seemed as if the globe was off its orbit.

"Southern Californians generally adopted the Athletics, to the extent they had a rooting interest in the Bay Bridge series. Oakland rolled, winning the first two games. They were on a mission, to exorcise the demons of Kirk Gibson's monumental shot off Eckersley. But nobody remembered much of anything other than a major earthquake just as game three was about to start at Candlestick Park.

"The Bay Area re-grouped and the two teams ventured into the hinterlands to practice until it could be resumed. It was as anti-climactic as any event in sports annals. Oakland won two easy ones and that was that.

"Murray loved San Francisco's skyline, bridges, bay and mountains. He was not enamored of its people, its politics, its low rent anti-L.A. fans throwing garbage and screaming obscenities at Tommy Lasorda, a baseball ambassador who believed in God and loved his country. Over the years Murray found a certain amount of satisfaction in writing how Divine Providence seemingly smiled on the Southland while turning San Francisco into a symbolic pillar of salt.

"He wrote that Los Angeles hosted major sporting events almost annually—Super Bowls, Rose Bowls, World Series, NBA Finals, basketball rivalries for the ages, collegiate football wars, two Olympics—virtually without a hitch. The weather was always perfect, the fans well behaved (like they had been there before, which they had), the events well-ordered absent riots and disasters. But San Francisco, a place that got a major event only occasionally, seemed doomed by dame fortune in the form of a completely rare Pacific rainstorm (1962) and a 7.1 earthquake (1989).

"But try as Jim Murray might to put Northern California down, to put them off and laugh them away, they were comers by 1989. John Robinson's Los Angeles Rams thought they had a pretty good football team that season. Late in November they hosted the 49ers at Anaheim Stadium on Monday Night Football. Al Michaels informed the viewing audience that Joe Montana was having what some historians were beginning to say might be the single greatest season any quarterback had ever had.

"With the hometown fans cheering wildly and pub denizens doing the same, the Rams built a big early lead. Then came Joe. 11 years after he rallied Notre Dame to the lead at the nearby Coliseum (before Frank Jordan's field goal gave USC the win), this time Montana was completely unstoppable. If Michaels had a point that Montana was having the best season in history, he probably wrapped that up on this evening, which may have been the best individual game ever played. He passed for 439 yards, rallying San Francisco to a 30–27 win. The Rams were done.

"Los Angeles could not compete with Montana and the 49ers. When they met again in the NFC championship game, it was a joke. San Francisco 30, Los Angeles 3. Afterwards Murray wrote, 'I thought Joe Montana was human.' He 'glows in the dark.' Giving him the ball was tantamount to 'giving Rembrandt a brush or Hemingway a pen.' For 'Joe World' . . . 'good field position' is his 'own three-yard line.' He returned to the well worn but always brilliant comparisons: Spencer Tracey acting, Jascha Heifetz fiddling, Ty Cobb at the plate, and one of his obvious faves, the ballet artist Vaslav Nijinsky.

"Murray was not finished. After the 49ers utterly annihilated Denver in the Super Bowl, he wrote a column on January 29 that was so good picking out really good lines from it is impossible. It was one of those pieces where you read one line and figure that is the best one, but the next is just better. It was absolute vintage Jim Murray. First, he listed things 'that shouldn't happen.' Among them was clubbing baby seals and other obvious things. Then he added to the list 'the Denver Broncos in the Super Bowl.'

"'Where is the Humane Society when you need it?' he wrote. 'Where are those organizations against cruelty to dumb animals?'

"The Broncos 'went to their fate like guys going to the electric chair . . . Cagney did it better.' Then, 'It wasn't a game, it was an execution. It was the biggest mismatch since the Christians and the lions.'

"He urged Bud Grant and the Vikings to return in order to re-claim their 'Super Bowl record for futility.' The Broncos were 'the William Jennings Bryans, the Harold Stassens, Tom Deweys of football.' This was classic stuff. Murray refused to write down to his audience. Many Los Angelenos had no idea who Williams Jennings Bryan, Harold Stassen or Tom Dewey were, but he refused to 'dumb it down.' It has been reported by many readers and observers that a Murray column caused them to find a history book or a library in order to learn more. The Internet was not around until very late in his career. Had it been throughout his years at the *Los Angeles Times*, Jim Murray's on-line columns would likely have engendered more Google searches than any other source.

"'They should have a clause in the wire agreement with the league that they don't have to play in a game under 5,000 feet,' he wrote of Denver.

"'And they shouldn't play the San Francisco 49ers anywhere.'

"Not only were the 49ers better 'they looked better in their uniforms. . . . The outcome was as foregone as a tidal wave.' As for Joe Montana, he probably could 'walk on water' and bullets 'probably bounce off him.' Giving him tools like Jerry Rice and Roger Craig was like 'giving a lion horses.' Anybody who enjoyed the Niners' destruction of the Broncos probably enjoyed pictures of 'the German Army going through Belgium.'

"'The 49ers aren't a team, they're a scourge. A dynasty . . . an empire.'"

—*The Poet: The Life and Los Angeles Times of Jim Murray*, by Steven Travers

Dynasty

As described in this author's previous book . . .
"The San Francisco 49ers dynasty lasted from 1981
to 1994, or until 1998, depending upon one's
standards. With all due respect for great teams of
the pre–Super Bowl era (Wellington Mara's Giants,
George Halas's Bears, Curly Lambeau's Packers,
Johnny Unitas's Colts, Paul Brown's Browns) and
dynasties of the modern game (Vince Lombardi's
Packers, Tom Landry's Cowboys, Al Davis's Raiders,
Chuck Noll's Steelers, Bill Belichick's Patriots), the
49ers' run is the longest, most sustained, and most
successful in NFL history.

"The run includes two Hall of Fame quarterbacks
(Joe Montana, Steve Young) and three coaches (Bill
Walsh, George Seifert, Steve Mariucci). In addition
to the five Super Bowl victories, the Mariucci-Young
teams of the mid-to-late 1990s were excellent, albeit
not Super Bowl clubs. San Francisco survived transition, replacing legends with capable second acts. They
found a winning formula that stood the test of time.

"Of all the great teams and moments, one stands
out. That was the 1990 Super Bowl victory over Denver. If San Francisco was an empire, this was Caesar
returning to Rome parading the prisoners from Gaul.

"The 1981 club was a surprise champion. Many
argue that the 1984 club was better, but the victory
over John Elway and Denver in Super Bowl XXIV was
so enormous as to surpass all other glory.

"San Francisco won three World Championships
under Bill Walsh (1981, 1984, 1988). The '88 title
was a hard-earned one. The team teetered on the
brink, survived a less-than-stellar regular season, got
hot in the playoffs, and rallied to beat Cincinnati in
the Super Bowl.

"Walsh retired and was replaced by George
Seifert from Lincoln High School in San Francisco.
Seifert's hiring and success sheds light on an odd

fact, which is that Northern California is the 'coaches capitol of America.' The Bay Area is not to be confused with Orange County, Texas, or Florida when it comes to producing high school football talent (although few other geographic locations rank much higher in actuality). Perhaps it is the leafy affluence that produces academic success, and in football terms, winning strategic thought, but excellent coaches seem to spawn from the 415, the 510, the 408, the 925, and the 707.

"Dick Vermeil (UCLA, Rams Super Bowl champs) hails from little old Calistoga. Pete Carroll (USC national champs, Seahawks Super Bowl winners) went to Redwood High in Marin County. Walsh is from the San Jose area and coached at Washington High in Fremont before a long career in college and the pros. Paul Hackett, one of the architects of the 'West Coast offense' as a 49ers assistant, hails from Orinda. Bob Toledo, who had a good run at UCLA, is from San Jose and San Francisco State. John Madden (Raiders) and his boyhood pal John Robinson (USC, Rams) both came from Daly City. Walt Harris (Pittsburgh, Stanford) is from South San Francisco. Jack Del Rio of Hayward coaches the Raiders. Mike Holmgren, like Seifert, went to Lincoln High and was considered a better prep quarterback than San Jose's Jim Plunkett before riding the bench at USC and coaching Green Bay to the Super Bowl title. With the exception of Del Rio (an SC All-American and Vikings star), none of these men were considered great players at the college or pro levels.

"Seifert was a defensive expert, a guy with the perfect, quiet mind and demeanor to work with the more flamboyant, media-savvy Walsh. On a team of superstars, he was expected to maintain status quo, but he did more than that. Seifert is viewed by history as a guy who inherited greatness instead of developing it, but he deserves kudos because many coaches with talent find ingenious ways to screw it all up. He did not. The 1990 49ers indeed featured Holmgren as their offensive coordinator. Neither Holmgren nor Seifert 'rocked the boat,' so to speak.

"'The team had been together for so long that roles were already defined,' explained All-Pro linebacker Matt Millen (who came over after years of success with the Los Angeles Raiders), in *Super Bowl: The Game of Their Lives*. "The guy who stood tallest in the locker room was Ronnie Lott. . . . He was inherently a leader. . . . It drove him crazy when other defensive guys wouldn't play like he wanted them to play. He stuck to the defense, but I would say that Ronnie was the heart and soul of the entire 49ers team.'

"Millen referred to Montana as 'Joe Cool.' Lott was verbal. Montana was quiet, and in that quiet demeanor he led the team, giving them supreme confidence in themselves.

"Wide receiver Jerry Rice, by 1990 established not only as the finest wide receiver in the NFL but already eliciting commentary that he might be the greatest ever, was 'almost inhuman to me,' said Millen. 'I thought this guy was a freak of nature. No one could work like that and not be tired.'

"Rice had grown up learning how to catch actual bricks, thrown to him by his father, a mason. The opposite of Rice, both in terms of field position and personality, was the other talented receiver, John Taylor. Perhaps, had he possessed Rice's intensity, he would have been a Hall of Famer too, but he certainly enjoyed some big moments with the 49ers.

"Roger Craig out of Nebraska was a tremendous running back, complemented by the workmanlike Tom Rathman, who was willing to handle the role of blocker. Craig, like Rice, was literally a physical specimen, and he possessed focus as well.

"Millen, despite a great reputation forged in L.A., knew that on this team he needed to earn respect. Normally a physical player in practice, he had to adjust to the 49ers method, which did not focus on this type of approach, but in the games he, Lott, Charles Haley, and Michael Carter established their respective bona fides.

"San Francisco operated a revised 3-4, but with Millen taking over the middle and calling signals, they became a 4-3. There was little situation substitution and not much blitzing. Their philosophy can be compared to John Wooden's man-to-man defensive approach during the heyday of UCLA basketball. With superior talent, they did not need to rely on tricks or surprises. The 'Niners operated out of a 'man-zone' in which roles were specifically adhered to based upon a logical play progression. It was the kind of system that only works if the players have the size, speed, and ability to make it successful. Seifert was disciplined enough to let it operate in this manner, rather than push the proverbial 'panic button.'

"1989 was arguably Montana's best year, and the 1989 49ers offense is considered by many to be the best 'ever to grace the field in the National Football League,' according to Millen. Their legend had been made on a Monday Night Football game at Anaheim when Joe directed the team to a remarkable comeback win over the Rams. Montana's statistics generally are not as impressive as some of the other great quarterbacks, namely Dan Marino and John Elway, to name a couple. He is considered a 'winner' above all statistics, but in 1989 he put up impressive single-game and single-season numbers, carrying that into the postseason.

"After a 14-2 regular-season mark, San Francisco opened the playoffs with Minnesota, who had humiliated them in 1987. Montana directed a total conquest of the Vikings, 41–13.

"John Robinson's Rams were next. Perhaps they held out hope the team that led San Francisco well into the second half before collapsing a month and a half earlier could maintain that kind of effort for four quarters. Instead, San Francisco dominated from start to finish, 30–3. In many ways the game capped the changing sports dynamic of the San Francisco–Los Angeles sports landscape. Prior to Joe Montana, the Dodgers dominated the Giants, and the Rams had their way with the 49ers. This mirrored the north-south sociology, with L.A. considering themselves superior, San Francisco green with envy because of it. Now it was different. Not only were the

Rams a pale 'rival' of the 49ers, but in 1989 both
Bay Area baseball teams, the A's and Giants, made it
to the World Series.

"For Millen, it was his third Super Bowl, having made it to New Orleans in 1981 and again to
Tampa in 1984, both with the Raiders. The 1990
Super Bowl was also in New Orleans; San Francisco's
fourth in nine years. They needed to win it in order to
match bragging rights of the 1974–1979 Steelers.

"Millen had been on a Raiders team that, according to myth at least, had partied in New Orleans
the week of their easy 27–10 win over Philadelphia
in 1981. The 49ers were much more corporate in
nature. Little in the way of high jinks was reported.

"The AFC champions were the Denver Broncos,
making their third Super Bowl appearance and second
with young quarterback John Elway, a hotshot from
Stanford. Elway possessed all the tools Montana did
not; size, speed, a rocket arm, all-around athleticism.
Going strictly by the book, there was no comparison.
Elway was the better prospect. But of course every
intangible favored Joe. That said, Elway was so good
and had been so close for several years now, it seemed
that his time had come. It was assumed that in order
to defeat Denver, San Francisco would have to win
an offensive shootout. But defensive coordinator Ray
Rhodes, team leader Ronnie Lott, and Charles Haley
made no such concessions. Lott in particular had
faced Elway when he was at USC. In his mind, Trojan
dominance would carry over to 49er dominance.

"When the hoopla finally came to an end and
the game started in front of 72,919 on January 28,
1990, at the New Orleans Superdome, Elway was off
and the Broncos were stopped stone cold. Montana
responded by moving San Francisco down the field
as if Denver was a high school team. It was 7–0 just
like that. Whether Denver tried a zone or man-to-
man, their defensive capabilities were no match for
San Francisco, especially rested after the NFC title
game—fully prepared, healthy, revved up.

"Elway led the Broncos to a field goal to make it
7–3, which served only to stir up the 49ers' offense

even more. A Bronco fumble was recovered by the 'Niners at mid-field. Montana led them in for a score, hitting tight end Brent Jones on a short pass to make it 14–3.

"In the first half, San Francisco used ball-control—utilizing Tom Rathman's running—blocking, and short-pass catching in combination with quick strikes. Jerry Rice broke free and scored on a Montana pass. At the half, it was all but over: 49ers 27, Broncos 3.

"'We had to guard against getting excited, although we knew we were the World Champs,' said Millen.

"Denver was a beaten crew, and they had no chance of regaining respectability in the second half. That was when Montana and company separated themselves from the pack. Their victory goes down in history as the most impressive Super Bowl win ever. In comparing Lombardi's Packers, Don Shula's Dolphins, Chuck Noll's Steelers, and other contenders, none match what San Francisco did.

"As the 'Niners turned the game into a track meet, frustration and defeat were etched on the Denver faces. In later years Elway said that the Denver coaches insisted that San Francisco would not throw in the middle, and prepared that way. Instead, Montana hit Rice and Taylor in the middle, attacking that area consistently.

"'How could we be so dumb?' lamented Elway.

"Taylor caught five TD passes to set a record. Montana was the MVP of the game, a 55–10 trouncing. It was his third such award, added to his 1989 Player of the Year and Sportsman of the Year honors. At one point, Millen tackled Elway and consoled him by saying, 'Hang in there, John.'

"In the aftermath of the Super Bowl, San Francisco had all the earmarks of being the finest pro football team ever assembled. Their stars were all young and in their primes, with no great injury problems. They had tied the four–Super Bowl record of Pittsburgh and were immediately installed as favorites to repeat in 1990. A fifth Super Bowl win would cement their place in history. No team had ever won three in a row, although the 1965–1967 Packers were three-time NFL champions (the first of those coming before the Super Bowl).

"It was the height of Montana's career. The 49ers could make a strong argument that they had the best quarterback (Montana), the best wide receiver (Rice), and the best defensive back (Lott) of all time. That argument holds up still to this day."
—*The Good, the Bad, and the Ugly San Francisco 49ers: Heart-Pounding, Jaw-Dropping, and Gut-Wrenching Moments from San Francisco 49ers History*, by Steven Travers

Football is not like other sports. A baseball player can hit anywhere. A football player is part of a system.

—49ERS ALL-PRO LINEMAN RANDY CROSS

So Close and Yet So Far

Since the first Super Bowl was played at the Los Angeles Memorial Coliseum in January 1967, no pro football team has ever won three straight. The Green Bay Packers won the first two, which when added to their 1965 NFL title still stands as the last of the "three-peat" pro football champions.

The 1971–1973 Miami Dolphins played in three straight Super Bowls, but lost the first one. Their bid for a third straight ended in the "sea of hands" loss to Oakland in the 1974 playoffs. Denver won two straight in the late 1990s, but with John Elway's retirement they did not have what it took to maintain dominance.

In baseball, three-peats are relatively common. The A's did it from 1972 to 1974, the Yankees from 1998 to 2000; just to name two modern champions. The Boston Celtics and the Los Angeles Lakers have done it with relative ease in the NBA. Since the creation of the Associated Press poll in 1936, it has never happened in college football. The California Golden Bears (1920–1922) and Minnesota Golden Gophers (1934–1936) managed to win various forms of the national championship, but the 2005 Southern California Trojans missed their aptly named three-Pete by virtue of a nine-yard Vince Young touchdown run with 19 seconds left in the Rose Bowl.

In 1990 the San Francisco 49ers entered the season heavily favored to capture that elusive third consecutive Super Bowl. Coach George Seifert was no longer a question mark, having directed his charges to the most impressive Super Bowl victory ever the previous season. At his disposal was less a football team and more of a display at the Hall of Fame museum in Canton, Ohio.

These were not "over the hill" Hall of Famers. These guys were carving their statistics and accomplishments into their plaques week by week. Joe Montana was the league MVP, passing John Brodie's team record to reach 34,998 career passing yards. His 3,944 yards were a club single-season record. Jerry Rice was at the height of his considerable powers. Ronnie Lott did not miss a beat. Pro Bowl linebacker and defensive end Charles Haley had 58 tackles and an NFC-high 16 sacks. Linebacker Bill Romanowski had 79 tackles, while cornerback Darryl Pollard recorded 74 (72 solo). Running back Roger Craig set the team career receptions record, breaking Dwight Clark's old mark of 506. Guard Guy McIntyre was a Pro Bowler.

San Francisco started 10–0 and won all eight of their road games. They finished 14–2, the best record in the NFL for the second straight year. They captured their fifth straight Western Division title. The Rams were not even a rival anymore. It was their eighth division championship since Montana and company led the 1981 team to the Promised Land, and the 11th since the 1966 merger. In that period, the Rams had won 8, Miami 13.

Before the season, there were some disruptions—holdouts, injuries, retirements, and of course the inevitable talk of "three-peat," a term that could not be marketed because Lakers basketball coach Pat Riley had patented the term, literally.

"There are always going to be disruptions," Seifert said. "Through the course of camp, and during the course of the season, we have to work with the players [who] are on hand and stay involved with our football. That's what we're here for. . . . These are all veteran players who have been a part of our program for some time. We look forward to them coming back and being part of this club again. . . . Just because they are involved in contract negotiations, and in some cases will miss some time in camp, I don't believe [that] will distract us from our ultimate goal. . . . We all have great expectations."

Offensive coordinator Mike Holmgren had his offense in place by 1990. The season opener was at New Orleans, and it looked like a Saints upset until San Francisco pulled it out with a late field goal, making it 13–12 before a stunned Superdome crowd of 68,629. A series of convincing and close wins followed, but throughout San Francisco always looked to be in control.

In November the Rams managed to win at Candlestick 25–17. A week later on *Monday Night Football*, a preview of things to come was held when Bill Parcells and his great defensive juggernaut, the Giants, came to town. San Francisco's 7–3 win made for a lot of nervousness. Here was one of if not the finest offensive machine ever: Montana, Rice, Craig, Holmgren, 55–10 over Denver, and in front of their fans they were held to a mere touchdown!

A chance to match the 1984 record of 15–1 was lost in game 15 when the Saints came marching in to San Francisco and took a 13–10 win. The 14–2 Niners dismissed Washington 28–10 in the first playoff game. As the team trotted off the field, the full house home crowd chanted, "Three-peat! Three-peat!"

For the second time in less than two years, events beyond the world of sports interfered with a San Francisco sports team. In October 1989 the Loma Prieta earthquake had shook up a Candlestick Park crowd, then broken up a World Series won by the Oakland A's over the San Francisco Giants.

The week of the January 1991 NFC championship game, the United States began an air war in Iraq. But despite concerns over the war, the game had to be played. Again, it was the New York Giants. In 1986 their defense dominated while quarterback Phil Simms led them to a Super Bowl victory. This time, Simms was out with an injury, replaced by the serviceable Jeff Hostetler. The face of their team was linebacker Lawrence Taylor, a larger-than-life pro football star whose appetites off the field were matched only by his ability to dominate on the field.

It was a "War of the Worlds," as Dennis Pottenger called it in *Great Expectations: The San Francisco 49ers and the Quest for the "Three-Peat."* A battle between the East Coast and the West Coast, between the philosophies of Parcells and—with all due respect to Seifert—Walsh, whose imprint was still all over the 1990 Niners.

It marked another New York–San Francisco grudge match, and would offer all the thrills of the classic 1962 World Series, won in seven games by the Yankees over the Giants.

There was another element of past-meeting-the-present in that the Raiders lost to the Buffalo Bills in the AFC title game, played before the NFC match. In 1971 the Raiders lost to Baltimore in the AFC championship game the same day the 49ers lost to Dallas. In 1984 the 49ers lost to Washington in the morning, but the Raiders earned a Super Bowl berth in the afternoon. The 1991 Raiders loss to Buffalo eliminated the intrigue of an L.A.–San Francisco Super Bowl. A Giants victory meant an all–New York state game.

San Francisco started the title bout with a drive resulting in a Mike Cofer field goal. New York lost their shot at a touchdown through self-inflicted wounds, settling for a field goal to end the first quarter at 3–3.

In the second quarter Hostetler hit tight end Mark Bavaro on key strikes, and Matt Bahr's field goal gave the Giants a 6–3 lead. Montana then led the 49ers on a late drive to send the teams into halftime tied 6–6. In the third quarter Montana hit John Taylor for a long catch-and-run touchdown over Everson Walls, the same defender who failed to stop Dwight Clark from making the Catch in 1982. A Giants field goal made it 13–9.

In the fourth quarter, holding a lead with the ball, Montana fumbled amid a furious rush from Taylor and Leonard Marshall. Montana was forced out of the game with an injury. Hostetler, who earlier looked to have been forced out by injury, returned looking chipper. Then Bill Romanowski came up limping and was out of the game.

The Giants managed another field goal to narrow the score to 13–12. With 5:47 left, Steve Young was in. Roger Craig fumbled, and Taylor recovered it at the New York 43 with 2:26 left to play. The Giants drove into field-goal range and broke 49ers hearts with a Matt Bahr kick to end the dreams of a third straight title, 15–13. They went on to beat Buffalo on a wide Bills field goal try to take their second Super Bowl in five years.

Roger Craig (the football version) was a 6',
222-pound running back who came to the 49ers
in the second round of the 1983 NFL Draft from
Nebraska. He and Jerry Rice had great work ethics.
Craig's chiseled body was almost a work of art that at
one time graced many a bus stop and billboard when
he did underwear advertisements in the City. He was
All-Pro in 1985 and 1988. His last year was 1990.

Fourteen 49ers players were selected All-Pro in
1990.

Saviors

THE MAN MOST IDENTIFIED IN THE MEDIA WITH SAVING THE SAN Francisco Giants franchise from moving to Tampa, Florida, after the 1992 season is Safeway magnate Peter Magowan, who presided over the club's main ownership duties well into the 2000s. He eventually left, leaving Larry Baer as the face of the current Giants. Baer has earned his way to the top of an egalitarian organization with skill and smarts. He is a City native, Cal graduate, and one-time "announcer" for the Oakland A's when Charlie O. Finley was such a cheapskate he used the university radio station to "broadcast" A's games, barely reaching Berkeley city limits. Baer was *Moneyball* before the book or movie. He went to Harvard Business School. It was his skills in this area that first helped him form the ownership group saving the club from Tampa in 1992–1993. He came in with Magowan after having worked in marketing in the 1980s. The Baer-Magowan friendship stretches back decades, and at the center of it was a shared love of the Giants. Eventually he was asked to take over the day-to-day duties. He has been responsible for the daily operations and decision making of the team since 1992, a consistent role for two decades now.

Baer said during a busy 2012–2013 off-season of attention and great fete over the architects of this success, "This run has been crazy. It's wonderful and so many people in the community have benefited from this new golden age."

Baer was quick to point out that his original involvement in the club was strictly an effort to keep the Giants in San Francisco, which he was emotionally invested in as a fan.

"Peter Magowan and I got together on this. He was on the Giants' board and I was at CBS in New York in August of 1992 when it looked like the Giants were gonna move. I sought Peter out, and we agreed to put together a group, so what happened was this group prevailed on this issue. As for the question of who would run it, we turned to Peter because he knew the most about baseball and was the youngest."

Baer may have played some ball in little league or high school, but other than fandom this was never his expertise. Today, however, he is integral to all decisions, on and off the field. The record speaks for itself.

Ownership of a major professional sports franchise today is an expensive proposition. There are men like Baer, who become indispensable. The Giants' ownership group lacks any of the flamboyance or controversy of Al Davis, Charlie O. Finley, and Eddie DeBartolo, or others such as Jerry Jones and George Steinbrenner. Asked whether this low-key approach is a trend or strategy, Baer replied, "There is not a strategy or trend. I'm the CEO and operate on the CEO model. As the CEO I report to a board, in which not everyone is equally involved. Jerry Jones and Al Davis operated on a different CEO model. They were owners who operated across the board at a CEO level and managing level. Jones, Davis, Eddie DeBartolo; they were different. In our case, our ownership group chooses not to put themselves out there. They are not involved in the day-to-day business. It comes down to the difference between CEOs and owners, and the nature of the two roles.

"Charlie Finley ran the team. The Giants' ownership group charged me with running the team, and their role is to approve or disapprove of what I do with the team, so it's just a matter of being a different model."

Building the new stadium privately was a daunting obstacle to overcome various factions.

"Going in we were just concentrating on how to acquire the team," recalled Baer. "There was no plan about a new stadium, because the new single most important thing was how to keep the team from moving to Florida.

"There was no political desire to build a new stadium with public funds. Remember, the question of a new Giants stadium lost four ballot measures. So it was only after we were able to acquire the team that we could even think about a new stadium. So we needed to figure out a plan, a recipe. There was a lot of work and research that went into it, we found there were a lot of questions to answer about where to locate it; the City, the peninsula? What type of deal would it be?"

The acquisition of the Giants from Bob Lurie, and successfully keeping the club in San Francisco until Pacific Bell Park could be built and completed in 2000, remains one of the great, monumental achievements in San Francisco sports history. The credit goes to many people, but at the top are Peter Magowan and Larry Baer.

Normally, when you take a survey, asking, "Why didn't you go to the game?" it's because the team isn't winning. At Candlestick, it was because "We don't like the ballpark." That was more important than winning and losing.

—GIANTS OWNER BOB LURIE, WHO LOST MONEY
YEARLY IN 18 YEARS OF OWNERSHIP

The only thing that gave it any character was the weather, the elements. What was special about Candlestick other than the wind? From an architectural point of view, there is nothing to characterize it as unique.

—EX-GIANTS OWNER PETER MAGOWAN

The team would have been put up for sale and sold, and the buyer would have been from out of the area and National League baseball would have disappeared forever.

—PETER MAGOWAN ON TAKING OVER OWNERSHIP OF
THE GIANTS AFTER THE 1992 SEASON

The OJ Scandal

O RENTHAL J AMES S IMPSON WAS NOT OFFICIALLY A MEMBER OF THE S AN Francisco 49ers when, on June 17, 1994, he and his pal, another San Francisco native and ex-49er named Al Cowlings, got in a white Bronco and apparently tried to make a Steve McQueen–style "escape to Mexico," as in the Sam Peckinpah film *The Getaway*.

He was also not officially a member of the USC Trojans or the Buffalo Bills. At the time, he was officially only a member of the Screen Actors Guild and the Riviera Country Club. Official or not, however, all those organizations—USC, the 49ers, the Bills, not to mention the Potrero Hill Boy's Club, Galileo High School, and City College of San Francisco—jealously regarded him as a member in good standing of their respective "families."

OJ of course "went Hollywood." He was a hero in New York. But he is San Francisco's, just as Joe DiMaggio belonged to the City despite Big Apple iconization and a Tinseltown marriage with Marilyn Monroe.

So when OJ went down in flames, the City by the Bay looked inward and asked some hard questions. KNBR talkshow host Ralph Barbieri, a local guy predisposed to like OJ and even to believe that a criminal had to be proven a criminal beyond all shadow of doubt before judgment be rendered, did not buy the Los Angeles jury's "not guilty" verdict for a second. He, like so many others, pronounced the man guilty in the court of public opinion.

That did not stop OJ supporters from coming to his defense. One caller told Barbieri that he had to stop referring to him as "guilty" and "fallen," apparently not because of DNA or the weight of evidence against him, but because "OJ's from the neighborhood, man."

Barbieri was flabbergasted at that logic, but it is a pervasive argument that continues to percolate in the various "neighborhoods" that may resemble the one OJ grew up in, but "escaped" from the first minute he had the chance.

The "neighborhood" of specificity is Potrero Hill, a gritty, mostly black section of public housing set in the hills overlooking Candlestick Park and the Hunter's Point-Bayview. The conundrum of this neighborhood is that it, like much of San Francisco, consists of spectacular vistas that might mean million-dollar homes in another city. In San Francisco, even the projects are esthetically pleasing.

His mother raised OJ. His father mostly was not around. He often hung out around Candlestick, frequently enough to befriend the great Willie Mays, who followed his high school and junior college career with interest, declaring, "You have an unusual talent."

That talent came to fruition at City College of San Francisco. OJ had attended Galileo High School, which is basically a middle class school located in the City's North Beach section. Historically, North Beach was home to Italian immigrants. DiMaggio grew up there and "attended" Galileo, although in truth he flunked out and started playing professionally for the San Francisco Seals at age 16.

OJ normally would have gone to Balboa or Poly, but he was getting in a lot of trouble as a youth. He ran in a "gang," which by today's standards would be considered tame compared to the guns-and-drugs culture of modern inner city Crips life. He was sent to Galileo in the hopes that the environment would straighten him out, and for the most part it did. His boyhood friend from the neighborhood, Al Cowlings, tagged along for the ride.

By the time OJ entered Galileo, however, the Italian population was dispersing to the suburbs, mostly Marin County. The football teams OJ played on consisted of a large number of Asian Americans. "Asians just aren't very big," OJ wrote in his autobiography. "They didn't block much so I was on my own."

OJ played defense. As a running back, he was not yet developed. As a student, he was lackluster despite a charismatic personality that made him the leader wherever he went. There were no college scholarships offered.

OJ considered joining the Army, but his high school coach told him to get some education and use football to do it; that the Army was just a form of social welfare and "you'll never get anywhere by having people give you things."

Whether the Army-as-welfare analogy had merit or not, OJ decided to give football, and education, another try. He enrolled at City College of San Francisco (CCSF). CCSF was just another junior college, but OJ's two years there spurred them into something very unusual.

San Francisco in the years since then has certainly not been a hotbed for prep sports. In the Bay Area, the players tend to come from the east bay, San Jose, and the peninsula. The real focus of high school sports is in Southern California: Orange County, the San Fernando Valley, the L.A. suburbs, and inner city. Great juco sports programs have, over the years, emerged in the Southland, as untold numbers of great high school stars, not quite ready for prime time, hone their skills for a year or two before getting drafted in baseball or taking an athletic scholarship someplace.

Despite little actual San Francisco talent to draw from, CCSF built on the OJ legend to become without question the greatest junior college football tradition in American history. They draw from not only the entire Bay Area, but all over America, as well. Countless players from Texas, Florida, Ohio—some after leaving high-profile four-year programs after their freshman years—come to CCSF, drawn not only by the program's success but the chance to live in an interesting city.

As CCSF has developed into something beyond superlatives, so too has another unlikely local program. De La Salle High School of Concord, located in the East Bay, won 151 straight games and is, like CCSF, the finest program in the nation at its level. The greatness of CCSF and De La Salle has had the effect of diminishing bragging rights in the Southland, where folks tend to think of themselves as a little bigger, a little better, a little brighter.

This state of affairs owes itself in no small part to OJ. His numbers at CCSF were staggering, almost cartoonish. After his freshman year, he was considered the biggest recruit in the nation, but his grades were still lagging. He had put in little effort in high school, little more as a college freshman.

Arizona State was willing to waive their requirements and let him into school, but no others were. Considering how many academic rejects play big-time collegiate sports, it is staggering to consider just how bad OJ's grades must have been up to that point, if nobody was willing to let this kind of superstar into their programs.

Enter Marv Goux, the fiery assistant football coach at USC. Goux got wind of OJ's decision to enter Arizona State. He flew to San Francisco and counseled OJ that "good things come to those who work for it." He said that if he would hang tough for one more year at City College, bring his grades up and play another year of J.C. ball, then he would have the chance to achieve his dream of becoming a Trojan.

OJ was more than a man among boys his sophomore year at CCSF. He was a giant among pygmies. Indeed, he did transfer with a full scholarship to USC, and the rest, as they say, is history.

OJ led Troy to the 1967 national championship and won the 1968 Heisman Trophy. An analysis of his 1967 season reveals that he should have won the Heisman that year, too, instead of UCLA's Gary Beban. His pal Cowlings followed him to USC. A talented lineman in his own right, Cowlings became a member of USC's famed "Wild Bunch" defensive front, named after a 1969 Sam Peckinpah movie.

In 1969 OJ was the number one draft choice in the NFL, picked by the Buffalo Bills. He signed for a huge bonus and within a few years was the best player in the league. In 1973 he broke Jim Brown's all-time single-season rushing record, becoming the first player to run for more than 2,000 yards. Others have done it since, but OJ achieved the feat in a 14-game season. The league went to 16 games in the late 1970s.

At the height of his career, OJ was not only the best player in the NFL, but had many people actively considering the possibility that he was better than Brown, the greatest pro football star in history. Injuries slowed OJ down, and a review of his career reveals that as great as he was, he probably fell a little shy of Brown's greatness. Others have surpassed his records in the years since, but in his heyday he was something to behold.

OJ's career was made in little Buffalo, a small town in western New York that suffers from some of the worst weather in pro football. The

California kid, who played in sunny Los Angeles as a collegian, achieved his bona fides playing in snow and sleet, which served only to add to the legend.

In an era of "Broadway Joe" Namath in New York, glamour teams in Los Angeles, Oakland, Miami, Pittsburgh, and Dallas, the biggest superstar of them all was OJ Simpson.

OJ left Buffalo in 1978 and came home to San Francisco. The Niners had floundered, but hope was held out that he was still a great runner who could lead the team he rooted for as a kid to glory. It was not to be. OJ played two years at Candlestick Park (he was a teammate of Joe Montana's in 1979). His skills had deteriorated rapidly. He was a shadow of his old self. He was cheered on by the "49ers faithful," but unable to produce on the field.

In 1979 Cowlings joined him on the 49ers. The OJ-Cowlings friendship is very unique, in that they grew up in the same neighborhood, playing Pop Warner, high school, junior college, college, and professional football together.

OJ retired for a career in the movies. This was a natural transition that had started when he went to "Hollywood's school," USC. He acted in a number of films while still playing pro football, including *The Klansmen* and *Towering Inferno*. It is in examining the OJ persona, his screen image, his personal charisma, where he is separated from other athletes, and where his eventual fall from grace is made so astounding.

He is a unique and iconic American personality. There had never been anything like him before he came along. He was *perfect*! First of all, OJ was one good lookin' dude; his personality was charming, his allure and his appeal universal. His Hertz commercials, in which OJ runs through an airport in a full suit, with a little old lady yelling, "Go, OJ, go," is a classic in the advertising genre. But OJ was highly intelligent, too. Not intelligent as in Ivy League intelligent; not a guy who was going to hold an audience in a discussion of the Middle East peace— "although I had been to Detroit a couple of times," as he joked on *Saturday Night Live*—but intelligent in the manner of friendly conversation, articulate, a smiling presence.

OJ became an announcer, joining for a time the famed *Monday Night Football* crew of Howard Cosell and fellow USC alum Frank Gifford. His performances were never great, but his comic turn as the unfortunate Nordberg in the *Naked Gun* franchise is very funny stuff.

His friends, other than Cowlings and some old teammates, tended to be corporate sponsors, USC alums, the Hollywood crowd. OJ became a golf addict, a constant presence at the exclusive Riviera Country Club in the posh Pacific Palisades-Brentwood enclave of L.A.

He had married his childhood sweetheart, Marguerite, bringing her with him to USC. At first, the "family man" act played well at USC, as if OJ's wife would "protect" him from all those beautiful coeds.

OJ started a family and went into the professional ranks, but fame, travel, money, and temptation were too great. He philandered, and the marriage ended in divorce. In 1977 OJ went to a restaurant and flirted with a beautiful blonde girl from Orange County named Nicole Brown.

She was thrilled to get the attention of such a superstar and was encouraged to play this hand for all it was worth, which is what she did. She and OJ were married. They had a family. They lived what seemed to be a perfect life in Brentwood. Nicole had money, a "rich and famous" lifestyle, and trendy friends and clothes. OJ lived a life most just dream of: golf, parties, fame, adoration . . . and any woman he wanted.

The marital infidelities caused problems. Like the couple in The Eagles' "Life in the Fast Lane," OJ and Nicole had checked into the Hotel California, but they could "never leave." An arrangement of sorts was entered into. There were rumors that Nicole played around as well. She became friendly with a number of OJ's handsome pals, fueling speculation further.

In 1989 OJ became enraged about something, and struck Nicole. She called 911 and told the operator that she was afraid Simpson would kill her. OJ was arrested and given probation and some anger counseling. Nobody wanted to hurt the great OJ. It was "understood." He cheated on her, she cheated on him. Alcohol was involved. Drugs were involved. OJ was a hero to millions, still had an acting career. The veneer was maintained.

The tabloids and psychologists have tried for years to get to what set OJ off on June 12, 1994. He and Nicole were separated by then, but he was still a part of her life. She loved him and could not break from him completely. Despite having a *Playboy*-party lifestyle, OJ was tied to Nicole, and no other woman had a hold on him in that manner. The speculators, trying to figure it all out, said that OJ was infuriated by Nicole's sexuality, but was particularly appalled by her dating young, pretty men. No longer young, no longer the symbol of American sports heroism, OJ seemed to be particularly frustrated by this dynamic.

Enter Ron Goldman. His role in the OJ case is still a bit of mystery to this day, but it appears that he was little more than an innocent victim, virtually a bystander who happened to be in the wrong place at the wrong time. Goldman was young and handsome, like so many a Hollywood wannabe working as a waiter in a trendy Brentwood bistro while waiting for his big break in the movies or modeling. On June 12, 1994, OJ attended a dance recital at his daughter's school, but was not invited by Nicole to a dinner afterward. Goldman waited on Nicole and her party. He knew her from frequenting the restaurant, knew who she was. They flirted. Beyond that, nobody really knows.

Perhaps OJ was infuriated at being cut out of the celebration of his daughter's dance recital. Perhaps the smiling, alluring Goldman capturing Nicole's attention was too much for him to take. Perhaps he had been planning it for weeks, for months. Perhaps, also, he did not commit the crime. Others have completely discounted this possibility, but the "guilty beyond a shadow of a doubt" is a heavy burden on the state. The evidence against him is overwhelming, but in the interest of truth, justice, and fairness, there remains a scintilla of possibility that the crime was committed by another.

Scintilla: a bit, a tiny part, very little.

The facts in a nutshell are these: OJ bought a knife at an L.A. knife store that was similar to the one used in the crime. He lived a few blocks away from Nicole, who stayed in their Brentwood home. Kato Kaelin, who lived in the guesthouse out back, heard a noise. Nicole left her watch at the restaurant. Goldman found it and drove it to her house to return it. An assailant emerged and killed them with a knife. It was a gruesome double-murder.

If OJ did it, he likely would have been hiding in the bushes. Whether he came to kill Nicole, and Goldman just happened to show up, or whether Goldman was more involved and therefore targeted by OJ, is not definitive.

OJ was scheduled to fly to Chicago that night. A cab took him to the airport. The taxi driver said he was sweating profusely and appeared agitated. The next day the bodies were discovered. He was called and asked to return to L.A. The news hit the world like a bombshell.

The speculation immediately began to center on whether OJ had done it. The LAPD considered him the prime suspect from the get-go. A few days after the murder, for reasons that neither OJ, Al Cowlings, nor anybody has ever adequately explained, Cowlings put OJ in the back of a white Bronco and drove south, apparently with the intent of "escaping" to Mexico. The authorities got wind of it. Cell phone calls were made communicating with the car. It became public, and a bizarre slow speed chase on rush hour L.A. freeways, which opened up like the Red Sea, played itself out for the world's cameras. It was as crazy a sight as many people have ever observed. Eventually, the car returned to Brentwood, where OJ surrendered to authorities.

A trial was held. It was one of the most racially divisive events in modern American history, coming on the heels of the Rodney King beatings and 1992 L.A. riots. A downtown L.A. jury acquitted OJ in 1995, to the consternation of millions. The verdict satisfied nobody.

In recent years, there was more Shakesepearean irony added to this American tragedy. Two decades have passed. OJ was able to protect enough of his assets to live a golf course life in Florida, occasionally granting interviews in which he vowed to find "the real killers," and even emerging at sports shindigs to gladhand with the curious. To many young people, he is a strange figure, but to those old enough to recall his heyday, his story is utterly incredible. He was not merely a "big name" or a "star." He was *the* guy who had it all, a symbol of the new, better America. He was a universally loved figure with offers of a free lunch from coast to coast.

As mentioned, the evidence against him was overwhelming. It is the consensus of most that, had they sat on the jury that judged him, they would have found him guilty, but absent video evidence the smallest possibility resonates in a tiny segment of the population that somehow it was a drug deal gone bad, a Mob retaliation, or some other explanation can be attached.

The defense's assertions of a police frame based on racism have been discredited and carry no weight at this point with people capable of clear thinking. OJ's life as he knew it ended: movie stardom, hero status, athletic glory recalled at USC, Bills and 49ers old-timers' days. If OJ is innocent, then he must live with the consequences of a monumental twist of fate. If he is guilty, then he must live with himself and God.

Then came perhaps the most bizarre episode of them all. Simpson tried to write a book called *If I Did It*, possibly a confession of sorts, but an outraged public prohibited its publication. Perhaps it was a sort of "confession," but the book rights were awarded to the Goldman family, still owed millions in a civil judgment they won over OJ. They wrote a book in OJ's "voice" called *If I Did It: Confessions of the Killer*, but the "If" in the title was overshadowed by a huge red "I," making the title ostensibly *I Did It*. Then, almost as if to punish himself, Simpson went to a Las Vegas hotel room to retrieve memorabilia he believed was rightfully his. He brought some losers along to help. Guns were involved. The caper went awry and OJ was arrested. His "friends" turned on him. He was convicted of a crime that, in any other case, would have resulted in a warning, or probation, but the world, including the Nevada prosecutors, was determined to give him the jail time for this crime he had not done for the 1994 murders. It is in a small cell in Nevada that OJ sits and ponders.

—◦—

Although recent 49ers teams in the Denise DeBartolo–John York era threatened, it is hard to say any team was worse than OJ's 1978 squad. They were 2–14. The hated Rams beat them twice. They started 0–4. Coach Pete McCulley was fired nine games into the season, replaced by Fred O'Connor. Eventually, OJ was sidelined in favor of Paul Hofer.

—

Frankie Albert was a Stanford All-American. Bill Walsh had two tenures at Stanford. Steve Mariucci coached at Cal. Terry Donahue coached at UCLA. The 49ers often looked to the Pacific-10, now the Pac-12 Conference, for coaches and executives. After George Seifert stepped down, in the mid-to-late 1990s the 49ers basically "stole" Mariucci from the California Golden Bears, where he had marginal success but was considered a hot coaching prospect. Mariucci coached good teams in San Francisco, continuing success with the team Walsh and Seifert had built. Walsh came back to the front office, eventually turning things over to Donahue. When it was all said and done, Walsh's absence coincided with the team's failures.

—

Many pro football cheerleaders in recent years are dressed in outfits, and perform routines, that seem more suited for dimly lit establishments that have DJs, bouncers, a stage, and a pole. The 49ers Gold Nuggets cheerleaders squad has maintained a wholesome reputation over the years. Their members are young women from the community: school teachers, secretaries, college students.

Super Bowl XXIX: 49ers 49, Chargers 26

In January 1994 Dallas defeated San Francisco 38–21 in the NFC championship game.

"That loss catapulted us to the next year, our championship year," recalled quarterback Steve Young. "We could not deal with that loss. It was too devastating. No one talked about it at all. To this day we haven't dealt with it, and it's probably a good thing. In some strange way, we accepted it."

In 1994 San Francisco rolled to an NFL-best 13–3 record. William Floyd was the Rookie of the Year, Ricky Watters was an All-Pro running back. They brought in some major stars: Ken Norton Jr. from Dallas, Rickey Jackson, Gary Plummer, free agents Richard Dent and Toi Cook, and of course the great "Neon Deion" Sanders.

At midseason, the 49ers beat Dallas 21–14, propelling a 10-game winning streak, playoff victories over Chicago and Dallas, again at home, and a trip to Miami to face San Diego in the Super Bowl.

It was Young's first Super Bowl as a starter, but he felt no pressure.

"Seriously, by the time I'd gone through the whole thing—taking over the quarterback job from Joe Montana—there was no way anything could ever be like that," said Young. "Even the Super Bowl. I'd faced real media pressure before. Talking about football and a big game—that was nothing!"

When the game started, Young hit Rice for a quick-strike touchdown. San Diego went three-and-out. Watters went up the middle for the Niners, there was a short pass to Floyd, and Young scrambled for 20 yards to midfield. Watters then caught a pass at the Charger 30, evaded tacklers, and at 14–0 the game was all over but the shouting.

San Diego managed a score, but the 49ers responded with an impressive drive and scoring pass to Floyd. A deflected punt later gave San

Francisco the ball in Chargers territory. Young maneuvered the offense inside the 10, then hit Watters on a short pass, 28–7. It was 28–10 at the half, with the TV audience rapidly losing in market share.

San Francisco was virtually perfect. They suffered no turnovers and only 10 yards in penalties. In the second half, Young passed them within sight of the goal, where Watters ran in for their only rushing score. Rice would finish with three TDs.

Young's fifth touchdown pass made the score 42–10. Number six was a quick slant to Rice in the fourth quarter. Young broke Montana's record for TD passes in a Super Bowl, set five years earlier. The 49ers defense intercepted Chargers quarterback Stan Humphries three times.

Just as Young had replaced Montana late in the Super Bowl blowout of Denver, Elvis Grbac replaced Young while he and his teammates whooped it up on the sideline.

"After the game, in the locker room, everybody was ecstatic," recalled Young. "I can't describe the feeling."

'Niners tight end Brent Jones, Steve Young's best friend on the team, was a local guy from nearby University of Santa Clara, which is not exactly a "football factory."

Best Winning Percentage of 49ers Coaches

George Seifert, 76.6 (1989–1996)
Jim Harbaugh, 69.0 (2011–2013)
Buck Shaw, 63.8 (1946–1954)
Bill Walsh, 61.8 (1979–1988)

Top All-Time 49ers Quarterback Ratings

Steve Young, 101.4 (1987–1999)
Joe Montana, 93.5 (1979–1992)
John Brodie, 72.3 (1957–1973)

49ers Top QBs by the Numbers

Completion percentage: Steve Young, 65.8
(1987–1999)
Yards: Joe Montana, 35,124 (1979–1992)
Touchdown passes: Joe Montana, 244 (1979–1992)

The North versus the South

On December 10, 1949, the National Football League announced a merger with the young All-American Football Conference. With that, Baltimore, the Cleveland Browns, the Cleveland Rams, and San Francisco went from the old AAFC to join the established NFL.

The 49ers were, in essence, the first "big-league" team on the West Coast. The San Francisco Seals, along with other teams in the Pacific Coast League, had long dominated minor league baseball. USC, California, and Stanford had at one time or another been powerhouses in college football, as well as other sports. UCLA was knocking on the door.

The 49ers had of course already been in business as a professional football team in the AAFC. In Los Angeles, a team called the L.A. Dons had existed, but beginning in 1950, the 49ers rivalry with the Rams began in earnest. Two teams had played in Cleveland, with the Browns dominating the city. The Rams sought greener pastures at the Los Angeles Memorial Coliseum, where they were an immediate Hollywood hit.

While the Niners could lay claim to being the first big-time professional team, they quickly found themselves taking a backseat to the Rams. San Francisco had originally been the West Coast city. Gold was discovered not in Southern California but in Northern California. Sacramento was chosen as the state capital. San Francisco, some 90 miles to the west, was established as a major seaport, a center of trade and commerce. Los Angeles was a sleepy Spanish pueblo, its desert population kept small because of a lack of fresh water.

The transcontinental railroad connected the East Coast and the Midwest not with Los Angeles but with San Francisco. It was built over the rugged Rocky and Sierra Mountain ranges. It could have been built through Texas, Arizona, Nevada, and the Southern California deserts, which would have been easier from an engineering standpoint. It was not, though, because the major political backer of the railroads was Illinois senator Abraham Lincoln. Senator Lincoln opposed slavery and was determined that the biggest achievement of the young country would not be accomplished on the backs of slaves, who surely would have done much of the work, at least in the southern states.

After the Civil War, the demographics of San Francisco and Los Angeles began to take shape. San Francisco was the destination of northerners from Boston and New York who had supported the Union. Los Angeles took on a more Confederate flavor.

The University of California was built as a land-grant public university in Berkeley. In nearby Palo Alto, Leland Stanford, one of the major railroad men of the era, created a private university. Natural rivalries in sports emanated between California and Stanford.

There was not enough population to justify a major public university in Los Angeles, but the Methodist Church, in cooperation with other religious denominations, did found the University of Southern California, a private school, in 1880.

Everything changed in the early 1900s. L.A.'s "city fathers" decided they wanted to be a major metropolitan center. To do that, they needed water. City engineer William Mulholland arranged for an aqueduct to divert water from the Owens Valley to Los Angeles. As the country mobilized by train, by automobile, by airplane, and through two world wars, the population grew and grew and grew. The basin was boundless, allowing for growth to outlying areas. The Bay Area, on the other hand, was naturally enclosed by mountain ranges with a body of water in the middle of everything.

USC wanted to compete in football with Cal and Stanford. Prior to World War I, they periodically played those schools, but were not considered big time. The best football in the country in the years prior to and during World War I shifted not to Los Angeles, but to the Pacific Northwest, where the University of Washington had a 63-game unbeaten streak.

World War I had a major impact on Southern California. In 1919 UCLA was founded as the Southern Branch of the University of

California. USC bid to become a major football power. They joined the Pacific Coast Conference. The L.A. Memorial Coliseum, as well as the Rose Bowl in Pasadena, were erected.

In the early 1920s California built their Memorial Stadium, and Stanford Stadium was constructed. Stanford tried to get the Rose Bowl shifted from Pasadena to its new stadium, but Pasadena's successful completion of the Rose Bowl stadium kept the game in the Southland.

The Cal teams of the early 1920s were the greatest college football teams ever seen up to that time, and to this day one of the best dynasties in history. The "Wonder Teams" captured three straight national championships (from 1920 to 1922), largely on the strength of the first "recruits," who had been "shipped" by train from Los Angeles and San Diego. It was the first time a college had actively found players from outside the area and persuaded them to come to their school to play ball. Until then, teams were fielded on the strength of whoever showed up for tryouts. Stanford under coach Pop Warner captured the 1926 national championship and bid for supremacy with their Berkeley rivals.

USC was unable to beat Cal and fared little better with Stanford, thus ensuring the firing of "Gloomy Gus" Henderson because he could not defeat the Golden Bears. They tried to hire Knute Rockne away from Notre Dame, but had to "settle" for his friendly rival, Howard Jones, and a yearly home-and-home arrangement with the Fighting Irish.

This had the effect of turning USC into a national powerhouse. In 1932 the Olympics came to Los Angeles, establishing L.A. as a sports capital.

Natural PCL rivalries existed between the Seals, Mission Reds, Oakland Oaks, Sacramento Solons, Los Angeles Angels, Hollywood Stars, and San Diego Padres. World War II led to population growth in the entire state. The Rose Bowl at first was a game that invited southern teams, then Big 10 schools. Fans of those teams came, saw, and often stayed, reinforcing this demographic.

After World War II, California was recognized as an electoral juggernaut, leading to the rise of junior senator Richard Nixon, the vice president from 1953 to 1961 and president from 1969 to 1974. Conservatism took hold in the West. Arizona senator Barry Goldwater became the face of the movement.

In the 1960s political divides were further created in response to the Vietnam War and campus protests. This led to the election of Republican Ronald Reagan as California governor and then president. The Rams had moved from Cleveland and entered the NFL with the 49ers.

The first game ever played between the new Los Angeles Rams and the 49ers was on October 1, 1950, when 27,262 came out to Kezar and saw coach Buck Shaw's Niners beaten 35–14. At the Coliseum a little over a month later, L.A. prevailed again by a score of 28–21.

Movie glamour enveloped the Rams in the form of quarterback Bob Waterfield, a local hero from Van Nuys High School and UCLA. Waterfield was a fine signal-caller, but it was his girlfriend who had everybody going gaga. Jane Russell, the star of *Gentlemen Prefer Blondes*, was at the time one of the major sex symbols of a sex-obsessed era. Her star was made in maverick filmmaker-aviator Howard Hughes's film *The Outlaw*, which scandalized America by revealing Miss Russell in a low-cut blouse while the camera kept creeping closer.

Individual rivalries revolved around the question of who was better, the Rams' Elroy "Crazy Legs" Hirsch or San Francisco's Hugh McElhenny? Things came to a head in 1957, the first playoff year in 49ers history. Coach Frankie Albert's 49ers defeated Los Angeles 23–20 in front of a sellout crowd of 59,637 at Kezar Stadium. On November 10, 102,368 packed the Coliseum to see the Rams extract revenge, 37–24. Sellouts at Kezar and crowds in the mid-90,000s marked the remaining years of the decade, with enormous attendance in the years since.

The Coliseum has reconfigured its capacity several times over the years. In the 1940s and '50s it held well over 100,000 fans, and topped the century mark in games between the Rams and 49ers, USC and Notre Dame, and the Trojans and Bruins. In the early 1960s the stadium was renovated slightly, making for a capacity that has at various times ranged from 92,000 to around 94,000.

In 1961 coach Red Hickey installed the shotgun, which was used effectively in dismantling Los Angeles to the delight of a Kezar sellout of 59,004 by a 35–0 score. But two weeks later, Chicago coach Clark Shaughnessy figured it out in a 31–0 whitewashing of San Francisco. It was a devastating setback, and the Rams got revenge before 62,766 in L.A. on November 12, winning 17–7.

This marked a reversal in fortunes. The 49ers floundered. Their stadium was a laughingstock. Still, all was not lost. Quarterback John Brodie was widely respected as one of the best in the game, as was All-Pro safety Jimmy Johnson. Despite having better teams, Los Angeles did not dominate San Francisco in head-to-head competition.

The Rams of this era featured the famed "Fearsome Foursome" of Roosevelt Grier, Merlin Olsen, Deacon Jones, and Lamar Lundy. Then in 1969 the Rams twice knocked the 49ers off. Quarterback Roman Gabriel won the league MVP award. In 1970 San Francisco served notice that they would not be an also-ran any longer by defeating Los Angeles in convincing fashion 20–6 before 77,271 at the Coliseum.

However, when the teams met in San Francisco, L.A. returned the favor, 30–13. The Rams suffered a series of strange defeats under new coach Tommy Prothro, failing to win the Western Division of the new NFC, while San Francisco, at 10-3-1, earned its first trip to the postseason since the 1957 debacle with Detroit.

In 1971 and 1972 San Francisco won the division two more times playing at Candlestick Park, but were unable to beat the Rams. The Rams looked at times like a great team, but faltered too often, failing to capture a postseason berth in either of those years.

The next year San Francisco got very old very fast. John Brodie was on his last legs, while new Ram coach "Ground Chuck" Knox instituted a strong rushing attack with Lawrence McCutcheon, along with ball control quarterback John Hadl, dominating regular season play. Over the next years, Los Angeles extended their winning streak over San Francisco to 11 games (from 1970 through 1975).

The conundrum of the rivalry was symbolized by San Francisco's ending the streak with an improbable 24–23 win over the Rams in front of a throng of 78,995 Coliseum faithful. The 49ers were a dismal 5–9 team. The 1975 Rams were thought by some at the time to be the best pro team not to win, or at least not play in, a Super Bowl. Led by superstar defensive end Fred Dryer, the talented Hacksaw Reynolds, and Jack

Youngblood, the '75 Rams were 12–2, having allowed the second fewest points ever in a regular season until that year.

The clubs split their 1976 wins in a season that saw Monte Clark's team go 8–6 with Jim Plunkett at quarterback. Pat Haden took over for James Harris in L.A. Haden had signed, along with USC teammate Anthony Davis, with the Southern California Sun of the now-defunct World Football League (who played their games in Anaheim). Now, on the Coliseum turf where he led Troy to glory, he led the Rams to a division title, although their victory against San Francisco came in the Candlestick game. A crazy, rare Southern California rainstorm turned the NFC title game into a mudbath loss to Minnesota, a team that bedeviled L.A. in numerous postseason games of the era, often with weather favoring the Vikings, whether in Minnesota or California.

Over the next four years, as the Bill Walsh–Joe Montana transition took shape, San Francisco played Los Angeles competitively, but never beat them. Ray Malavasi took over the reins in Los Angeles, but the franchise changed drastically during this time.

The Rams brought in Joe Namath, the legendary quarterback who had led the New York Jets to a historic Super Bowl win over the Baltimore Colts in 1969. Hobbled by knee injuries, "Broadway Joe" was supposed to become "Hollywood Joe," but he did not "do business," to use a trade term.

The Rams won with their patented running game and great defense, trademarks of their team for years. From 1977 to 1979, they utilized different quarterbacks in the wake of the failed Namath experiment. In 1979 Vince Ferragamo, an L.A. kid from Banning High School (who briefly played at Cal) caught fire. The Rams beat San Francisco 27–24 and 26–20, en route to a "home" Super Bowl appearance against Pittsburgh at the Rose Bowl. Ferragamo was spectacular, but the combination of Terry Bradshaw-to-Lynn Swann was better.

In 1980 a huge shift in Southern California sports occurred when the Rams moved to Anaheim Stadium in the suburbs.

This left the Coliseum vacant, in a way. USC continued to play there, but UCLA moved to the Rose Bowl, leaving the Coliseum to USC and the Raiders, who moved to L.A. in 1982. Several games between the

Raiders and 49ers at the Coliseum in the 1980s had strange overtones to them. Enormous crowds came out, but a gang element, centered on the Raiders "bad boy" image and silver-and-black color scheme, lent criminality to the proceedings. Watching the 49ers do battle on the Coliseum in games against a team other than the Rams was disconcerting, although they enjoyed their fair share of success.

But what was most disconcerting was the change in the Rams' ownership structure. In 1979 Carroll Rosenbloom, an expert swimmer, went for a dip in mild Florida waters and drowned.

His wife, a former Las Vegas showgirl named Georgia Frontiere, assumed control of the team. The rightful owner of the Rams was Rosenbloom's son, Steve, but Frontiere manipulated the records and won a power struggle. Nobody has ever proved that she killed her husband for his money, but many throughout sports suspect just that.

"Georgia will meet her Maker," Rams star Fred Dryer said in 2000. "She will be judged for her actions."

Frontiere immediately pulled up roots, leaving the venerable Coliseum, trashing 30 years of Rams tradition, glory, and success, for the green pastures of Orange County. As if by divine intervention, the rivalry with San Francisco, which was barely even a rivalry when the team first moved to the Big A, switched gears. It became a rivalry again, then became something, like most everything the Walsh-Montana-Lott 49ers did in the 1980s, that was dominated by San Francisco.

The 1981 World Champion 49ers could point to several turning points. After losing the opener to Detroit and Game 3 to Atlanta, they found themselves beating Dallas handily and holding off Green Bay in Wisconsin, always a tough task. But their 20–17 win over the Rams marked the beginning of their wild ride, enthusing the Bay Area over their chances.

A home loss to Cleveland was followed by a 33–31 victory at Anaheim, and the team never looked back. As the 1980s developed, the 49ers-Raiders games began to take on more meaning, but by the decade's end, both the Raiders and Rams were in San Francisco's shadow.

The nail in the coffin came on January 14, 1990, at Candlestick Park. In a 14–2 campaign, one of their losses had come at the hands of Los

Angeles, 13–12 in San Francisco. The Rams were led by coach John Robinson, who presided over a successful running game in Anaheim just as he had at USC.

The Rams advanced to the NFC title game, but were embarrassed by Montana and his mates, 30–3. San Francisco went on to more Super Bowl glory, then made a successful transition to Steve Young, winning another Super Bowl and more divisions in another winning decade.

The Rams dropped deeper and deeper into a hole. Frontiere was a laughingstock, which was the best thing people had to say about her ("gold-digging femme fatale" being a more serious handle). Hated by an entire region, she packed up the Rams' bags following the 1994 campaign and moved to St. Louis.

At first, it looked like a desperate move. Her team was desultory, fan acceptance lukewarm; the 49ers continued to dominate. Then in 1998 the world went topsy-turvy when her team won an improbable Super Bowl.

In the years since then, as the league has realigned divisions to match regions, the Rams-49ers rivalry sadly is, for the most part, a thing of the past. "Beat St. Louis!" does not resonate with San Franciscans as "Beat L.A.!" does. The Rams' 2016 return to the Southland offers hope that the rivalry will be a great one someday.

Jack Reynolds got the nickname "Hacksaw" when, after a tough loss at the University of Tennessee, he took a hacksaw to his Volkswagen, cutting it in half.

In 1969 the NFL's Most Valuable Player was Rams quarterback Roman Gabriel. John Brodie, despite leading the league in passing in 1965, was still a less heralded signal-caller, but in 1970 Brodie was named the NFL's Player of the Year.

Cornerback Bruce Taylor was the 1970 NFL Rookie of the Year.

The Rams, after dominating the 49ers for years, must have been chagrined to see Charles "Tree" Young, Wendell Tyler, and Hacksaw Reynolds—all former Rams—become stalwart Niners on Super Bowl champions. It all happened on Georgia Frontiere's watch.

The December 1, 1989, *Monday Night Football* game at Anaheim Stadium, in which Joe Montana led San Francisco to an incredible 30–27 comeback win over the Rams, was in many ways the last straw, leading to the eventual, dismal loss of the team to St. Louis five years later.

Rams quarterback Jim Everett was supposed to lead the Rams to victory. Instead, despite great potential, the former Purdue star and his team continued to be patsies at the hands of the Steve Young–led 49ers. Talkshow host Jim Rome was merciless in his assessment of Everett, calling him "Chris Everett" in an emasculating reference to women's tennis player Chris Evert. In 1994 Everett had enough, physically attacking Rome during an in-studio interview.

The Greatness That Is, Er, Was the Raiders

THE OBVIOUS, NATURAL RIVAL OF THE SAN FRANCISCO 49ERS ALWAYS was the Los Angeles Rams. It was a fierce rivalry in the 1950s and early 1970s. In the 1960s the Rams were a dominant team, the 49ers an also-ran. When the 49ers tanked from 1973 to 1980. In the 1980s much of the edge was lost when the Rams went to Anaheim, where crowds sat on their hands and San Francisco established themselves as the football version of Patton's drive through the Rhineland. But when the Rams took off for St. Louis, it was over. Who cared anymore? It was a cryin' shame.

The 49ers have played many tough games, within their division, their conference, and in the postseason. But two teams aside from the Rams, and in fact with the Rams in St. Louis more so than ever, emerged in the historical memory as major rivals. Geography only plays a part in it. The former San Diego Chargers and Seattle Seahawks occupy the same coast and time zone, but until Pete Carroll arrived in Seattle, neither had ever emerged as a big 49ers rival.

Two teams have. The Raiders, partly because of their physical locale (the rivalry may have gotten more heated when they were in L.A.). The Cowboys, because of the fierceness of playoff games in the 1970s, 1980s, and 1990s.

The 49ers were none too happy when the Oakland franchise was awarded to the brand-new American Football League in 1960. For 14 years San Francisco owned the growing market. When the AFL was announced, it looked at first like Minneapolis would get a team, but at the last moment they got an expansion NFL club, leaving Oakland available.

The Raiders certainly did not pose much of a threat at first. Somebody suggested that they be called the Oakland Señors, which begs the question as to whether there would ever have been such a thing as Señor

Nation? At first, the Raiders—the name was a combination of somebody on the Oakland City Council having been a Texas Tech Red Raider alum, the seafaring nature of Jack London's old town, and the riff on "pirates"— played home games at Kezar, and even Candlestick, to little fanfare.

Then they switched to a glorified high school field in Oakland named after an undertaker. But the 49ers were poor, and there was hunger for quality football. The east bay long had no identity. "Lost Generation" writer Gertrude Stein stated "there is no there there." But that was before the Raiders came along.

When Al Davis took over as coach, then AFL commissioner, then Raiders managing general partner, all bets were off. He quickly turned the Raiders into a team that was vastly superior to the 49ers. They were exciting, the 49ers dull. Then Oakland built a modern stadium, the Oak-land–Alameda County Coliseum. It was so much better than Kezar—or Candlestick, for that matter—as to be beyond dispute. Long before Joe Namath led the "Super Jets" to victory, the Raiders' superiority over San Francisco erased any real question that the American Football League was as good as the established NFL. It was.

Oakland had the Raiders, the Coliseum, then the A's. San Francisco had a bad Niners team, a bad stadium, and hippies urinating all over the park, which had no parking, by the way. Where was the comparison? There was none. They played each other in preseason games, and they were not normal exhibitions. Local pride was on the line.

Naturally, in the first year of the new AFC-NFC arrangement, in which there were interconference games between old AFL-NFL teams, the final game of the regular season was San Francisco at Oakland. It was an immediate barnburner.

To the delight of the league, the Raiders and 49ers both won their respective divisions. The great hope had been that the New York Jets and Giants would be natural rivals, but the Jets faltered. That arrangement has never met the intensity of the 49ers-Raiders feud.

There were fewer two-city—or even two-area—teams in pro football than there were in baseball. There were the Giants and Jets in New York and the Raiders and 49ers in the Bay Area. Chicago and Los Angeles had one team. Washington was close to Baltimore. San Diego sat by itself, never attracting much attention from L.A. even though the Chargers started out there. The Cowboys and Oilers played in the preseason and in the 1970s it got rough when University of Texas Heisman winner Earl Campbell played for Houston, but it never took much beyond that.

Social strata, envy, sophistication, blue collar versus wine drinkers, and of course the cold relationship that marked Lou Spadia and Al Davis gave the Raiders-49ers battles extra tension. In 1970 the crowd at the Coliseum was out for blood, but San Francisco needed a win to capture the division. They beat a Raiders team that had already clinched 38–7 in front of Oakland's loyal fans in a driving rain.

This created great hope that the two teams would meet in Super Bowl IV. It was an open year, with no dominant teams. Both advanced past their first rounds but lost in their conference title games to end the dream.

Throughout the 1970s, the Raiders were a storied team, filled with legendary players, Hall of Famers. The 49ers floundered. The move to decrepit Candlestick was a slight improvement over Kezar (or was it?). But in the late 1970s Davis and NFL commissioner Pete Rozelle openly feuded over a legal issue called "eminent domain." The Los Angeles Coliseum was opening up with the Rams' rumored move to Orange County. The Raiders had a few down years, and the 49ers improved.

In 1980 the "greatness that is the Raiders," as Davis called it, was evident in their Super Bowl–winning performance. They seemingly rubbed it in the 49ers' faces by doing it with the recycled Jim Plunkett. In 1981, however, everything seemed to have swung San Francisco's way. Oakland had a down year. The 49ers were golden with Montana leading them all the way. When Davis announced his move to L.A. in 1982, it seemed like Rome outlasting Hannibal. The 49ers had won the long battle. In truth, the rivalry became hotter than ever.

Naturally, the first regular season game ever played between Jim Plunkett and the brand-new Los Angeles Raiders in the L.A. Coliseum was against Joe Montana and the defending Super Bowl champion San Francisco 49ers.

The Raiders, at least in those first years, fit L.A. like a glove. There was tremendous bitterness in Oakland, of course, but incredibly their fan base traveled, stayed loyal, and of course expanded in the Southland. All their games, home and road, were televised and broadcast on the radio, with longtime favorite Bill King still calling the action. The uniforms were the same, the coach, owner, players, and personnel the same; even the stadium name—Coliseum—was the same.

In a hard-fought struggle, Los Angeles prevailed 23–17 to the delight of their "new" fan base. They put together an excellent season before getting upset by the Jets in front of more than 90,000 in a Coliseum playoff game. The 49ers stumbled badly at 3–6 in the strike-shortened season. In 1983, even though the two teams did not meet, it was as if Davis and the Raiders were telling San Francisco—along with Rozelle and all of pro football—"Hey, we're L.A., we're dominant, we're still the winningest team in pro football!"

What rubbed salt in the 49ers' wound even more was the fact that a team that had played in the cultural backwater of Oakland now played in big Los Angeles. The 1983 Raiders captured their third Super Bowl title. Through the first half of the 1980s, the two best teams in football were the 49ers and Raiders. San Francisco rebounded to win the championship in 1984. The teams met again before 87,006 at the Coliseum in 1985 in a game that had all the earmarks of a rubber match.

Montana shut up the huge L.A. throng in a smashing 34–10 San Francisco victory, featuring all the tools of their Super Bowl greatness, not to mention a new receiver named Jerry Rice.

It would seem that was it, since San Francisco captured three Super Bowls in the next decade while the silver-and-black have never recaptured the "greatness that is the Raiders."

In 1988, however, a year that saw the Raiders stumble and San Francisco capture the "brass ring," Los Angeles won a defensive struggle at Candlestick 9–3. In 1994 the Super Bowl champion 49ers embarrassed Los Angeles on Monday Night Football when Jerry Rice broke Jim Brown's all-time touchdown record in a 44–14 trouncing.

When the Raiders moved back to Oakland in 1995, they were trying to recapture lost magic. They never have. Jerry Rice became a Raider and the team went to the Super Bowl after the 2002 season, but they folded after losing coach Jon Gruden. The preseason games and the occasional regular season contests do not have the intensity of the old L.A.–San

Francisco wars. Both teams were down until recently. Jim Harbaugh's hiring in San Francisco elevated the Niners. Whether the Raiders will find their place in the sun again is an open question. Jack Del Rio's hiring has resuscitated hopes in Oakland just as San Francisco has sunk.

After the Raiders won the Super Bowl in 1977, the Oakland–Alameda County Coliseum put up a sign that read "Oakland: Home of Champions," trumpeting the three World Series titles of the Oakland A's (1972, 1973, 1974); the Golden State Warriors (who played in the next-door Coliseum Arena), winners of the 1975 NBA title; and the Raiders. Additional east bay champs: California's football team won four national championships (1920, 1921, 1922, 1937), its baseball team two (1947, 1957), its basketball team one (1959), and its track team one (1971, but taken away for NCAA violations). Until the 49ers won the 1982 Super Bowl, the west bay claimed only two University of San Francisco basketball titles (1955, 1956), a couple of dusty Stanford national championships in football (1926, 1940), one in basketball during the Paleolithic era (1942), and little else.

Jim Plunkett led Oakland to the 1980 and 1983 World Championships after failing in San Francisco. Ronnie Lott played for the Los Angeles Raiders after a stellar career in San Francisco.

The Computer That Was Dallas

THE 49ERS' RIVALRY WITH THE DALLAS COWBOYS HAS BEEN A HORSE OF an entirely different color from the one they have had with the Raiders. For one, the Raiders and Cowboys, aside from the fact that they are two of the winningest franchises in NFL history, are two teams with different images from top to bottom. Dallas is "America's team," which is different from the "Raider Nation." The Cowboys, in theory at least, are squeaky clean, while the Raiders offer a criminal element . . . on the field and off. Of course, the Michael Irvin–led Cowboys of the 1990s were on as many police blotters as rosters. The Tom Landry teams were parodied as a façade, their coach a "plastic man" with a greater interest in computers than human interest. Several tell-all books and movies parodied Landry and the Cowboys. Then there are the cheerleaders. The Dallas Cowboys Cheerleaders are all-American girls. In Oakland, they could be found in *Hustler* or partying with the notorious Ken Stabler. In L.A., the Raiderettes were notorious for breaking the rules against fraternization with Raiders players.

The Cowboys are a team, like Notre Dame in college, that seems to have a rivalry with everybody. In the 1960s it was with the Green Bay Packers. In the early 1970s it was with the 49ers. In the mid-1970s it was with the Washington Redskins and the Pittsburgh Steelers. In the early 1980s and 1990s it was with the 49ers again.

The rivalry has always been infused by the cross-cultural differences of San Francisco and Dallas, California and Texas, "blue state" politics versus "red state" politics. Mayors and governors have gotten involved, betting cases of Napa Valley wine against boxes of USDA prime steak.

In 1970 the 49ers were an offensive powerhouse, led by quarterback John Brodie and receiver Gene Washington (both Stanford men). Dallas was a team in search of itself. In 1966 the Cowboys behind quarterback "Dandy Don" Meredith had advanced to the NFL title game, only to have Meredith's intercepted pass into the end zone with no time left deny them victory at the hands of the Packers.

Dallas was back in 1967, but this time it was the infamous "ice bowl" in Green Bay, the game where narrator John Facenda made his famous "frozen tundra" description. Cowboys wide receiver Bob Hayes was so cold he ran pass routes with his hands tucked into his shirt. Again, Dallas had victory swiped from them when Packer quarterback Bart Starr snuck over for a touchdown, 21–17.

The reason coach Tom Landry was given the moniker "plastic man" was because he rarely smiled, had little rapport with his players, and was one of the first coaches to rely on computerized information, for which he was lampooned. In truth, Coach Landry was a Christian who cared for his players but did not suffer fools well. Football coaches at every level eventually adopted his methods. His players found out he was a compassionate man who was there for them in later years when the money and the fame were not.

By 1970 he and the Cowboys were working on a reputation for not winning "the big one." That team was called the "Dallas Doomsday Defense." They recovered from a 38–0 Monday Night Football shellacking at the hands of the St. Louis Cardinals to finish 10–4, good for the division title. Quarterback Craig Morton, an All-American at California, was a utilitarian pro. In the first playoff game, Dallas showed no offense, but allowed none either in a 5–0 win over Detroit. The 49ers surprised the 12–2 Minnesota Vikings on the road, returning to Kezar considered somewhere between even and the favorite to beat the Cowboys.

Dallas stuffed Brodie all day long. Morton was as good as he needed to be. Recalcitrant running back Duane Thomas, who represented a new kind of black athlete in the 1960s and 1970s, pointedly refusing to play for "the man," nevertheless ran wild for the ball control Cowboys. The Niners scored a TD too late in a disappointing 17–10 loss. It was the final pro game at Kezar (although the high school "turkey day" game is still played there every Thanksgiving). The team and its fans would bid Golden Gate Park and the hippies adieu in favor of Candlestick the following year. The crowd, as if bound to live up to its rough reputation, was surly and drunk for the most part, chanting "Hurt Morton" as the game got away from the home team.

The Cowboys went to Miami where they lost to Baltimore in what to this day is probably the sloppiest, worst-played Super Bowl ever. They had every chance to win but blew it time and again, further adding to Landry's "can't win the big one" reputation.

In 1971 Dallas moved into Texas Stadium and replaced Morton with young hotshot Roger Staubach, who had done four years in the Navy before coming to the league. Staubach—disciplined, religious, and hard-working—was Landry's kind of guy. Meredith had been a hell-raiser. Morton was a party animal, too, although he later became as religious as Landry.

The 1971 Cowboys are considered one of the better teams in league history. It took them about seven games to find their groove and adjust to Staubach, who could throw, run, and think on the run, a rare combo, but when they hit all cylinders there was no stopping them. The 11–3 Cowboys hosted the 9–5 Niners after both teams advanced past the first round. Dallas chewed San Francisco up and spit them out, 14–3.

In 1972 the idea that a rivalry existed between the two teams seemed incongruous. The Cowboys ran their three-year playoff mark against San Francisco to 3–0, but the game was so wild as to reverberate through the ages. The 49ers led 28–13 entering the fourth quarter. Staubach, the Super Bowl MVP and future Hall of Famer, had been benched for inef-fectiveness but was brought back and led Dallas to 17 points and a 30–28 win that ripped the hearts out of the 49ers. They never recovered, and would be a loser until the Joe Montana years.

That was when the rivalry resumed. Dallas achieved glory in the 1970s, although Super Bowl victories over Pittsburgh eluded them. The 1977 Cowboys, at 12–2, were a juggernaut that dismantled Denver, led by their old quarterback Craig Morton, 27–10 in the Super Bowl.

By 1981 Staubach was retired, but Danny White offered a major challenge to San Francisco. In a see-saw battle for the ages, Montana led San Francisco downfield with the clock ticking away, hitting Dwight Clark with the Catch to clinch the 28–27 win. The roles were reversed.

This time, the heart had been taken from Dallas, and they would not recover until the Troy Aikman era.

It was during this period that the rivalry hit its peak. Dallas fans were gaga over the return to glory of their beloved Cowboys, but victory in those days meant traveling a hard road through San Francisco. In 1992 and 1993 Dallas did just that. In so doing, Aikman established his Canton bona fides, Steve Young proved he was not yet at Montana's level, and Montana—sitting on the bench or playing in Kansas City—saw his legend grow in the City.

In 1994 Young's ascension to superstar status, despite years of glowing statistics and winning records, was not secured until Aikman and Dallas fell 38–28 at the 'Stick. Victory over San Diego in the Super Bowl was an afterthought.

In the years since, Dallas fell slowly but surely. San Francisco maintained a strong NFL presence, but Green Bay became the team to beat. Eventually, both teams became also-rans, with the rivalry spiced up not by legendary games for all the marbles, but by inane acts of unsportsmanlike conduct.

The San Francisco–Dallas rivalry mirrored the larger California-Texas sentiments that have marked the two states, both of which entered the United States in the mid-19th century. In 1988 the Dallas Mavericks pushed the Los Angeles Lakers to seven games before losing in the NBA finals. In 2006 the Texas Longhorns knocked off the Southern California Trojans in a BCS Rose Bowl game that was probably the best college football game ever played. Texas is oil patch from the Gulf of Mexico to its northern borders. California outlawed most oil exploration after a spill off Santa Barbara years ago. Party affiliation has switched. Texas used to be filled with LBJ Democrats, California with Reagan Republicans. Today Texas embodies "red state" Republican politics. California is reliably "blue state" Democrat.

"Neon Deion" Sanders was a mercenary in San Francisco and Dallas. Ken Norton Jr. led San Francisco to the 1994 World Championship after leading Dallas to the 1992 and 1993 titles. He later joined his '95 49ers defensive coordinator, Pete Carroll, on Carroll's staff at Southern California.

The "Steroid Era"

Considered "wilderness years" for Dusty Baker and the San Francisco Giants, in 1995 the club went 67–77 in a schedule shortened by the insidious strike, followed by a 68–94 season in 1996.

Barry Bonds was as good as ever on a losing club. He led the National League in walks (120) and on-base percentage (.431). He scored 109 runs, hit 33 homers, drove in 104, had 292 total bases, slugged at a .577 rate, had 70 extra base hits, and tied for the league lead in assists with 12. Again, he was the league's leading vote-getter for the All-Star Game (one-for-three batting third with an RBI at Veterans Stadium in a National League win, having bested Mark McGwire in the Home Run Contest the previous day).

He became the first Giant since his father to hit 30 homers and steal 30 bases, and on June 28 he stole a base against Colorado to make him and his dad the greatest father/son stolen base combination in history, with 783. Maury and Bump Wills had held the previous record.

In 1996, the club would unload Williams, leaving Bonds exposed in a weak lineup. That did not stop him from playing some of the best baseball of his career. He joined Jose Canseco on the 40/40 Club, set the league record with 151 walks, intentional walks (30), RBI ratio (4.0), and home run ratio (12.3). He started and went 0-for-2 in the All-Star Game at Cleveland, won the Gold Glove for the sixth time, and was Player of the Month in April (32 RBIs). Bonds hit .308, with 42 homers, and 129 RBIs. Had his team contended, he would have been a fine MVP candidate.

"Barry might make two or three mistakes over the course of the year," Willie Mays told *USA Baseball Weekly* in the spring of 1996, "and that's when I talk to him. Other than that, he knows what he's supposed to do."

When Mays was asked to help arrange for an interview with Bonds, Mays knew where to draw the line.

"Not Barry—Barry's in his own f——-g world," Mays says.

"You can't get under my skin no more," Bonds had said to a small crowd of reporters in the clubhouse. "My life is a lot different and better now."

"He's made a conscientious effort—I've seen him signing autographs more this spring," Baker said shortly thereafter. "Sometimes Barry is tough to deal with, but most of the times he's a gentleman. He ain't phony or fake about anything."

Is it phony or fake to be courteous?

"I think what happened to Albert Belle last year [surliness probably cost Belle the MVP award] made him realize that sometimes you have to open up and let people get close," Tony Gwynn told *USA Baseball Weekly*. "He fights the media off, and he does it with players in the league, too."

At the 1995 All-Star Game in Texas, which was Bonds's fifth such appearance, Gwynn, Ozzie Smith, and Bobby Bonilla tried to get their friend to relax with the press.

"We were telling him, man, you've just got to loosen up, you've got to relax and be yourself. Let them see what you're all about," Gwynn said. "I said, 'Here's an opportunity for you to let these people get close, but will you do that?' No. And he said, 'You're right—I won't.' I know what's going on up there [in Bonds's head] and I can be a little more sympathetic than most people. I still say he's the best player in our league, without a question."

That spring, Bonds was asked about hitting 50 homers and stealing 50 bases.

"No, I don't think so," Bonds said. "I'm not that strong."

However, he was by this point in his career upgrading his workout regimen, supervised by personal trainer Raymond Farris. Farris also trained former NFL running back Roger Craig and all-world wide receiver Jerry Rice.

In four months, Bonds had lowered his body fat to 8 percent from 12 percent, and was bench-pressing 315 pounds, up from 230. He had increased his explosiveness by running sprints. He now looked more muscular, more defined, more powerful, with bulging biceps stretching his jersey's sleeves.

"I thought I was in great shape the way I worked out before because I was putting up the numbers I did," Bonds said in *USA Baseball Weekly*, "but I was out of shape. I wanted to prove to myself that I could do it and I'm happy with the results, but it doesn't guarantee success. I don't care how many weights you lift—you can lift until you're blue in the face—it doesn't guarantee success.

"I don't put a whole lot of emphasis on my training program. I don't say that it's going to win me an MVP."

Bonds by this time was officially referring to himself in the third person.

"I'm like Tony Gwynn now," Bonds continued, laughing. "If he hits .340, it's like, 'So? That's Tony.' If Barry Bonds hits 30 home runs and steals 30 bases, it's 'So? That's Barry.' It's harder for people to recognize it now because if somebody has one good year out of his career, it overshadows what I do consistently."

"The years he didn't win the MVP," Gwynn said, "if I had those years, I'd probably win it. That's the hole you dig for yourself. If you're more consistent than anybody in the National League and you do the same thing for five years, sometime around the third year, there's no glamour to it. He's just doing what he should be doing.

"It's going to take an ungodly year. In Barry Bonds' case, it might take 50–50 for him to be an MVP again. That, and the fact that he could do that and his team would probably have to win, too."

"If I ever did try to do that," Bonds said of a prospective 50–50, "I'd hit about .220. You'd have to be willing to give up something for it and I'm not willing to give up anything. I like the 30–30 and hitting .300 and driving in 100 and scoring 100. To me, that's as complete as you can be."

"He sees things quicker than any other player except Hank Aaron," Baker said. "He sees a pitcher flaring his glove on a changeup and he'll come back to the dugout and say, 'Did you see that?' Other guys don't see that until the sixth inning, if they see it at all. And once you can see it, you'll always be able to see it."

"I just know the game well, I guess," Bonds said. "I don't try to evaluate every little thing that other people are doing. I just try to keep myself mechanically sound and if they make a mistake and put it within that square, then if I'm mechanically sound, it doesn't really make a difference what they throw."

"He's probably more comfortable in those [clutch] situations than he is with nobody on in the first inning," Matt Williams told *USA Baseball Weekly*. "Playing against him and playing with him for the last couple of years, nothing he does surprises me. The more you see, you just accept that he's a special player."

"I think it's just that I don't like to lose," Bonds said. "I want to be up in that [clutch] situation to have a shot at it, but I don't have dreams about the World Series or having the bases loaded or nothing like that. My dreams are 9-0 and we're winning in the World Series rather than having a situation where there's a noose around my neck. I try to look at things a little easier than stressful."

"It's like in hockey in an overtime game, you anticipate Gretzky will score," Baker told the media. "In basketball, you know Michael Jordan is going to take the shot. In football, you know Jerry Rice is going to catch the pass. That's the real superstar—when everyone knows he's going to get the ball and he still scores or makes the play."

Bonds also addressed his reputation.

"I feel the press puts a stamp on certain players and once they stamp you as a 'bad person,' then that's what they feed on and there's nothing you can do about it," Bonds said. "I know in my heart the type of ballplayer I am and the type of person I am.

"Every time they say, 'Well, people say,' everyone knows it's just, 'The press says.' I mean, be honest—they didn't do a survey, they didn't really ask anybody?

"As many people as they say don't like you, I have that many people who do like me, so I don't worry about it."

In this respect, Bonds hit the nail on the head. Most of his "bad reputation" had been based on his relations with the media. He was occasionally standoffish with fans, and not always available for autographs, but this can be attributed to time constraints. He does have love in his heart, and a genuine desire to help people in need.

In the off-season, he joined Baker on an eight-game tour of Japan, where he hit .292 with a homer while the Major League All-Stars posted a 4-2-2 record.

In 1997, Baker and new general manager Brian Sabean had reorganized the club into a surprise contender again. How they did it is still something of a mystery. Second baseman Jeff Kent, who had played college ball at nearby California, was a solid fielder with pop, but nobody was predicting MVP awards, or consideration for Cooperstown, in his future. Matt Williams, on the other hand, was very much a player carrying those kinds of expectations, but Sabean, in one of his early moves, traded him to the Cleveland Indians for Kent.

In fairness, it was a good trade for Cleveland, who went to the World Series with Williams, but they were more or less forced to trade him to Arizona because Williams's children, separated from him by divorce, now lived in the Phoenix area and he wanted to be near them. He then won a world title with the Diamondbacks.

Sabean had none of the goodwill reserve he now has, and was lambasted for dealing Williams for Kent, Jose Vizcaino, and Julian Tavarez. "I'm not an idiot," he said at the time. But Kent's arrival in San Francisco marked a new heyday in Giants baseball annals. Undoubtedly, the arrival of Barry Bonds was the biggest thing in town. The building of Pacific Bell Park may never have taken place without him, but Kent's bat in the lineup increased Bonds's production, as well as Kent's. In 1997 the new second baseman slammed 29 home runs and drove in 121 runs.

"We had some fierce, fierce competitors," recalled Baker of 1997. "We left spring training thinking: we have a chance to go to the dance."

On July 31, 1997, at the trading deadline, Sabean acquired Wilson Alvarez, Roberto Hernandez, and Danny Darwin from the White Sox for Keith Foulke and some minor leaguers, none of whom panned out.

"I still can't believe it to a certain extent," exclaimed Sabean.

"I couldn't believe we were getting guys of this quality," said Baker.

Sabean was excoriated first for the Williams trade, and got little love for the midseason transactions, but in retrospect he established himself as the greatest general manager in San Francisco, if not all of franchise history, by dint of the moves he made in 1997.

It was also a key year in Dusty Baker's career. In 1993, the first-year skipper appeared to be a miracle worker, but when two journeyman pitchers (Bill Swift, John Burkett) have career 20-win years, and your star (Bonds) has a season favorably comparable to the best seasons of Babe Ruth and Ted Williams, miracles can happen. In 1997 first baseman J. T. Snow was a defensive whiz, but the lineup was often patchwork and their opening day pitcher was Mark Gardner.

Mark Gardner?

How did they really do it? Well, Kent's 121 RBIs, Snow's fancy glovework, third baseman Bill Mueller's .292 batting average, and Shawn Estes emerging as a top pitcher with 19 victories, a 3.18 ERA, and 181 strikeouts in 201 innings, certainly contributed, but the short answer is: BARRY BONDS. The Giants' superstar hit .291 with 40 homers, 101 RBIs, 37 stolen bases, 123 runs scored, 145 walks, and started in left field in the All-Star Game (stealing a base). He hit *two* inside-the-park home runs against San Diego on September 21.

"We all knew Barry would drive the bus, get the attention, and we'd just be passengers, doing our job," recalled Snow.

It was one of those seasons that occasionally manifest themselves; an average club that never quite goes away, like Rocky Balboa refusing to get knocked out of the ring, until it is September and you look up and see the name "San Francisco" only two games back in the standings.

That was where they were when the Los Angeles Dodgers arrived at Candlestick Park with 12 games left on the schedule. This was the Dodgers' opportunity to put San Francisco away in front of the Giants' own fans, to wrap up the division and get ready for the playoffs. Instead, they were like Butch Cassidy and the Sundance Kid staring at the posse always within tracking distance of them, asking, "Who *are* those guys?"

Bonds hit a homer in his first at-bat, and the Giants won eight of their last 10. Bonds had seven home runs and 14 runs batted in. But the moment that is best remembered was a home run by little known Brian Johnson that beat Los Angeles, igniting the crowd in one of the most cherished memories of the dilapidated old ballyard.

The date was September 18, 1997, and 52,188 fans packed Candlestick on a perfect Indian summer day. In the top of the 12th inning, Rod Beck pitched out of a bases load, no out jam to preserve it. Johnson's shot off Mark Guthrie won it 6–5.

"You always dream of hitting game-winning homers, but you don't expect them," said Johnson. Johnson was a local guy from Oakland who played baseball and quarterback on the football team at Stanford. His career has little in the way of highlights, but among Giants fans his name resonates with names like Bonds and Kent. His knock took all the air out the Dodgers, in the tradition of Bobby Thomson's "shot heard 'round the world," Willie May's single off Ed Roebuck in '62, and Joe Morgan's 1982 last-weekend blast. The club finished 90–72 and beat fading Los Angeles by two games to win the West outright.

"When they made the playoffs, there's a shot of Barry running into the infield, waving his arms in pure joy, and the little boy in him came out," former teammate Matt Williams told *Sports Century*.

In the postseason, it was the same old story.

San Francisco faced the upstart, recent-expansion, wild card Marlins in the first round Division Series. Florida featured Bobby Bonilla and a host of free agent stars cobbled together for a one-year run by Blockbuster Video owner Wayne Huizenga, who spent $89 million. By midseason, he was ready to sell the team because he said he was losing millions despite a 30 percent increase in attendance.

Bonds had three hits in three straight losses to the eventual World Champions.

"At the time, we didn't know it, but looking back, I don't think there's any doubt the play-offs that year was beating the Dodgers," recalled Krukow.

"I remember during the playoffs, walking into the locker room, and Barry was under a sea of microphones, and his eyes were red and it hurt," observed actor Robert Wuhl.

Barry had made a guest appearance on Wuhl's HBO comedy, *Arli$$*, about a craven sports agent. In the episode, Arliss says he wants him as a client because other players of less talent get more endorsement money than he does. Arliss asks him why that is?

"I'm too nice a guy?" replies Bonds.

"From time to time, I'll wear my ring, and he's taken it off and looked at it," Bonilla told ESPN. "And he's not said much, he just won't talk about it."

"There's times I just can't take the abuse anymore," said Bonds. "Everybody expects so much, and that's a lonely place to be."

The abuse? Bill Clinton took abuse during the Monica Lewinsky scandal. A kid who comes home each day to a drunken father who beats him suffers abuse. It is quite the stretch to imagine this million-dollar baseball player experiencing legitimate "abuse."

"Barry says whatever he feels," said Josh Suchon of the *Oakland Tribune* to ESPN. "He doesn't care if the manager gets upset, his teammates get upset, and he definitely doesn't care if the media gets upset."

"He made the guy from *Sports Illustrated* wait for four days before he talked to him," recalled Mark Whicker of the *Orange County Register*, referring to the infamous *SI* cover, "I'm Barry Bonds, And You're Not."

"I said to his father, I said, 'Bobby, how come you're such a nice guy and your son's such a jerk?'" recalled Hall of Fame Chicago scribe Jerome Holtzman.

"Reggie Jackson was that way, too," recalled veteran beat writer Ron Bergman of the *San Jose Mercury News*. Bergman had covered the A's in the 1970s, and wrote a book about Charlie Finley's dynasty, *The Moustache Gang*. "But Reggie loved the press and knew how to work it."

"A lot of players don't like dealing with us," added Whicker. "Barry Bonds is one of the few who's honest about it. He's got a Michael Jordan type of presence, but he doesn't have a Michael Jordan type of diplomacy."

In 1998, Bonds created the 400/400 Club.

"He comes up to me and says, 'Well, I've done it, I got you off the list,' and I said to him, 'The only thing you've done is make up the best father-son combination in baseball history, and believe me, father is first,'" said Bobby on ESPN.

Is there any doubt that the two were rivals? That Bobby, for all of his fatherly pride, still held on to his own position versus his son? Can one imagine that Barry sniffed arrogantly when Bobby said that to him?

"He might be the most confident individual in sports," said Bonilla. In a radio interview around 1999, Bonds was infamously quoted saying, "I'm not arrogant, I'm good."

"Both Griffey and Bonds saw the good side and the bad side of being the sons of fathers in the Major Leagues and of being superstars," said the *Chronicle*'s Henry Schulman on *Sports Century*. "I think they both would sell their souls in order to win a championship."

In 1998 baseball came back from the 1994 strike, led by big Mark McGwire's record-breaking home run production. Baker's club won 89 games, and after 162 regular season contests, their postseason fate was still undetermined. Tied with Sammy Sosa and the Cubs for the wild card berth, they had to go to Wrigley Field for a Monday playoff, which they lost.

Bonds, as usual, was spectacular in the regular season, but he had to go home disappointed again. Batting cleanup at homer-friendly Coors Field in the All-Star Game, Bonds hit a three-run, 451-foot home run off Bartolo Colon. That made for the first-ever father-son home run combination in All-Star Game history.

For the record, he hit .303 with 37 homers and 122 RBIs. He had 44 doubles, a career high. He set a league record by getting on base *15 consecutive times* during a key August-September stretch. During this run, he was nine-for-nine with two doubles, two homers, and six walks.

On April 26 he hit his eighth grand slam. On May 28, Buck Showalter walked him intentionally *with the bases loaded*! He also did something on August 2 that he rarely did, which was charge the mound after being hit by Philadelphia's Ricky Bottalico, earning him a three-game suspension.

1998 may have been the year of McGwire and Sosa, but *Sports Illustrated* still recognized Bonds's greatness:

"It's hard to talk baseball these days without having words like McGwire, Griffey, homer and Yankee dominate the conversation. But don't let the hubbub surrounding the Maris chase and the other record onslaughts obscure the real man of the '90s. Barry Bonds. The Giants outfielder isn't having his strongest statistical season, but he still looms large as the decade's most productive player."

With all of this as backdrop, if *Game of Shadows* by *Chronicle* scribes Mark Fainaru-Wada and Lance Williams (2006) is to believed, 1998 was the year Barry Bonds made a fateful decision, motivated by race and jealousy. Baseball insiders—the *Sports Illustrated* piece, for example—understood that Bonds was the best player in the game. Indeed, experts generally agree that he was the best player of the decade (1990s), but in his mind all the media attention and glamour was going to Sosa and "the white boy," McGwire.

McGwire and Bonds had been squaring off against each other since Big Mac was a Trojans superstar and Bonds an Arizona State All-American. McGwire was the "squeaky clean" kid, admired and loved. USC fans chanted "Bail Bonds" at Barry because his father was always getting arrested for drunk driving on the Bayshore Freeway. McGwire received standing ovations on the road. Fans and opponents came out early, staring in awe while he launched massive batting practice home runs. He was a hulking Paul Bunyan of a man, a mythic figure. While there was rumor and random intelligence, few really, truly new what Bonds apparently learned that year: McGwire was on steroids.

Steroids had been around for years. Ken Caminiti was little more than a journeyman until he got on "the juice," which made all the difference in his winning the 1996 National League MVP award, and may well have led him to addiction and early death. Steroids weaken hearts and livers. To use it is to risk early demise, a Faustian bargain many are willing to take for fame and fortune. Jose Canseco had been on it since the early 1980s, and according to him he started McGwire on it. Sosa had elevated himself from a near bust to a superstar, it is now learned, through 'roids.

In 1998, Barry Bonds was a first-ballot Hall of Fame lock, sure to break the 500-homer mark in a few years. It was not enough for him. Apparently a "white boy" getting the attention he craved was the final motivating factor. When he went to Victor Conte and BALCO, a Burlingame steroids supplier, and had his personal trainer, Greg Anderson,

begin a program of procurement, ingestion, and attendant training regimen—this more than Canseco, McGwire, Sosa, or Caminiti—changed
the very nature of sports, and not for the good. This is Barry Bonds's
legacy, and it kept McGwire, Sosa, and a laundry list of others out of the
Hall of Fame. It was the "steroid era."

Ellis Burks hit .306 in 1998 after coming over from
Colorado on July 31.

Jeff Kent had played for Cal's 1988 College World
Series team under coach Bob Milano. He and
Bonds quickly formed the best one-two punch
since Mays-McCovey.

In 1998, closer Robb Nen saved 40 games on a
team that made it to a one-game playoff for the
National League wild card with Chicago at Wrigley
Field. Nen was a high school football/baseball teammate of first baseman J.T. Snow at Los Alamitos High
School in Orange County. Both Nen's and Snow's
fathers were ex-pro athletes. Dick Nen was a big
leaguer; Jack Snow a football star for the Rams. Nen
made the All-Star Game in his first year replacing
Rod Beck, and finished with a 1.72 ERA (0.43 at
Candlestick/3Com Park).

*To say that Beck struck out Zeile, then got Murray to hit a ground-
ball to Kent, who relayed home to Johnson for one, who then relayed
to Snow at first for the double-play does not begin to describe that
moment in Giants history. You probably had to be at Candlestick to
feel your innards shake from the noise, and to see Beck, memories of
his 1993 heroism hanging in the air, brought back to life again. On*

the short list of Candlestick moments that defined Giants fans, their ballpark and their team, and the unique confluence of all three, there aren't many above this.

—SAN FRANCISCO GIANTS: 50 YEARS, BY BRIAN MURPHY,
DESCRIBING THE GAME WITH LOS ANGELES ON
SEPTEMBER 18, 1997

Will you please not put Rod Beck in the game today?

—A LITTLE GIRL'S PLEA TO MANAGER DUSTY BAKER, IN
RESPONSE TO BECK BLOWING A LEAD VERSUS ATLANTA, GIVING
UP FOUR RUNS IN A 5–4 LOSS, PRIOR TO THE SEPTEMBER 18,
1997, GAME IN WHICH BAKER PUT BECK IN WITH THE SCORED
TIED AT FIVE, AND AFTER LOADING THE BASES, HE PITCHED
OUT OF THE JAM BEFORE BRIAN JOHNSON'S HOMER WON IT IN
THE BOTTOM OF THE 12TH INNING

Everyone was gasping for breath. I remember thinking I just needed to get on base. Get a hit, a double—something—and win this thing. . . . It was as if I were in a bubble. A force field. I could see everything. I could feel the vibrations. I knew it was loud, but what I was experiencing was a peaceful moment. . . . I'm so appreciative that people remember me, that I am associated with something positive.

—FORMER SKYLINE HIGH AND STANFORD QUARTERBACK
BRIAN JOHNSON ON HIS GAME-WINNING HOMER VERSUS THE
DODGERS, SEPTEMBER 18, 1997

That was a moment you'd have a hard time scripting.

—FORMER GIANTS BROADCASTER TED ROBINSON
ON JOHNSON'S HOME RUN

I have no desire to go anyplace else, and the Giants have been kind enough to sign me to three- or four-year contracts. . . . I was in Acapulco a couple of years ago, and a guy came up to me and said, "Where's Kruk?" And I went, "I have no idea where Kruk is." And he was stunned because he thought he was probably right around the corner.

—Longtime announcer Duane Kuiper on his relationship with the Giants and partner Mike Krukow, a former San Francisco teammate

―~◆~―

I think we were both lucky because we both had radio shows as players and the Bay Area was used to our voices and our perspectives. . . . Kuip had played in the big leagues for 10 years and I played 13. We prep ourselves the same way now that we prepped as players. . . . I think the drama of baseball is something that builds slowly.

—Mike Krukow on the Kuiper-Krukow broadcasting team

Farewell to the "Prison Yard"

IN APRIL 1999, BARRY BONDS'S EX-WIFE SUN BONDS WON A STATE appeals court ruling that overturned their prenuptial agreement and granted her half of the All-Star's baseball earnings during their seven-year marriage.

The couple had signed an agreement the day before their wedding in February 1988 in which they relinquished the right to community property and agreed to keep future earnings separate. That meant Sun Bonds would not share in 50 percent of Bonds's salary, which was $8 million per year when they divorced in December 1994.

Bonds's agent had warned her that there would be no wedding without her signature. The agreement included several typographical errors and appeared to be altered.

In addition, Sun Bonds, a Swedish immigrant who had been in the United States for only a month, did not understand English well and was only advised by a Swedish friend while Bonds was represented by two lawyers and a financial adviser, the court said.

The ruling concluded that Mrs. Bonds did not voluntarily agree to the prenuptial agreement.

Sun Bonds's lawyer, Paige Wickland, said Mrs. Bonds would not get half of everything Bonds earned during the marriage, but that her client would receive half the money and property that remained from his earnings when the couple separated in May 1994.

The ruling is "very important because more people are doing premarital agreements and they should be fair and fairly procured," Wickland told the press.

In this case, she said, "one side had everything, had all the money and got all the benefits of the agreement. . . . There was no one who was looking out for her benefit."

This was the sort of headline that was always knocking against the image of Barry Bonds; indeed, causing in his mind the motivation to just "show 'em" with a display of force so spectacular that it could not be denied. This was precisely what motivated Ted Williams, who felt if he was so good, so awesome, so over-the-top great, that greatness would make the Boston scribes he feuded with literally "shut up" once and for all. Anybody advising Williams or Bonds on such a strategy need only remind them it is not a good strategy to pick a fight with anybody who "buys ink by the barrel," or in the Internet age, can write anything he wants, read by anybody in the world, at any minute of every day, all at the click of a keyboard. Williams himself called the press the "knights of the keyboard."

Bonds could not simply be judged for his baseball prowess. He was judged for his personal life, his brashness, his arrogance. In 1999, he experienced injuries that limited him to 102 games. He suffered from left elbow pain, groin problems, and knee inflammation. At the time, the ailments actually were thought to have been the determining factor in his future success, since it made him re-evaluate his body, his workout regimen, his stretching routine, and his diet. He felt that his routine in 1996 was making him too tired, so now he would begin to accommodate his age. The result was, literally, history.

The fans and media were stunned at Bonds's change in appearance, beginning in 1999. His father had the build of a lithe track star, as his sister had been at the Tokyo Olympics. Barry's early physique resembled his dad. Over the next couple of years he would more resemble McGwire and Canseco. At first everybody praised him for his newfound dedication. But Bonds's 1999 injuries—he was virtually never hurt before that—are in retrospect tell-tale signs of steroids. Groin problems, inflammation, elbow, and ligament pain—these are some of the odd bodily results of steroid use. McGwire himself had suffered similar injuries in the early 1990s, but had figured out a regimen that worked for his body type, as Bonds would.

In '99, Bonds knocked out 34 home runs in the team's last season at Candlestick Park. On October 1, he had arthroscopic surgery on his knee, performed by Dr. Art Ting. The successful procedure repaired his cartilage and removed inflamed tissue. Bonds had gone under Ting's knife in April to remove a bone spur and repair the damaged tendon in his left arm. Prior to that season, he had played 888 of 908 regular season games with the Giants, but injuries kept him out of the All-Star Game. Baker's squad played winning baseball, but it was not enough to reach the Division Series.

In 1999, Major League Baseball announced their All-Century Team.

"When Griffey was named to the All-Century team, where was the outrage when Barry Bonds was left off?" asked Steve Hirdt of the Elias Sports Bureau in 2002 on *Sports Century*, of contemporary Ken Griffey's selection. Griffey, a great star but apparently clean of steroid use, was a player whose career was eventually overshadowed by the "juicers."

"Bonds had a much higher slugging percentage, a much better on-base percentage, 400 more walks than Griffey and twice as many stolen bases, yet people just said, 'Yeah, Griffey, sure, he's gotta be on the team.'"

"Barry Bonds is one of the greatest players of all time," said renowned announcer Bob Costas. "He's on a relatively short list. I don't think the public's embraced him the way they embraced Ken Griffey Jr., but his career accomplishments place him on that list."

"They're very similar players," Seattle manager Lou Piniella said. "They're both multitalented. Both can beat you with their bat, their glove and their legs.

"When I had Junior here, I thought that because of the more demanding position he played and the age factor that he was the one. But that's not to take anything away from Barry."

"It's unfair on my part to compare Barry to Griffey because I never [previously] played with Griffey," said Seattle outfielder Stan Javier, who had four seasons with Bonds. "Barry is one of the most complete players to ever play the game. He has 400-plus home runs and more than 400 steals—no one else has come close to that. He'll probably hit 600 home runs, and steal between 550 and 600 bases.

"To me, if you compare both at their peaks in their careers, I think Barry is the better player because of his speed."

Then there is the question: Which is the best father-son combination, Barry and Bobby or Ken Senior and Junior? Bonds and his father, Bobby, are the all-time leaders in father-son home runs, stolen bases, and RBIs. Neither Barry nor Junior had ever played in the World Series.

"I saw Barry after we won the World Series in Florida," former Pirate coach Rich Donnelly once told a reporter. "I saw his look and he was jealous. It was like, 'I have everything but I don't have that.'"

"That's got to drive him, to get to a World Series," Rickey Henderson said of him. "He's done everything in baseball except reach the Promised Land. In the postseason, he hasn't been too successful, and he wants to get there and come through when the chips are down and show that he's a money player, too."

Bonds said the same thing in an interview with *Sports Illustrated*, denying that the attention Mark McGwire and Griffey received or any statistical milestones motivated him.

"If I never reach another milestone and the Giants finally win a World Series—that's all I could ask for," he said. "I'd be complete."

By 1999, Bonds had become a creature of habit. His regular pre-game routine was to take some light batting practice, then go in the back of the clubhouse, lie down, and take a nap. He woke up about 7:25 for a 7:35 game.

"The game is easy for him," Donnelly said. "He's playing with the best players in the world, and he looks like that one 12-year-old in Little League who's better than everyone else."

Bonds had a lot of bounce back, too. He once took a swing, grimaced, took a few steps, and fell to the ground in pain with a sprained joint in his lower back. He rode off the field on a cart. Everybody said he was done for a while, but after four games he was back. He hit a homer his first game back.

His ability to hit the ground running after injuries and layoffs separated him from McGwire. Big Mac almost always slumped for a time after coming off the disabled list. Bonds was not intimidated by inside heat, either.

Oakland's Tim Hudson once threw up-and-in at Bonds. He homered into the upper deck.

"All you do is wake up the lion when you throw at my head," Bonds told reporters.

Shawn Estes was asked once about Bonds's relations with reporters.

"I think Barry is making more of an effort to be liked, I really do," Estes told the writers. "But if it looks like a rat and smells like a rat, it's probably a rat. At 30-something years old, you're never going to change who you are, deep down."

Donnelly once told a story, however, that spoke to Bonds's inner beauty.

"My daughter passed away in 1994 with a brain tumor when she was 17 years old," Donnelly said. "I remember one day when she was 15 and she was supposed to meet me at the car after the game, and she showed up late. And when I asked why, she said, 'I just had the nicest talk with Barry Bonds. He told me how I should be when I grow up, how I shouldn't use drugs, how I should go to school.'

"And I said, 'Are you sure you were talking to Barry Bonds?'"

Donnelly said that when he told Bonds about his daughter's death, he cried.

"He can be the meanest guy a writer's ever seen and he can be the warmest, most considerate guy, too," Donnelly said. "And you'll ask, Is he the same guy? Yeah, he is.

"He's an enigma."

As more than one writer and player has said, Barry is Barry.

—◆—

San Francisco has a checkered past. One story concerns a man who was born in Japan, but raised in San Francisco. He moved back to Japan while still in his youth, and was recruited by the military to return to San Francisco as a spy in the late 1930s, prior to World War II. When he arrived in the City, he was met by the sight of the Bay Bridge, a span that extends from San Francisco to Treasure Island and Yerba Buena Island, where the 1937 World's Fair was held. The bridge then goes through a tunnel, and spans again from the island to Oakland across the bay.

In an apocryphal story, the man tells his handlers that they should rethink their plans about going to war with America. Any country capable of building such a structure, he tells them, is capable of "doing anything."

Candlestick Park, which opened in 1960, was another story. Vice President Richard Nixon was a big sports fan, but his analysis of stadiums was not very good. When he dedicated the Los Angeles Memorial Sports Arena, later known as the "Clip Joint," where L.A.'s second basketball team played their games in cheap surroundings, he called the place the "best" basketball facility in the country. Up in San Francisco, Nixon said Candlestick was "the finest baseball stadium in America."

It was the worst. After playing two years at Seals Stadium, the club had moved into their new facility, which immediately looked old. What happened was a story of political graft and corruption. San Francisco mayor George Christopher had a sweetheart deal with construction and land magnate Charlie Harney. Harney had tons of dirt, but no place to put it. They decided that they would use it to create landfill at Candlestick Point. All they needed was a buyer.

Enter New York Giants owner Horace Stoneham. "Horace used to like a toddy," said movie producer Edgar Scherick, who started *Monday Night Football* before a dispute with Roone Arledge forced him out of it, and thus on to Hollywood. "So did his buddy, Chub Feeney."

According to the legend, Stoneham was shown Candlestick Point on a windless morning, but was knocking 'em back at the cocktail hour, by which time gale force winds were blowing across his future stadium. Stoneham liked all the land, because he was convinced that he had to have a lot of parking. That was a big sticking point. He somehow did not notice that only one freeway came close to the stadium, and that fans would have to traverse narrow ghetto streets to get to the place.

It was a big, gray concrete mausoleum. When the Oakland–Alameda County Coliseum was built in 1965, it was immediately identified as a much more pleasant place to attend a sports event. Only the most diehard Giant fan expressed any love for Candlestick. Fans avoided the place, unless the team was good. It cost the team untold millions.

Politics in San Francisco range from liberal Democrat to Socialist, to be kind. Local government is slightly more organized than post–World War II Italy. Getting anything done in such an atmosphere is, at best, problematic.

Consequently, efforts to build a new stadium spelled frustration for Bay Area fans for decades. Politicians and citizens groups always brought up issues of the homeless, the schools without heat, and other social dilemmas that needed to be attended to before a stadium could be built with tax payer funds.

Eventually, plans to build a new park in the City were scrapped. The idea was to build one somewhere in the South Bay. San Jose and Santa Clara, considered "Giants country," seemed logical choices. So, ballot measures went up for votes. What happened? They were defeated every time.

It was left to Magowan, the businessman, to organize an effort to build a stadium using mainly private funds. The result was Pac Bell Park, which opened in 2000, and does more to wipe out the image of San Francisco as a town of bumbling politicos than any other symbol in recent memory.

Bonds from 1993–1999: .302, .617 slugging percentage, 38 home runs per year, 106 RBIs, 30 stolen bases a season, and in 1998 he was the first player to hit 400 homers and steal 400 bases.

So, 2000 was a whole new ballgame. Barry Bonds had as much to do with a stadium being built as any player since the Babe and Yankee Stadium (the "House That Ruth Built") in 1923. In their first year, the club sold out every single game in the 40,800-seat park to finish the season at 3,315,330 in attendance.

Those who say baseball is boring and has lost fan support are out of their minds. It is the most popular sport in America, if not the world. San Francisco is not the only city that sells out every single game. Toronto had done that in the late 1980s and early '90s. Cleveland, Texas, Colorado, Atlanta, and other stadiums have done the same thing in various seasons. You *cannot get a ticket* to Fenway Park. Baseball games are televised every night on ESPN, Fox, and on local stations.

Pro basketball teams play 41 home games and have a hard time selling out 16,000-seat arenas. Pro football teams play eight home games, and maybe they sell out, maybe they do not. Here is baseball, played day in, day out, and they fill stadiums with enthusiastic fans over and over again.

The game is recession-proof, scandal-proof, and, incredibly, strike-proof.

—•—

After getting off to a bad start in their new yard against the Dodgers, no less, the "fabulous Baker boys" went on a tear to beat Los Angeles by 11 games. In 2000, Bonds hit 49 home runs. Kent hit 33 with 125 RBIs, capturing the Most Valuable Player award. In 2001, Bonds broke McGwire's home run record with 73. The club lost to the Angels in the 2002 World Series. In 2003 the BALCO scandal broke out, first when an FBI investigator revealed details, which were researched and revealed by Mark Fainaru-Wada and Lance Williams in their newspaper reporting of subsequent court hearings, eventually in *Game of Shadows*. Bonds won four straight MVP trophies (seven in his storied career), broke Hank Aaron's career home run record in 2007, and after his retirement, San Francisco captured two long-elusive World Series, in 2010 and 2012.

It seems that in 14 years the Giants accomplished all the things they could not attain in some 40 years at Candlestick. It was old, decrepit, wind-swept, dirty, built on corruption, hated by many, yet to those who loved the Giants, it holds memories that linger long and sweet.

—•—

J. T. Snow hit 24 homers with 98 RBIs in 1999, the last year at Candlestick. He won Glove Gloves in 1997 and 1998.

—•—

Retired San Francisco Giants Numbers

24—Willie Mays
27—Juan Marichal
36—Gaylord Perry
30—Orlando Cepeda
44—Willie McCovey

—◦—

61,389 fans were at the last game at Candlestick Park on September 30, 1999. Juan Marichal threw out the first pitch. The Dodgers won, 9–4. The team's marketing slogan all year was Lon Simmon's home run call: "Tell it good-bye." San Francisco's final record at the 'Stick: 1,775–1,398.

—◦—

Proposition 6 (1996) paved the way for the building of Pac Bell Park.

—◦—

The ubiquitous "Murph" was as much a fixture at Candlestick Park as the notorious winds and cold. When the stadium closed its baseball doors in September 1999, Mike Murphy was the Giants' employee with the longest service with the club.

—The Giants Encyclopedia, by Tom Schott
and Nick Peters

—◦—

I loved moving out of Candlestick. Football was such a problem. They used our clubhouse from August on and made it tough. What a thing: no more football!

—Mike Murphy

—◦—

Another episode was when the batting cage was lifted by the wind and dropped almost 100 feet from its initial position.

—100 Things Giants Fans Should Know Before They Die, by
Bill Chastain

—◦—

We used to feel sorry for the fans, not ourselves.

—Willie McCovey

The only difference between Candlestick and San Quentin is that at Candlestick they let you go home at night.
—Ex-Giant Jim Wohlford

Good riddance. I don't even want to look at a post card of this stadium.
—Ex-Dodgers outfielder Rick Monday, 1999

That's where I'm going, I told myself. In another week, I'll be there, sitting in the stands with Dad, watching the Giants in person.
—Searching for Candlestick Park, by Peg Kehret

Jon Miller is the best announcer in baseball . . . in his price range!
—Giants announcer Jon Miller doing a dead-on impersonation of legendary Dodgers play-by-play man Vin Scully

It was Heaven on Earth. People would badmouth it, and I couldn't understand what they were talking about. Cold? Well, San Francisco is cold.
—Jon Miller on Candlestick Park

Like Candlestick, it's known to feature a breeze or two.
—World Champs: San Francisco Giants, by Roland Lazenby, on Pac Bell Park

TO the Whiner

Terrell Owens is probably not as bad a guy as some make him out to be, but he sure makes it hard to believe otherwise. How good was he? From a strictly physical standpoint, his ability was world-class, but his off-field (and on-field) antics prove that distractions can indeed take away from a player's contributions.

Some years ago he appeared in a commercial that "shocked" viewers watching *Monday Night Football*. In an ABC ploy meant to advertise football and the hot series *Desperate Housewives*, blonde bombshell Nicollette Sheridan appears wearing a towel and a lustful expression, all alone in the locker room, except for TO. She tempts TO not to go out and play football, the implication obviously being that wild times are to be had with her, *sans* the towel which is shown falling to the floor.

What all of this says is not clear. TO shrugged off the sideline pundits and went on his merry way, which included on-field highlights, commercial endorsements, and notoriety. He has never really *hurt* anybody, although he has certainly set a few football teams back when they needed him to buckle down. Nobody would begrudge him the money he made or the fame and fans he enjoyed.

TO's career can be judged to be one filled with many exciting highlights, but ultimately he is viewed negatively. As great as he was, he played on teams that might have gone all the way, or at least farther than they did. TO's disruptive ways are, in the end, one of the reasons some of those teams failed. In a team game, this is not a good legacy.

Like Randy Moss, TO never led a team to a Super Bowl championship to completely shed his image. Rightly or wrongly, he is viewed as a player who helped get teams close to the title, then prevented those teams from attaining the title. A contemporary, one-time teammate, and semiadversary, Donovan McNabb, on the other hand, was viewed as a guy who gave every measure of himself to help his team win. Receivers like Fred Biletnikoff and Jerry Rice; quarterbacks like Ken Stabler and Joe Montana; these players are viewed as winners who went beyond their natural abilities. TO is heretofore viewed as wasting his many gifts.

TO was the first son of Marilyn Heard. Most of Marilyn's childhood was spent in fear and silence. Marilyn's mother, Alice, was cruel to her children, raising them in a confined environment with little love or support. Marilyn wasn't allowed to play with other children, and had to come home directly after school. If she didn't, she would pay the price.

Marilyn had Terrell when she was 17 years old. A neighbor 14 years her senior, L. C. Russell, who lived across the street with his wife and kids, was the baby's father. After Terrell, Marilyn had a girl named Latasha. She was married to the infant's father for a brief time. Then in the early 1980s came two more babies, Sharmaine and Victor, fathered by another man.

Terrell often stayed with his grandmother Alice. He was whipped regularly. For all the abuse, however, Terrell loved Alice, viewing her as a second mother. Alice's marriage fell apart and she drank heavily. Terrell was forced to watch out for her. One time Alice was so intoxicated, she put her purse in the oven and burned all her money. She bought Terrell a go-cart, but they recklessly drove on the highway.

When Terrell turned 12, he befriended a girl across the street. Her father noticed and confronted him, warning Terrell that the girl was actually his half-sister. Thus the youngster learned who his father was.

Terrell loved football, idolizing San Francisco star Jerry Rice. Alice opposed his playing, but Marilyn supported him. Marilyn often found herself back in Alice's house with Terrell, but she eventually moved into a beat-up two-bedroom home. Terrell stayed with Alice because there simply wasn't room for him in the cramped dwelling.

At Benjamin Russell High School, Terrell lettered four times in football and track, accumulated three letters in basketball, and one in baseball. He actually didn't start for the football team until his senior year. He even thought about quitting the sport, but his coaches talked him out of it. He had great, untapped ability.

Tall, lanky, and fast, Terrell's skills were overlooked, but the University of Tennessee at Chattanooga went after the multisport star. With the Moccasins, Terrell lined up at forward on the basketball team for three years, including five starts for the UTC squad that qualified for the NCAA tournament in 1995. In his senior year, he anchored the school's 4x100 relay team.

In football he wore number 80 in honor of Jerry Rice. His biggest day came against Marshall, when he set a school record with four TDs. He caught 58 receptions for 836 yards and 6 touchdowns, earning second-team All-Southern Conference honors. He was regularly double-covered as a senior and had a less stellar season: 43 receptions for 666 yards and a touchdown.

At 6'3" and more than 200 pounds with speed, Terrell was drafted by San Francisco in the third round (89th overall) of the 1996 draft. The 49ers had traded up to pick J.J. Stokes out of UCLA, but he disappointed. It was a chance to play with Rice and quarterback Steve Young.

George Seifert was the head coach. Pete Carroll was the defensive coordinator. Bill Walsh returned to the front office. The team appeared to be a Super Bowl contender. Defensively, Bryant Young was among the league's best on the line, while Tim McDonald and Merton Hanks were solid at the safety positions.

When Stokes went down with an injury, Terrell caught four passes for 94 yards, including a 45-yard touchdown. In the final 10 games, he posted 32 receptions for 488 yards and four touchdowns, second on the team to Rice. The Niners finished second in the NFC West at 12–4. Young suffered two concussions. In the playoffs, they were beaten by Brett Favre and the Green Bay Packers.

Seifert retired and was replaced by Steve Mariucci. Carroll took over as the head coach at New England. Young was turning 36, and Rice would soon be 35. Running back Garrison Hearst was brought in. On defense, the front seven was strong, but the secondary was average.

Injuries to Rice and Young increased the focus on Terrell (four TD receptions), and San Francisco started 4–1. The defense responded, too. Owens became most dangerous after catching the ball with 60 receptions for 936 yards and eight touchdowns.

San Francisco finished 13–3, good for first in the NFC West. In the playoffs, they beat Minnesota 38–22. Owens, Rice, and Stokes matched the Vikings' Randy Moss, Cris Carter, and Josh Reed. The Packers, however, defeated them 23–10 in the championship game. It was their fifth defeat in the last four years versus Green Bay. Terrell caught six balls for 100 yards.

In 1998 Rice returned, coach Steve Mariucci promised to open up the passing attack, Dana Stubblefield left via free agency, while Young and Junior Bryant were still a terrific duo up front. In the defensive backfield, R. W. McQuarters, San Francisco's first-round pick from Oklahoma State, looked to settle in at one of the corners.

The 49ers started strong with blowout wins in their first two games, ranked first in the NFL in rushing and passing. Terrell became a star. He escorted Hearst into the end zone on a 96-yard touchdown run for an overtime victory over the New York Jets. Two months later, he led the Niners over the Giants, hauling in a 79-yard touchdown pass, while Hearst rushed for 166 yards.

Trailing Green Bay 27–23 in the playoffs, Steve Young guided the Niners downfield, and with three seconds left, he crouched under center for a final snap from the Packers' 25-yard line. After tripping over a teammate's foot, he spotted Terrell near the goal line and fired a strike. Terrell got hammered as the ball reached him, and he somehow managed to hold on to deliver a thrilling 30–27 win. The Falcons, however, beat them 20–18 to go to the Super Bowl.

In 1999 the team signed running backs Charlie Garner and Lawrence Phillips, and also added Charles Haley to bolster the defense. But Young was out with a series of concussions, and Rice's yards-per-catch dipped to a career low. Mariucci turned to quarterbacks Jeff Garcia and Steve Stenstrom. After a 3–1 start, they dropped eight straight, ending 4–12. Owens had 60 receptions for 754 yards and four touchdowns. Young announced his retirement, leaving the team to Jeff Garcia.

Ahmed Plummer from Ohio State and Jason Webster from Texas A&M joined the defensive unit. Early in the 2000 campaign, the Niners visited Dallas. San Francisco jumped out to a big lead, and built it further on a touchdown pass to Terrell. Unable to control his emotions, he sprinted to the star in the middle of the field in a celebration that clearly offended the Cowboys. When Terrell scored again and repeated his actions, some on the opposing sideline had seen enough, including George Teague, who blindsided the San Francisco receiver.

Thus was "TO" born.

The 49ers suspended TO for a week and fined him $24,000. He reacted angrily. The media savaged him. National sportstalk host Jim Rome made blistering fun of TO's "star" turn. The team went downhill fast. Rice was showered with praise and ovations, in contrast to the treatment accorded TO. But TO stole the show. Running free all day long, he logged an NFL-record 20 receptions for 283 yards against Chicago. TO finished 2000 with 97 receptions and 1,451 yards, scoring 13 touchdowns. Terrell earned a trip to Hawaii for his first Pro Bowl. Garcia blossomed, too.

Still vilified in the press, TO began to feud with Mariucci in 2001 after Jerry Rice left to become an Oakland Raider. Teammates avoided him in the locker room.

When San Francisco blew a 19-point lead in Chicago, losing in overtime after TO mishandled a pass that Bears free safety Mike Brown intercepted and returned for the game-winning score, he accused Mariucci of protecting good friend Dick Jauron, the Chicago head coach whose job was on the line. The comment left people to ponder two possibilities. One: that it was a stupid comment. Two: that TO might actually be, simply, stupid. Neither possibility served him publicly. It definitely was of no value in his relations with the coach.

The Niners still finished 12–4. TO recorded 93 receptions for 1,412 yards and 16 touchdowns. He was selected to the Pro Bowl for the second time, and earned first-team All-Pro honors from the Associated Press, but San Francisco lost to old nemesis Green Bay 25–15 in the playoffs. TO caught just four passes, and a ball that would have given San Francisco a lead was tipped away. In the locker room, center Jeremy Newberry overheard TO openly complain and advised him to keep quiet. TO's response: demand a trade.

In the off-season, with no trade in the offing, Mariucci tried to patch things up. Playing in Seattle in a key 2002 division showdown, TO hauled in the game-winning touchdown in the 28–21 victory. Then he pulled a Sharpie out of his sock, signed the ball, and handed it to his financial adviser sitting in an end zone luxury suite rented by Shawn Springs, the cornerback he had just beaten. America was unimpressed. Seahawks coach Mike Holmgren said he dishonored the game. ESPN analysts Sean Salisbury, Dennis Green, and Tom Jackson ripped him. TO's reaction: to bring a camera crew into his home like a rap star showing off his "crib." America was less impressed. TO's reaction: to blame his unpopularity on racism. America's conclusion: TO is either an idiot or doing an excellent imitation of one.

On the field he was spectacular, at least as a regular season player in games that did not mean everything: a career-high 100 receptions, 1,300 yards, and 13 touchdowns. The Niners went 10–6, finishing first in the weak NFC West.

Down by 14 points at halftime against the Giants in the first playoff game, TO started spouting off. They fell further behind 38–14. But TO showed leadership, reeling in nine passes for 177 yards and two touchdowns, plus a pair of two-point conversions. San Francisco won 39–38 in miraculous fashion.

Then Tampa Bay crushed them 31–6. Mariucci was fired. Dennis Erickson, who had turned down the USC job in 2000, leaving it open to the third or fourth choice (Pete Carroll), was brought in. After a loss to Minnesota, TO went into a screaming rage. He made the Pro Bowl with 80 receptions, 1,102 yards, and nine touchdowns. Mainly he spouted off about how unhappy he was. Nobody was impressed with anything about him at this point other than his God-given abilities.

He was traded to Baltimore. Infuriated, he forced a settlement in which he ended up at Philadelphia in a three-way deal including the Ravens. He confirmed the low opinion of his moral character when he complained during the preseason about not seeing the ball enough, and in an interview with *Playboy* hinted that Jeff Garcia was gay. Garcia subsequently dated a *Playboy* Playmate.

TO's actions in Philadelphia were moronic, starting with *actually arriving late for the first game.* In the volatile Philly atmosphere, TO played spectacularly on the field.

Against the Bears, TO did six sit-ups for each of his TD catches to that point in the season. Cleveland fans reigned disrespect on TO, causing him to tear down signs berating him. In a 15–10 win over Baltimore, he mocked Ray Lewis's "squirrel" dance, gyrating in the end zone after a touchdown that put the contest on ice.

TO touched off a firestorm of controversy with the racy promotion with Nicollette Sheridan. Ultimately, amid league pressure, Terrell apologized, as did ABC and Sheridan.

Then TO suffered an injury prior to the playoffs. Quarterback Donovan McNabb led them to a 27–14 win over Minnesota. TO was unavailable in that or the NFC championship game win over Atlanta. Donovan showed he was the team leader and Philly did not need TO.

TO played fairly well in the Super Bowl, but his injury ultimately may have made the difference in the 24–21 loss to Tom Brady and New England.

After the Super Bowl, he dumbly criticized everybody and everything. He had reached new heights of selfish egotism. Eventually, despite obvious talent, the decision was made that his character faults overshadowed his ability. He was run out of Philly on a rail and ended up in Dallas, where he continued to say and do ignorant things.

Dennis Erickson was once a golden boy, but his story is indicative of how the coaching game can take strange twists and turns of fate. Erickson succeeded Jimmy Johnson as coach at the University of Miami, winning a national championship in 1991. He led Oregon State to the Fiesta Bowl, where the 11–1 Beavers trounced Notre Dame. When the USC job became vacant, Erickson was the top choice of athletic director Mike Garrett. He turned down what was traditionally one of the most prestigious jobs in the profession. Since that time, Pete Carroll (Garrett's third or fourth choice) was being compared to John McKay and Howard Jones (and after a Super Bowl win for Seattle, Bill Walsh and Paul Brown). Erickson had zero success with the 49ers, was fired, and had zero success at Idaho, where his salary was a fraction of what he made in his heyday, but he enjoyed some winning season at Arizona State. He is a mercenary.

Denise DeBartolo York and Dr. John York were not the worst owners in pro football history, it just seemed that way. Denise's brother, Eddie, took over a bad franchise and helped turn them into the greatest dynasty pro football has ever known. Denise and her husband, York, then put a power play together. True, it was not as bad as what allegedly went down with Georgia Frontiere, taking the Rams from Carroll Rosenbloom and stealing it from his son, but the DeBartolo-York combo was, well, unimpressive. In their tenure they oversaw the transformation of the greatest dynasty ever into one of the worst eras in 49ers history. Finally, their son Jed York came along to save the day. Or so it seemed at first.

Did you know that Alex Smith, San Francisco's number-one draft pick in 2005, played at Helix High School in San Diego, where he was a teammate of Reggie Bush? Utah's Smith, USC's Bush and Matt Leinart, and Oklahoma's Adrian Petersen and Jason White, were all finalists for the 2004 Heisman Trophy. The only reason Bush did not make two straight Helix High number-one picks in 2006 was because of a last-second question about a house owned by his parents. He went number two to New Orleans. Hall of Fame basketball star Bill Walton also led Helix to a state record for consecutive victories in 1970 that was broken in the early 1980s by Drake High of San Anselmo.

Mike Shumann, a member of the 1981 World Champion 49ers, became a well-respected San Francisco TV sportscaster. Gary Plummer, a linebacker on the 1994 49ers world champions, became the team's radio color analyst.

Top 10 49ers Nemeses of the Candlestick Era

1. Roger Staubach, Dallas Cowboys
2. Troy Aikman, Dallas Cowboys
3. Russell Wilson, Seattle Seahawks
4. Lawrence Taylor, New York Giants
5. Fred Dryer, Los Angeles Rams
6. Raymond Lewis, Baltimore Ravens
7. Brett Favre, Green Bay Packers
8. Mike Singletary, Chicago Bears
9. Emmitt Smith, Dallas Cowboys
10. Duane Thomas, Dallas Cowboys

Doldrums

THE 2002 NFL SEASON BEGAN WITH THE DIVISIONAL REALIGNMENT. The 49ers gained two divisional rivals, the Seattle Seahawks and Arizona Cardinals, while former divisional foes Atlanta, New Orleans, and Carolina moved to the newly formed NFC South. The team's production dropped from the previous year, Jeff Garcia went from having 31 and 32 TDs in the previous two seasons, to only 21 in 2002. The 49ers defense struggled at times, but they won the NFC West for the first time since 1997, with the division-clinching game coming on a last second touchdown pass to Terrell Owens against the Dallas Cowboys. They finished 10–6. In the 2002 NFC playoffs they hosted the New York Giants. The Giants had a 38–14 lead late into the third quarter. The Giants' defense was highly ranked, but San Francisco started to chip away.

By the final minute in the fourth quarter Jeff Garcia had led the team back from the 24-point deficit. Giants quarterback Kerry Collins then led a drive in the game's final minute to put the Giants at the 49ers' 23-yard line with six seconds left for a shot at a game-winning field goal. Trey Junkin, who had been signed by the Giants that week, had a bad snap so holder Matt Allen attempted a desperate pass down the field, which fell incomplete but there was a flag on the play. The initial thought by spectators and the Giants was a clear pass interference, but it was to an ineligible receiver so the game ended like that. The next day the NFL said the referee blew the call and it was pass interference. A press conference was made and a reporter asked 49ers head coach Steve Mariucci about his thoughts on the NFL, saying they blew the call.

"Bummer," he replied. It was the second biggest comeback victory in NFL playoff history, the 49ers winning 39–38. The 49ers lost the next week to the eventual Super Bowl Champion Tampa Bay Buccaneers in the Divisional round, 31–6. This was the last postseason appearance for the 49ers until the 2011 playoffs. Steve Mariucci, whose published statements about his degree of power in the organization had frayed already-strained relations with management, was fired by John York, despite a winning record.

The 2002 season marks the final ending to a long run of success begun with the hiring of Bill Walsh prior to the 1979 season. While there had been a few bumps in the road marking the end of Steve Young's career, the growing pains of his successor Jeff Garcia, and the trials and tribulations of the mercurial Terrell Owens, for the most part the San Francisco 49ers from 1981 to 2002 mark as great a two-decade run as pro football has ever known.

Alas, the departure of the Giants from Candlestick Park into the fabulous Pac Bell Park, only accentuated the deficiencies of the 'Stick. Symbolic or not symbolic, the desultory performance of the 49ers in the years after the Giants left made their need for a new stadium more and more glaring.

The 2003 season was one of turmoil for the 49ers. The 49ers finished 7–9 and missed the playoffs for the first time in two seasons. The team finished the 2004 season last in the NFC West Division with a 2–14 record, tying a franchise worst and finishing last for the first time since 1979; ending what had been the NFL's longest active streak for not finishing last in a division. With the worst record in the NFL the team secured the rights to the first pick in the NFL Draft. Dennis Erickson and GM Terry Donahue were fired.

Mike Nolan, the son of Dick Nolan, who had led the team to three consecutive playoff appearances from 1970 to 1972, was brought in. Alex Smith from the University of Utah was selected with the first overall pick of the 2005 NFL Draft. It was a pick predicted by most, though many thought the 49ers might select local product Aaron Rodgers of the University of California. Smith's rookie season was a disaster, producing only one touchdown against eleven interceptions. The team finished fourth in the NFC West for the second consecutive year, with a 4–12 record.

Frank Gore from the University of Miami did emerge as a star, rushing for a franchise record of 1,695 rushing yards, which led the NFC in

2006, along with eight touchdowns. He was awarded his first Pro Bowl appearance. However, the team finished 7–9, their fourth consecutive losing season.

Middle linebacker Patrick Willis was named the 2007 AP NFL Defensive Rookie of the Year. Quarterback troubles plagued the 49ers. On October 20, 2008, after a 2–5 start, Mike Nolan was fired. Assistant head coach Mike Singletary, a Hall of Fame linebacker with the Chicago Bears, was named as the interim head coach. Singletary proved to be a fan favorite when after his first game as head coach he delivered a memorable postgame interview. Singletary said of their loss: "right now, we've got to figure out the formula. Our formula. Our formula is this: we go out, we hit people in the mouth."

The team went 5–4 overall under Singletary, winning five of its final seven games and ending the season with a 7–9 record. After the last game of the season, Singletary was named permanent head coach by Jed York, who had been appointed as team president just days before. Jed York is the oldest son of John York and Denise DeBartolo York.

On April 25, 2009, the 49ers selected Texas Tech wide receiver Michael Crabtree, and posted an 8–8 record. Frank Gore collected his fourth consecutive 1,000-yard season, a 49ers record. Vernon Davis and Patrick Willis took star turns, but the 2010 season was a disaster. They started 0–5, Singletary was fired, and finished a sad and disappointing 6–10.

Harbaugh and Kaepernick:
The Dawning of a New Age

In 2011, Jim Harbaugh was named the new head coach of the San Francisco 49ers. Born in 1963, Harbaugh's father Jack was a football coach, and the family lived in Ohio, Kentucky, Iowa, Michigan, and California. He attended high school in Ann Arbor, Michigan, and Palo Alto, California, when his father was an assistant coach at Michigan and Stanford. After graduation from high school in Palo Alto in 1982, Harbaugh returned to Ann Arbor and enrolled at the University of Michigan, playing quarterback for the Wolverines, starting for three seasons. As a fifth-year senior in 1986, he led Michigan to the 1987 Rose Bowl and was a Heisman Trophy finalist, finishing third.

The Chicago Bears selected Harbaugh in the first round of the 1987 NFL Draft. He played 14 years as a quarterback in the NFL, with Chicago from 1987 to 1993, the Indianapolis Colts from 1994 to 1997, the Baltimore Ravens in 1998, and the San Diego Chargers in 1999 and 2000. He first became a regular starting quarterback in 1990 with Chicago. In 1995 with Indianapolis, he led the Colts to the AFC Championship Game, was selected to the Pro Bowl, and was honored as NFL Comeback Player of the Year.

From 1994 to 2001, while still playing in the NFL, Harbaugh was an unpaid assistant coach at Western Kentucky University, where his father Jack was head coach. In 2002, he returned to the NFL as the quarterbacks coach for the Oakland Raiders. Harbaugh returned to the college ranks in 2004 as the head coach at the University of San Diego. After leading San Diego to consecutive Pioneer League championships in 2005 and 2006, he moved up to Stanford in 2007 for four seasons and led the Cardinals to two bowl berths, including the 2011 Orange Bowl. Immediately afterward, Harbaugh signed a five-year deal as head coach of the 49ers.

Harbaugh's first season was a huge success. After 10 weeks the 49ers were 9–1, highlighted by road wins against the Philadelphia Eagles, where the team came back from a 20-point deficit in the second half, and the previously unbeaten Detroit Lions. The 49ers defense became one of the most intimidating in the league, particularly against the run; not allowing a 100-yard rusher or a single rushing touchdown until week 16 of the regular season. Alex Smith blossomed in the new system, reviving his career while San Francisco finally ended their nine-year playoff drought, finishing 13–3.

They defeated the New Orleans Saints 36–32 after a touchdown pass from Smith to Vernon Davis in the closing seconds of the game, but lost to the eventual Super Bowl Champion New York Giants, by a 20–17 score in overtime after two critical fumbles by backup return man Kyle Williams.

In 2012, the 49ers were predicted to be the NFC West champions and possibly make a run for the Super Bowl. Starting the season 6–2, the 49ers went on to face the rival St. Louis Rams in week 10. Alex Smith suffered a concussion in the second quarter and exited the game. He was replaced by 2011 second round pick Colin Kaepernick, who led the 49ers back to tie the game.

Born in 1987 in Milwaukee, Wisconsin, to Heidi Russo, a blonde who was 19 years old, almost broke and single, his African-American birth father was out of the picture. Russo placed her son for adoption with Rick and Teresa Kaepernick, a white couple who had two kids already—son Kyle and daughter Devon—and were looking for a boy after having lost two other sons to heart defects. Kaepernick became the youngest of their three children. He lived in Fond du Lac, Wisconsin, until age four, and attended grade school in Turlock, California.

Kaepernick won several punt, pass, and kick competitions mainly on his passing ability and had a 4.0 GPA at John H. Pitman High School in Turlock, where he was a three-sport star who passed up a promising baseball career as a pitcher in order to play football.

He was the MVP of the Central California Conference in football, leading his school to its first-ever playoff victory. In basketball he was a first-team all CCC selection at forward and led his 16th-ranked team to a near upset of the number one-ranked Oak Ridge Trojans in the opening round of playoffs. In that game Kaepernick scored 34 points but Ryan Anderson scored 50 to beat the Pitman Pride.

Kaepernick was a star baseball pitcher, receiving several scholarship offers in that sport. He was a two-time California all-state selection, listed as a draftable prospect on Major League Baseball's website in the class of 2006. He earned Northern California athlete of the week honors as a pitcher, and was reported to throw 92 miles per hour. He was a member of the Brewers Grey squad in the 2005 Area Code games and in his senior year Kaepernick pitched two no-hitters. Kaepernick was 11–2 with an ERA of 1.26, 97 strikeouts and 39 walks, and was drafted in the 43rd round by the Chicago Cubs.

But football was his first love. The major programs passed on him and he ended up at the University of Nevada. Kaepernick made his mark in a 49–41 loss to arch-rival Fresno State, then nearly engineered an upset of mighty Boise State in one of the highest-scoring games in NCAA history (a 69–67 loss in four overtimes). The game was nationally televised on ESPN and was deemed an "instant classic," re-aired on the network's ESPN Classic station in the following days. He compiled 243 yards passing with three TDs and rushed for another 177 yards and two scores.

During the contest, Kaepernick earned high praise from ESPN's Bill Curry (the former Georgia Tech and Green Bay Packer center and University of Alabama and University of Kentucky head football coach) as having perhaps the best game by a red-shirt freshman quarterback he had ever witnessed. As a sophomore Kaepernick became just the fifth player in NCAA history to pass for 2,000 yards and rush for 1,000 or more yards in a single season. On November 26, 2011, Kaepernick led his team to a 34–31 overtime victory against previously undefeated Boise State, snapping a 24-game win streak that had dated back to the 2008 Poinsettia Bowl.

Nevada head coach Chris Ault would later call this game the "most important win in program history." During this game, Kaepernick surpassed 1,000 rushing yards for this season, becoming the first player in NCAA history to have over 2,000 yards passing and 1,000 yards rushing for three consecutive seasons. Against Louisiana Tech, Kaepernick joined Florida's Tim Tebow as the second quarterback in FBS history to throw for 20 touchdowns and run for 20 in the same season. Kaepernick was named WAC Co-Offensive Player of the Year.

Now the starting quarterback for the 49ers, Kaepernick led a blowout of the Chicago Bears 32–7. Harbaugh chose Kaepernick as the starter the next week against the New Orleans Saints, despite Smith being cleared to play. A quarterback controversy began. Despite Smith leading the NFL in completion percentage (70 percent) and passer rating (104.1), Kaepernick was considered more dynamic with his scrambling ability and arm strength. He eventually started the rest of the season, going 5–2. Kaepernick set the record for rushing yards for a quarterback in the playoffs with 181 rushing against the Green Bay Packers. The 49ers defeated the Green Bay Packers and the Atlanta Falcons in the playoffs, advancing to Super Bowl XLVII, but were denied their sixth Super Bowl win against the Baltimore Ravens, who were coached by Jim's brother John Harbaugh, 34–31. Smith was dealt away.

The 49ers finished 12–4 in the 2013 regular season and entered the playoffs as a wild card, with their first game at Lambeau Field against the Green Bay Packers. On January 5, 2014, San Francisco defeated the Packers 23–20. On January 12, the 49ers defeated the Carolina Panthers 23–10, thus advancing to their third straight NFC Championship game. However, the 49ers' season ended at CenturyLink Field in Seattle, when a pass intended for Michael Crabtree was tipped by Seahawks cornerback Richard Sherman and intercepted by Seahawks linebacker, Malcolm Smith. They lost to their division rivals and Harbaugh's arch nemesis, Pete Carroll, the eventual Super Bowl champion Seattle Seahawks, 23–17.

The 49ers move to Levi Stadium in Santa Clara beginning in 2014 meant the end of Candlestick Park. Possible musical events were mentioned for the 'Stick, and others speculated that the Giants could play an exhibition game as the Dodgers had at the L.A. Coliseum in 2008, the 50th anniversary of their arrival in Los Angeles.

But the old gray lady had served her purpose. It was not a great stadium, but it had seen great sporting events in two sports. Now finally football could move, as baseball had, into the 21st century.

—◆—

The 'Stick, as it is known, has few rivals in terms of history, dilapidation.

—Jim Carlton, *Wall Street Journal,* 2013

—◆—

This is what we know, and this is all we know.

—San Francisco fan Joe Lenoir

—◆—

It was our dump.

—Ron Kroichick, *San Francisco Chronicle,* December 22, 2013

49ers of Silicon Valley

THE SILICON VALLEY IS A SCHIZOPHRENIC PATIENT, A CONTRAST OF military research mixed with 1970s hippy culture, whose greatest innovator, Steve Jobs, claimed to be a European-style Socialist who ran his company as if it was European . . . as in a rock quarry slave driven by the Roman Empire 2,000 years ago.

Much of Northern California's inexorable rise owes itself to the Silicon Valley. But one icon of San Francisco lagged behind. The 49ers fell into a state of disrepair, its ownership after the exile of Eddie DeBartolo a joke. They were mediocre on the field, and Candlestick, now standing in comparison with AT&T Park, looked more atrocious than ever.

After one last season at Candlestick Park in 2013, the 49ers moved into a state-of-the-art facility in Santa Clara, the apex of the Silicon Valley. It is the money, the political power, and the savvy of the technology sector that drove the decision to build a stadium not in the City, but on the peninsula. In 2016, the 49ers hosted the greatest of all sporting events, the 50th Super Bowl, and for two weeks the entire Bay Area from the wine country to San Jose was spotlighted in an economic boom of unprecedented proportions.

But the 49ers have not merely benefited from geographical proximity to technology; they have adopted it and made use of it to improve the fan experience, project and highlight the new stadium's bells and whistles.

First, there was Jed York,* who tried to prove that just because one's parents are incompetent, one need not follow their footsteps. Then there was Jim Harbaugh, driven by a thousand personal demons asserting that he was not an NFL-worthy quarterback, that Pete Carroll was all the rage and he was not in his collegiate class, that the pros would never stand for his intensity and demands.

After a long pro career, BCS glory at Stanford, and then success in San Francisco, we can say: wrong, wrong, and wrong again.

Finally, there comes Colin Kaepernick, undervalued from the start, the tattooed Christian soldier out of mid-level Nevada who now at first ascended to the throne once sat in by such kingpins of the quarterback position as Frankie Albert, Y. A. Tittle, John Brodie, Joe Montana, and Steve Young.

We looked with great anticipation toward the tantalizing possibility that in 2016 San Francisco would do what no NFL team has ever done: host the Super Bowl in its home stadium. Obviously, as far as the fans are concerned, success on the field is paramount, The heroes would be the orchestrators of that success, Harbaugh the sideline genius, Kaepernick the runnin', gunnin' quarterback, and a cast of blockers and tacklers.

But as any Giants fan can attest, the stadium experience is so prevalent that today it practically rivals on-field excellence when it comes to elevation of a franchise; its value, its imprimatur as a business/entertainment entity.

It is here where the 49ers again were thought to take the lead, using the tools at its ready disposal right there in the Silicon Valley tech shops they share a neighborhood with. Right now, San Francisco is considered the leader when it comes to technical innovation. When they got into Levi Stadium, it would be like a kid playing in a candy store.

Bill Walsh, easily one of the most innovative football minds ever, was famously said to model many of his techniques after technology gurus of

---

* The text from here until the end of the chapter has been adapted from an article that appeared in the September 2013 issue of *Gentry* magazine ("If You Build It—Smart . . . . They Will Come," Steven Travers). It is reprinted here with permission.

the halcyon 1980s. Now the club has gone from imitation to hiring of the top technical minds available.

Former team president and co-owner Gideon Yu was once a major player with Facebook, YouTube, and Yahoo—pinnacles of social media, video sharing, and search capability, respectively. Yu oversaw the club's tech touchstones, making use of them not merely in terms of fan experience or club promotion, but in the area of player development.

Michael Lewis's *Moneyball* certainly outlined some of the modern innovations, but the Internet has done more to improve scouting than any single factor. A scout need not watch a prospect or an upcoming opponent in person. He can find it using any number of services available, streaming video of almost any athlete he wishes to watch on demand to his phone, laptop, or computer. A player can instantly watch video of himself, studying flaws and changes over time, while at the same time instantly observing his next opponent in a variety of situations, conveniently organized at his fingertips.

The fan experience is exponentially improved by technology, which Yu said is "fundamentally trying to rethink everything about live sports." CEO Jed York was asked why men like Yu choose to revolutionize football the way they revolutionized technology.

"Because they made a lot of money they did a lot of cool things before they turned 40 years old and they don't want to go play golf six days a week," he replied, adding that the Niners were in a "lucky situation" because independently wealthy men like Yu were not motivated by pure salary. They did not need to compete with everybody else for their services. The 49ers were a challenge for these savants, which York said they view as being like a "startup." He said he receives resumes from people willing to work for half of what they made "at Google or Cisco or wherever."

Ex-Facebook director Dan Williams saw his new position as 49ers tech chief as "a passion play," adding that while a place like Facebook, which as the film *The Social Network* demonstrates can resemble a soap opera, there is a timeless joy to sports and the fan experience that goes with it. The chance to "develop a stadium" he would attend clinched it for Williams.

The club is ahead of the curve when it comes to stadium operations and marketing, but only time will tell whether the club's drafts will shape up as superior in large measure because of technology. In this supercompetitive business, no team in the league can afford to fall behind. The NFL is actually quite strict, in light of the Patriots' improper use of video surveillance a few use years ago, which has resulted in limits on the placement of iPads during games.

"We don't know the technical aspects," admitted general manager Trent Baalke. Baalke felt that the team's Silicon Valley location made it "foolish" not to be on "the cutting edge," but the money and stakes were so high that no team can possibly allow itself to lag behind, whether they are in Seattle, Los Angeles, or Santa Clara. Scouting will always be an inexact science, not as easy to master as, say, the ability to spot unused seats that can be sold to a fan willing to pay more to improve his on-site location, or the use of StubHub to purchase seats at the last minute, downloaded on location to a phone app.

Aside from fan mobilization, Yu foresaw the use of apps and text messages to increase fan noise, maybe even individualization of the ancient form of razzing. The possibility of abuse is predictable, too. Imagine a section of fans located near where a particular player is standing on the sideline. Suddenly they are all provided some embarrassing information about his recent brush with the law, or racy photos of his model girlfriend.

49ers COO Paraag Marathe wanted to actually knock down walls at the team's facility, more closely mirroring the atmosphere of companies like Apple. Yu added that one distinct advantage of the team's Santa Clara location was that when he attended things like youth sports events, techie fathers and mothers of other kids approached with ideas, some of which were quite good.

Technology's role in player development—centralization, player data, height/weight, times—are standard, not something the Niners have discovered that other teams have not, because they are not operating a few miles from the Mecca Steve Jobs created. 49ers chief tech officer Kunal Malik emphasized that paperless information sharing is now standard, adding that the real innovation will come from old school experts who get a taste of what technology can do for them, which he said will "push them to dream even more."

If true innovation in player development lies ahead, it comes in the form of what Yu called "open sourcing." We have seen some form of this, particularly in baseball. Fantasy leagues, computers, and Bill James created a new fan, derided as Ivy League non-jocks in *Moneyball*, but some form of word recognition and algorithm trending could result in various tipping points manifesting themselves in the form of, for instance, the decision to draft or trade for a particular safety or wide receiver. This thinking undoubtedly will be met with resistance, but it is already part of advertising, political campaigning, and even national defense, where "chatter," game theory, and even gambling odds have been used to fight the War on Terror. After all, it was military innovation that gave birth to the Silicon Valley in the first place.

—◦—

York is a married Notre Dame graduate with a stylish half-beard. He is handsome yet youthful. A former analyst with Guggenheim Partners in New York, he moved back to the Bay Area and worked his way up in the organization, learning all aspects of the operation, beginning as an apprentice to the equipment manager. This is not unlike the way Otis Chandler was brought in at a young age out of Stanford to learn how the *Los Angeles Times* was run from the ground up.

"His father meant well but he was like a bull in a china shop," wrote Glenn Dickey of John York, who even offered Bill Walsh "advice."

Jed became team president in 2008. Today he has grown into the job and has an air of confidence about him, largely because of his role in the building of the $1.2 billion Levi Stadium. Jed worked relentlessly with local interests to overcome political obstacles to a stadium being built, which history tells us are formidable in the Bay Area.

York said he did not want to spend $70 million on a scoreboard that would be "obsolete in a few years," but rather wanted a stadium that was "central to the grid" and allows for on-site fan interaction, to improve the overall experience.

"You don't want to be tech for tech's sake" but rather get into the game, York said, "different from other people," giving fans the chance to "opt in or not opt in." They planned to create photo replay ability using Sony products that allowed fans to see highlights on their devices, not related to what is on the scoreboard video screen.

The club developed a strong partnership with Sony, begging the question, why is the new facility called Levi Stadium instead of Sony Stadium? The decision to give naming rights to an iconic, old San Francisco company instead of a Japanese firm was a stroke of genius.

Sony chief executive Kazuo Hirai had absolutely no problem with the stadium's name. He knew that fans would be using Sony products and wished to create a "really new experience" through technology.

"We will increase fan enjoyment of the content by creating for them things for fans to read up on while watching games," he stated.

"Yes, using the stadium feed, the fans should be able to see the replays,'" York said, explaining that he hopes fans will get additional angle from the traditional network feeds, because of added tech access the stadium shall provide.

The league may limit this ability, but technology may make it impossible to stop.

"The fans will not just plug into the network feed," he said.

The key to success will be to see that, if fans are not tech-savvy, they can still enjoy the game, and need not rely on having an app on their phones.

"If you want to focus on a specific player, or the offensive line, you can use technology, and we will make it available for you to do so from your seat," York added, but did not want this to seem a mandatory part of the fan's participation. This seemed to combine the stadium experience with the TV viewer experience, the best of both worlds.

"Obviously there will be a lot of branding opportunity for Sony," said Hirai. "We want to rent out some of our products on the spot for branding purposes."

Hirai agreed there is a synergy between entertainment and technology that fits its model and partnership with football. He said there are aspects that are "uniquely Sony" that make the stadium experience better.

Sony owns content and has "relationships with content creators" that were brought into this partnership.

"Technology will be used in the uniforms, using cameras on uniforms, censors monitoring player heart rates and stuff, to reduce concussions, and allow fans to understand game better," said York.

He believed the ultimate goal was to create a "sense of community at the game. We want the experience to start from before you leave your house, to getting the best route to the game, the best place to park, the best healthy food options, where to pick it up, where lines are shorter; a complete experience making it better." York also chided, "We know the Silicon Valley better than Seattle, to start with," in response to a question whether the 49ers experience would be better than at Seattle, which already boasted the state-of-the-art Century Link Field. He added that the money saved from investing in scoreboard technology would be put into bandwidth. Cell phone access at large sporting events, with tens of thousands of fans using them, is notoriously bad. Stadium-wide WiFi access is the just the first step.

Apple, Google, Yahoo, and HP all chipped in $30 million toward hosting the Super Bowl. Google executive chairman Eric Schmidt promised a "fundamentally deeper" game experience.

San Francisco mayor Ed Lee was initially disappointed in losing the stadium to Santa Clara, although the fault is not with him but his predecessor, Gavin Newsom, but he was fully on board since not just the City, but the entire region, will benefit from a fan experience he said will "completely transform" itself from previous events. This certainly far outdistanced the area's one and only Super Bowl, the 1985 49ers triumph over Miami at ancient Stanford Stadium. The February 2016 event promised to bring in $300–500 million, 7,500 media members, and a 10,000-person tailgate party.

Moscone Center hosted the "NFL Experience," and over two weeks it is estimated that the Super Bowl was worth $4.1 million in free advertising.

"This is the kind of international event we love hosting," says Mayor Lee.

—————

The 49ers' foray into stadium technology is only part of the new trend in sports toward all things innovative. ESPN is planning to subsidize wireless coverage for its app users, a new cost-sharing plan that will revolutionize the bandwidth industry, which will "bring value to our customers," said Verizon Wireless chief executive Dan Mead.

Forty-one million people watch content on their phones. Sixteen million watch ESPN exclusively on the phone. Paul Gallant, the managing director at Guggenheim (where York worked), warned that the FCC might investigate too incestuous a relationship between content providers and wireless phone companies. Verizon had a case pending in federal appellate court.

Mead compared the proposals to Amazon essentially paying the connectivity costs on Kindle books, which Mead saw as a "possibility to expand" beyond current parameters.

Individual athletes are now making their forays into this brave new world. Giants catcher Buster Posey was involved in "Buster Bash," a home run derby mobile game.

Hall of Famer Joe Montana was releasing "iMFL," a football fantasy app.

"With their growing numbers on social media, they have the power to build something that they can co-own versus just giving their name out as part of a licensing deal," said John Shahidi of start-up RockLive.

The tablet app market was projected to grow to $84.5 million in 2013, according to analyst Carl Howe of the Yankee group. Howe recommended that athletes actively endorse and get involved in the business, that just lending a celebrity name will not result in success (pointing to a recent example, Mike Tyson).

"This space is exciting," said Montana. "I'm the kind of geek that will kick your butt."

Los Angeles mega-talent agency Creative Artists took the lead in brokering this new synergy. Eliran Sapir of Apptopia said this market is no longer in its "early days," hearkening to how the Internet bubbled in 2000.

"The era of the garage developer is over," Howe said.

—◦—

As for the San Francisco 49ers, after three years at Levi's Stadium, it is too early to judge their new digs. It is better than Candlestick, but that is not a high bar. Parking is not better. Stadium access is not better. Fan enthusiasm, for varying reasons, has so far not lived up to the greatest moments at the 'Stick. Jim Harbaugh was allowed to leave, greatly tainting Jed York's reputation; the team has floundered; and Colin Kaepernick has become a polarizing figure who has not come close to his early promise or performance.

The team is looking at an uncertain future, not unlike the pioneers who settled the golden paradise of California in the 19th century. If this state has any chance of regaining its footing after years of struggle, this may be its key.

Bibliography

2000 San Francisco 49ers Media Guide. San Francisco: San Francisco 49ers, 2000.

Alston, Walter, with Jack Tobin. *One Year at a Time.* Waco, TX: Word, 1976.

Angell, Roger. *Five Seasons.* New York: Simon & Schuster, 1977.

———. *Game Time: A Baseball Companion.* Orlando, FL: Harcourt, 2003.

———. *Late Innings: A Baseball Companion.* New York: Simon & Schuster, 1972.

———. *The Summer Game.* New York: Viking Press, 1972.

Atlas, Ted. *Candlestick Park.* Charleston, SC: Arcadia Publishing, 2010.

Baseball Encyclopedia, The. New York: Barnes & Noble Books, 2004.

Baseball Encyclopedia, The. New York: Macmillan, 1996.

Berra, Yogi. *The Yogi Book: "I Really Didn't Say Everything I Said!"* New York: Workman Publishing, 1998.

Berra, Yogi, with Dave Kaplan. *Ten Rings: My Championship Seasons.* New York: William Morrow, 2003.

Berra, Yogi, with Tom Horton. *Yogi: It Ain't Over . . .* New York: McGraw-Hill, 1989.

Bitker, Steve. *The Original San Francisco Giants.* Champaign, IL: Sports Publishing L.L.C., 2001.

Bjarkman, Peter C. *The New York Mets Encyclopedia.* Champaign, IL: Sports Publishing L.L.C., 2003.

Black Book Partners, LLC, 2004.

Bouton, Jim. *Ball Four.* New York: World Publishing, 1970.

Bouton, Jim, with Neil Offen. *"I Managed Good, but Boy Did They Play Bad."* New York: Dell Publishing, 1973.

Breslin, Jimmy. *Can't Any Here Play This Game?* New York: Viking, 1963.

Brosnan, Jim. *Great Rookies of the Major Leagues.* New York: Random House, 1966.

Carlton, Jim. "Fans Wax Nostalgic before Candlestick Is Snuffed Out." *Wall Street Journal*, December 19, 2013.

Chadwick, Bruce, and David M. Spindel. *The Giants: Memories and Memorabilia from a Century of Baseball.* New York: Abbeville Press, 1993.

Chastain, Bill. *100 Things Giants Should Know Before They Die.* Chicago: Triumph Books, 2011.

Cramer, Richard Ben. *Joe DiMaggio: The Hero's Life.* New York: Simon & Schuster, 2000.

Creamer, Robert. *Stengel: His Life and Times.* New York: Simon & Schuster, 1984.

Devaney, John. *Tom Seaver.* New York: Popular Library, 1974.

DiMaggio, Joe. *Lucky to Be a Yankee.* New York: Grosset & Dunlap, 1947.

Drucker, Malka, with Tom Seaver. *Tom Seaver: Portrait of a Pitcher.* New York: Holiday House, 1978.

Durso, Joseph. *DiMaggio: The Last American Knight.* New York: Little, Brown, 1995.

Eig, Jonathan. *Luckiest Man: The Life and Death of Lou Gehrig.* New York: Simon & Schuster, 2005.

Einstein, Charles. *Willie's Time.* New York: J.B. Lippincott, 1979.

———, ed. *The Third Fireside Book of Baseball.* New York: Simon & Schuster, 1968.

Enders, Eric. *100 Years If the World Series.* Barnes & Noble Publishing, 2003.

Eskenazi, Gerald. *The Lip: A Biography of Leo Durocher.* New York: William Morrow, 1993.

Ford, Whitey, with Phil Pepe. *Few and Chosen: Defining Yankee Greatness across the Eras.* Chicago: Triumph Books, 2001.

Fost, Dan. *Giants Past and Present.* Minneapolis, MN: MVP Books, 2010.

Fox, Bucky. *The Mets Fan's Little Book of Wisdom.* Lanham, MD: Taylor Trade Publishing, 2006.

Fox, Larry. *Broadway Joe and His Super Jets.* New York: Coward-McCann, 1969.

galesayers40.com

Giants 2001 Media Guide. San Francisco: Giants Media Relations Dept., 2001.

Gitlin, Marty. *San Francisco Giants.* Edina, MN: ABDO Publishing Company, 2011.

Golenbock, Peter. *Amazin': The Miraculous History of New York's Most Beloved Baseball Team.* New York: St. Martin's Press, 2002.

Grabowski, John. *Willie Mays.* New York: Chelsea House Publishers, 1990.

Graham Jr., Frank. *Great Pennant Races of the Major Leagues.* New York: Random House, 1967.

Gruver, Edward. *Koufax.* Dallas: Taylor Publishing, 2000.

Gutman, Bill. *Miracle Year 1969: Amazing Mets and Super Jets.* Champaign, IL: Sports Publishing L.L.C., 2004.

Hano, Arnold. *Willie Mays.* New York: Grosset & Dunlap, 1966.

Helyar, John. *Lords of the Realm.* New York: Villard Books, 1994.

Herskowitz, Mickey. *A Hero All His Life.* New York: HarperCollins, 1996.

Hirsch, James S. *Willie Mays: The Life, the Legend.* New York: Scribner, 2010.

History of USC Football DVD.

Hodges, Gil, with Frank Slocum. *The Game of Baseball.* New York: Crown Publishers, 1969.

Hodges, Russ, and Al Hirshberg. *My Giants.* Garden City, NY: Doubleday, 1963.

Honig, Donald. *The National League: An Illustrated History.* New York: Crown Publishers, 1983.

Houk, Ralph. *Ballplayers Are Human, Too.* Charles Dexter, ed. and trans. New York: G.P. Putnam's Son, 1962.

Johanson, Matt, and Wylie Wong. *San Francisco Giants: Where Have You Gone?* Champagne, IL: Sports Publishing L.L.C., 2007.

Kahn, Roger. *Joe and Marilyn: A Memory of Love.* New York: William Morrow, 1986.

Kaplan, Jim. *The Greatest Game Ever Pitched: Juan Marichal, Warren Spahn, and the Pitching Duel of the Century.* Chicago: Triumph Books, 2011.

Kehret, Peg. *Searching for Candlestick Park.* New York: Cobblehill Books, 1997.

Knapp, Ron. *Sports Great: Will Clark.* Hillside, NJ: Enslow Publishers, 1993.

Koufax, Sandy, with Ed Linn. *Koufax.* New York: Viking Press, 1966.

Kroichick, Ron. "It Was *Our* Dump." *San Francisco Chronicle*, December 22, 2013.

Kroner, Steve. "A Stroll Down Memory Lane." *San Francisco Chronicle*, January 19, 2014.

Kuenster, John, ed. *From Cobb to Catfish*. Chicago: Rand McNally, 1975.

Leavy, Jane. *Sandy Koufax*. New York: HarperCollins, 2002.

Lee, Bill, with Richard Lally. *The Wrong Stuff*. New York: Viking Press, 1983.

Lee, Bill, with Jim Prince. "Spaceman." *Baseball Eccentrics*. Chicago: Triumph Books, 2007.

Lichtenstein, Michael. *Ya Gotta Believe!* New York: St. Martin's Griffin, 2002.

Leventhal, Josh. *The World Series*. New York: Tess Press, 2004.

Livsey, Laury. *The Steve Young Story*. Rocklin, CA: Prima Publishing, 1996.

Los Angeles Dodgers 2001 Media Guide. Los Angeles: Los Angeles Dodgers, 2001.

Lott, Ronnie, and Jill Lieber. *Total Impact*. New York: Doubleday, 1991.

Macht, Norman L. *Tom Seaver*. New York: Chelsea House Publishers, 1994.

Mantle, Mickey, and Phil Pepe. *Mickey Mantle: My Favorite Summer 1956*. New York: Doubleday, 1991.

Mantle, Mickey, with Mickey Herskowitz. *All My Octobers: My Memories of 12 World Series When the Yankees Ruled Baseball.* New York: HarperCollins, 1994.

Marichal, Juan, with Charles Einstein. *A Pitcher's Story*. New York: Doubleday, 1967.

Marichal, Juan, with Lew Freedman. *Juan Marichal: My Journey from the Dominican Republic to Cooperstown*. Minneapolis, MN: MVP Books, 2011.

Markusen, Bruce. *Tales From the Mets Dugout*. Champaign, IL: Sports Publishing L.L.C., 2005.

Mays, Willie, as told to Charles Einstein. *Willie Mays: My Life In and Out of Baseball.* New York: E.P. Dutton, 1966.

Montana, Joe, and Bob Raissman. *Audibles*. New York: William Morrow, 1986.

Montana, Joe, and Richard Weiner. *Art and Magic of Quarterbacking*. New York: Henry Holt, 1997.

Murphy, Brian. *Never Say Die: The Francisco Giants—2012 World Series Champions*. Petaluma, CA: Cameron + Company, 2013.

———. *San Francisco Giants: 50 Years*. San Rafael, CA: Insight Editions, 2008.

Honig, Donald. *The National League*. New York: Crown Publishers, 1983.

Newhan, Ross. "Vintage Seaver." *Los Angeles Times*, July 5, 2007. latimes.com/sports/la-sp-seaver5jul05,1,3895492,full.story.

New York Times *Book of Baseball History, The*, foreword by Red Smith. New York: The *New York Times* Book Co., 1975.

NFL. *The First 50 Years: The Story of the National Football League*. New York: Simon & Schuster, 1969.

Official 1969 Baseball Guide. St. Louis: The Sporting News, 1969.

Official 1970 Baseball Guide. St. Louis: The Sporting News, 1970.

Official 1972 Baseball Guide. St. Louis: The Sporting News, 1972.

O'Neal, Bill. *The Pacific Coast League*. Austin, TX: Eakin Publications, 1990.

Palmquits, Matt. "49er Stripper Video." sfweekly.com, June 15, 2005.

Parrott, Harold. *The Lords of Baseball*. New York: Praeger Publishers, 1976.

Pearlman, Jeff. *The Bad Guys Won!* New York: HarperCollins, 2004.

Peary, Danny, ed. *Super Bowl: The Game of Their Lives.* New York: Macmillan, 1997.

Peters, Nick, with Stuart Shea. *Tales from the San Francisco Giants Dugout: A Collection of the Greatest Giants Stories Ever Told.* New York: Sports Publishing, 2003.

Plaut, David. *Chasing October: The Dodgers-Giants Pennant Race of 1962.* South Bend, IN: Diamond Communications, 1994.

Plunkett, Jim, and Dave Newhouse. *The Jim Plunkett Story.* New York: Arbor House, 1981.

Pottenger, Dennis. *Great Expectations.* Rocklin, CA: Prima Publishing, 1991.

Reichler, Joseph. *30 Years of Baseball's Great Moments.* New York: Crown Publishers, 1974.

Rice, Jerry, and Michael Silver. *Rice.* New York: St. Martin's Press, 1996.

Ritter, Lawrence. *The Glory of Their Times.* New York: Macmillan, 1966.

Ritter, Lawrence, and Donald Honig. *The Image of Their Greatness.* New York: Crown Publishers, 1979.

Robinson, Ray, ed. *Baseball Stars of 1965.* New York: Pyramid Books, 1965.

———, ed. *Baseball Stars of 1970.* New York: Pyramid Books, 1970.

Russell, Jesse, and Ronald Cohn. *Willie McCovey.* Edinburgh, Scotland, 2012.

Schott, Tom, and Nick Peters. *The Giants Encyclopedia.* Champaign, IL: Sports Publishing, 1999.

Seaver, Tom, with Marty Appel. *Great Moments in Baseball.* New York: Carol Publishing Group L.L.C., 1992.

Seaver, Tom, with Martin Appel. *Tom Seaver's All-Time Baseball Greats: The Inside Scoop on Baseball's Best.* New York: Wanderer Books, 1984.

Seaver, Tom, with Rick Hummel and Bob Nightengale. *Tom Seaver's 1989 Scouting Notebook.* St. Louis: The Sporting News Publishing, 1989.

Seaver, Tom, with Dick Schaap. *The Perfect Game.* New York: E.P. Dutton, 1970.

Shamsky, Art, with Barry Zeman. *The Magnificent Seasons: How the Jets, Mets, and Knicks Made Sports History and Uplifted a City and the Country.* New York: Thomas Dunne Books, 2004.

Smith, Robert. *Baseball.* New York: Simon & Schuster, 1947.

Smith, Ron. The Sporting News *Selects Baseball's Greatest 100 Players.* St. Louis: The Sporting News Publishing, 1998.

Stein, Fred, and Nick Peters. *Giants Diary: A Century of Giants Baseball in New York and San Francisco.* Berkeley, CA. North Atlantic Books, 1987.

Stout, Glenn. *The Dodgers: 120 Years of Dodgers Baseball.* New York: Houghton Mifflin, 2004.

———. *Yankees Century: 100 Years of New York Yankees Baseball.* New York: Houghton Mifflin, 2002.

Suchon, Josh. *This Gracious Season.* San Diego: Winter Publications, 2002.

Travers, Steven. *Angels Essential: Everything You Need to Know to Be a Real Fan!* Chicago: Triumph Books, 2007.

———. *A's Essential: Everything You Need to Know to Be a Real Fan!* Chicago: Triumph Books, 2007.

———. *Barry Bonds: Baseball's Superman.* Champaign, IL: Sports Publishing L.L.C., 2002.

———. "City Bids Genius Adieu." *San Francisco Examiner*, April 20, 2001.

———. "A Conversation with Fred Dryer." *StreetZebra*, January 2000.

———. *Dodgers Essential: Everything You Need to Know to Be a Real Fan!* Chicago: Triumph Books, 2007.

———. "The Giants' Power Hitter." *Gentry*, March 2013.

———. *God's County: A Conservative, Christian Worldview of How History Formed the United States Empire and America's Manifest Destiny for the 21st Century.* Unpublished.

———. *The Good, the Bad and the Ugly Los Angeles Lakers.* Chicago: Triumph Books, 2007.

———. "If You Build It Smart . . . They Will Come." *Gentry*, September 2013.

———. "L.A./Orange County Prep All-Century Teams." *StreetZebra*, January 2000.

———. *The Last Icon: Tom Seaver and His Times.* Lanham, MD: Taylor Trade Publishing, 2011.

———. *1969 Miracle Mets: The Improbable Story of Baseball's Greatest Underdog Team.* Guilford, CT: Globe Pequot Press, 2009.

———. "No Humility Here." *San Francisco Examiner*, May 15, 2001.

———. *Once He Was an Angel.* Unproduced screenplay.

———. "Once He Was an Angel." *StreetZebra*, 1999.

———. *One Night, Two Teams: Alabama vs. USC and the Game That Changed a Nation.* Lanham, MD: Taylor Trade Publishing, 2007.

———. *The Poet: The Life and* Los Angeles Times *of Jim Murray.* Washington, DC: Potomac Books, 2013.

———. *A Tale of Three Cities: New York, Los Angeles and San Francisco in the 1962 Baseball Season.* Washington, DC: Potomac Books, 2009.

———. "Time to Give Barry His Due." *San Francisco Examiner*, April 18, 2001.

———. *The USC Trojans: College Football's All-Time Greatest Dynasty.* Lanham, MD: Taylor Trade Publishing, 2006.

———. *Summer of '62.* Unproduced screenplay.

Tuckman, Michael W., and Jeff Schultz. *The San Francisco 49ers: Team of the Decade.* Rocklin, CA: Prima Publishing, 1989.

Walsh, Bill, and Glenn Dickey. *Building a Champion.* New York: St. Martin's Press, 1990.

Will, George. *Bunts.* New York: Touchstone, 1999.

Wise, Bill, ed. *1963 Official Baseball Almanac.* Greenwich, CT: Fawcett Publications.

Whittingham, Richard. *Illustrated History of the Dodgers.* Chicago: Triumph Books, 2005.

World Champs: San Francisco Giants 2012: From Mays to Marichal to Posey and Cain. Birmingham, AL: D.M.D. Publications, 2012.

Yankees 2000 Information and Record Guide. Bronx: New York Yankees Media Relations Department, 2001.

Zimmerman, Paul D., and Dick Schaap. *The Year the Mets Lost Last Place.* New York: World Publishing, 1969.